To Flourish or Destruct

To Flourish or Destruct

A Personalist Theory of Human Goods, Motivations, Failure, and Evil

CHRISTIAN SMITH

The University of Chicago Press
Chicago and London

Christian Smith is the William R. Kenan, Jr., Professor of Sociology at the University of Notre Dame, where he directs the Center for the Study of Religion and Society and the Notre Dame Center for Social Research. He is the author or coauthor of several books, including *What Is a Person?* and *Soul Searching: The Religious and Spiritual Lives of American Teenagers.*

The University of Chicago Press, Chicago 60637
The University of Chicago Press, Ltd., London
© 2015 by The University of Chicago
All rights reserved. Published 2015.
Printed in the United States of America

24 23 22 21 20 19 18 17 16 15   1 2 3 4 5

ISBN-13: 978-0-226-23195-2 (cloth)
ISBN-13: 978-0-226-23200-3 (e-book)
DOI: 10.7208/chicago/9780226232003.001.0001

Library of Congress Cataloging-in-Publication Data

Smith, Christian, 1960– author.
    To flourish or destruct : a personalist theory of human goods, motivations, failure, and evil / Christian Smith.
        pages cm
    Includes bibliographical references and index.
        ISBN 978-0-226-23195-2 (cloth : alkaline paper) — ISBN 978-0-226-23200-3 (e-book)
1. Persons.   2. Motivation (Psychology).   3. Good and evil.   I. Title.
    BF503.S53 2015
    153.8 — dc23

                                                                    2014025470

♾ This paper meets the requirements of ANSI/NISO Z39.48–1992
(Permanence of Paper).

Contents

Some think there is no such thing as human nature.
For some people this idea becomes translated as,
"everything is possible for man," and in that they find some hope;
for others, "everything is permissible to man,"
and with that they abandon all restraint;
and others, finally, "everything is permissible against man,"
and with that we have arrived at Buchenwald.

—EMMANUEL MOUNIER, *Personalism*

Acknowledgments

Numerous valued colleagues and friends read and provided helpful feedback on parts or the whole of this book's manuscript. These include Doug Porpora, Brian Brock, Bill Hurlbut, John Evans, Heather Price (who also helped to design some figures), Roy Bhaskar, Jason Springs, Atalia Omer, Steve Vaisey, Margaret Archer, Keith Meador, Margarita Mooney, Nicolette Manglos, Mehrdad Babadi, Brandon Vaidyanathan, Hilary Davidson, Trish Snell Herzog, Brad Gregory, Todd Whitmore, and Mark Chaves. Meredith Whitnah, Katherine Sorrell, Cole Carnesecca, Daniel Escher, and Karen Hooge provided a helpful group discussion of the drafts of the final two chapters. Very early on, Chris Eberle posed some provocative ideas about the inescapable nature of beliefs that helped get gears turning in my mind. I am grateful to them all for their insights, support, and critical ideas. Part of this book was written while on an Alan Richardson Fellowship at Durham University, in Durham, England, awarded by the Department of Theology and Religion. Many thanks to the Department and Durham University—in particular to Matthew Guest, Paul Murray, Douglas Davies, and Richard Song—for helping to provide me the time, space, and good conversations that helped moved this book toward publication. Thanks also to the University of Notre Dame for providing me a semester's leave to work on this book, during a spell in North Carolina and on the Richardson Fellowship. I presented overviews of this book's argument in two lectures—the Cheryl Frank Memorial Lecture at the International Centre for Critical Realism at the University of London, and the annual Alan Richardson lecture at Durham University—and received helpful questions and suggestions by the audiences of both, for which I am grateful as well. Thanks also to the John Templeton Foundation for funding and organizing a two-day discussion of this book's manuscript in Fort

Lauderdale, Florida, by an excellent group of sociologists and philosophers, which also helped clarify and strengthen my argument—and especially to Mike Murray for his role in making that happen. The critical discussion there by Omar Lizardo, Phil Gorksi, Chris Eberle, Christian Miller, Karsten Stueber, Gabriel Abend, Gabriel Ignatow, John Churchill, and Kimon Sargeant at that meeting was invaluable, as were their many written comments supplied after the meeting. I offer my sincerest thanks to all of these good people. Finally, Doug Mitchell is, of course, a wonderful editor with whom to work. My hat's off to him with deep appreciation for his support of my work.

Introduction

This book advances a personalist account of human beings to help us better understand and explain human persons, motivations, interests, and the social life to which they give rise. My account offers an alternative to the standard views in contemporary sociology and most of the rest of social science, which I think are generally impoverished. The models of human beings that dominate sociology and other disciplines are not only lacking on certain points, they are also misdirected and misleading on crucial issues concerning human being, motivations, interests, and action. If I am right, much of social science is working with and propagating defective ideas about human beings in social life. As a result, social science understandings and explanations are compromised by these defective models of human beings on which they depend. And the social sciences are teaching those who come under their influence problematic ideas about one of the most important subjects of scientific knowledge: human beings, ourselves. We need to expand our range of vision and imagination to develop different ideas about what human beings are, in order to improve social science and the truthfulness of what social science teaches others.

Viewed in terms of analytical themes concerning human persons, this book seeks to answer three big questions. First, what *basic motivations and interests* generate and direct human action? Second, what is by nature *good* for human beings—that is, what are real human *goods*? Third, how should we understand and explain the lack of goodness—sometimes even the definite *destructiveness* and *evil*—that are so prevalent and damaging in human life? I raise these three questions together because good answers to them must be developed and understood together. One cannot ask and answer well any of these questions, ultimately, without addressing them all. We will see that answering them well requires that we engage not only social science and social theory but also some history and philosophy. This inquiry thus transgresses standard academic boundaries that segregate traditional disciplinary compartments.

The question about human motivations and interests is fairly straightforward. Why do people do anything they do? What moves or compels people to action? What does anyone do when they wake up from sleeping, and why do they do that and not something else? To answer such questions, we need some theory of human beings and the nature of their interests. These, I will argue, are an important part of what gets people to act, to do whatever they do with their lives. Considering basic questions about motivations and interests also proves to be a good way to examine and evaluate the general assumptions and arguments about human beings embedded in different social science models.

Motivating This Inquiry

Why do we need a better theory of human personhood, motivations, the good, and destruction? Not all social scientists even believe that motivations matter. Some think the social interactions, structures, and institutions that social science studies have little to do with people's motivations. Motives are personal, unobservable subjectivities that do little to predict behavior, so they can be ignored. That view, I will argue, is wrong. It is impossible to explain human social life without recourse to motivations of some kind. The only question is, how should we best understand the nature and operation of human motivations? If this is correct, the better our understanding of human motivations, the better will be our social science explanations.[1]

Stated differently, this book seeks to better theorize the microfoundations of social life, yet not from the rational-choice perspective that has dominated microfoundations discourse. No social science can be any better than the microfoundations it presupposes, even when the subject of study is focused on the macro or meso levels. Herbert Simon rightly noted, "Nothing is more fundamental in setting our research agenda and informing our research methods than our view of the nature of human being whose behavior we are studying."[2] Some social scientists simply ignore the question of microfoundations. Others attend to microfoundations but adopt models—such as rational choice theory—that are defective, and as a result their explanations turn out to be problematic. One of my purposes is to better theorize the microfoundations of social life, to develop a model more true to reality, in order to underwrite more believable and fruitful social science understandings and explanations.

Just as important as the need for social science to work with a good theoretical microfoundation of social life is the need to better describe and defend the reality of human personhood. If human actions are indeed motivated, yet our theories fail to account well for motivations, then our social scientific descriptions of human persons are not only inadequate but also distort our self-understandings of persons. That can have big negative moral and political consequences. Any humanistic society presupposes that people are to a significant extent the responsible agents of their own actions. If we lose a thick sense of the reality of motivated action, we lose a humanism worth defending.[3] If it is true that people's activities are *not* significantly motivated and directed by their own personal "centers with purpose,"[4] then their status as particular *subjects* in the world is diminished. People become mere objects. B. F. Skinner, for example, correctly notified us in 1971 that his behaviorism revealed a humanity existing "beyond freedom and dignity." Happily, we eventually realized that behaviorism is deeply misguided. But the same kind of potentially pernicious implications emanate from a variety of other theoretical schools of thought in social science. And one aspect of such views is the ignoring, discounting, or misrepresenting of the role of personal motivations in human action. If humans are actually not significantly motivated to action but are instead, say, driven by social forces to behave, then their humanity necessarily reflects a very different status and quality than that believed by realistic humanism. And that has real moral and political implications. The same is true if people are actually merely enacting social roles into which they have been socialized, behaving in ways determined by their genes or neural systems, or cloaking purely instrumental acquisitions of wealth and power with what (falsely) seems to be genuinely sociable behavior. If we want to live in humanistic societies, we need to actually *be* (ontologically) the kind of persons that justify humanism and to recognize that fact about ourselves. Regrettably, much of social science undercuts such a view. My purpose is to push back on behalf of the reality of human personhood, with an account I think more truthfully describes our humanity and justifies a robust humanism.

But why ask about the human good or human goods? A tendency in Western modernity—particularly in its politically liberal, individualistic modes—has been to replace questions about what is good with questions about what is right.[5] Even if real goods exist, many argue, inquiries about them only produce disagreement and conflict. Others deny outright the existence of any human good, recognizing only infinite possible goods determined by individual desires and cultural invention. In either case, this view says, what really matters in the end, what should focus our attention is the

right, not the good. In practical terms, society should do no more than protect the right and rights by ensuring equal opportunity, just procedures, individual self-determination, individual civil and human rights, and so on.
Questions about what is good are not "society's" to answer but must devolve
to individuals to decide for themselves in private.

The human good, however, cannot be so easily set aside. We cannot even
begin to argue for prioritizing the right over the good without a more fundamental sense of what actually *is* good. Why do liberal values deserve to
be protected, instead of some others that people may prize, such as natural
hierarchy, racial superiority, male domination, conquest, empire building,
or something else? Protecting equality, fairness, autonomy, and civil rights
only makes sense given the true value of a certain substantive vision of what
is humanly good. And in this world, that vision cannot be taken for granted
as obvious, since many people and cultures do favor antiliberal values. So
questions about the human good persist, even in societies that would prefer
to avoid them.

Many people today think that what is good for people is whatever they
think is good for themselves. Everybody must decide what is good for his or
her own life. I suggest that this view is wrong. It is both empirically untrue
and impossible to affirm honestly without heading into theoretical and practical places that few of us, I hope, are prepared to go. Human goods are not
simply up to each individual to decide. There actually *are* real, true human
goods. The implications of that are immense. Humans stand to attain lives
and societies of greater flourishing and genuine happiness by realizing those
goods. Humans in that case have something like a natural, objective, nonrelative standard for what is in their own interest to achieve, to move toward,
to actualize.[6] It is not all individually determined or culturally constructed
or morally relative. Human flourishing, well-being, and the resulting happiness are in some important sense given by the facts of reality, specified and
guided by the nature of things. I am aware that such ideas are difficult for
moderns and postmoderns to accept. But that does not make them wrong. It
only means that these ideas need to be retrieved, explained, and defended in
order to correct our current misunderstandings.

Why do we need a theory of human failure, brokenness, destructiveness,
and evil? That does not sound very social scientific. I ask in reply: must this
question really be answered, after the horrific twentieth century? Something
like brokenness, malice, and evil are undeniably widespread and seemingly
ineradicable facts of human life, which continually produce consequences of
immense personal and social pathos and destruction. Little of life can be experienced without encountering these grim realities. And very little of interest

in the social sciences can be studied without encountering and trying to make sense of them. Only a social science that is single-mindedly determined to remain neutral, objective, uncommitted, amoral, and truly disengaged from real human concerns—that is, a morally nihilistic social science—could imagine that better understanding the destruction and evil in the world is irrelevant to its concerns.[7] Let us remember that social scientists are human persons too, and, in our wielding of ideas, we are relatively powerful and therefore responsible people. Unless we are prepared to become absolute moral relativists or skeptics and embrace all that implies—and I hope we are not, and in fact think that nobody, not even social scientists in their own scholarship, ever is[8]—then we cannot avert the question of brokenness, destructiveness, and evil and still make good sense of life and the world.

Four Standard Accounts and a Fifth Upstart

I have said that a personalist account of human beings, motivations, and interests proves better than the available alternatives. But what are those alternatives? We can simplify a bit and say that the dominant, general models of human beings embedded in different major approaches to understanding and explanation in sociology (and much of social science more generally) are four in number.[9] To those I add a fifth, newer approach to explaining human beings, one that externally presses upon social science today through the disciplinary imperialism of intellectual entrepreneurs in the natural sciences.

First, especially in sociology we often adopt the model of human beings as *dependent norm-followers*. This approach, which takes a macroperspective, assumes that the primary fact of social life is "society," on which individual people are dependent through socialization for the cultural and institutional norms, values, and meanings that govern their goals, choices, and behaviors. People are the cultural products of their societies. Prominent representatives of this approach, broadly conceived, include Émile Durkheim, Talcott Parsons, Clifford Geertz (read in macroterms), Mary Douglas, adherents of an older cultural society, and most structural functionalists. The deep social philosophy behind this model is social collectivism, influenced in important ways by traditional conservatism, corporatism, counter-Enlightenment thought, nationalist Romanticism, and strands of early neo-medievalism and gothic revivalism. Plato, Edmund Burke, Georg Hegel, Joseph de Maistre, Johann Gottfried von Herder, Wilhelm von Humboldt, and Ferdinand Tönnies stand in various ways in the far background of this approach.

The second major model of human beings found in sociology and many of the other social sciences is *materialist group-interest seekers*. This approach also takes a macroperspective, assuming a kind of rational egoism in partial solidarity operating at the group level, which produces collectivities that ally with and vie against each other in order to increase their mostly material, shared advantages. This view emphasizes objective material interests that divide human social groups, social institutions as fields of struggle on which are waged the conflicts of contending groups to realize their interests, and unstable situations of domination, oppression, subordination, and exploitation that result. Prominent representatives of this approach (in various ways) include (much of) Max Weber, Robert Michels, Ralph Dahrendorf, C. Wright Mills, Charles Tilly, and Theda Skocpol. The deeper social philosophy behind this model derives from Niccolò Machiavelli, Thomas Hobbes, Carl von Clausewitz, various rationalist philosophers, Karl Marx, and Vladimir Lenin.

The third major model of human beings in sociology is that of *rationally acquisitive individuals*. This approach shifts down from the macro- to the microview. Here, the primary unit of human life is the autonomous, self-interested, rational, individual choice maker who spends his or her life engaged in strategic decision making and actions designed to increase material well-being, power, security, domination of others, and social status.[10] "Society" here is the aggregate of relatively stable sets of social exchanges that arise from individual actions. Prominent representatives of this approach (in various ways) include George Homans, the early Peter Blau, Gary Becker, Michael Hechter, and James Coleman, among many others. The deep social philosophies underwriting this model of humans are utilitarianism, political liberalism, and secular rationalism. Thomas Hobbes, David Hume, Adam Smith, John Locke, John Stuart Mill, Auguste Comte, Ludwig von Mises, Friedrich Hayek, and various game theorists stand in the background here, in diverse ways.[11]

The fourth model operating in contemporary sociology and other pockets of social science is of human persons as *communicative, interacting meaning-makers*. This approach largely rejects the previous models, emphasizing instead the continuous flow of microinteractions among purposive, symbol-wielding agents who are most basically seeking to construct and sustain meaningful definitions of reality, identities, and respectable relationships in their lives. "Society" here is the aggregation of empirical patterns of interactions among meaning-constructing actors. Prominent representatives of this approach (in various ways) include George Herbert Mead, Charles H. Cooley, W. I. Thomas, Herbert Blumer, Clifford Geertz (read in microterms), Peter Berger, Harold Garfinkel, Erving Goffman, Alfred Schutz, Sheldon Stryker, and Anthony Giddens. The background philosophy to this model of human beings is American pragmatism, sometimes influenced by existentialism, phenomenology, hermeneutics, and ordinary-speech philosophy; some Scottish enlightenment moral philosophers, such as David Hume, Frances Hutcheson, and Adam Ferguson; and strains of German phenomenology. Standing in the background here, in other words, are thinkers such as Wilhelm Dilthey, Alexius Meinong, Franz Brentano, William James, Charles Peirce, John Dewey, the later Ludwig Wittgenstein, and Edmund Husserl.

These four are the main operative models in social science today. But a fifth model of human beings that we should also recognize views humans as *evolved neuro-genetic-biochemical behavers*. In this approach, humans are assumed to be nothing more than biological organisms that happen to embody more highly evolved (that is, more complex and capable) functions compared to other biological organisms. Those organisms and their functions are best understood and explained by reducing their complexity to their most elementary genetic, neural, and chemical parts and processes. Reproductive fitness in processes of evolutionary natural selection determines and explains the nature and behavior of all living organisms, including humans and their social lives. People and their societies are the complex products of biologically grounded forces of natural selection. Prominent representatives of this approach when it comes to social science include Robert Sloan Wilson, Edward O. Wilson, Richard Dawkins, Daniel Dennett, Steven Pinker, and John Tooby. The background philosophies of science and metaphysics that underwrite this model of humanity are metaphysical materialism and naturalism, positivism, empiricism, atheism, and behavioral genetics. (No particular deep *social* philosophy, except perhaps social Darwinism, backs this approach, since everything social here is reduced to the neuro-genetic-biochemical.) Standing in the further background here in various ways are Charles Darwin, Herbert Spencer, and William Hamilton.[12] We have to recognize this model not because it is dominant in social science, but because it is hegemonic in the natural sciences and increasingly presses from the outside upon social science. Most social scientists today seem to endorse this paradigm and model when it comes to the natural sciences but reject it when it comes to their disciplines. Whether they will be able to sustain that clear distinction against the influences of imperialistic natural scientism is uncertain. With the ascendency of the integrated neo-Darwinian evolutionary approach in the natural sciences and major recent advances in genetics, neuroscience, and bioengineering, some vocal natural-science advocates are proposing to dissolve the above four approaches in the social sciences with the solvent of this fifth model as a comprehensive, unifying (totalizing) theory.[13]

For brevity's sake, I have laid out five broad models by which to map out the big theoretical terrain of philosophical anthropology in the social sciences.

Partisans of them may complain about distinctions and nuances I have failed to represent. Of course we may parse out subtypes within the models, and greater nuance is always possible. But the underlying perspectives and logics of these five approaches still retain a broad internal coherence that groups them into theories with real family resemblances. So I think we can generalize fairly about their main contours in this way.[14] I will not spend many words in what follows further describing these models, since they are already quite familiar, much written about, and firmly institutionalized in social science. I will instead focus mostly on advancing and describing my own personalist theory as an alternative to them.

The Personalist Alternative

Personalist social theory views the five models of human beings above—and their associated ideas about interests and motivations—as inadequate. Critical realist personalism, my constructive alternative, understands humans rather to be *natural-goods-seeking persons*. Such an account, I argue, is more realistic, theoretically coherent, and intellectually and morally more fruitful. It embraces what is helpful yet rejects what is problematic in the five rival models. It underwrites better social science and realistically explains more of our actual human experience. Large numbers of persons acting in accordance with this personalist theory also proves more generative of the kind of just, peaceful, equitable, free, humanistic societies in which (I hope) most of us, for good reasons, would like to live and have our progeny live. If I am correct, then we should be motivated to seriously consider these issues, work through the arguments, and embrace the personalist account I propose here.

Personalist theory claims that all adequate understandings of human life must take seriously the fact that human beings are *persons* and not something else. This requires that we understand what persons *are*, what distinguishes them from nonpersonal entities. It is not enough to know something about human bodies or genetics or social interactions. We need to understand more of the fullness of what it means to *be* a person. Only by understanding the personhood of human beings will we adequately be able to understand and explain people and their social relations, because humans cannot be properly understood apart from their personhood.[15] To ignore personhood is to evacuate the central and most important features of the basic unit that social science studies.[16] That creates a major blind spot that prevents us from seeing important facts we must observe if we wish to adequately understand human life. To ignore human personhood is to self-compromise our own ability—as social theorists, social scientists, and persons trying to negotiate ourselves and life—to understand ourselves as particular kinds of beings in the larger order of reality.

Not every social theory places persons at the theoretical center, and not every theory that purports to take persons seriously understands what personhood means. Sociological and philosophical approaches that sidestep, "de-center," or dissolve persons, that oversimplify assumptions about persons, or that engage in reductionisms that compress persons into nonpersonal components must be refused. Instead, social processes and structures must be understood and explained with reference to the nature, capacities, and tendencies of human persons from which they emerge—even when those processes and structures through emergence are distinctly real and possess causal capacities greater than the persons whose activities animated them.[17] Personalism thus demands that we believe and work with a thick, realistic notion of human personhood.[18]

The nature of human persons also provides direction and substance to moral judgments and normative reflections on what is good in human life and society. Personalism advances claims concerning facts and values, descriptions and prescriptions, empirical happenings and moral norms. We cannot do moral philosophy or normative political theory well without accounting for the personhood of humans. The reality of persons is a central, ineliminable, and defining fact when it comes to human life. So any attempt to understand life, whether descriptively or normatively, for scholarship or personal or social living, must grasp and work with a good account of personhood. Personalism is not merely of theoretical and analytical scholarly interest. It has personal and political implications. If personalism's claims are correct, for example, then political liberalism, libertarianism, traditional conservatism, social pragmatism, some versions of communitarianism, and all forms of authoritarian, statist collectivism (whether on the right, such as national socialism, or the left, such as communism, or those inspired by revolutionary varieties of Rousseau[19]) are more or less inadequate, for various reasons. The personalism offered here does not harmonize with these ideologies and political programs. How and why this is so will become clearer as my account develops.

When I say "personalism" in this book, I mean a specific version of the broader personalist tradition of thought that I am particularly interested in developing. Different versions of personalism have been advanced over the last two centuries.[20] Here I pick up important insights in some of them, which I try to integrate and develop into a robust theoretical account of human beings and social life. Personalism in this book is actually shorthand for the more accurate label, "critical realist personalism." An even more precise name might be "teleological and phenomenologically serious critical realist personalism."[21] Consistently using those terms would grow tedious, however, so I usually simply refer to personalism or personalist theory.

This book also explores questions concerning the ideas of *basic* motivations and interests. It examines what previous studies have said about them and what might be reasonable to believe on the matter. The question concerns whether one master motivation or set of fundamental motivations exist out of which arise the many nonbasic motivations we observe in life. I will argue that one set of motives does exist. I identify what I believe are the multiple, basic human motivations for action. I then consider their nature and the ends toward which they are oriented. I develop an argument about the ends of human action as teleologically oriented toward what is good for humans, the human good. That then raises the larger question of what, if anything, actually *is* good for humans, and whether all humans everywhere may possibly share a telos or end that represents the true good of persons. I propose at that point to answer that question by relying on a classical notion of happiness—which is perhaps better called human flourishing, well-being, or thriving, in order to emphasize the richness and complexity of the kind of happiness in question (as opposed to standard, thin, modern notions of happiness based on self-reported, transient emotional states).

I will also suggest that the happiness and flourishing of any given person is inextricably tied up with their promoting the happiness and flourishing of *other* persons. This will establish a particular framework grounded in an ancient tradition of philosophy. That will enable us to connect the disparate matters of the vast variety of human motivations for and interests in action, their rootedness in certain basic motivations for action, namely, human goods, toward the realization of human flourishing. I will thus attempt to show that my account of human motivations and interests, grounded in the pursuit of human goods, is linked to an alternative and much improved understanding of human persons and human social life, relations, and institutions. Not only does this alternative account provide social science with a better model of human beings than the other models noted above, it also provides us with a better account of what we all *are* as human persons, how we should live our lives and why, and what a good society looks like.

The kind of account of human motivations and actions I advance in this book raises a specific, difficult problem, however, which does not much trouble the five rival accounts described above. That is the problem of human selfishness, stupidity, laziness, deception, and malice. The benign form of the problem involves explaining why people in fact often do *not* seek what is good. In its darkest form, the problem is about explaining human evil. This problem confronts my account of human motivations and action with this question: If human motivations are ultimately oriented toward the achievement of basic human goods, which are constitutive of a real human good, then why do so many humans seem motivated not to pursue what is good, but instead what is bad, what often leads to the failure, compromising, and destruction of themselves and others? If my personalist account is correct, it has to answer this query: If humans are in their actions ultimately oriented toward the realization of the deepest kind of human happiness and flourishing, then why are so many people unhappy, and why do people willfully behave in ways that (they sometimes actually know will) make themselves and others unhappy, which will lead to stagnation and destruction instead of well-being? The standard social science accounts of human beings either have no burden to answer these questions (because they do not address them) or else they offer unsatisfactory answers. My project, therefore, must confront the problem of human failure, destruction, and evil, explaining them in terms that are consistent with my larger theory. I seek to offer humanly true and satisfying reasons why goods-oriented motivations can and do produce bad human actions and outcomes.

Personalism's Promise

Personalism brings to sociology a number of theoretical advantages. One is an account of human beings that avoids the long-standing problems generated by the oppositions of individualism and social holism, the micro and the macro, and agency and structure. Many think these problems have been solved in sociology, but I think that is wrong. The nub of personalism's solution to this problem comes with this recognition: all persons are radically dependent upon the social for their existential *development* and flourishing, but persons are *not* dependent on the social for their *ontological* personal being. Human persons themselves innately have all of the natural equipment to be the persons they *are* as persons, without any essential contribution from society or culture. Yet they remain radically dependent upon society for their natural personal potential to survive, grow, and thrive. Persons need from social life the care, nourishment, and training to develop and flourish. The implications of getting these distinctions right are huge. Such an account, the discerning reader will see, depends upon the crucial distinctions between being and becoming, ontology and existence, the real and the actual, full potential and variable realization. It also depends completely on understanding emergence. These are categories that modern social theory rarely uses, which explains some of our problem.

Another advantage personalism brings to sociological theory is a better account of human motivations and interests that give rise to actions and practices.[22] Many sociological theories tend either simply to ignore or discount the question of human motivations for action, supposing it to be unimportant, or they do offer accounts of motivations for action yet define them in such one-dimensional terms that we must judge them to be inadequate to reality. On the question of human interests, for example, some approaches dismiss the very idea as superfluous, believing that people's "interests" are merely variable and relative cultural constructions handed to people by society, not natural and real facts. Other sociological approaches take natural human interests seriously, yet they poorly specify what those interests are.[23] Personalism as an alternative contends that human action and practices are in fact driven by real motivations and interests that are grounded in the nature of reality and necessary to identify and understand if we wish to comprehend and explain social life and social structures. Those motivations and interests are directly tied to the nature of human personhood, requiring us to understand and center the reality of persons. They are also real and natural, not mere cultural constructions. They are, furthermore, teleological, oriented toward ends having to do with goods and excellence of human life, toward which people, in personal processes of development, move (or do not move). In this, personalism seeks to offer a significant contribution to sociological theory.

A third advantage personalism brings to sociological theory is a coherent normative and moral perspective on human life. Personalism not only does not disregard normative questions in theory, it also refuses to allow morality to be segregated off from descriptive and explanatory social theory. It rejects the modern divorce of *is* from *ought*, fact from value. It recognizes that many descriptive claims entail concepts and ideas that raise and engage normative claims.[24] This is true, personalism insists, of all social theories, whether they admit or deny it. Personalism names that relationship, embraces the reconnection of fact and value without collapsing the distinction, and advances an account of morality and the good that it proposes to be most true to reality.[25] Personalism also advances an approach that bonds together what Western modernity has chronically pulled apart as isolated polarities. It holds together both the light and the dark sides of human nature and experience, the personal good and evil. For the last four centuries, Western social theory has dissolved the creative tension that older accounts maintained between the bright and the dark sides of human being. Lacking a larger framework that could sustain both together in dynamic tension, the centrifugal intellectual forces of modernity have pulled apart humanity's goodness and evil and pushed them in opposite directions.[26] As a result, optimistic humanist accounts have highlighted the genuinely impressive, intelligent, accomplishing, and admirable features of human beings—all the while underplaying humanity's pestilent side. At the same time, darkly pessimistic antihumanist accounts have correctly emphasized humanity's bestial irrationality, puny insignificance, and destructive malice—while ignoring or discounting the impressive side of humanity. Both kinds of accounts are partly right in their own ways, but incomplete, and wrong when taken alone. The only account worth taking seriously is one that brings both sides of humanity, the light and the dark, together into one coherent picture. Personalism does that.

Other Theoretical Resources

It is worth noting two other theoretical perspectives that shape the kind of personalism I advocate. First, this book's argument is guided by *critical realism* as a metatheory of science. Critical realism believes in ontological realism, epistemic perspectivalism, and judgmental rationality, all held together. This means that much of reality exists and operates independently of our human awareness of it (ontological realism), that human knowledge about reality is always historically and socially situated and conceptually mediated (epistemic perspectivalism), and that it is nonetheless normally possible for humans over time to improve their knowledge about the real, to adjudicate rival accounts, and so to make justified truth claims about reality (judgmental rationality). All three of these beliefs must go together, critical realism says, to keep (social) science on track. Stated negatively, critical realism rejects ontological antirealism (that "reality" is itself a mind-dependent, human construction), epistemological foundationalism (that a bedrock foundation exists for human knowledge that is indubitably certain and universally binding on all rational persons), and judgmental relativism (that all truth claims are relative and impossible to adjudicate).

Critical realism offers an alternative to positivist empiricism, hermeneutical interpretivism, and postmodern deconstructionism. It says that social science should not only want to know how measured variances are statistically associated, for example, or what human symbols mean to people, but more fundamentally to understand the ontological character of what exists in reality and how it works causally to produce the facts and events we experience. Therefore, we must inquire into matters such as what human beings *are*, ontologically, what causes their actions, and what is in fact good and bad for humans—to the limits of our ability to understand such concerns. Many sociologists long ago ceased caring about ontological questions, and many today are skittish about causality. But it is impossible to do good sociology while bracketing ontology and sidelining causality. We have to be ready to investigate ontological matters in social life—to examine what is real, what exists, what capacities and limitations things have, and so on. And we have to be ready to make justified causal claims—about how certain entities exert forces or powers that cause other things to happen. Ontology and causality are needed to do good sociology, and critical realism provides the framework for doing that well.

As mentioned above, critical realism also reconnects facts and values, toward overcoming the standard is/ought divide. The modern propensity to divorce the descriptive and the normative ritualistically appeals to David Hume and against the "naturalistic fallacy." But Hume has been misread on this point, and moderns have wrongly partitioned the empirical and the moral.[27] Critical realism takes another approach, saying that reality is ultimately of one piece and that while the whole comprises both distinctly factual and normative dimensions, these interpenetrate one another and cannot be fully separable. Our empirically descriptive and analytical observations often naturally entail normative and moral implications. And our normative and moral outlooks and judgments inescapably refer to the nature of reality as best as we can empirically describe, understand, and analyze it. We do not need to confuse or merge the factual and the normative in order to free them from their hermetically sealed isolation chambers to interact with one another. The point is not that no difference exists between descriptive and normative statements. The point, rather, is that the two cannot be divorced from each other, as if each must operate in a separate realm of ideas outside of which the two may never meet. *That* modern philosophical idea does not work.

Critical realism has much more than this to say about these points, and about emergence, reductionism, downward causation, the difference between the real, the actual, and the empirical, causation, explanation, social mechanisms, retroduction, complexity, the epistemic fallacy, the role of theory, and more. Some of this will be explained in the next chapter. But beyond these few points I cannot go here. Good expositions of critical realism are available elsewhere, which interested readers should consult.[28] Suffice it for now to acknowledge the central role that critical realism plays in forming the argument that follows.

This book also relies as a second theoretical resource on a broadly neo-Aristotelian view of human life. That means it takes seriously this premodern intellectual tradition as modern thinkers have mediated it. Contemporary Western academics usually work only with assumptions and ideas that have developed since the seventeenth century. I find that to be parochial and debilitating. Modern beliefs and ideas have hardly solved all of our human problems or brought about the kind of world that early modern thinkers aspired to realize. Some modern ideas I think are patently abject failures, and consequently the world we inhabit is something of a mess. In my view, we have no good reason, as long as we are discerning about it, not to consider human intellectual accomplishments and approaches from across history, beginning with the ancients—to be "looking for friends in history," as Mencius put it.[29] Aristotle, I think, is one premodern well worth considering, revising, and renewing for use, even in our contemporary world. Western modernity is, of course, itself in part *defined* by a wholesale rejection of Aristotelian thinking, starting in the seventeenth century. Justified as that rejection may have been on the matter of Aristotle's "natural philosophy," I think it was unwarranted when it came to understanding major dimensions of *human* life. Following many others of late, I seek here to retrieve the Aristotelian tradition in ways I think help us.

Crucial in any Aristotelian account is the notion that certain aspects of reality are oriented and operate *teleologically*, that is, toward ends that are proper to their being.[30] It is not necessary to adopt the view and language of Aristotle's own natural philosophy about the nonhuman material world. It is possible to believe that modern natural science was essentially correct in rejecting that part of Aristotle.[31] Because of the reality of emergence, however, the living human world is qualitatively different from the inanimate world in crucial ways. Human life in fact does entail a significant teleological character in a way that does not apply to oak trees and comets. *People* do confront an existence that involves ends proper to their humanity. Such a view is heretical in contemporary social science. But this teleological heresy deserves to challenge and overturn the problematic, established, modern social science orthodoxy of humanity-without-proper-ends. I do not take the fact that an idea existed before the sixteenth century to itself be an automatic refutation of it. While I adhere to many modern ideas, I also find certain premodern ideas insightful and illuminating. In fact, I believe that some of them are true. Our criterion for adjudicating ideas should not be whether they are modern or premodern, but rather how well they seem to illuminate and explain reality for us. Having spent most of my life as a modern discounting the idea of humans possessing a natural human telos or purpose, I have more recently come to believe that this idea is actually correct. So this book is devoted in part to developing this idea of natural human goods and purposes and to exploring how they relate to the sociological question of basic human interests and motivations giving rise to actions and practices.

One of modernity's conceits concerns its own novelty. Modernity's self-image has always included the belief that all of its issues, outlooks, and experiences are new—which is presumed to also mean better and true. The word "modern" itself means "just now, as pertaining to present times."[32] So part of being modern is to think that modernity made a radical break from the past, started history over, and grapples with life in a radically new way. But that is mythology. Many of the positions with which we are concerned in this book, both for and against, are rooted in developments of late medieval Christendom,[33] and those in turn reflect positions first laid out in the classical age. There is nothing new under the sun. Modern thinkers simply too often have amnesia or suffer historical obliviousness. By setting personalist theory and its alternatives in a broader historical framework, we can see more clearly both the issues that are at stake and the problematic intellectual moves generations past made that set us up for some of our current troubles.

Human Nature?

What I have said so far suggests that I intend somehow to speak to the question of "human nature." That is correct. I realize that "human nature" is an antiquated term for many, often associated with illegitimately essentialist views of humanity, if not archaic religious doctrines of human sin or optimistic Enlightenment or Romanticist doctrines of human goodness. Illegitimately essentialist views of humanity do exist, but the theory this book advances is not one of them.[34] In any case, nobody really, consistently believes in a totally nonessentialist view of humanity, or else there would be no identifiable subject to have a view about. Those who claim to do so are either confused or inconsistent about what "essential" means, or are simply fooling themselves. Everyone, including social scientists, holds views of "human nature," whether they realize it or not. And those views govern how they make sense of the world. The real question, then, is whether or not our views are good ones. Since no social scientist can theorize the microfoundations of social life without coming down somewhere on the issue of what we might as well call human nature and its implications for motivations for action, I say it is better to come down somewhere after having brought it out into the open and thought about it long and hard, rather than ignoring it and then arriving somewhere by default that is therefore more likely to be problematic.

Why do people so strongly resist "essentialistic" accounts of humans? The main motive seems to be their moral objection to abusive uses of essentialistic accounts in the past. Understandable. But just because some or even many versions of essentialist views of humanity are wrong and have been used for oppressive purposes does *not* mean that *every* account of human being that attributes some essential features or characteristics to humanity is wrong. Rather than uncritically throwing out all views of human nature as "essentialist" by definition, on the assumption that they will necessarily be pernicious, we should instead work harder to discriminate between true versus erroneous accounts of human nature. In fact, to eradicate *every* account of human nature is, ironically, to place oneself in the position of total helplessness against aggressive forces of exploitation and oppression.[35] The very ideas of and judgments against exploitation and oppression must presuppose some notion of what is good and right for human beings, in relation to which other things are judged to be exploitative and oppressive. And that requires some idea of what human beings are like, what their condition is, what they need, what is beneficial for them, what causes them to thrive or destruct. And those matters concern exactly the nature of human being, human nature. I thus proceed without apology using the terms "human nature" and "the nature of human being."

That then forces us to define what we mean by "natural" and "naturally." I mean by them the stably characteristic properties, capacities, tendencies, and limitations of any entity by virtue of its ontological character. The idea is that specific parts of reality are what they are and not other things. By virtue of being what they particularly are, specific parts of reality possess certain characteristic features, causal powers, dispositions, and limitations (and not others) that adhere in their being. Many such properties, capacities, tendencies, and limits are not accidental but help constitute the entity. For example, it is the nature of water to be liquid and clear, to be capable of certain things, such as dissolving salt and extinguishing fires, and to tend to boil and evaporate into a gas at a specific high temperature and to freeze into a solid at a specific low temperature. Everything in reality has some kind of nature, in this sense, insofar as every entity possesses and can express particular characteristics, capacities, and tendencies by virtue of simply being what it is. That is partly what makes them humanly knowable entities in the first place. If they had no stably characteristic properties, capacities, tendencies, or limitations, how could we even know that they existed as "entities" to begin with, much less anything reliable about them? For my purposes, when such features, capacities, and disposition are not accidental, random, or unstable, but stably typify the entity by virtue of its ontology in ways shared by all entities of that type, we can refer to them as their nature.[36]

This approach simply recognizes that some parts of reality are neither (entirely) humanly "constructed" nor readily susceptible to intentional human change. Reality itself has a certain "grain" in its structure and tendencies.

Reality and its many parts and systems operate in accordance with a variety of patterns and regularities, sometimes (in the natural world) even constants and laws. Human beings are not exempt from these regularities. We humans involve and function through and up to certain natural characteristics, capacities, tendencies, and limitations that do not depend for existence on human beliefs and cultural practices—which, by contrast, we should think of as "mind dependent" and "constructed." Humans have a nature, a human nature, as I mean that here. It is human nature, for instance, to tend strongly to seek to avoid death (except under the pathological condition of severe depression), just as it is natural for human bodies to seek to repel threats to health and to heal themselves when infected or injured. Some moderns and postmoderns may not like humans having a nature, since modernity is all about human autonomy and control, and postmodernism about difference, fluidity, and self-creation, but that does not change the reality.

Believing that reality involves real entities with real natures, however, does not commit us to reifying categorical differences and inequalities as "natural" that are in fact institutionally caused. Human persons do have the natural capacities for memory and creativity, for instance. But humans with a certain shade of skin color are *not* naturally superior in morality or worth to other humans of different skin shades, despite some asserting and believing otherwise. Mere claims to certain observed features of life existing "by nature" and so requiring legitimation and cooperation are not self-validating. The question is whether such claims are true or not. Our goal as human observers, especially in science, is to learn what is true about what is real. It is true that reality is comprised of entities with *natural* features, capacities, and tendencies. We do no good categorically denying that fact simply because sometimes it is put to uses that are cruel and unjust. The fitting response to a certain truth being *abused* is not to deny the truth wholesale, but to condemn and reject that abusive use, to stop abusing it now, and to be more careful to understand and use it properly.

To observe that real entities have real natures also does not mean that they always, consistently behave in particular ways. My approach is not deterministic, especially when applied to certain spheres of life. Some parts and systems of reality, especially those involving inanimate entities, seem to operate in highly regular, even determined ways. Other parts of reality, especially those involving many living entities, entail natural capacities for bounded indeterminacies. And some animals, especially those with more complexly developed capacities for consciousness, cognition, volition, and affect—and, among those, especially human persons—possess natural powers enabling them to partly transcend deterministic causes or laws.[37] This, of course, is the root of the notions of human freedom and agency. Therefore, real differences in degrees of determination and indeterminacy, order and chaos, consistency and variety inhere in the nature of reality itself. In which case, overcoming determinism does not require negating or transgressing the very nature of things, since the determinate and indeterminate nature of reality is innately specified and limited by natural reality.

Finally, observing and believing that various real entities have particular real natures also does not commit us to the additional belief that the *characteristics* of entities are immutable in the long run. Some entities do change in their natural characteristics, capacities, and features over time. Sometimes this is due to transformations that take place over the life course of a specific entity, such as human females' normal inability and then ability and then inability again to conceive and bear children at different points in life. But most of these kinds of transformations are part of the normal development of the natural, innate potencies of the things in question—that is, the entity qua entity does not change. Entities can also change their natural characteristics, capacities, and features over time because certain of them are particularly developed or selected upon, whether randomly or intentionally. Certain wild animals, for instance, can be domesticated through selective breeding to be well suited to human domestic life. But that also relies upon crucial, natural, stable characteristics of the animals in question, including the operation of genetically grounded behavioral dispositions selected across generations. Even then, some animals, such as snakes, crocodiles, and scorpions, cannot be domesticated, as their particular natures will not allow it. "Nature," as defined here, concerns traits that are stable and common across kinds of entities, but not absolutely immutably. The key concept is "stably characteristic," not "eternally permanent." But even when the nature of some entities does change, those transformations usually happen slowly and transpire in accord with the larger order, direction, and regularity of the nature of reality within which those entities exist.

The personalist theory I propose therefore concerns stable and anthropologically universal features of humanity. Accounts that, by contrast, emphasize characteristics or tendencies that are particular only to some civilizations, cultures, or historical periods and concern only contingent and accidental features of humanity, not universal ones. That is not what I am after.[38] Still, human nature may well not have been constant for the entire history of *Homo sapiens*. To specify the scope conditions of my account, I propose the conservative boundary of human life since the Neolithic revolution, beginning circa 9500 BC, as the human existence to which it applies—although I suspect it also applies as far back to *Homo sapiens* many tens of thousands of years ago.[39] But I am content to specify a more limited time frame of relevance. I am thus not claiming to theorize protohuman and human life for all of its existence on earth, but for most of known human history and certainly as it matters for us today.

The Purpose of Theory

Some colleagues have told me that "American social scientists will not be interested in issues like human personhood or critical realism unless they can be shown how it will make a direct difference in the ways they conduct their empirical research." Otherwise, apparently, most social scientists will ignore it as "just theory" and keep doing their empirical work the same old ways. Perhaps. But so much the worse for social science, then. The ultimate point of conducting good empirical research in social science is to develop well-informed general theories about how social life is constituted and how it operates. What exists and how does it work? That is the ultimate scientific question, the proper final end of any research. Good general *theory* is actually the ultimate *goal* of social science, the true end point, the final standard for having eventually succeeded in empirical work. By contrast, a show-me-the-practical-empirical-research-payoff-now-or-I'm-not-interested mentality wrongly inverts the purpose of research and theory. It demotes theory to mere prolegomena for empirical research, perhaps the source of some orienting axiom or hypotheses to test. Theory of course inescapably informs empirical research. All data are theory laden, and so on. But to view theory generally as mere prologue to what "really" counts in sociology (that is, incessant empirical investigation) is misguided. What finally counts in social science, what would indicate ultimate disciplinary success, is the formation of theories that could tell us generally how social life is composed and how it works, in a way that would well interpret and explain empirical social reality to us as we live our lives. Otherwise, social science amounts to only so much gathering and cataloging of empirical facts, something like sophisticated journalism. Unless empirically formed general theory is the goal of social science, then social science is underachieving and failing in its highest purpose.

Maybe many in social science have given up on general theory. That simply tells us that something about our scholarly business-as-usual has gotten off track. If so, there is reason to step back and reconsider what we are doing. If many social scientists have lost interest in general theory, then understanding why brings us back to the philosophy of social science. For most of the twentieth century, mainstream American social science was defined by the dominant philosophy of positivist empiricism. But positivist empiricism is a theoretical failure, an inevitable disappointment when it comes to theory. Positivist empiricism teaches that real theory takes the basic form of "If A → B," or (probabilistically modified and statistically elaborated) "If A → (more likely) B (ceteris paribus)." Under this kind of influence, mainstream social science has set itself the task of identifying such universal and "middle range" covering laws of social life amenable to that form—whether or not it is realized or admitted that this is what is actually going on. The problem is that there exist few if any such laws of social life—not even of the middle range. Social life just does not work that way. That is what decades of accumulated inconsistent and inconclusive empirical studies have demonstrated. In short, general social theory *of the positivist empiricist kind* has failed, and where it has appeared to have succeeded, it usually turns out to be boring. No wonder many social scientists who remain under the (residual or active) influence of positivist empiricism's assumptions cannot get enthusiastic about general theory. Better, under those conditions, it seems, to just keep cranking out empirical studies.

But suppose we actually want to get somewhere with general social science theory. It would be necessary to drop positivist empiricism as a background philosophy and to replace it with critical realism. Critical realism has little to do with discovering invariant or probabilistic conjunctions between observable events or conditions that take the form of "If A → (probably) B." Theory in critical realism is about formulating conceptually mediated descriptions about what social reality is composed of ontologically, in both its observable and nonobservable dimensions, and how causally it works to produce real facts and events of interest. That shifts the question away from, for example, "What variables tend to be associated?" toward, "What is real in social life, and how do its parts work causally to generate outcomes of importance?" We become less concerned with correlations (what goes together) and inferences (hypothesized connections) and more concerned with social ontology (what is) and real social causation (how social entities exert real capacities and tendencies by virtue of their natural powers and limitations to produce particular outcomes through the operation of real causal mechanisms). If social science hopes to revive good general theory, it will have to be on this critical realist, not positivist empiricist, grounds.

As it turns out, critical realism also has big implications for how empirical research should be conducted. But "immediate empirical payoff" cannot be the starting point. Nor can it be the impatient criterion for whether anyone should spend the effort to learn big, alternative theory. We need to get theory and empirical investigation back into their proper places and to start thinking in critical realist terms. *Then* we in our empirical research will see the need for change and opportunities for improvement. At which point, the main question will be not what immediate difference it makes, but instead whether we will be ready, willing, and able to actually change the ways we conduct and report empirical research. Critical realism makes big differences, but it takes time, patience, and investment to understand what, why, where, and how.

Why Ontology?

Some social scientists also react to accounts such as this book's by asking, "Why do we need all the ontological baggage? Can't we get rid of the ontology and do our work just as well?" The answer is no. We need the ontology. The right ontology is in fact nothing like "baggage," a metaphor that suggests that we could somehow pack lighter or bring nothing with us at all and so travel easier. The right ontology is instead more like the map that tells us where we are and how to get where we want to go. Ontology, by a critical realist account, describes for us the kind of terrain we move in and indicates different ways we might go about exploring it. Getting rid of ontology is like going on an important trip without a map or directions or GPS. One easily gets lost, however much other baggage one is toting. From a critical realist perspective, eschewing ontology is one reason why the results of the social sciences over the past century have been less than astounding.

In fact, everyone in social science operates with *some* ontology or other. The option of dismissing ontological assumptions is not available to those who want to understand and explain human behavior and social life. Most often, those who wish to operate with little to no ontology simply end up making their own operational ontology invisible to themselves and (sometimes) to others. But that does not make their de facto ontology disappear. It simply means that it cannot be inspected and evaluated. That hardly seems like an honest and responsible way to conduct scholarship. So even if ontology is baggage, scholars who think they have left it behind are in fact lugging around plenty of it—they have simply grown used to it and may not see the ways the wrong baggage may be dragging them down. Critical realism asks everyone to bring their operational ontological assumptions and models out into the open, to own up to them, to consider how they affect scholarship for good or ill, and to subject them to the criticism of others and the test of reality. As a matter of principle, that itself does nothing to establish that a critical realist ontology provides the best theoretical description of reality. Doing that takes a lot more inquiry, evidence, and argumentation. There is of course more than one ontological account deserving consideration. What this says, however, is that if someone does not like critical realism's account of ontology, it is not adequate to simply call for the dismissal of ontological considerations entirely. They need instead to advance what they think is a better ontology, argue for it, and answer the critiques of rivals. Ontology just doesn't go away.

Final Thoughts

This book is a work of *retrieval*. My argument may seem new and unusual for some readers. But anything seemingly different and unusual here is not so in the sense of daringly pushing, Prometheus-like, into original, uncharted intellectual territory. What may seem novel is provided rather by recovering ideas that many moderns have forgotten. "Retrieval" suggests that something has been left behind or lost that has a value worth returning to reclaim, renew, and bring back to the present. What I intend to retrieve for our purposes especially is the idea of the reality of a natural human good and a real human telos. Along the way, I believe we will also find much else of value to retrieve for social science and beyond. And in so doing I expect that we will likewise find that we have reclaimed and renewed something of our own value as humans.

This book can also be considered a work of experience seeking understanding or, less succinctly, human experience seeking self-understanding. The highest value of social science for humanity, I think, is not accurately predicting future events or discovering the laws of social life for use in social engineering. Social science's greatest value, rather, is to serve as a medium of self-reflexivity for human persons and societies. We humans are not only the subjects of our actions but also often the objects of our own knowledge, reflection, and evaluation. We not only think and evaluate as selves, we also think about and evaluate *ourselves* as selves. Good social science provides people in social groups and institutions truthful knowledge about themselves as persons and the social entities they comprise and inhabit, with which they can then reflect about their conditions, experiences, and possible futures. What are we? What is actually happening among us? Why did X, Y, and Z happen in our experiences? How can we better understand the true character of our social lives? When it comes to answering these kinds of questions beyond the complexity-level of interpersonal relationships, something like a disciplined, systematically methodological social science is needed. Social science's greatest contribution to the societies that sustain it with resources, therefore, is simply reporting back to those societies what really is going on in and among them, why and how so, and with what apparent consequences. That is the service of social self-reflexivity that is so valuable when performed

well, a service worthy of the resources invested in it. This book, as a work offered to contribute to the common good in exactly this way, seeks to expand
and enrich human personal and social self-understanding by reflecting upon
human experience and hopefully as a result making better sense of it. Human
experience is real, even if not self-interpreting, and can be highly informative
when reflected upon well. Self-understanding is thus the conceptually mediated, reasoned, theoretical comprehension of ourselves and our world in
response to our personal and collective experiences over time.

Developing a personalist social theory opens up a lot of big questions.
It is like starting out on a weekend morning intending to fix a leaky bath-
room faucet and ending up having to tear out most of the walls and fixtures
and renovating the entire mess from the studs out. The ideas of personalism
evoke big thoughts debated in many other theories and fields. So beginning
at any one place in personalism inevitably pulls a lot of intellectual issues
onto the floor. I will do my best to address a breadth of issues adequately
while keeping the argument manageable. We start off discussing the nature
of personhood and social life and soon find ourselves ankle deep in other
weighty matters, such as solidarity, autonomy, finitude, freedom, causation,
progress, and determinism. Developing a theory of personalism necessarily
raises ontological and epistemological questions from philosophy, pulls us
into arguments about political theory, and forces us to think about the nature
and meaning of modernity. Any adequate general theory requires as much.[40]
Hopefully readers find personalism refreshing and challenging. At the same
time I do not seek to offer here a theory of everything or to comment on every conceivably related question. A variety of relevant and important issues
I will recognize but leave undiscussed. That may be because personalism has
no particular stake in the matter. Or it may be because personalism has a real
stake but addressing it would take us well beyond the reasonable scope of a
book. Subsequent works will have to take up matters left unaddressed here.[41]

Stating outright the main targets of my critique in this book should help
readers to see key threads woven through my developing argument. In social science, my opponents are social situationists, antirealist social constructionists, antimentalist theories, and any approach that seriously discounts
people's subjective beliefs and motivations for action. More broadly, I am
challenging certain versions of the theory and culture of liberalism, those that
strongly emphasize individualism and personal autonomy.[42] Most broadly, I
am taking on social scientists and philosophers who are more influenced by
Thomas Hobbes, David Hume, and Immanuel Kant than by Aristotle.[43] As
to the situating of my argument in the larger field of general theories, readers
will soon realize that my personalism is positioned within the broad natural

law tradition. My account would not unfairly be understood as a secular analogue to other natural law accounts that may be religiously oriented. Thus secular readers should be able to find my argument entirely convincing, even though it is also arguably compatible with certain theological outlooks. Thus, to be clear, this book is not about religion, but rather the nature of human personhood and its implications for social science and beyond.

Finally, it is perhaps worth saying on a personal note that I do not come to personalism naturally. Personalism is allied to a kind of humanism that holds onto hope in the face of horror. A superficial reading of what follows might suggest that personalist theory is best suited for the kind of people who "like people," that it sits especially well with anthropological optimists and naively happy humanists. Not so. My own natural personal disposition is misanthropic. I find bleak antihumanistic theories quite compelling, although in the end I know they are descriptively incomplete and morally impossible. It would be easier for me to take a dark and dismissive view of my own species than to be a balanced personalist. Yet in the end personalism impresses me as the most honest and reasonable view of humanity and society. Any candid, fair, complex reading of humanity and society demands an account acknowledging the dark, broken, inhuman side of people and life. Personalism possesses the resources to name and explain those dark features, without going overboard, without also losing sight of the light. Attending to this reality of human brokenness will lead us well beyond the normal boundaries of standard social science theory. We need that. Contemporary social science in the United States suffers a variety of problems.[44] In addition to its disconnection from and oftentimes ignorance of larger, crucial philosophical questions, another problem is its common, uneasy belief that moral issues can be bracketed away and social science conducted as an objective or neutral affair that does not wrestle with what is good, right, true, and virtuous. I see that situation as impossible and irresponsible, and so I try to work against it. However successful or not I may be in that, it is perchance worth saying that what led me to embrace personalism is our human reality, in all of its rich complexity and stark contrasts, and not any of my own personal proclivities toward (against) most other humans. I hope that readers, in view of reality, also find personalism similarly illuminating and compelling.

A Brief Roadmap to the Chapters

Chapter 1 sketches certain basic ideas comprising the personalist theory this book assumes and develops, summarizing for present purposes some of what I have argued at length elsewhere.[45] Chapter 2 presents my constructive theory of human motivations for action, emphasizing the necessity and feasibility of an account of motivations and defending the centrality of beliefs in human personal and social life. Chapter 3 offers a rational reconstruction and critique of "social situationism," a strong theoretical and analytical current in contemporary sociology, which I show to be untenable, although capable of being revised to be realistic and useful. Chapter 4 examines the assumptions about human nature and motivations held by Émile Durkheim, Karl Marx, and Max Weber, demonstrating the importance of beliefs about human nature for their larger theoretical projects, and evaluating the strengths and weaknesses of their accounts of motivations. I focus there on the "*Homo duplex*" model of human beings, which I contrast with my personalist account of persons. Chapter 5 explores the question of whether human personhood involves any "basic" goods that might define core human motivations. I argue that the nature of human personhood involves six identifiable, basic human goods that define basic human motivations and interests—all of which are oriented toward human flourishing. Chapter 6 then develops a personalist theory of human flourishing, grounded in a neo-Aristotelian, teleological framework that takes seriously both the enjoyment of favorable social-structural conditions *and* personal effort and learning. Chapter 7 then turns to explain why and how human failure, destruction, and even evil happen in a world that naturally orients human persons toward flourishing. Altogether, the chapters make a case for the need to take seriously the reality and nature of subjective human motivations for generating action, to resist problematic versions of social situationism, to define carefully the relationship between distinct persons and their social environments, to identify which goods are by nature basic to human life, to develop a teleological account of human flourishing that defines objective human interests, and to understand how the natural human telos of flourishing can be compromised and destroyed by failure, destruction, and evil.

Critical Realist Personalism—Some Basics

Critical realist personalism grounds and centers its theoretical reflections in the nature, capacities, limitations, and implications of real human personhood. Humanity's personal being is the starting point, substantive focus, and explanatory reference for understanding the constitution and operation of human personal and social life. To describe, understand, and explain features of human life well—from the simplest actions to the most complex global institutions—one must begin by thinking about what persons are, can do, are motivated to accomplish, are not able to do, and what their actions and interactions produce through emergence as social facts. I have written in depth about the nature of persons elsewhere, but readers of this book may benefit from a restatement of some of the basics of personalist theory.[1]

The center and touchstone of personalist social theory is the human person. Every social theory and philosophy has some structuring framework, guiding metaphor, or thematic reference that organizes how it describes and explains reality. Thomas Hobbes, for example, focused on the problem of creating order in a chaotic and conflicted world. John Locke wrote of the problem of cultivating a free citizenship in the face of overbearing states. Jeremy Bentham emphasized the maximizing of human pleasure and minimizing of pain. Karl Marx made the means and relations of material production his interpretive key. Émile Durkheim framed his thinking around the problem of social solidarity. Talcott Parsons's theoretical touchstone was the functional survival and well-being of social systems. Pierre Bourdieu was centrally concerned with the dynamics of the social reproduction of inequality.[2] By comparison, the central organizing theoretical principle and reference of personalist theory is the human person.

The Reality of the Person

The most basic belief underlying personalist theory is that human persons are real entities with ontological being that exist in nature. Persons and personhood are not mere names we give to gesture toward something that seems real but in fact is a mere appearance or fabrication. By calling ourselves "persons" we are not simply evoking a fiction of folk psychology that has no substantial referent. The word "persons" refers to real entities, that which we humans ontologically are. Personhood is a real thing, what philosophers call a "natural kind." Persons have being naturally, as a particular kind of entity with characteristic capacities, features, and tendencies that are distinct from nonpersonal entities. Persons are one particular part of the larger order of reality in the nature of things. They are not human cultural constructions (although our theories about them, which is different from the "them" about which we have theories, are human constructions). Furthermore, the personhood of persons cannot be disaggregated in a reductionistic operation to some lesser or simpler collection of parts, without a loss of ontological essentials. The personhood of persons is irreducible.[3] So when we ponder what related to human social life might be real, what actually exists, what belongs to a human social ontology, human persons are among them as primary facts. Human life never could be constructed and lived in some places or times in a way in which personhood was absent. Where there are living humans we find persons.[4] That is because personhood is a particular, natural, and central aspect of human being.[5]

By "humans" I mean living members of the human species—*Homo sapiens*—at whatever stage of development in the life course. By "reality" I mean all that belongs to that which has being, the sum total of what exists. By "real" I mean possessing ontological being and thus occupying a part of the totality of all that exists in reality. Included in the real are both material things and nonmaterial entities that possess causal powers.[6] Thus no material object is not real, and nothing that can exert causal force on other objects is not real. Nonmaterial entities—such as gravity, radio waves, force fields, beliefs, and desires—may therefore be real if they possess causal powers.

What would an argument against the reality of human personhood sound like? One version might be that "persons" are mere epiphenomenal imaginings or cognitive illusions wafting off of the brains of the material bodies of *Homo sapiens* about themselves or other humans. Such a materialist account might say humans are bodies and nothing but bodies, mere matter and electrical signals and the stream of conscious perceptions and cognitions that arise from them—but nothing existing above and beyond those material elements, despite our imaginings of them.[7] Another personhood-denying view, compatible with the materialist account above, would argue a social-constructionist line, that personhood is merely a cultural invention of some people in some times and places, not real or universal. The constructed idea of personhood is simply a cultural imposition on human bodies, merely one way to look at what human beings are. In which case, we might want to call some people "persons" in social contexts that recognize the term, but have no good reason to claim that all humans are persons or that personhood itself is a real, natural entity.

Personalism denies both of those positions. For one reason, personalism rejects classical materialism (the doctrine that nothing exists except matter) as a general metaphysical presupposition and exclusive criterion defining the contents of reality. The causal criterion of reality recognizes nonmaterial entities possessing causal powers as belonging to the real. Many things that are not material do possess capacities to exert causal forces to make things happen in the world. And, by a causal criterion of reality, that makes them real. Personhood endows humans with causal powers that are not reducible to the material bodily elements from which personhood emerges, and so causally equipped and cause-exerting persons are real. Accounts that seek to expunge such nonmaterial entities from reality yet explain without them how reality (supposedly) works end up having to engage in more intellectual reductionism and contortions than justifies the initial presupposition of metaphysical materialism. Materialism is a mere *presupposed* doctrine—the kind that constrictively functions to define the basic rules of the scientific game in ways that determine in the first place what could count as a fact and so what could possibly ever be discovered and recognized. So it seems best to many of us simply not to presuppose it, since other good reasons and evidence argue against it. Personalism thus contends that nonmaterial entities can exist and do exist, and very important among them are human persons.[8]

The Centrality of Persons

In personalism, social structures and societies are not prioritized analytically or morally over persons. Particular features of human relationships or institutions are not privileged in explaining humans and social life. Specific analytical questions about social order or change are not the starting point. Rather, personalism is driven by a realist account of what persons are ontologically, what persons are capable of causally, how finite persons are limited in their causal capacities, and what personhood entails as genuine goods for persons to pursue teleologically. The rest flows from there. In personalism, the real, natural character, capacities, tendencies, interests, and ends of human persons, and the constructed cultural and institutional outcomes to which those naturally give rise, are what organize and shape how personalism describes and explains human social life. The cultures and the social, economic, and political institutions, structures, processes that people develop and pass on are first and ultimately made sense of by the nature, capacities, goods, and limits of human persons.

From a personalist perspective, a crucial test of any theory about human social life is whether it in principle, at least, comports with what we know about and experience as persons. Not every theory needs to discuss persons explicitly. But every theory needs in principle to be able to explain, if asked, how its account fits with what we best understand about personhood. The question is one of compatibility and coherence, not completeness. Not all theories need to spell out their positions on personhood. But they should be able, in principle, to unpack their respective assumptions and theories in ways that are compatible with the central role of human persons as described by personalism in social life. Theories may operate at a very abstract or macro level. That is fine. The question is whether they are capable of providing an account of how and why they work at that level in light of the reality of human persons. Theories that can are worth further consideration. But theories that try to explain important features of social life while blackboxing the nature, interests, capacities, tendencies, goods, and ends of human persons are problematic, perhaps worth learning from selectively but not deserving full acceptance.

The principal reason behind this position is the personalist belief that human persons are the primary actors in and agents of human social life. The actions of persons are what animate, energize, and drive social life. Of course, social structures and institutions also emerge into real being at an ontologically higher level than that of persons as a result of emergent human activity. The social does exist at a higher level than the personal in the "strata" of reality, just as both of these exist at a higher level than the cardiovascular or neurological. And those social structures and institutions by virtue of their sui generis emergent properties and capacities possess specific downward causal powers that persons do not possess. But all social structures and institutions are *emergently* dependent upon the ongoing activity of human persons, whereas human persons are only *contextually* and *developmentally* dependent upon the social structures and institutions that nurture and sustain (or perhaps exclude, exploit, and destroy) them.[9] This is a crucial distinction. By emergently dependent I mean having no source of being other than that given through upward emergence. By contextually and developmentally dependent I mean actually having a different source of being—different from upward emergence working from a lower level—but still needing the higher level as a context necessary for the nurturance and sustenance of that being. Thus personal being emerges up from human bodies, not downwardly from social structures. Yet persons depend upon social structures and institutions to survive and realize the fullness of their personhood, so they are contextually and developmentally dependent but not emergently dependent upon them. In this sense, while both personal and social realities possess and exercise different real causal powers to influence the world, human persons are ontologically more basic and original sources of life and energy in the social world than are social structures and institutions.[10] Therefore, any good social theory should in principle be able to explain why and how it works analytically and explanatorily in relation to the principle source of social life and activity, human persons. Otherwise it is a theory floating inexplicably above the level of reality from which its components draw their being.

This account proceeds within a different framework from the individualism/social holism debate of a generation ago.[11] Personalism rejects social holism as an account of human social life. No social being exists apart from the activities of persons, which emergently give rise to the social. Holism itself was an equally troubled pendulum swing away from problematic atomistic individualism. But the real problems of a rival do not make its counterpart valid or sensible. Framed in terms of that debate, personalism also rejects individualism. Society, social institutions, and social structures are not simply nominal labels attached for convenience purposes to what is really nothing more ontologically than individuals behaving and interacting. Social institutions and structures are real in their own right; they exist in reality, sui generis, possessing real ontological being through emergence, which endows them with their own causal features and capacities.[12] The social exists at a next-higher "level" of reality above the personal. So despite its emphasis on the centrality of persons, personalism cannot accept an individualistic social theory. Since that older holism/individualism debate, more recent social theorists have proposed other ways to address similar issues. For some time, the matter was framed as a "micro/macro problem." Anthony Giddens tried to dissolve the holism/individualism, micro/macro problem with his theory of structuration. James Coleman took a rational choice approach in linking individual agents to macro social processes.[13] All of these offered advances in understanding, in their own ways. But none are ultimately satisfactory from a personalist perspective, for reasons that will become clear as this book unfolds. Suffice it for now to say that personalism derives its understanding and explanation of social life from the nature of human persons, yet without discounting the reality and power of social structures and institutions.

A Realist View of Reality

Critical realist personalism provides us with certain conceptual distinctions that are essential for making sense of reality, on which the argument of this book relies. One set of distinctions is among the real, the actual, and the empirical. The *real*, as noted above, is what exists—material, nonmaterial, and social entities that have structures and capacities. The real exists whether we know or understand it. It possesses objective being apart from human awareness of it, even when parts of it are not expressed in existential actuality. The *actual*, by contrast, is what happens as events in the world, when entities that belong to the real activate their powers and capacities. The actual happens in time and space, whether any person experiences it or not. The *empirical*, by contrast again, consists of what we humans experience or observe, either directly or indirectly. By definition, empirical matters are actualities that are observed or felt. Thus what we observe (the empirical) is not identical to all that happens (the actual). The actual comprises much more than the empirical. And neither the actual nor the empirical are identical to all that has existence (the real). There is also more to what is real than what *happens*, and to think otherwise is to engage in the fallacy critical realists dub "actualism." The empirical is always a subset of the actual, and the actual is the outcome of operations of entities that belong to the real. The three must not be conflated or else we fall into problems.

Maintaining these distinctions enables us to understand that certain objects and entities can and do exist even if they are empirically not observable at particular times and places (for example, beliefs, values, and desires). It is only when they activate their causal powers in ways producing events in time and space that they become actual, and thus potentially observable. (Of course, the causal powers of other real entities may counteract or neutralize their causal powers, in which case their effects may not become actual, even though their real causal capacities are operating.) Just because we do not see or cannot experience or measure something at some place and time in the actual, that does not mean it is not real and potentially or actually exercising causal powers. To think otherwise is to conflate the real with the empirical.

Personalism begins with a set of assumptions about reality that is both commonsensical and intellectually defensible. Most generally, it assumes that independently of human consciousness, a reality exists that is differentiated, ordered, complex, and stratified. Reality is all of that which exists or has being. The existence of much, though not all, of reality—including things like galaxies, oceans, maple trees, frogs, and nitrogen—is not dependent upon human consciousness. These parts of reality would exist whether or not humans recognized, thought about, or understood them. So only some of reality is dependent for its existence on human consciousness, things like people's beliefs, for example. What is this larger reality like? Reality is, first of all, *differentiated*. It does not consist of one indivisible monad, but of different parts, including planets and toads (among those that are not mind-dependent) and families and armies (among those at least partly dependent upon human consciousness for their existence as institutional facts). Those parts that altogether comprise reality are also *ordered*. They stand in relationship to and interaction with many other parts in ways that are normally stable across space and time. That is in part what makes it scientifically understandable. Reality is also *complex*, not simple. Its many parts are normally related in intricate, interdependent ways, so that a change in any one part usually has consequences for other parts, making most parts causally subject to potential influences by many other parts.

Reality is also *stratified*. Subsystems of reality cluster together as if in "layers" operating "above" and "below" other subsections. By subsystems of reality I mean particular types of interdependent parts that operate together, such as atoms interacting in molecular systems, biological organs operating in body systems, and human persons interacting in social systems. These subsystems are not literally spatially higher and lower, but it is common to use this language metaphorically. What makes different subsystems of reality "higher" and "lower" are not their different coordinates in three-dimensional space. The different strata instead exist and operate in what we might call "multidimensional unified space." What makes different subsystems of reality higher and lower is, first, their dependence (or lack of dependence) for existence on the operation of simpler subsystems "beneath" them, and, second, their susceptibility to being potentially causally influenced by more complex subsystems operating "above" them. This may sound impossibly abstract. But we see, study, understand, and embody this happening everywhere, all the time. Subatomic systems give rise through emergence to atomic systems, which give rise to molecular systems, which comprise various kinds of matter. Cells interact to give rise to organs, which combine in particular ways to make bodies, from which arise living agents of action and interaction, from which emerges social systems. The being of each subsystem depends on the existence and operation of the subsystem below it, and, in turn, may possess the downwardly causal capacity to influence the subsystem(s) below it. The living humans that depend for existence on their bodies (which in turn depend on their bodily organs, which in turn depend on their organic cells, and so on) can, from their particular level as agents, downwardly intervene casually upon their bodies, organs, and cells, by, for example, killing cancerous cells, protecting heart function by altering diet, or committing suicide.

Human persons are one particular kind of entity existing among many others in the larger reality that is differentiated, ordered, complex, and stratified. By virtue of their emergence into being from the operation of systems below the level of personhood (bodies, organs, cells, molecules, atoms, and such), persons are entirely dependent upon and simultaneously ontologically different from and irreducible to the systems of reality below them.[14] By virtue of their own nature, capacities, and tendencies, persons also interact and operate in ways that give rise to levels of reality above that of personhood, such as social realities, including the political, economic, familial, and so on. Persons are thus neither the highest nor the lowest level of reality, as we understand it. But persons are real and do possess natural properties, capacities, tendencies, and limitations proper to their being as persons.[15]

Some contemporary thinkers find talk about "entities" problematic, objecting to the idea that distinct objects exist that have particular, discrete essences. Understood properly, however, talk about entities is legitimate and necessary. An entity is simply something that has existence, that has being and so is and exists. The word "entity" derives from the Latin word *ens*, meaning being. To believe that some entities exist in reality is a necessary presupposition for even having a discussion about how we should properly talk about things. For if entities did not exist, then who would even be having this discussion and why would it matter?[16] Nor does believing in and talking about entities force us to accept misguided essentialist accounts of reality that claim that some of what are only humanly constructed, historically and culturally limited institutional facts are actually natural, fixed, necessary facts. Those kind of claims simply confuse the general fact that some entities exist that possess certain particular natures—which is true—with some specific claims that certain entities possess certain particular natures, which are actually false because those entities do not possess those natures (when that is true). To buy into antiessentialism wholesale because particular claims about the nature of some entities have in fact been wrong, oppressive, and damaging at the retail level is wrongheaded. We need to think more carefully than that.

The Ontology of Personhood

Personalism is not content to describe what persons are like, analyze how they act, or explain or predict their behavior. Personalism wants to know what persons *are*. That is an ontological question; one that social science often dodges. But by ducking out on ontological questions, social science undermines its own ability to understand and explain social life. The central task of any science is to describe well the nature of what exists and how it works to produce outcomes of interest. If social scientists are scientific, therefore, their job is to do that when it comes to human beings and their social lives and institutions. So we must ask, what are humans? If our answer is that humans are most importantly persons, then we must further ask, what is a person? What are the important components, capabilities, tendencies, goods, purposes, and limitations of persons? And we must also ask, of what does human social life consist? What are its key component parts? How are they ordered and disordered? What causal powers do different kinds of social entities possess? What consequences in human life do they produce? From our answers to these basic questions we must develop theoretical accounts that enhance our descriptive and analytical understanding and explanations of humans and human social life.

What is a person? By "person" I mean the particular kind of being that under proper conditions is capable of developing into (or has developed into) a conscious, reflexive, embodied, self-transcending center of subjective experience, durable identity, moral commitment, and social communication who—as the efficient cause of his or her responsible actions and interactions—exercises complex capacities for agency and intersubjectivity in order to develop and sustain his or her own incommunicable self in loving relationships with other personal selves and with the nonpersonal world.[17] Elsewhere I have unpacked and examined the individual elements of this definition in detail.[18] I will not repeat that here. Meanwhile, as this book develops, different aspects of this definition of the person will become more meaningful. For present purposes, it is enough to claim that a description of the ontology of persons is possible (even if necessarily complex) and that we need to venture a specific description of this kind to build a larger personalist social theory. Perhaps my proposed definition is inadequate. Perhaps a better description of personal ontology can be offered. All human knowledge, by critical realism's account—that affirms epistemological fallibilism—is imperfect and subject to improvement. If a better description of the ontology of personhood can be made, I will gladly embrace it. The point is not to territorially define and absolutely defend particular views. The point is to improve our shared, conceptually mediated understanding of what exists and how it works. In the meantime, however, I proceed by stating, defending, and developing the best account I currently have, as stated above, in hopes of moving the larger inquiry forward.

The discussion thus far implies that persons are complex beings. What it means to be a person is not simple. It involves many aspects and parts that are not only related to each other in complicated ways but are also dynamic in their mutually influencing systems of feedback and adjustment. To be a person is to possess and experience qualities of depth, multiplicity, and intricacy that could never be fully transparent or fathomed. The personhood of humans entails so many dimensions, powers, goods, interests, activities, enigmas, and paradoxes that persons can never be fully described, determined, or controlled. Human personhood cannot therefore be compacted down to one or a few key features that could supposedly represent the essence or simplicity or resolution of persons.

The Emergence of Personhood

An important idea of critical realist personalism is that human personhood is a reality that exists emergently, coming into being through a process of emergence. As I explained at length elsewhere, emergence refers to the process of constituting a new entity with its own particular characteristics and capacities through the interactive combination of other, different entities that are necessary to create the new entity but which themselves do not contain the characteristics present in the new entity.[19] Emergence involves the following: First, two or more entities that exist at a "lower" level interact or combine. Second, that interaction or combination serves as the basis of some new, real entity that has existence at a "higher" level. Third, the existence of the new higher-level entity is fully dependent upon the two or more lower-level entities interacting or combining, as they have and could not exist without them doing so. Fourth, the new, higher-level entity nevertheless possesses characteristic qualities (for example, structures, qualities, capacities, textures, powers) that cannot be reduced to those of the lower-level entities that gave rise to the new entity possessing them. When these four things occur, emergence has happened. The whole is more than the sum of its parts.[20]

Personhood is emergent. The personal nature of human beings is not some discrete substance residing somewhere inside the human body that in principle could be spatially located in some organ or other bodily area. Nor is personhood an independent being or spirit that could be separated from the living body. The best surgeon could not locate and remove the personhood from humans. The best exorcist could not "cast out" the person from a human being or body, even assuming that exorcisms happen. Personhood is an emergent fact of human existence, "arising" emergently from living, active human bodies, and in each case infusing and partially governing living human bodies. Living humans therefore do not "have" persons somewhere inside of them. Living humans *are* persons. Their own vital life principles present in and as bodies from the very start proactively develop bodily grounded capacities and functions that give rise through emergence to full expressions of personhood.[21]

The emergent nature of personhood means that persons cannot be equated directly with the various human capacities and functions that through emergence give rise to them. Personhood cannot be reduced, for example, to human capacities for rational thought, language use, or meaning making. Personhood instead is that which proactively brings the latter capacities into being and function. Just as the characteristic features and capacities of water (liquidity, capacity to dissolve salt, ability to extinguish fires, and so on) cannot be properly explained by merely looking at hydrogen and oxygen as individual substances, human personhood cannot be understood as the mere collection of certain human capacities. Personhood emerges as its own ontological reality sui generis in relation to those capacities, and the empirical realization and expression of personhood depends on their unfolding and exercise. But personhood cannot be reduced to those capacities.

I must introduce an important distinction between two ways emergence operates. The first I call "proactive" and the second "responsive." The difference between them concerns whether the agency generating and guiding the interactions of lower-level parts that constitute the emergent reality belongs to the emergent reality or is external to it. With proactive emergence, the emergent entity involves some governing agency and power to cause the development and behavior of the relationally interacting parts on which the emergent entity is dependent for being. With responsive emergence, by comparison, some agent other than the emergent entity causes parts to interact relationally, which then constitutes the emergent entity. A simple example of *responsive* emergence is an inkjet or laser printer. The printer is an emergent reality consisting of more than the sum of its printer parts and possessing causal powers to effect changes in the world, such as printing clean words on a page. But the emergent printer was not the agent that caused the printer to create itself. The agent was the printer manufacturer. The printer exists through emergence because another agent, the manufacturer, designed and assembled printer parts in such a way to produce an emergent printer that it knew would be a printer and print. Emergence here is responsive insofar as it exists as a response to the operations another's agency achieves. Responsively emergent entities are thus the *objects* of emergent processes and outcomes caused and guided by another agent.

By contrast, *proactive* emergence involves cases in which the agency of the emergent operations resides in or is the emergent entity itself. Here the emergent entities are the *subjects* of the emergent processes and outcomes on which they depend. Take, for example, the emergent bodily life of a tiger. The tiger's bodily organism as a single whole is in fact emergent from the relation of its various body parts and could not exist apart from them. But those body parts were developed and coordinated in the first place by the tiger's life organism. Before the parts ever existed, the tiger existed at first as a single-cell organism. The whole of its unified life precedes and produces the parts. And that organism contained within itself the capacity as a self-governing and self-developing agent of life, of its *own* life, to draw on nourishment, develop its parts, and coordinate them together in such a way as to produce emergently the normal, mature tiger organism it becomes. Tiger ontology (real being) was the agent of tiger ontogeny (organic development). This is one example of *proactive* emergence, in that the primordial core of the emergent entity was the proactive agent causing its emergent existence. In this case, the agency consisted of the tiger's life principle or energy operating through causal genetic DNA processes. Clearly, to mark the conceptual contrast, the tiger as emergent entity did not come to exist because some other agent caused its parts to develop and come together. A Dr. Frankenstein–like zoo owner, for instance, did not assemble tiger parts to produce an emergent tiger organism to show zoo visitors. The agency behind the emergence rather adheres in the emergent entity. How that happens is amazing and mysterious, as embryonic zoology shows.

This means that primal versions of wholes can in some cases precede parts in time. Developing emergent wholes can be the proactive efficient-cause agents of their own temporal development. When thinking about proactive emergence, we should picture densely compacted bundles of vitality, coded direction, and intelligence unfolding their natural abilities and tendencies through developmental processes. As the parts complexify, so does the whole. Think analogously of an oak tree growing from an acorn. Think of a brown caterpillar encapsulating itself in a chrysalis and soon emerging as a yellow butterfly. No other agent makes these happen.[22] The entities themselves contain the causal powers and directions to develop in these ways. Importantly, the developmental process does not produce the emergent entity, but instead the other way around. Nor, again, does another agent cause the developmental process, especially before birth, but rather the emergent entity itself.

Human persons are *proactively*—not responsively—emergent realities. Persons are not subsequent products of purely physical processes, the final outcomes of a temporal series of events governed by other agents at the end of which persons emerge. To the contrary, personhood ontologically adheres in the human from the start—even if in only the most nascent, densely compacted form possible—acting as the causal agent of its own development. This, of course, is part of what makes personhood what it is—namely, comprising a self-subsistent, self-governing center of being, direction, and purpose. This is also where the human agency comes from that good sociological thinking rightly acknowledges and theorizes. This, too, is why people are never the mere passive consequences or products of social forces, however powerful social forces are. Here we see the difference between persons being developmentally but not ontologically dependent upon society as important. This very proactive, not responsive, nature of personal emergence makes personhood not a possible, optional, high-end addition or accessory in human existence but rather fundamental and ineradicable in and for human being itself. That is not to say, for instance, that human bodies per se are persons—that would be a reversion to a reductionistic, flat-reality mentality. The real, including the human reality, is complex and stratified, existing and operating at least in part through emergence and downward causation. Human bodies, capacities, and persons are in reality intimately connected but are not identical.

Understanding the proactive emergence of persons, therefore, provides an account closely connecting personhood to the body, yet without conflating the first with the second. It explains how and why bodies and persons are not the products of other agents who have put them together and developed them into existence, but rather are the emergent products of their own inherent life being, energy, and direction. Proactive emergence also tells us how and why it is that the personhood of humans is not a temporally subsequent development that depends for existence on the prior development of bodily capacities—even if the mature *realization* and *expression* of personhood does depend on those developed capacities. And that explains how and why personhood is not a matter of greater or lesser degrees in any given case, but rather of full existence of being (and all that this implies) or no existence at all. Nobody is 10 or 45 or 80 percent a person. All living humans are 100 percent persons in ontological being, even if not in the empirical realization and expression of that real personhood—a distinction that proves to be important for thinking about personalist ethics.

My larger argument for prioritizing the person over the social may be difficult for some sociologists to believe, since much of what we do is to show how society shapes and directs people. In fact, "society" has an immense power to *dominate* most people, often not for their personal good.[23] But it would be a mistake to conclude from these facts that society is the more basic ontological reality or that human beings are dependent upon society in all ways and are its "constructions" or "products." We need to work with more careful distinctions than those. A central argument of this book concerns essential asymmetries between social and personal realities. Societies and persons are radically different kinds of things, with very different sources, properties, powers, and limitations. Persons are developmentally and contextually, but not ontologically, dependent upon the social—despite society's shaping, directing, and dominating powers. Nevertheless, social life is to persons always temporally preexistent and transcendentally necessary—and as such asymmetrically dominant over people.[24] While persons are not created ontologically by society, but rather emergently from biology, they nonetheless are always from conception "thrown"[25] into a preexistent social (dis)order. And that gives the social world colossal powers to shape people contextually and developmentally, even to dominate them (but also to cultivate their personhood and provide the means for exercising agency). Recognizing that the social is temporally and existentially prior to the social, and a transcendental necessity for personal survival and development (even though it is also ontologically secondary to persons) enables us to avoid an idealist voluntarism that is sociologically naive. At the same time, the distinctions made here enable us in social theory to avoid the equally false idea that people as the constructions or products of society are ontologically dependent on the social.[26]

Against Reductionism

Reductionism is a ruinous move many thinkers in various sciences make. Its approach is to claim that an emergent entity can be best understood and explained by reducing it to its lower-level component parts, from which the entity came through emergence into being, and then proposing a description or explanation only with reference to those parts and not the emergent new whole. In short, reductionism asserts that an emergent reality is in fact *nothing but* the parts from which the reality emergently came into being and can only be explained in terms of them—an act of radical and unacceptable compaction. Critical realist personalism is resolutely antireductionistic.[27] From a personalist perspective, reductionism is intellectually fatal to a realist ontology. Reductionism must be resisted in order to prevent reality—which is multidimensional, multileveled, and highly complex—from being flattened and oversimplified by a heavy-handed conceptual outlook. Opposing reductionism is not merely one among many conceptual pieces of a complicated personalist theoretical scheme. Antireductionism is a nonnegotiable, live-or-die commitment necessarily bound to key crucial critical realist ideas, especially emergence, the stratification of reality, and downward causation.

What does reductionism look like when applied to humans? Human beings, one version of reductionism says, are nothing but the material elements (carbon, hydrogen, and such) that compose them. Human minds, another asserts, are nothing but packs of neurons and neurotransmitters. One reductionist sees nothing in the experience of human love but the operation of hormones and pleasure neurotransmitters at work. Another sees little else in human behavior than selected-upon genes pushing people to act in certain ways. Still another claims that human morality amounts to nothing but cultural inventions designed to promote domination and social control. Other reductionist approaches argue that human social relationships are simply means by which resources flow through social networks, or that all apparent acts of kindness, altruism, and generosity are nothing but self-interested strategies to indirectly maximize pleasure or reproductive fitness. Such applications of reductionism to humanity have the effect of flattening, oversimplifying, degrading, distorting, and dehumanizing the reality of human persons—even if there are partial truths in them. Persons become nothing but material animals, operant responders to external stimuli, egos repressing ids, carriers of selfish genes, organic machines processing information, rational and self-interested utility maximizers, sustainers of webs of meaningful definitions of situations, strategic accumulators of power and status, or some other person-falsifying fiction.

Reductionist claims take this standard form: "I know that you and other people normally think that P is really a complex matter of A, B, C . . . X, Y, and Z. But I as a scientist who knows the real truth of the matter tell you instead that P is really nothing but e" (or k or s or whatever other oversimplified idea). Reductionism squashes complicated, emergent complexity into its simple, preemergent components, and then thinks that its account better describes and explains reality. Reductionism's fatal move is to fail to see all of the new properties, capacities, and tendencies that come into being at higher levels of reality through processes of emergence, which do *not* exist at the lower levels of reality from which the higher comes emergently into being. Reductionism proceeds as if emergence simply does not happen—and in ignoring emergence, it misrepresents reality. It says, in its most ridiculous form, that water is really "nothing but" H and O, for instance. But doing that fails to see one of the most important factors at work in the way things actually *are*, which produces the kind of reality we have. In the case of water, it fails to see that the covalent bonding of H_2 and O bring into being an entirely new substance—water—with properties, capacities, tendencies, and limitations of its own that do *not* exist at the level of H and O.

Reductionism thus, through this misguided and misguiding intellectual move, strips reality of all of its real, upwardly emergent features, powers, and operations. It takes a world that is multidimensionally differentiated, complex, and stratified and turns it into a simple fact or operation. It takes beings that are absolutely invaluable and turns them into $4.50 worth of material. Personalism insists that "nothing-but" reductionism is unacceptable, because it mis-recognizes the way reality is put together and mis-describes the very reality it claims to illuminate and explain. It pronounces on reality with a stunning obliviousness to emergence and falsifies everything important that emergence produces. When applied to persons, reductionism must especially be resisted and denounced, because it inevitably depersonalizes human beings.[28] And that, personalism says, is not only bad science but also a moral crime.

Personal Centers with Purpose

Persons are by nature "centers with purpose." To be a person that is reasonably well developed in existential expression is to exist and operate as a governing center of consciousness and action oriented toward pursuing certain purposes. The centeredness of persons is what enables us to coordinate and integrate the immense number of sensory, cognitive, affective, volitional, and other inputs, experiences, and outlooks into relatively unified, singular lives and life projects. Being personal centers of that kind prevents our lives from being chaotic jumbles of disconnected and conflicting sensations, awareness, thoughts, desires, feelings, and so on. The centered nature of our personal being thus prevents the unbearable confusion to which our myriad human capacities and tendencies would lead us, if they were not integrated and coordinated in relatively unified experience, identity, and action. A natural feature of human personhood is thus the integration and coordination that comes with being "centers of."

That persons are centers means that they are not mere conglomerations, inventories, or compilations of diverse features. There is at the core of the person a centering, interior focal point of personal being, consciousness, and activity. Persons exhibit structures of internal organization that provide a hub or nucleus of coherence and continuity of awareness and action. It is not that persons are perfectly unified, harmonized, or consistent internally. We are not. Personal being involves certain degrees of internal disconnection, disjuncture, and lack of integration among parts. People's structures of belief and patterns of behavior, for example, do not always consistently add up. But those disconnections always operate relative to what for all normal persons is a more dominant controlling center of coordinated mental and physical activity. If such an organizing personal center of coherence and direction were not prevailing, then the very idea and experience of disconnection and lack of integration would be meaningless. It is only against the governing center of personhood that elements of internal disjuncture can be recognized and problematized. That human beings are centers does not preclude the influence of unconscious activities on human actions. But neither does the real unconscious eliminate the fact of personal centeredness. A moment's reflection by the (presumably sane) reader on their own subjective experience of personhood will validate this point about the person being and having a "center of" coordinated awareness and activity. It is precisely the breakdown of such a "center of" in the forms of multiple personality disorder, schizophrenia, and other psychotic thought and identity disorders that we judge that human personhood itself is being threatened by pathological, person-damaging forces. The normally developed person, by contrast, operates primarily out of a deep, single, centered nucleus of being, self-governance, and self-direction.

Personal centers also have natural *purposes*. However unfashionable the idea might be in science today, personalism holds that personal human life really involves natural purposes, real teleological ends that properly belong to persons by nature. Of course, very many people's purposes in life are culturally learned and so vary across social contexts—one person purposes to be a rock star, another to fulfill their life in the untouchable caste. Those we can think of as culturally relative, constructed, specified, and guided purposes. But not all human purposes are of that kind. Some human purposes proper to the nature of personhood are real, natural, and universal. They are also more basic than the kinds of purposes just noted (see chapter 5). Sometimes people think and behave in ways that deny or violate these real, natural, and universal human purposes. But that itself does not make them unreal, unnatural, or nonuniversal. It simply means that those people are thinking and living in denial or violation of the real nature of their personhood. That (living in denial of reality), too, is a real capacity of human personal being, which is sometimes actualized empirically (see chapter 7).

Ontological Being and Existential Realization

Personalism insists that all living human beings are ontologically persons, fully and completely, with all of the implications the status of personhood entails. Personal being in fact is what develops through the maturing human body from the start of life toward its own greater actualization and expression, moving through proactive emergence toward realizing and enacting its essential nature in human development over the life course. What varies in human life, then, is not the *being* of personhood, which belongs to the real and exists either completely or not at all. What varies, rather, is the extent to which that real personhood is actualized, realized, and expressed, something that concerns not the real but the actual and empirical.[29]

Real personhood can in some abnormal instances remain significantly unrealized in the realm of the actual, although below a certain threshold of realization life stops and personhood perishes. A fetus that because of genetic anomalies stops growing properly, for example, will encounter severe limits to the actualization of his or her real personal being, and may die as a result of body dysfunctions. A severely physically and mentally disabled child may live much longer but will also face profound limits on his or her potential to bring to full actualization his or her ontologically real personhood. The disabled child is fully a person, but the degree of actual realization and ex-pression of that real personhood will be constrained. Furthermore, real per-sonhood that has already been significantly realized in life experience can also later become severely damaged or deteriorated in the extent of its actualiza-tion and expression. A brilliant "renaissance woman" who is a scholar, an artist, and an athlete, for example, may as a result of an automobile accident fall into a coma. As a living human, she remains 100 percent a person, even while in a coma, but the realization and expression of her personhood in actuality has become radically damaged and may never return. Likewise, a degenerative nervous disorder may dramatically roll back the actualization of personhood previously realized by a prize-winning scientist, undoing much of the realization of his personhood expressed in the realm of the actual while doing nothing to change the ontological reality of his personal being in the realm of the real. But these we all recognize as abnormalities and pathologies, not the normal, right, or good course of affairs. In most lives, the 100 percent, ontologically real personhood of living humans finds itself more or less able to significantly develop, realize, express, and enjoy his or herself in actuality. The more that is able to happen, the better it is, and the more the human good is potentially achieved.

Distinguishing the fully is/is not nature of the ontological presence or reality of personhood in living human beings from the more-or-less char-acter of the realization, actualization, and expression of that personhood, in this way, accomplishes a number of important things for us conceptually. It enables us to identify and protect the personhood of persons who are not at their physical and mental optimum, allowing us to admit the full extent of their developmental immaturity, malformation, damage, or degeneration without thereby excluding such people from the circle of humans recognized as persons. It also provides a crucial *developmental* framework for understanding the natural tasks and purposes of human life, not only setting up a descriptive account of life-course-oriented social institutions but also giving orientation to questions about what makes for a morally good human life and society. Here again the is and the ought, the factual and the normative, the analytical and the moral closely interact.[30] Most importantly, distinguishing the existence of personhood as ontologically real from the variable realization of it in actual experience gives us a conceptual language that describes well the reality of personal being and experience that truly exists. This is not simply one among many possible ways to talk about things that are ultimately unconcerned with what is real and true. This distinction names a real difference adhering in the nature of reality, which presents to our knowing human minds a descriptive understanding that (we are justified in believing) truthfully corresponds to reality we seek to understand.

Another way to make this point is to say that human persons—unless they are radically damaged—naturally possess within the province of their given personhood all of the necessary "equipment" to become and live as flourishing persons. This point is terrifically important and its full significance must be grasped. Persons normally come into being in the world naturally equipped with all of the necessary potential systems, capacities, and teleological orientation to develop into fully realized persons. The components and powers required for persons to develop the full realization of their personhood come innate with the person from the start—although those powers are sometimes diminished in cases of persons who are radically damaged. Persons do not need subsequent to their conception anything from the outside that is necessary and essential for their personhood per se. All dimensions of human personhood come "fully installed," so to speak, in inconceivably compact and dense potencies given from the first hour of life. Nothing substantively new to personhood per se needs to be added from outside. What persons need from the outside are humanly and materially nurturing environments in which their natural, innate capacities for personhood can develop, grow in health, mature, and thrive.

Thus while all living human beings are ontologically fully persons at all times of their lives, all human beings nevertheless vary in the course of their lives in the degree of the empirical development and realization of their natural personhood. The first has to do with absolute real being, the second with the variable empirical actualization and expression of that being. Thus the ontological personhood of human persons is in no way provided or completed by any outside agent—except in origin by Mother Nature or God—and certainly it does not come from "society." That is to say, the personhood of persons, once present, is not ontologically dependent on anyone or anything outside of the person (even though the person is always developmentally dependent). Personhood comes already provided in full and complete being-in-potential, bundled in unimaginable density in the natural components of the human body. Personhood comes, once first established, as inherent "equipment" that only needs in the course of natural development to unfold, evolve, and become mature and shaped well by the right kind of human and material environments. What persons crucially need from the outside, then, are nurturing contexts to foster the greater realization of personhood. In short, human personhood per se, once conceived, is *ontologically* self-given, self-existent, self-carrying, and self-developing, even though contextually and *developmentally* persons are extraordinarily dependent on external environments for proper nurture, love, and training.

Persons in Social Relations

Following the previous points is the realization that, far from being autonomous individuals, distinct human persons are naturally, inescapably, and radically dependent on a nurturing human and material world around them for love, protection, nourishment, teaching, development, recognition, affirmation, direction, discipline, and much more—not only to survive but also to realizing or actualizing empirically any of the potentialities of personhood. Again, such nurturing environments never create, construct, or supplement personhood per se. All that is required to be a person comes at conception, as just noted, fully intact with all the necessary equipment and potencies of personhood bundled in an innate compaction of living personal being. Instead, such nurturing environments provide the many vital contexts and resources needed for that innately given personhood to live, grow, unfold, and hopefully eventually thrive in empirical existence.

For this reason and others, human persons are naturally, innately, and inescapably *social* beings who depend upon social relationships for their ongoing life and development. That humans are social animals is a commonplace observation. But it deserves more examination. Personalism recognizes at least two ways that humans are social animals. The first is that humans are *dependently* social creatures. They are necessarily social in this sense because from the start of life to its end humans depend on other humans for sustenance, nurturance, protection, fellowship. In this way people are dependent on other people simply to survive and grow. Without any social relationships from the start, human persons would wither and die. Sociality is thus a functional requirement of survival and health for the kind of embodied animal that humans are. But humans are social in an even deeper, more profound way: they are also *constitutionally* social because living in social relationships with other persons expresses what persons *are*. Social relationships are not simply instrumental means to sustain life and health. They are that too, but they are much more. It is not the case that if only people could be materially self-sufficient then they would not need other people to be persons. To be a person is constitutionally in part "to develop and sustain one's own incommunicable self in loving relationships with other personal selves."

We must be careful and precise in our claims here to avoid falling into error. Social relationships do *not* construct or constitute human persons. The fullness of ontological personhood is, again, given in being from the start. But living with and in social relationships *is* constitutive of the nature and meaning and expression of personhood. To be a person *is* in part to be and live in social relationships. Existing in that social condition and so living in those personal, I-Thou relationships are centrally and essentially part of what it is to be a person.[31] Personalism thus understands the social nature of human beings to be not merely instrumentally and functionally necessary, a kind of strategic and tactical way of operating in the world as an otherwise-independent self, simply to get what one wants and needs from the human and material environment. There is a kernel of truth in that view, but taken alone it is insufficient and misleading. That is because human persons are not merely dependently social animals, which they are, but also *constitutionally* social creatures. Personal sociality is not merely required to survive but more significantly central to what the point of survival *is*. Persons do not merely use others in relationships to maintain their lives, in order to be able to pursue some other impersonal goal, like increased pleasure or securing more material goods. Persons are steeped in personal social relationships as a good end in itself, because that is what any normal, thriving person simply is and does.[32]

Crucial to personalism as a project, therefore, is correctly specifying the nature of particular persons in their social relationships with other persons. Overemphasizing the autonomy of particular persons from other people and institutions is a problem, both as accurate empirical description and for its implications for personal morality and social ethics. But problematic, too, is overemphasizing the dependence on or subordination of person to other people and institutions. Liberalism and individualistic social theories tend to err on the one side here, while collectivism and many macrosociological theories tend to err on the other. Personalism seeks to carefully describe the relationships among persons and between persons and institutions in a way that well informs the theoretical elaboration it underwrites and the moral conclusions it draws.

All human persons, personalism says, definitely have a nature—a personal human nature. But no persons have lived or will live in a presocial "state of nature." Rather—except for the rare exceptions, such as single humans shipwrecked on deserted islands, the success of which presupposes learning from prior social relations—all persons at all times live in and with social relationships. From the very start of human personal existence, all persons have lived with and in relation to others. It begins with a most intimate personal relationship with our mothers, in whose womb we were all were conceived and nurtured until birth. And, unless people have lived the most dreadful of lives, from which they would likely not have survived or developed much, all persons grew up in webs of personal social relationships—of family, clan, kin, neighborhood, village, town, school, team, or something else. These kinds of significant social relationships, every sociologist knows, are absolutely necessary to socialize and "humanize" new members of society so they can grow up to be functional adults.

However, a crucial personalist insight insists that we may not rightly say that "persons are the products of their societies," if by that we mean that people acquire their personhood through their social relationships. People's personhood in its ontological reality is a natural fact of their human being, from start to end. And all living human beings are persons. This being the case, it is impossible for society to be the source of our personhood. Social relationships and institutions do not confer, create, or construct persons any more than they do brains. Persons are a natural kind of ontological reality originating in innate human being at the start of life and developmentally unfolding in time-space existence. So the standard sociological mantra that "people are social constructions" is wrongheaded. Such a claim gives far too much creative power to "society" to somehow generate personhood and impart it to human bodies. It fails to recognize the fact that human personhood per se springs naturally from the ontological reality that constitutes things human, and that social relationships can only, though always crucially do, foster or obstruct its development and flourishing.

Personalism claims that "the individual" in fact does not exist, that "individuals" are a myth of liberal and utilitarian theory. It denies that the liberal individual is real. The individual is not what a human being is, but rather a construction of a misguided theoretical tradition, foisted upon humanity by intellectual visionaries and ideologues.[33] "The individual" is a liberal construction that makes the world ready for the advance of capitalism and a kind of liberal democracy that serves the desires of certain groups at the expense of a proper human self-understanding. And, since the fiction of the individual departs so far from the reality of the person, that foisting has required a great deal of ideological indoctrination and practice in various institutional settings to make it seem remotely plausible and attractive to people.[34] Personalism, in opposition, flatly denies the alleged reality of "the individual." It calls out such an account as empirically false, destructive, and morally irresponsible. Personalism advances a quite different account of human beings, one that is more realistic, social, and humane. And in this, personalism is determined not to allow real human persons to ever be confused with liberalism and utilitarianism's fictional individual.[35] Therefore, personalists as a practice refuse to refer to distinct human beings as "individuals." That very term inevitably carries with it a heavy baggage of assumptions about atomism, autonomy, egoism, instrumentalism, rationalism, competition, and more, from which the word cannot be purified. So for the sake of clarity and precision in theoretical denotation, personalist theory refuses to utter the term "individual" and uses instead the language of "persons" or, when necessary, "distinct human beings."[36]

Causal Realism

Critical realist personalism is causally realist.[37] That means believing that causes of states of affairs and events exist, even when we cannot see them.[38] In this it is neither causally antirealist nor skeptical about causation. What happens in life and the world is the result of causes that produce outcomes. Causes, however, need *not* be rigid, deterministic, mechanistic forces. People's beliefs can be causes, desires can be causes, values can be causes. And all of reality's causes work their way out in a host of different contexts in immensely complex ways to produce a variety of kinds of outcomes. All of this means that any science, including a human or social science, is about the business of understanding causes. Science, I have said, is about learning what exists in reality and how it works. Critical realist personalism believes that causes are among the things that exist in reality. The second part of science's interest (how it works) concerns causal explanation. What it means to explain how something works is to show how it produces certain processes or outcomes. And showing that means describing the various causal forces that together exert influences that change the state of other things (or maintain them against the power of change-inducing other forces). In short, science seeks to discover and describe what causal capacities, tendencies, and limitations different parts of reality possess that, when activated, under certain conditions produce certain effects or results.

Critical realist personalism applies this causal realism to human persons. Many thinkers of humanistic, hermeneutical, and even other personalist bents have historically shied away from the application of causation to human experiences and actions.[39] Immanuel Kant argued that the possibility of human freedom requires a disconnect from the deterministic forces of natural causation. But personalism sees no need to protect human persons from life in a causal universe. That is in part because personalism does not understand causation as necessarily deterministic but rather about tendencies. Some causes in the natural world may be thought of as deterministic. But many causes are not so. The critical realism that underwrites the kind of personalism I advance here views causation as involving natural powers, capacities, limitations, and tendencies—not linear, closed-system, deterministic forces. And these causal factors critical realism observes often operate in extraordinarily complex and interactive ways and in many different kinds of settings and environments to produce various, complicated, and often unpredictable outcomes. Many operative causal forces also end up producing no observable effects, according to critical realism. Furthermore, with human personhood in particular arise many unique powers and capacities that by nature are characterized by openness, creativity, agency, freedom, and unexpectedness. So personalism is entirely comfortable understanding human persons not as transcending but instead as embedded in and shaped by a causally operative world.

The causal power of human motivations to produce action also need not compromise the fact of real human agency involved in action. When engaged in motivation-causing actions, persons remain the purposeful agents of many of their own significant motivations and actions. By "human agency" I here mean the capacity to exercise personal powers and capabilities to cause events to happen in the world.[40] Agency always involves the exercise, often purposive, of causal capacities and transformative powers to influence outcomes in life. Real causes operating to produce social life need not compromise or negate human agency. A causally oriented social science does not need to eliminate more humanistically oriented assumptions, studies, and approaches to human life.[41] Freedom and determination are not opposites. Agency and structure need not compete directly against each other for influence. Strong causal influence and real human self-determination and choice are compatible. Any social science (and normative political or moral) theory that is to prove adequate to human reality must find a way to transcend these false dichotomies and describe the more integrated, compatibilist reality that is at work with structure and agency.[42] The causal realism advanced here in no way undermines the reality of human agency—quite the contrary.[43]

Furthermore, much of reality normally operates in "open systems" in which immensely complex causal forces operate within and across levels of reality, through emergence and downward causation, in ways that make determinism irrelevant for all practical purposes. The number of "moving parts" in any context is immense, the causal powers of most of them are many, the particular conditions that trigger various powers may or may not be present, and the assorted combinations of different causal forces interacting only increases the complexity of influences and outcomes. To worry about determinism in such a reality is pointless. If anything, the bigger problem is the challenge of understanding the massive complexities of reality's workings. Finally, even when causally influenced under fairly controlled conditions, many parts of reality do not respond with consequential effects in predictable, linear, ways. There is a major difference between law-like regularities and tendencies. Critical realism only posits the reality of natural tendencies of entities in responding to various causal influences. Exactly how and to what degree those triggered tendencies may be expressed will often be a function of the character of the individual entity in question as it interacts with the variety and combinations of causal forces that are influencing it. Often the magnitudes of effects are variable approximations of theoretical expectations, rendering a deterministic universe not threatening.

Finally, on the matter of causal mechanisms, it is worth noting that personalism is not the only theory that refers to "causal mechanisms."[44] The latter has become prevalent in American sociology in recent years. But much of sociology's talk about mechanisms lacks coherent intellectual justification. This recent interest seems to have been stimulated by the 1998 publication of Peter Hedström and Richard Swedberg's book *Social Mechanisms*.[45] That was a step in the right direction, at least in raising some important questions. Yet Hedström and Swedberg did not get mechanisms quite right.[46] And it is not clear how many sociologists have even studied that book closely. A great deal of mechanisms talk in sociology today proceeds with a weak theoretical foundation for explaining exactly what mechanisms are and why and how sociologists (particularly those also influenced by positivism) could or should believe in them. In effect, these sociologists are importing a theoretically foreign concept into fields and practices governed by a dominant, alien, neopositivist empiricism.[47] Since critical realism provides solid grounds for making sense of the reality and operation of social causal mechanisms, if the current mechanisms-focused trend is to last (and be improved, as it should) and prove useful over the long run, it will require a regrounding in the metatheory of critical realism.

Motivated Persons

Personalism tells us that most human actions are motivated. It provides us with an account of human motivations and interests that give rise to actions that pertain to all persons (is universal), it is grounded in the nature of reality (is natural) and yet is broadly open to a variety of paths, realizations, and expressions (is culturally variable within bounds). Human motives and interests are not ultimately to maximize pleasure and minimize pain. Nor are they simply to define reality and share meanings. Humans are not properly described as basically motivated to obey the norms of society, nor interested in acquiring more possessions, power, and security. Some of those may fit into the true motivations and interests of human persons, either as genuine goods pursued or as distorted versions of them. But they are not themselves realistic or satisfactory accounts of the basic motivations and interests of persons. According to personalism, instead, humans should be understood as possessing the motivations and interests to ever more fully realize in their existence the fullness and flourishing of their personhood. The true purpose of human persons is to be persons well. It is to become more fully, in time and space, better-realized expressions of the persons we ontologically already are. The purpose of persons is to develop and unfold our given personhood in ways that move us toward real personal excellence, thriving, flourishing. It is, in Aristotle's phrase, *eudaimonia*, deep, genuine, life happiness, the result of a good personal life well lived.[48]

In this sense, what persons are properly up to in life, what their personal and social lives are actually about, is not extrinsic or alien to their being. The point of life is essentially to be and become what one already is by nature. That is-ness must also *become*. We must become good persons living well the lives we have, in accordance with the character, capacities, and limitations of our human being. So this essential human motivation and interest does not produce mere static maintenance. The existential realization of personhood never stands still. It is always either becoming or diminishing, developing or receding, in the course of personal existence. Personhood's lived, empirical expressions are ever dynamic. Life is always a journey, a quest, a struggle, an accomplishment that never ends until death. Every more specific human motivation and interest on which people act is some subsidiary aspect of or means toward achieving—whether genuine or misguided, about which more later—the true personal life purpose of being and becoming a person, a good, vibrant, healthy, flourishing person who is living, has lived, and will live well. Crucial in the previous sentence is the qualifying clause, "whether genuine or misguided." I am not saying that everything people are motivated to do or consider in their interest in fact produces a good personal life well lived. Much that people do is stupid, malicious, deceptive, and destructive. Personalism is not naive in this way. What I *am* saying is that all motivations and interests on which people act are in fact inescapably *oriented toward* the purpose of developing and realizing the goods inherent to personhood toward happiness and flourishing.

The distinction between people being "oriented toward" the good and people always acting good is key. The former means that people cannot avoid operating in relation to the good and under its influence; people always act in ways compelled to achieve what seems to be good, even when the "goods" sought are mere privations or mis-directions of genuine goods. Even when people fail and choose the bad, the continual reference point, orienting horizon, and "magnetic attraction" of their doings is nevertheless the proper human good. Unfortunately, it is also true that many people often do not know what actually leads to their personal thriving and happiness. Many also often do not exercise the prudence and wisdom to learn the virtues and discipline that are needed for persons to flourish and enjoy happiness. Some people also pursue the (mal)development of their own personhood in ways that are known to be destructive. Human ignorance, laziness, foolishness, compromise, and hatred are all too real (about which more in chapter 7). But none of that in any way overturns the inexorable reality that all human motivations and interests—whether wise or misguided, well directed or darkly destructive—are oriented toward and impelled by the basic human personal motive and interest in realizing in space and time the goods and fullness of personhood.

The Particularity of Persons

The particularity of persons is an important feature of personhood in personalism. For as many persons that have existed and do exist, each is distinctly particular. Despite all social relationships and interactions, and despite society's power to influence people, no person can be duplicated. Each in their personal being is (what some personalists call) "incommunicable." Who they are cannot be transferred to or replicated in someone else. Persons in their particularity are unrepeatable and inalienable. No person can be exchanged for another that is just like him or her. Particularity is indispensable to personhood. Each personal self is exactly their own being and not another. And this each person understands him- or herself to be. This is why, when a particular person dies, something unique and irreplaceable is lost to the world. It is also why, if we were either to encounter another person who is exactly our self or to morph ourselves into a perfect replica of another person, this would provoke a personal identity crisis of unnatural condition. But this does not happen, happily, because persons are naturally particular, incommunicable selves.[49]

The particularity of persons carries with it significant implications. One central task of all persons—objectively, whether they realize and act upon it or not—is to sustain their own particular, unique, personal being. The good of persons is realized in part by actualizing in experience the unrepeatable and irreplaceable character of their particular personhood. People not only are particular persons de facto, they also *ought* to be their own particular selves as a matter of what is good. This expression of differentiation in personal particularity is an authentic human good, when realized prudently in concert with other goods. That has implications for each person's sense of identity, purpose, and direction in life. The particularity of persons also has implications for the constitution of good social orders and articulation of worthy moral standards. On the one hand, personalism definitely emphasizes the truly common, shared, universal features of human nature, recognizing human solidarity. Not all in human life is about difference. But personalism simultaneously resists theories, practices, and institutions that treat persons as generic, interchangeable, or replaceable. Such approaches many people rightly call depersonalizing and dehumanizing. No good moral system or social order can violate the particularity and incommunicability of persons. Persons of course often legitimately replace other persons in social roles, job positions, and political offices. But relationships and social systems can also replace people in wrong ways that violate their personal particularity— without due process or consideration of the specific contexts and circumstances that are entailed in particular cases. Personalism provides an account that explains how and why that is wrong.[50]

In the same vein, personalism suggests that human personhood also involves an insurmountable mystery such that persons can never be exhaustively viewed, understood, and explained by science or any other discipline of inquiry. No science can fully plumb the depths of the person. People themselves cannot plumb the depths of their own personhood, with perhaps rare exceptions. The complexity, subjectivity, multidimensionality, qualitative subtleties, and depths of personhood are too immense and mysterious for an investigative science to fully master, model, and explain. That does not make an inquiry into the nature of personhood futile. The point is simply that ambitious aspirations of science to thoroughly explore, discover, map, and explicate human personhood are overreaching. We can learn, explain, and describe much about persons. But at many points the mysteries and ineffability of persons will overtake our scientific capacities—a fact we should happily accept.

Personal Dignity

A crucial, natural, ineradicable feature of human personhood is dignity. By dignity I mean the property of an inherent worth of immeasurable value that is deserving of certain morally appropriate responses by other persons. Dignity, personalism observes, inheres objectively in the nature of personhood, through emergence. It is not conferred by law or custom. It does not cease to exist when some people fail to recognize or properly honor it. Dignity is a brute feature that human persons possess by virtue of the essential nature of personhood. Where there are persons, they possess dignity. Personal dignity can be violated but it cannot be expunged. It can be denied but cannot be eliminated. The question is not whether dignity exists, any more than whether the Andes mountains exist. The question is whether human minds understand, acknowledge, and respond to the fact that human persons in reality possess dignity.

Human dignity therefore should not be regarded as merely an ethical or theological or philosophical opinion or assertion that is superimposed upon hard scientific knowledge about humans. Dignity inheres naturally in the emergent constitution of human personhood, including in the persons who are ignorant of or deny its reality. Dignity cannot be thought or wished away. It cannot be sold or negated by legal judgment. Dignity exists as a real and ineliminable dimension of human persons, just as reproduction does of living organisms and gravitational force does of physical mass. The dignity of personhood is a constitutive property of personhood, existing through emergence always as one of its essential and defining characteristics. Dignity is to personhood in this way as liquidity is to water and as the qualia of redness is to our perceptions of the color red. So the statement that "human persons possess a dignity, value, and worth beyond human measure" is, personalism maintains, not an ideology, an ethics, or a nice humanistic feeling but rather a true descriptive observation about an important part of reality. That truth bears important implications, so it must be said, accepted, and recognized in our theorizing.

Dignity recognizes and describes persons as innately precious and inviolable. Because of this dignity, human persons are naturally worthy of certain kinds of moral treatment by themselves and in their mutual relations—in particular, of respect, justice, and love. The ontology of personhood makes it morally true that persons are creatures that are worthy of being treated with respect, justice, and love. In the nature of things, persons should give other persons the recognition and honor of respect. Persons ought to provide other persons what they rightly deserve in justice. And persons should care for the genuine well-being of other persons in love. All of this pertains by virtue of the nature of human personhood itself, not because the state or society says so.[51] If these do say so, it is because they correctly recognize what is objectively true in reality, not because they have the power by declaration to make it true or untrue. Personalism, being a realistic theory, acknowledges that at the empirical, existential level many humans do not exhibit signs of their own dignity. Not only do many people not properly respect the dignity of other people, but many also live their own lives in ways that neglect or violate their own dignity. They do not behave as creatures of inestimable worth. They behave rather in ways that are self-neglecting and self-destructive. This means that such people either misunderstand their own dignity or are broken in ways that fail to make actual their real dignity. Here again we see another example of the difference between real ontological being and its existential realization.

Personalism contends in this that an immense qualitative gulf separates personal beings from all things not personal. To be a person is not merely to be a more complicated or interesting version of impersonal objects. It is to be radically different from impersonal objects. Persons possess and normally enjoy features, powers, capacities, and experiences that set them apart in entirely different dimensions of existence and value from nonpersonal things. To be a person is to be a unique "I" who addresses and is addressed by a unique "Thou," and many others besides. And every Thou that a person addresses and is addressed by is also personal, in infinitely different species of being than anything nonpersonal. Entities that are not persons are mere objects, things, articles. It is not that impersonal things have no value. They can have immense value, in various ways. But personal beings have value on an entirely different plane of existence.

Beyond the Individual and the Social Self

Personalism helps us to transcend the problematic individual-versus-society framework that has long shaped much sociological and political thinking. This frame reflects what is known as a *Homo duplex* model of humanity, which runs deep in Western thought and culture.[52] *Homo duplex* assumptions profoundly influenced sociology's founders, Marx, Durkheim, and Weber—as we will see in chapter 4. This model assumes that two basic realities exist—individuals and society—and that between them a primal opposition and divergence of interests operates. What individuals desire for themselves and of society is essentially different from what society wants of individuals. That oppositional dualism produces theories that not only oppose the individual versus society, but inevitably prioritize one over the other. Some theories emphasize individual autonomy, will, and choice. Others prioritize the collective or social over the individual. The same underlying dualism has troubled sociological theory in perennial conflicts over individualism versus holism,

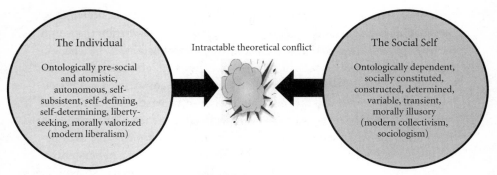

The Individual

Ontologically pre-social
and atomistic,
autonomous, self-
subsistent, self-defining,
self-determining, liberty-
seeking, morally valorized
(modern liberalism)

Intractable theoretical conflict

The Social Self

Ontologically dependent,
socially constituted,
constructed, determined,
variable, transient,
morally illusory
(modern collectivism,
sociologism)

FIGURE 1. The intractable conflict between the "individual" and the "social self."

the micro and the macro, and agency versus structure. Sociological theorists have long struggled to formulate a single, coherent account of social life that takes fully seriously both individual human agency and the constraining and directing power of social structures. The basic terms of this debate, we should note, are set by the deep cultural structures of Western modernity, of liberal individualism versus the collective of "society." In my view, those theoretical conflicts are irresolvable as normally framed, because the defining terms of the debates—individuals *versus* society—are misleading and problematic. The intractable nature of the problem is built into the very fundamental categories of the debate. This situation is depicted in figure 1. The theoretical Individual is by nature presocial, atomistic, autonomous, self-subsistent, self-determining, always seeking liberty and freedom, and valorized as representing the triumph of the human agent over all external forces of constraint and repression. The Social Self, by contrast, is socially dependent, socially constituted, constructed, and determined, variable, transient, and morally illusory compared to the valorized Individual. These are the core images of the human person that in sociological theory have led to intractable conflict.

Personalism tells us that we need to alter our basic conceivable units of reality, setting aside our standard individualist and collectivist ontologies of humanity and reconceptualizing the nature of human beings as *persons* in ways that avoid the oppositions of *Homo duplex*. That requires recognizing more clearly how persons relate to the social. Personalist social theory begins with one *basic* unit, the human *person*, from which all else, including the social, flows and has its reference. Human persons are understood as not the mere "individuals" of Western liberalism. For one thing, persons are *constitutionally social by nature*. Although they are not ontologically created by society, persons are innately social in their ontological being, in the existential realization of their being, and in the proper teleological ends of their personhood. Social existence is not something alien to persons, added onto personal life as some kind of subsequent experience or obligation placed on humans emerging from an innocent, atomistic state of nature. To be a person *is* to be social. Sociality is thus in persons' own essential interests. At the same time, the sociality of persons is not transferred to or constructed in persons by society, but is innate to the ontological essence of persons in their natural personhood and in the space and time of personal existence. That puts a stop to the idea that persons are ontologically dependent upon society for their being, character, and purposes. Persons are thus not under threat of being swallowed up or determined by a fundamentally oppositional force of society.

Furthermore, society in personalism enjoys no existence apart from the activities of other persons, which through emergence bring it into being. Persons do not by nature face an autonomous, alien being—society—that they must resist or else suffer its violation of their interests. Persons participate in and face society as the emergent product of their own life activities, inherited from the past, yes, but always in need of continual sustaining through ongoing activity. At the same time, however, the real, emergent ontological being of society is never denied or discounted as a mere epiphenomenal apparentness wafting off the real facts of human interactions. Through emergence, causally efficacious social facts become part of reality.[53] Personalism thus does not undercut the reality of society. In this way the individual and society are not opposed. Rather, persons are the basic unit in human reality, and the social has real emergent being with unique downwardly causal powers. It is neither inherently threatening nor does it have an autonomous holistic existence.

Finally, personalism resists falling into a naive, harmonious, organicist view of social life. Distinct subjects and objects are recognized in the boundaries that differentiate human persons from each other and from the rest of the material world they inhabit. Struggle and conflict are also crucial to a personalist account, although they are not finally located between individuals and society. The fundamental human problem is not how individuals can either resist the intrusions of or self-interestedly capitalize upon the incentives and opportunities society offers. The challenge is rather to develop and bring to fuller realization in time-space existence the manifold natural features, powers, and capacities innate to the personal being of persons. The concern is how to achieve through struggle and growth one's personal telos in view of the facts of both one's personal finitude and limitations and forces beyond oneself, which present not only opportunities but also obstacles to the achievement of one's telos. Put in Aristotelian terms, the real tension, problem, and challenge in life for persons is not how to be reconciled to the alien powers of society. The problem is how over the course of a life well lived to bring to realization the fullness of one's personhood in social and political contexts and so achieve genuine, deep, rich human happiness and flourishing. Society is of course always implicated in that challenge, but it is not the fundamental "other" of human personal life.

Many of the problems of sociological theory result from many of its debates for the last two centuries being badly framed by the background assumptions and categories of liberal individualism, and, as a reactive counterpart, collectivism or holism. The way to resolve those sociological problems is to recast the basic categories, by eschewing social collectivism or holism as surely as individualism. That means not framing our thinking within the terms and assumptions of *Homo duplex* conceptions of human life more broadly. That approach allows no way to understand a positive bond between persons and societies. That relationship is instead always construed as alien, detached, maintaining a distance, suspicious, instrumental, and opportunistic. This problematic individualistic liberal framework also evokes an opposite, reactive account, social collectivism or holism. Here the individual takes an ontological and moral second place to the whole, to the unity of "society." Social orders, systems, and structures are primal. Individuals exist as products of the social—outputs of the system—whose subsidiary purpose and function is to stand in dependent relation to the whole. This may take a conservative form in traditionalist organicism. Or it might take a radical form in Marxist communism. Or it might take a revolutionary form seeking a Rousseauian "general will." It may be theorized as the Parsonian structural functionalism of midcentury American social order, or a Luhmannian systems theory of European modernity. In every case, the collective proves to be ontologically and often morally more important than the individual. In abstract sociological theory, social collectivism or holism is bad enough. But when carried out in real sociopolitical programs—Marxist communism on the left, National Socialism on the right, or the French Revolution in a different direction—the results are predictably horrific.[54]

Personalism thus seeks to make a basic assumption-changing contribution. This kind of move is depicted in figure 2, showing both "The Individual" and "The Social Self" of sociological theory being negated and displaced by the personalist account of the human person. On the basis of this real human person, and not The Individual or The Social Self, sociological theory can advance to solve some of its deep theoretical problems and better relate itself to crucial human moral concerns.

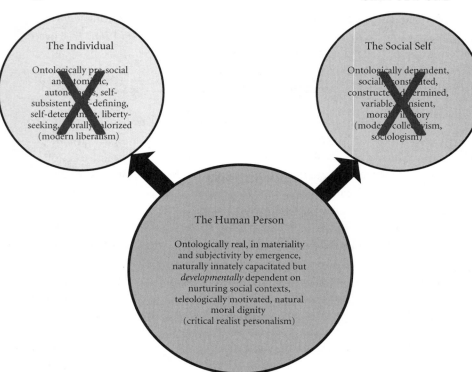

FIGURE 2. The person breaking the intractable conflict between the "individual" and the "social self."

Conclusion

Sociological theory has conceptually *centered* nearly everything imaginable—nearly everything, that is, except human persons. We have centered action and meanings. We have centered interactions, society, and practices. We have centered culture. We have centered social structures. We have centered the functional requisites of society and the means and relations of production. We have centered habits and habitus. We have centered pleasure, exchange, and utility maximization. We have centered social network ties and social influence. We have centered social norms and values. We have centered power and conflict. We have centered social roles, identity, and creativity. We have centered social interest, social class, social facts, and social knowledge. We have centered gender and rational choice and emotions. We have centered individuals. All of that. But we have never centered human persons. And that explains, I suggest, why sociological theory has never quite worked.

If we want to understand and explain human social life adequately in general theoretical terms, we must center human persons. If we center anything else—as sociology has so far seemed determined to do—we will fail. Human persons are the real and most important ontological constituents of social life. Persons are the pivot point of the human particular and the human universal, of the distinct and of the general. Persons are also the source of energy that motivates all human activity and generates social life itself. Persons, rightly theorized, account for the amazing capacities and severe limitations that humans constantly negotiate. Persons also account for the immense goodness and evil that is evident in human social life. So if we want to understand and explain human social life well, we have to come to grips with persons.

Immediately, again, some will object that sociology has long theorized social life from the perspective of individuals. Have not rational choice theory, symbolic interactionism, action theory, exchange theory, methodological individualism, identity theory, and many theories besides centered the acting, choosing, interacting individual as the basis of social life? Yes, that is my point exactly. Sociology has long theorized *individuals*, but rarely human persons. Individuals and persons are very different things. Therein lies much of the larger problem. The closest thing to persons that sociological theory has been able to imagine for more than a century is "individuals." But individuals are not persons. Individuals cannot perform in sociological theory as persons can. Individuals actually do not exist. They are a theoretical fiction imposed on human life and thought by particular versions of the social and political theory of Western liberalism. By contrast, human persons *do* exist in reality in all cultures, and all things humanly social emerge from the life and activities of persons—not of postulated individuals but of real persons.

This chapter has described some basic positions in personalism. Its purpose has not been to develop a full-blown personalist theory but to lay down some ideas needed to understand the arguments of subsequent chapters. We turn next to directly examining the question of human motivations for action, attempting to sketch out an account of motivations that comports with a personalist outlook and contributes to sociological theory.

Rethinking Motivations for Action

Why does any person do anything? When people wake up from sleep, what do they do with the hours ahead of them and why? By "do" I mean a wide range of activities in which humans engage, extending from somewhat mindless habitual motions to purposeful, determined actions. Is what people do coordinated toward any larger ends? Are humans trying to accomplish something particular with the spending of their lives? Or are people's activities random, disorganized, or arbitrary? These questions—about human motivations— are the focus of this chapter. My argument is that human actions are in fact motivated. So we have to understand the nature and workings of human motivations in order to comprehend and explain most human activities and, by extension, the social institutions and structures to which they give rise. I advance a personalist account of motivations to help achieve that end.

Do Motivations Matter?

The vast majority of human beings who now live and have lived for millennia on this earth would intuitively understand that most of their own and other people's actions in life result from their having been in some significant way personally motivated. Understanding the importance of motivations for action is the normal human condition, a view that all of historical understanding and our own phenomenological experience tells us is obvious and hardly needs defending.[1] By contrast, doubting that motivations matter for human action is the odd, marginal position, a skeptical outlook that has to be learned under very particular conditions—such as years of graduate school in certain disciplines. Most social scientists realize that personal motivations to action do matter in some important ways. Yet some doubt that people's personal motivations are particularly important for understanding and explaining their actions. For example, in their book on dramaturgical sociology, *Life as Theater*, Dennis Brissett and Charles Edgley write that "centuries of social psychological debate has only recently begun to apprehend [that] motives have nothing whatsoever to do with the alleged 'causes' of human conduct." Motivations, they say, are not "forces that stir people to act. Instead, motives are . . . utilized in certain encounters [merely] to justify or rationalize the conduct of persons." Motivations are "not . . . phenomena that reside in individuals," but are post hoc rationalizations demanded by social interactions in certain situations. So even to ask, "what makes people act the way they do?," they claim, "is the wrong question."[2] We will see more of this kind of outlook in the next chapter. How then should we think about these and other doubters about motivations?

Events happen in reality because forces exerted by real entities that have the causal capacities and powers to bring about those events cause them. A toxic vapor is given off by ammonia because chlorine added to it produces a chemical reaction that releases chloramine. A door breaks open because the police kick it in. A savings and loan bank goes bankrupt because its depositors make a rush on the bank to withdraw their money. All of these events are caused. They happen because some entities possess the causal capacities to produce the events, capacities that various environmental conditions trigger. Understanding the entities in reality and how their causal powers produce events is what science is about. Furthermore, the causal production of events requires the ongoing expenditure of energy to sustain them. Given the second law of thermodynamics, the natural forces of entropy tend by nature to diffuse energy, which leads to increased randomness, disorder, and breakdown. Nature tends to move from order to disorder in any isolated system. So maintaining order, structure, process, or action requires the ongoing conversion and expenditure of energy from some contributing system. Things do not simply happen. All movements are moved. Events require energy-activated efficient causes to bring them about.

Human actions, practices, and habits are events. They are not uncaused, but are caused by something or other. If we wish to understand and explain them, we need to understand what causes them. That involves identifying the specific sources and types of energy expended that function as the efficient causes of people's actions, practices, or habits. Most social scientists would agree with this description so far. Where some diverge concerns which real entities exert which causal forces. Some seem to believe that social forces cause human actions in ways that do not require motivations as causes. The idea of *motivated* human action, by contrast, says that some important process or force operating *within* actors—some capacity to exert causal powers to generate action that operate by or within human subjective consciousness and intention—provides the energy that plays an important role in producing the action.[3] It typically identifies these energy-expending processes with features of human *subjectivity*, such as desires, beliefs, and emotions. Motivated actions, in short, are movements that are caused by expenditures of energy derived from systems *internal* to conscious human beings and governed in some way by human subjective capacities. Most people across the great variety of human cultures and for all of known history have understood this.[4]

On what grounds might some social scientists discount the importance of motivations for human action? Let us consider the conceivable options. Some might say that actions are not caused by internal or subjective personal motives, but rather by macro- or microsituational social forces impinging upon people from the outside. Let us call this position "social determinism." Others might say that when it comes to human life (as opposed to nonhuman objects), identifying causes is simply the wrong and inappropriate form of explanation, that human life is really about meaningful symbols and interpretations and interactions, not actions that are "mechanically" caused in the way chemical reactions are caused.[5] Let us call this view "hermeneutical purism." Other skeptics say that the vast majority of what people do in life is not obviously ends-oriented, that people do not seem to pay much direct attention to what they are doing, that human doings are more like simple happenings than goal-driven undertakings, and that people are often terrible at discerning the optimal means to attain desired ends and explaining the reasons for their actions to others. Let us call this "empirical pessimism." Finally, other skeptics about motivations point to weak associations between what people say they value, believe, and desire and the ways they actually behave, when it comes to matters that should be influenced by those same values, beliefs, and desires. Let us label this view "doubtful decoupling." (Again, readers tempted to think that no sociologists adopt such positions should withhold judgment before reading chapter 3.)

These are all interesting ideas, some of which involve accurate descriptions of human life. But none provides good reasons to doubt that motivated human actions happen or that most people's actions are motivated. The first objection to motivation (social determinism) presupposes a false dichotomy and unnecessary zero-sum opposition between personal and social causes of action. It fails to recognize that social causal forces normally work in conjunction with and through processes of personal motivations.[6] Causal influences of social contexts provide or confront actors with opportunities, constraints, information, incentives, norms, expectations, routines, costs, benefits, public moralities, and the like, which are normally processed by human agents also engaged in motivated action.[7] So structure and agency are not mutually exclusive, competing forces in social life. Social structure is the emergent product of acting persons engaged in ongoing (usually) motivated activity.[8] Social determinism gives us no good reason to doubt that people's motivations often cause their actions.

Hermeneutical purism assumes a false distinction between how explanation works in human and nonhuman realms. Hermeneutical purists confuse the idea that certain important, explanation-relevant aspects of human life differ from nonhuman life (which is true) with the more comprehensive and indefensible claim that human actions cannot be causally explained. That relates to a false dichotomy between symbolic meanings and causal forces. Human beliefs, desires, purposes, and cultural meanings are causally powerful forces in personal and social life.[9] Among humans, meanings have causal powers to help generate action. And to grasp the causal significance of meanings requires engaging in the interpretive work of hermeneutical understanding. A causal social science does not need to be and should not be mechanistic (in a bad sense), deterministic, materialistic, or scientistic. Causation and human agency are not zero-sum rivals but, when understood properly, not only coexist but also require each other for action and explanation.[10] Each ultimately presupposes and needs the other. Furthermore, causation need not be deterministic. Critical realism's conceptual recognition of the reality of emergence helps to explain this, by showing how higher-order events and processes (such as human deliberation and action) are often not best explained by being reduced to lower-order ones (such as the dynamics of protons, neutrons, and electrons). Causation coexists with human meaning, agency, and freedom. Our account of human motivations as causes of action simply needs to take seriously symbolic meanings and human self-direction, the centrality of which in human life helps to set persons apart from nonpersons. We can thus embrace a causal approach to social science without abandoning all that is valuable in interpretive, hermeneutical approaches, or taking on problematic mechanistic, deterministic, materialistic, or scientistic ideologies.

The third possible objection, empirical pessimism, appeals to observations that are often true about human action, yet which do not tell us that motivations do not cause actions. That conclusion does not follow from the empirical evidence. People are indeed often distracted, confused, inefficient, and inarticulate when it comes to their activities. Sometimes people's behaviors do not seem very purposive, instrumental, or rationally deliberated. So what? That does not eliminate motivated human actions.[11] It only tells us that our theory of motivations must account for the dimensions of motivated action that are habituated, uneconomical, and operating below discursive consciousness.[12]

Finally, the doubtful decoupling view also rightly notes a recurring fact of human life: people's verbal professions seem often to not closely match their actions. People often say that they value X, but then fail to act in ways that would accomplish X. Again, however, that does not make motivations irrelevant to action. It merely tells us that the processes involved are more complex than a simple "motive → action" model would suggest. The skepticism of doubtful decoupling also often begins by expecting a strong relationship between social survey and interview measures of "values" or "beliefs" and people's real motivations—an often-unwarranted assumption.[13] Sometimes the seeming disconnect between people's professions and actions is not because these are not connected in people's lives, but because social scientists' methods are often poor at identifying and measuring people's real motivations. What deserves skepticism, when so, are not people's motivations but the adequacy of social science's methods. Sometimes claims about disconnects between professions and actions are also overstated. In fact, research over decades has shown moderate associations between professed values and intentions and people's actions.[14] But even when the claims are not overstated, there are good reasons—having to do with multiplicity and complexity— why people's actions may not closely match their professed values, beliefs, and goals. People are usually trying to negotiate the implications of myriad values, beliefs, and goals (not just the one that a survey asked about), which often creates conflicting purposes and compromises decision making. That does not mean that actions are not motivated, but simply that human life is complicated.[15]

In short, some social scientists may be tempted to believe that human actions can be explained without particular reference to personal motivations, but they are playing with a weak hand. I proceed, then, on the assumption— which I hope most of my social science colleagues share—that motivations do matter in generating people's actions.[16] And that means that we need a good, realistic theoretical account of motivations.

The Reality of Motivated Action

Human behavior and action come in a variety of types and expressions. Some of it, like sneezing, snoring, having seizures, tics, surges of adrenalin, nocturnal emissions, obsessive-compulsive disorders, and (in certain circumstances) screaming in fright, is essentially involuntary. Some of it, such as stepping off a pirate's plank into water full of sharks, is coerced and so involuntary in a different way. Certain other behaviors are compelled by strong biochemical drives or neurologically based illnesses or dysfunctions. Yet other human behaviors, such as somnambulism (sleepwalking), are performed at such low levels of consciousness that they cannot be rightly described as meaningfully intentional or purposive. Then again, certain highly obsessive or compulsive behaviors do not seem to be the result of motivated purposes or goals, even if they do appear somehow to be generated or driven by the actors engaged in them. And then some human behaviors and actions seem genuinely random and inexplicable—or at least we will not be harmed by having an analytical category for that possible type of action.[17] But those kinds of involuntary, nonpurposive, coerced, random, and externally driven behaviors and actions do not exhaust the range of types of important human action. In fact, they represent a minority of human doings. Besides them, another very important type of action is best described as motivated, as generated and propelled by motivations.[18] A social science that misses the centrality of motivated actions will therefore not be getting entirely right large swaths of human activities, in fact most of the kinds of human actions that are of greatest interest to and importance for social scientific understanding and explanation.[19]

Although life can sometimes feel confused, pointless, and frustrating, for the most part our actions seem to have some greater purpose and our lives some larger coherence. If they did not, there would be nothing to feel frustrated about and the pointlessness would not be noticeable. So most people, when asked why they engage in some of the significant doings in their lives, are not immediately stumped and reply, "Actually, I have no idea—none of this really makes sense or has purpose." Most people can and do offer more or less reasonable explanations of the meaning and purpose of their doings. They may not understand their own lives sufficiently—just because people profess something does not make it true or adequate—but most people, you and I included, normally want to, think we should, and usually do understand the meaning and purpose of most of our activities. That tells us something. I begin with the belief that a large amount (though not all) of human activity is motivated—that is, conducted more or less intentionally in pursuit of humanly meaningful interests, purposes, or goals.[20] By "motivations" I mean the causal energy and direction the organized patterning of people's desires, beliefs, and emotions provide that move people to choose, initiate, and often persist in particular actions or general strategies in specific contexts.[21] Following this understanding of motivations, I define purposive, motivated *action* as behaviors performed when (1) there is some goal G that person P affectively desires or intends to bring about, (2) P believes that by performing action A he or she will likely help achieve G, and (3) this (i) emotionally laden desire or intention for G, (ii) belief in the causal effects of A regarding G, and (iii) desire to employ the means of A *cause* P to do A.[22] What then are "reasons"? They are considerations that justify or explain certain actions to actors and others. Reasons come in two types, normative and explanatory.[23] Motivated actions can be thought of as actions that are carried out by actors who can in principle provide normative reasons for them. The reasons given thus provide an account for why an actor acted as he or she did, insofar as the reasons tell why the actor thought certain considerations counted in favor of the action. Social science explanations of people's actions may and should draw upon actors' professed normative reasons, and the explanations themselves will consist of an account of the explanatory reasons making the actions intelligible.[24]

The Ontology of Motivations

Human motivations for action are real and important. But what *are* they? Of what do they consist? The human capacity to engage in motivated action is grounded in the real, multiple, and interacting *natural powers* and *tendencies* of normal human personhood. Human persons naturally possess the capacities that interact and combine to produce the causal mechanisms by which motivations produce actions.[25] The ability, tendency, even inevitability of humans to act on the basis of action-generating motivations is thus a natural, inbuilt feature of the nature of normal human persons. Persons conceived as "centers with purpose" require and give rise to motivated action. Ontologically, human motivations to action consist of combinations of *beliefs, desires*, and *emotions*. Here I follow the traditional philosophical definition of the sources of human action focused on beliefs and desires.[26] To them, I add emotions for guiding and regulating the intensity of the energy involved in motivations for action, following recent findings in studies of emotions.[27]

Before proceeding, we should remind ourselves that although motivations are real, routinely experienced, and acted upon by all normal human actors, they *cannot* be directly observed in others, and so are not immediately empirically accessible outside of one's own experience. Nobody can directly look at, touch, hear, or taste other people's motivations per se.[28] They exist at a "deep" level of reality within the subjectivity of persons.[29] For consistent empiricists following the tradition of David Hume, this empirical inaccessibility of motivations makes their existence and real causal powers doubtful. But the Humean tradition is wrong on this point. Critical realism, by contrast, rightly legitimates us recognizing the reality of some immaterial, directly unobservable entities and processes, providing the most coherent way to recognize and understand real motivations. All normal, sentient human actors experience motivations phenomenologically. Motivations can also be indirectly observed and measured by their observable effects and by the (admittedly fallible) reports of human agents. Social scientists can furthermore believe in the existence and power of motivations for action by means of "inference to the best explanation" (IBE), considering all of the relevant factors involved.[30] Here, the mental operations of retroduction, abduction, and other mental experiments prove crucially helpful. We thus acknowledge up front the direct, empirical nonobservability of motivations, but nonetheless insist, for good reasons, on their reality, causal powers, and comprehensibility. Now let us examine each component of motivations.

Beliefs. By "beliefs" I mean a premise or proposition that people consciously or tacitly regard to be true. Stated more precisely, beliefs are mental attitudes of a certain kind directed toward premises or propositions, specifically, those that are taken to be true.[31] Beliefs concern what is traditionally labeled the cognitive aspect of mental life. Human beliefs encompass a wide range of attitudes and suppositions about what people regard to be true, only some of which are the result of or represented by active reflections or expressed propositions. Some social scientists doubt the theoretical importance of human beliefs in motivating, guiding, or explaining human action and social life, because they often conceive of beliefs in narrower ways. "Beliefs" are commonly thought to be something like "propositional ideas that people actively consider, adopt, reflect upon, and readily express when questioned"— the sort of thing one might expect as a confession of faith by an educated, committed Protestant. But that is only one possible kind of human belief, and an unusual one at that. In fact, beliefs come in a broad range of forms.[32] Philosophy provides a helpful hint here. When philosophers use the word "beliefs," they simply mean the specific kind of mental attitude toward things people regard as true.[33] Those beliefs may be mindful or thoughtless, vehemently defended or taken for granted as obvious, reflected upon or accepted without consideration, and objectively veritable or false.[34] Once understood this way, we see that people's beliefs are tremendously important in forming the way they live their lives.[35] But many if not most of the beliefs that exert that kind of causal power are not of the actively considered, propounded, explicitly propositional sort.[36] Most are highly mundane and simply operate in the background as attitudes or suppositions about what people regard to be true. *In principle*, all of people's beliefs *should* be able to be "surfaced" and expressed in propositional form. But in reality, only a small fraction of people's actual beliefs can be and are expressed that way.[37] A host of people's beliefs are real, truly believed, and powerfully influence their patterns of action, but that does not mean that people can or do bring them to conscious awareness for direct inspection and expression.[38] Beliefs are therefore powerfully governing of people's lives, but only some are the sort that people can express explicitly, for example, in research interviews or survey questions.

Desires. Human desires encompass a wide range of personal, subjective orientations to objects, conditions, and experiences.[39] By "desires" I mean a state of embodied mind or "pro attitude" that combines attraction and will toward some object, state of being, or experience. Desires concern what was traditionally labeled the "conative" aspect of mental life.[40] We must for an adequate theory of motivated human action understand human "desires" in a broad enough way to account for the actual range of kinds of them that people have and the different ways those desires enter into the motivational process.[41] Clearly, desires (at least those of which we are aware) are subjectively felt states, yet they are also grounded in the biological substrate of the body and brain.[42] For some people, "desires" means something like pressing yearnings, cravings, longings, or passions that exist in conscious awareness and that can be expressed in words if necessary. "I really want to buy a new car" and "I cannot resist ordering the chocolate cheesecake" are examples. But humans experience a broader range of desires than these.[43] Many desires operate in people's lives without their conscious awareness, immediate reflection, or capacity to be communicated with words. Sometimes people have desires that are literally unconscious, that have roots in relationships and experiences far beyond the access of normal memory or reflection (such as, for example, the un-self-reflective, knee-jerk reaction of resisting all authority figures). Sometimes people have significant desires that operate far in the background of their field of focused awareness that are rarely if ever recognized in the course of ordinary life, yet in principle are susceptible to retrieval, inspection, evaluation, and revision (such as people's cravings for recognition and status or physical affection). Then again, people often have many diffuse, unfocused, or generalized (though not strictly unconscious) desires that can nonetheless prove to be causally powerful in life (such as an interest in novelty and unconventional experiences, or the general wish to banish all insecurity and disorder in relationships). Desires too can be selfish and unselfish. A good theory of human motivations needs to adopt this broader view of the nature of human desires, both to be adequate to the reality and to be explanatorily satisfying when it comes to causes and outcomes.[44]

Emotions. Many theories do not include emotions as constitutive parts of motivations. And Western rationalism has traditionally warned people against the dangers and unreliability of emotions. However, the more we learn about the human brain, about the role of emotions in the real living of life, and reflect upon our own phenomenological experiences in light of those considerations, the more we see that emotions are inseparable from most desires, beliefs, judgments, and motivational processes. We have good reason to include emotions in our account of the ontology of motivations.[45] Few if any, in fact, are the operative motivations that do not comprise some emotional component.[46] Emotions are complex psycho-physiological experiences or states that environmental and biochemical forces generate.[47] Emotions concern what is traditionally labeled the affective aspect of mental and bodily life. Emotional experiences or states entail some kind of physiological arousal that is often (but not always) meaningfully interpreted in conscious awareness and expressed in culturally appropriate behaviors.[48] Both the physical body and subjective awareness are involved in emotions.[49] Various neurotransmitters and hormones, such as dopamine, serotonin, and norepinephrine, are centrally involved in emotions.[50] Emotions have incredibly complex relations to physiological operations of the brain as the underlying material substrate of affective subjective experiences.[51] Emotions are also often consciously interpreted as to their kind, cause, and significance. People normally try to regulate the expression and experience of their emotions to fit culturally normative expectations.[52] Some human emotions—often identified as happiness, sadness, surprise, fear, disgust, and anger—are believed to be basic and universal.[53] Others are more complex in their specific cultural definition and expression.[54] Crucial for present purposes is recognizing that emotions help to energize and direct human actions; they provide the affective dimension of the larger motivational ontology examined here.[55]

The etymological origins of the English word "emotion" are closely related to the word "motivation."[56] Emotions can powerfully propel actions and inhibit actions as they shape motivations in complex ways. "Emotion proper serves to facilitate or regulate action."[57] Emotions are integrally enmeshed in the basic motivational processes of "anticipatory states and seeking systems."[58] Emotions involve a "power of teleology" involved in the "established fact" that "emotions . . . motivate. . . . Emotions are essentially implicated in our capacity to live a coherent and reasonably well-regulated life; unless you care, your life will be a mess; and whether or not you care is surprisingly neatly attested by your galvanic skin response [i.e., measurable emotional reactions]."[59] Emotions are "judgments of the body" that can be nonpropositional and subjectively felt, that help people both "know that" about life and "know how" to live life, all of which helps comprise and govern motivations for action.[60] "Emotions can be, or help make up, the cause of something we do."[61] Jon Elster observes the "fairly robust fact about emotions that each of them goes together with one or several spontaneous action tendencies that, if unchecked, will result in action."[62] Any study of human motivations for action must thus take emotions seriously.[63] It is not my purpose to explore the many specific human emotions and ways they interact with beliefs and desires to comprise motivations. My interest in emotions is more modest: to argue that emotions as a "substantive psychological category"[64] belong to a proper account of the ontology of human motivations.[65] Motivations are constituted in part by human emotions.[66]

My overall ontology of motivations thus relies upon the traditional three-part view of human mind comprised of the cognitive, conative, and affective—going back at least to Plato's three components of the human mind. Various modern thinkers have criticized this view of humanity's "three faculties" of mind, but I find those criticisms to be ineffective. There are of course different ways to map out the faculties, functions, and dimensions of human mental life. But I believe the threefold concept of beliefs, desires, and emotions well captures real distinctions. And, despite criticisms, many findings of contemporary neuroscience are validating this traditional, three-faculty view.[67] For instance, studies of the supplementary motor area (SMA) of the brain are demonstrating the tight connections between the functioning of conative desires and intentions, cognitive belief representations, affective dispositions and emotions, and bodily motor activity.[68] In short, the traditional view, long under a cloud of suspicion, is being revalidated by good natural science.

The Teleological Orientation of Motivations

Teleology has come in for a beating in the social sciences. Set against the backdrop of a rejection of Aristotle in science centuries ago—particularly since Francis Bacon's *Novum Organum* (1620)—and the broad rejection of organic models of society since then, teleology was more recently attacked as part of the broader critique of Parsons's structural functionalism in the 1960s and 1970s. The argument then was that we cannot rightly explain the actions of people and institutions by reference to their supposed functional contribution to the telic end of the survival and well-being of "society" as a whole—a critique with which I agree. Today, the primary explicit exponents of teleology in human life are rational choice theorists, who presuppose that all people are oriented toward the end of increasing if not maximizing their benefits, rewards, or utility.[69] That too tends to give teleology a bad name in other sectors of social science—and with good reason with regard to rational choice theory.

Yet my argument is inescapably and unapologetically teleological. Most of human activity is oriented toward the (greater) realization, achievement, or fulfillment of desired goods. And the (greater) accomplishment of those goods lies in the future, in the distance, ahead in life. The structure of the human motivational condition, therefore, is teleological, that is, oriented toward the achievement of some unrealized, future end (although the goods pursued are much more complex and specific than the "rewards" of rational choice theory).[70] Human life is oriented toward certain ends, which motivations provide the energy, direction, and focus to realize or fulfill.[71] We commit no theoretical crime by thinking teleologically. But we need to focus the telic emphasis of our theories not on "society" (as with functionalism) but on *persons*, on what they are trying to achieve in their lives—and, by extension, institutions, insofar as they are constructed, sustained, led, and represented by persons, and so can be rightly said to be purposively pursuing ends. To get it right, we must also properly specify the telic ends toward which persons live. Rational choice theory is not wrong in believing that people are teleologically motivated. It is wrong primarily in the combination of narrowness or vagueness of the ends it assumes people are motivated to achieve.

Sometimes in sociological theory teleology and causal approaches are opposed. The allegation is that teleology has to do with being pulled into the future, whereas causation is concerned with forces driving from the past. But that is a false opposition. In fact, teleology and causation are compatible, necessary, and complementary. Properly understood, causation need not have to do with some kind of deterministic push from temporally preceding forces. Causation is about the activated operation of various capacities and powers possessed by different entities, both sentient and nonsentient, that often (though not always) work to produce change or maintain continuity in reality, in the context of the operation or force of other activated powers and capacities. That may work in some cases according to a kind of Newtonian mechanics, which reflects no apparent teleological processes at work. But in other cases, including many human contexts, causation may involve the perceptions and powers of intention, interests, desires, and purposes, which reflect clear teleological aspects.[72] Human action, in short, is often both caused and teleologically motivated. Telic interests and purposes can and do function as causes, just as causal processes can and do operate in people's teleological motivations toward ends.

Adequate Complexity

A good model of human motivations and action must be both *complex* enough to account for the actual complications of the reality in question (the

nature of motivated human action) and *broad* and stable enough to be useful across the full range of types of motivated human actions. By *complex*
I refer to a feature of (natural or social) systems in which distinct and in-
terdependently related parts are adaptive to dynamic changes in each other
and in their environments—sometimes producing what complexity theory
calls "dancing landscapes." That can make them difficult to understand and
model. Many social science theories often sacrifice adequate complexity for
the sake of parsimony. Some also sacrifice definitional inclusiveness and
breadth of applicability for the sake of "working" (often only) in particular
contexts. An adequate model of motivated human action, however, has to
satisfy the criterion of adequate complexity by relaxing the imperative for
parsimony enough to account conceptually for the important complications
involved in the matter.[73] An adequate theory must also be general and stable
enough to work in making sense of motivated human action broadly, not
simply in particular cultures, contexts, or time periods.[74]

Multiplicity and Incommensurability. We can start by recognizing that motivations are irreducibly *multiple* and often *incommensurate.*[75] Motivations
are potentially complementary or conflicting, but never unitary or simple.
In chapter 5, I explain the reasons for this multiplicity of even basic human
motivations. For now suffice it to note that no realistic or useful theory of
human motivations can proceed on the assumption that all significant motivations can be reduced to one, single underlying, latent, or general basic or
megamotivation. Despite that, however, it has been common in the history
of social science for theories to posit or focus on *one* dominant, if not exclusive, interest or motivation. Monomotivational assumptions are standard in
sociology, for example, if and when motives are actually addressed. Certain
strands of normative, functionalist, and cultural theories presuppose that the
single important motivation in social life is the human desire to follow social
norms or make meanings. Parsons's work, for example, keyed on the motive
of following socialized norms.[76] Many conflict-based theories are built on
the assumption that humans are universally and, for all practical purposes,
exclusively driven in actions to increase their wealth, power, security, and
status. Marxism, for example, posits the centrality of control over material
production. Symbolic interactionism emphasizes either the generation and
sustaining of intersubjective meanings or, alternatively, the maintenance of
credible public moral identities. Ethnomethodology stresses the motivation
to create orderly communications. Hedonic theories claim that all motivations lead back to the "pleasure principle." Rational choice theory posits rational egoism's motivation to maximize benefits and rewards relative to costs,
presuming that all ends and goods can be fit on a commensurate scale of

"utility."[77] Anthony Giddens says that the most elemental human motive is to sustain "ontological security." Randall Collins explains human social life in terms of the pursuit of emotional energy.[78] And so on. In short, sociologists, when they pay attention to motivations, often feel compelled to identify one single motivation by which to explain social life generally. What they usually end up doing instead, however, is only partially explaining some limited dimensions of social life and sometimes not very well.[79] Monomotivational theories oversimplify and ultimately fail to explain social life without having to engage in major conceptual and empirical qualifications or contortions.[80] They usually prove in the end to be either empirically false or theoretically vacuous or tautological.

So an adequate theory of motivated action must recognize that human motivations, even basic motivations, are multiple.[81] Human action is usually deployed to try to satisfy numerous, different, often competing motivations.[82] Motivations are also complex. They do not usually organize into simple or neat sets, but are instead fraught with complications, intricacies, and difficulties.[83] Finally, the multiplicity and variety of many actual human motivations, whether basic or otherwise, are sometimes not commensurate, in that they entail enough qualitative differences between them that they cannot be compared, weighted, or evaluated on shared scales of importance, consequence, or value. Nonetheless, different sorts of motivations often conglomerate into clusters or sets that are more or less internally coherent. Sometimes different human motivations complement each other and so can be satisfied with one action or set of actions. But oftentimes the action implications of those sets of motivations conflict with one another. Whether the imperatives of different motivations complement or conflict may depend on the time horizon of the ends and actions involved. Or they may depend on the particular conditions or situations in which actors find themselves. In any case, a good social science theory of motivations must see them as characterized by multiplicity, complexity, incommensurability, and the possibility of various combinations of synergy and tension among them.

As a result of this multiplicity and complexity of motivations, a great deal of human life consists of actively managing, balancing, and adjudicating the multiple, complex, incommensurate, often-conflicting motivations and actions to which they do or would give rise. We all know this from lived experience. Because human motivations for action are not singular, simple, easily comparable, or routinely convergent in their action-implications, the ordinary business of living life turns out to be not simple or easily focused and negotiated. Daily life consists significantly of people managing the innumerable causal energies and directions of myriad sorts of motivations that push and pull in different directions for different reasons and with different intensities, kinds, and durations of force. Normal human existence thus involves managing personal subjective "coordination and control centers" that process immense flows of perceptions, definitions, associations, desires, emotions, evaluations, and the like, in order to deploy adequately functional plans of action. This is why people have to recurrently sort out their own mixed motives, decision trade-offs, ethical dilemmas, temptations, and compromises, as well as engage in various forms of mental self-control, suppression of desires, sublimation, displacements, denials, rationalizations, "self-talk," and the like. This also provides the basis for various kinds of tragic situations and lose-lose outcomes in life. Overloaded personal systems of motivations management are also in part why people become "overwhelmed" in life and need rest, sleep, and diversion to recover and make better decisions and take better actions.

Variance in Conscious Awareness. Human motivations for action also vary in the extent to which they are represented in conscious awareness, being sometimes *conscious* and entailing focused concentration, sometimes *habituated* and *latent* in consciousness, and sometimes *unconscious* and even *denied.*[84] Not all real, causally powerful motivations are or need to be operating in the forefront of conscious minds. The beliefs, desires, and emotions out of which motivations are constituted are not always or often present in immediate consciousness. Some, like "I really want to pass this test," are immediately conscious. Others operate further in the background of conscious attentiveness, such as those compelling one's driving to work (which *is* motivated, even though people rarely have to explicitly think, "I need to get into my car and drive to work now in order to perform my job so that I can sustain myself financially").[85] Yet other motivations may be inaccessible to the person's conscious awareness, such as, for example, a desire to succeed as a surgeon as a means to impress a demanding parent for whom one never felt quite good enough. Motivations can move people even when they are not at the center of their minds' consciously focused attention.[86] These three levels of human un/consciousness are depicted graphically in figure 3 (the proportions are suggestive, not intended to represent actually measured distributions of un/conscious activity). Of all human sentient, cognitive, affective, and volitional activity, we have reason to believe that focused consciousness—that about which people have direct attentive awareness—involves lesser amounts of content and mental activity.[87] The human capacity for focused, conscious attention and mental processing is highly limited and consumes large amounts of subjective resources. To use a computer analogy, people can only upload into and process a limited amount of information in their cognitive random

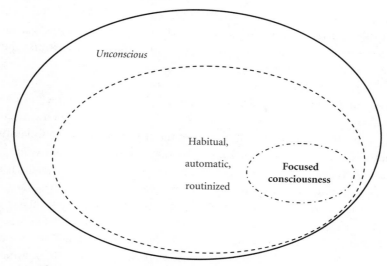

FIGURE 3. The conscious, habitual, and unconscious in human subjective activity.

access memory (RAM) at any given time. Even when operating at full capacity, conscious awareness can handle only a limited amount of information, so shifting to new information in focused consciousness requires pushing other content out of focus.

By contrast, the human capacity for habitual, automatic, routinized mental and physical activity is vast. Humans enjoy immense capacities to efficiently process mental activity and deploy bodily actions without having to focus on them while they operate "in the background."[88] Human interests are able to organize a variety of habits and routines that operate on "automatic pilot."[89] This dramatically increases the amount of activity in which humans are able to engage, despite the limited capacities of focused consciousness. The dashed line between focused consciousness and the habitual, inertial, and routinized in figure 3 indicates the porous boundary separating the two, by which the former is able to deploy and retrieve from the latter; the content and meaning of the habitual, inertial, and routinized are often not far from being able to be recalled into focused consciousness.[90] Finally, human subjectivity also includes a dimension that is inaccessible to the actor's conscious awareness at any particular point in time—although, in principle, with work, elements of the unconscious are capable of being brought to consciousness. This human unconscious is real, active, and often causally potent. But in its deep subjectivity, it remains beyond the access and inspection of conscious awareness. Again, the boundary separating the unconscious from the habitual is somewhat porous.

My account thus does not assume that all human action is consistently "purposive," in the sense of being animated by *conscious* intentions to achieve goals that are valued and actively pursued. Only some human action is purposive *in that sense*, even if all action is purposive in a broader sense, as I argued above. A massive amount of human action is not, but is rather habitual, inertial, and routinized or driven by subconscious processes, such as emotional "transference" or the operation of an unacknowledged defense mechanisms. In other words, we can recognize the reality of "motivated habitual actions." Most human actions that are habituated and latent in consciousness nevertheless have *origins* in motivated, purposive action; and the original and often current motivations generating them usually can, when questioned, be brought to awareness and explained. Much human action *is* habitual.[91] Yet merely because habits allow actors to not always have to deliberate cognitively about their purposes does not mean that habituated actions are not motivated. Most habitual actions *are* motivated. Most actions on "automatic pilot" once had to have been *put* on automatic pilot by a motivation that produced that effect. "The beliefs informing the action do not disappear merely because they are not consciously reflected upon each time. . . . Our beliefs and intentions can be variously located within our consciousness."[92] And when what eventually became habitual—what people "can do in their sleep"—was first being learned, the actions involved took some conscious, focused, deliberate, motivated effort to acquire and execute. Some habitual actions may simply be mindless and purposeless. But most are oriented toward some desired purpose that once set them into motion and that partly helps to sustain them. As Colin Campbell notes:

> Habitual acts . . . are merely "decayed" versions of earlier "true" actions and obviously have to be understood as such. If, therefore, conduct as presently performed appears to lack any accompanying subjective meaning, it is still the case that it must have been so accompanied at the point in the past when the actor learnt how to do it. The action characteristics of habitual conduct necessarily stem from the same source as those for "true" action—that of the mind of the actor.[93]

Many people's habits have also been intentionally chosen and purposefully formed to help achieve some desired outcome. Social scientists sometimes talk about people's habits as if they are bad-to-neutral behaviors. People in this view are seen as having "fallen into" habits or having simply "developed" habits mindlessly. In other cases, habits are viewed as larger social practices of life—"the habitus"—imposed by social orders on individuals who then act them out. Habits thus conceptualized are either replacements for mindful action or expressions of social domination. But habits can be much more than that. Habits sometimes are practices intentionally taken on by persons that help to achieve the realization of goods. Habits, in short, can express virtues (as well as vices). This reminds us that people are not always merely the passive receivers and performers of habits that befall them. People can and do choose to develop certain habits and to break others, as means to help them better realize the kinds of personal lives they wish to lead and achieve the kind of goals they have set for themselves. Habits of this kind are not simply mindless behaviors inscribed upon human activity by chance or society. They may be means deployed toward certain goals, disciplines chosen by persons that help realize teleological ends.

"Motivated unconscious actions" also exist. Many human actions that are driven by unconscious or denied motivations have biographical *sources* in the consciously experienced world and may be susceptible with help to being surfaced for examination and evaluation. Actions whose motivations are inaccessible to consciousness also normally have temporal connections to real-world facts, events, and relationship, even if in the distant past. Not all of the human unconscious needs to be understood in terms of a Freudian psychodynamic model—contemporary psychology takes us well beyond that.[94] Most of the content of the human unconscious is not random or preprogrammed. Most has been embedded in areas of the mind beyond conscious inspection by past experiences living in the world, potentially going as far back as infancy—indeed, arguably, accumulating in human brain structures for millions of years of human history. So unconsciously motivated actions are not compelled by free-floating, random, or materially determined forces, but by dynamics that in principle may be traced back to experiences, perceptions, and reactions rooted in lived reality.[95] This means that people's actions can be motivated even when the motives are unconscious. That said, however, my concern in this book is not to explore the human unconscious, even when it comes to motivations, so the focus of what I write in this text will not reflect the proportions of space represented in figure 3—other works at other times perhaps by other authors will have to analyze more thoroughly the role of the unconscious for human motivation and action as related to critical realist personalism.[96]

Variance in Intensity of Importance and Commitment. Motivations also vary in the extent to which they are important to the persons who hold them. That variance operates on a continuum from persons hardly caring about them, to their being life commitments for which actors are prepared to die. People can be motivated in ways that reflect the smallest of interests, importance, and commitments. In such cases, people may be willing to "give it shot," but are also ready to quickly abandon the action with little sense of loss. In other cases, people's actions reflect interests and commitments believed to be of major importance, which few or no other motivations can trump.

Variance in Temporal Durability. Motivations for action vary in their durability over time, on a spectrum from highly fleeting motivations, to highly stable and long lasting. Some motivations are brief impulses that quickly pass, whether or not they are satisfied. Others stick with people for various periods of time and then eventually are satisfied or fade. Yet other motivations are long enduring, sometimes permanent in human personalities, governing fundamental personal orientations and strategies over entire lifetimes. Theories of motivated action that constrain the motivational time horizons to some artificially "typical" range (P wanted X, P worked to get X, P got X) underestimate the capacity for both fleeting and lifelong motivations to generate significant action in different contexts and ways.

Variance in Internal Coherence of Motivational Sets. Specific motivations for action vary in their coherence with other personal motivations, differing in the degree to which they are isolated from or well integrated into larger webs or structures of personal motivation systems. Nothing in a realist theory of motivated human action requires that any of people's particular motives are well integrated into or driven by the force of a coherent, bounded, organized, systematic scheme of ideas or desires. Particular motivations may be linked to coherent ideologies or worldviews. They may belong to larger systems of compatible desires and beliefs. But they need not be. Oftentimes particular motives are not. Motivations can be integrated, but they can also be idiosyncratic.[97] They may cohere in a larger structure of ideas and wants, or they may operate in what seem to be random or inconsistent ways. We need not predetermine the coherence level of people's motives as a standard for being considered real or important, but instead see systemic coherence as an open question. A motivation is a motivation if it moves action, regardless of how random, incoherent, contradictory, consistent, or integrated it may be in relation to other motivations.[98]

Variance in Degree of Internalization. Human motivations for action also vary in the extent to which they are personally internalized or are prompted or highlighted by influences outside the person. Some motivations ("intrinsic") are central to integrated personal selves and are the basis of self-determined actions. These internalized motivations prompt voluntary actions because of the inherent satisfaction for the actor of the motivated activities per se.[99] Other motivations ("extrinsic") are more externally prompted and driven, triggered and directed by actors, situations, and rewards outside of the personal actor, beyond the enjoyment of the activities in and of themselves.

These can include what some scholars call amotivational states, external regulation, introjected regulation, identified regulation, integrated regulation, and intrinsic regulation.[100] But even when they lean in an extrinsic direction, such motivated actions are not simply replaced by the determinative power of "social forces," as if in a zero-sum game. Again, social forces normally work on and through the real motivations of persons.

Variance in Intentionality of Appropriation. Motivations also vary in the degree to which they are actively or passively learned or adopted, on a spectrum from passive absorption through unconscious acquisition, to embrace through purposeful choice. Not all motivations for action need to be of the sort that are purposefully considered and intentionally embraced by the people who are moved by them to action. Many motivations for action are internalized through a variety of means over long periods of time, including ways about which the persons involved have limited awareness and control. Motivations are not limited to those that people appropriate with full awareness and intention with regard to their purpose, power, and consequences.

Solitary and Repeated Actions. Motivations also vary in the extent to which the activities they cause are solitary or repeated in patterns of action or practices. Motivated actions vary across a spectrum of degrees of repetition, from singular isolation to continual reiteration. Motivated actions may be isolated, performed only once. Most actions, however, are not singular, but come as patterned, repeated practices.

Temporal Development

Motivations are also often complex when considered in their temporal formation. An adequate theory of motivations needs to describe the complexity of motives when viewed in "cross-sectional" light (synchronically) and also to take a temporal view that describes how motivations develop within time (diachronically). Motivations often form in a multifaceted, developmental process of strengthening movement toward action. This usually involves the developing stages of wishes, current concerns, intentions, decisions, and implementation. The process by which motivations generate action, in other words, does not normally involve a complete 0-to-1 movement, from having no motive to that of a full motivation immediately acted upon. Motivation is often an internal developmental process involving multiple steps between the spark of initial desire to the final taking of action,[101] represented as a full-blown process as follows:

> initial belief(s) → wish formation → becoming a current concern → forming intentions → deciding → acting

This motivational process can happen nearly instantaneously or can take a long time to develop. It can also be initiated and then stalled or aborted.[102] The process itself involves moving the purpose of the possible action to greater centrality in attention, importance, and commitment.[103] Understanding this helps us to see how and why a variety of contextual factors often complicate and neutralize motivated action in time.[104]

The temporal development of motivations does not stop once a motivated action has occurred, however. Life is a continual flow of personal being in experience, action, practice, and habit. In that flow, people's motivations are in dynamic motion. Some motivations are satisfied and so discharged and dropped. Some are satisfied and sustained to continue to achieve their satisfaction. Some are satisfied and give rise to new, similar or related motivations. Some motivations are frustrated and either abandoned or modified. Some motivations are over time in experience heightened in their conscious focus. Others are moved into the background of awareness. Depending on people's experiences, they may integrate certain motives into larger, coherent motive sets. Others may split out particular motives from previously coherent sets, concentrating on one motivation and dropping the previously related ones. In short, because people's beliefs, desires, and emotions can and do continually change—slowly and quickly—their motivations are also ever in motion. The simple model depicted above, which analytically represents the temporal development of one motive, usually operates at various points in a complex process for every motivation operating in every person. And a big part of what it is to be personal "centers with purpose" is to learn how to form, manage, and act well upon the motivations that are ever developing, causing activity, and realizing ends (or not) in life.

Excursus: In Defense of Beliefs

Some social scientists believe that the content of people's beliefs does not count much in shaping their actions and behaviors.[105] I cannot count the number of thesis and dissertation committees I have served on in which other faculty members declared during the defense, "Forget what people supposedly believe subjectively. That predicts nothing. Focus instead on actual behaviors." People's beliefs, at least some social scientists believe, do little work helping us to understand and explain their lives. What really matter are things like social network ties, habitus and habituated practices, cultural repertoires of action, immediate social situations, or organizational embeddedness. By contrast, taking people's beliefs seriously is associated with outdated ways of explaining human action, often connected to Parsonian functionalism, which emphasized the central role of "subjective" attitudes, values, and norms. Rarely do scholars come right out and bluntly declare, "People's beliefs do not matter" (although Durkheim does, as we see in chapter 4, along with some others observed in chapter 3), but the antimentalist bias behind such a view is present in contemporary sociology. It is also manifest in the *absence* of attention to beliefs, rather than explicit dismissive statements about beliefs—by the neglect of attention to the role of beliefs in personal and social life, much of social science sends the powerful *implicit* message that beliefs can be ignored without negative consequences. The belief that beliefs do not matter has a deep and wide-ranging history. The philosophy of empiric*ism* (distinct from simply being empirical[106]) in its strong form counts beliefs as ontological fictions since they cannot be empirically observed. Positivism—advocated by the man who coined "sociology," Auguste Comte—also leads to the discounting of beliefs, since beliefs are subjective and unobservable. The philosophical position of "dispositionalism" has also claimed that a belief may be equated simply with the disposition to act as if that belief is true.[107] Philosophical "interpretationism" also eschews a view of beliefs as psychological structures of representation and instead defines beliefs as what an outside observer might attribute to an actor based on their behavior. Rooted in this deeper history are more recent sociological schools and approaches that discount the importance of beliefs for understanding and explaining human life.[108] And a body of (I think problematic) social psychological research has concluded that the relationship between people's professions and actions is nearly random[109]—although Nancy Snow has nicely shown how inappropriate and artificial much of the social psychological experiments are that social and philosophical situationists point to as validating evidence.[110] There are, however, a number of things wrong with the idea that the content of beliefs do not matter in generating or explaining people's actions and behaviors.[111]

First, the belief that beliefs don't matter is self-defeating, insofar as *that is* a belief that might affect the actions of anyone holding it (for example, turning the explanatory attention of social scientists away from people's beliefs and toward other factors). Simply by espousing such a theoretical position, anyone believing it shows it cannot be true. Social science itself is obviously informed by various kinds of beliefs about what is real, important, useful, moral, and effective in research, publishing, and teaching. In the absence of beliefs governing actions, what kind of account could possibly explain people's activities?[112] What kind of discipline would be suited to offering that kind of explanation? It would have to appeal to noncognitive biological mechanisms, of the sort that explain the activities of bacteria and worms. Explanation would reduce to something like elementary biology or nonvertebrate zoology, if not even more rudimentary than that.[113] But real people obviously do hold beliefs that make a huge difference in what we must account for as we seek to explain their actions and behaviors.[114] And that is why, even if some social scientists may have lost confidence in the explanatory relevance of human beliefs, many others proceed in their scholarship assuming that beliefs are important in human personal and social life.

Social scientists who doubt the importance of people's belief for understanding and explaining their actions commit basic errors that make their outlook confused and untenable. One error is conflating the concepts of beliefs, attitudes, values, norms, and other subjective entities. The dismissal of the importance of beliefs is sometimes expressed in critiques of the explanatory usefulness of people's values or attitudes or norms. But these are not the same things. Just because studies may show that people's attitudes are loosely related to their behaviors in certain areas of life does little to demonstrate that beliefs do not matter. Even granting that attitudes and values and cultural norms are poor predictors of people's actions—which I do not necessarily believe—does not mean that beliefs too are largely irrelevant. These are often different sorts of items, and any theorizing about them must be clear in its reference to and claims about them.

Another error scholars who claim that people's beliefs are decoupled from their actions and behaviors make is confusing people's actual beliefs with what people report discursively to others when asked about their beliefs related to the actions in question. Actual beliefs and reports about beliefs are not the same things. It may be that many people do not act in accordance with how we might reasonably deduce they ought to act based on what they say about a topic. But that does not mean that beliefs did not help give rise to their actions. It means that people often do not act in accordance with how we might reasonably deduce they ought to act based on what they say about a topic in question. And that is a different matter. So social scientists may be justified in claiming that what people say often does not predict how they act. But that is different from thinking that people's beliefs do not matter.

Beliefs are subjective entities referring to things people consciously or tacitly regard to be true. Only some beliefs are represented by active reflections on expressed propositions that can be readily formulated into language. People are normally highly limited in their own awareness of their beliefs, in their capacity to bring to consciousness the complex fullness of their relevant beliefs, and in their ability to represent their beliefs in words. Hence, the real possible disconnect is between people's beliefs and their *talk* about their beliefs, *not* between their beliefs and their actions. To think otherwise is to wrongly assume that people's discourse thoroughly and accurately reflects their beliefs.[115] Locating the real disconnect in the right place leaves us without reason for thinking that people's beliefs do not matter for action. The severe limits on people's ability to express beliefs in words are problems inherent to studying human beings, with which social science simply has to do its best to deal. They are not, however, indications that beliefs do not matter.[116]

Another error made here is erroneously assuming that action outcomes should be influenced by one or a small number of seemingly relevant beliefs that are identified by researchers as those that should govern the action in question. For example, sociologists might ask if people believe that "it is good to engage in voluntary charitable giving to nonprofits," and then compare their answers to their actual charitable-giving behavior. When they find a low correlation between the belief profession and the behavior, they may then conclude that people's beliefs do not matter. But that is based on the tenuous assumption that actions that are governed by beliefs are so governed by one or a few beliefs that can be formulated in a simple proposition about that action. Yet we know that reality is more complicated than that. People may believe it is good (or not) to give money away, and those beliefs may have some bearing on their giving behavior. But normally many other beliefs also influence their financial giving behavior. If someone genuinely thinks it is good to give money away but does not actually give much, that could be because they *also believe*, say, that they are currently at risk of financial bankruptcy, that their first fiscal responsibility is to take care of their own family, that the recipients of their donations may be wasting money, that they already gave at the office (whether or not they did), or that much wealthier people have a greater responsibility to give than they do. In which case, it would be wrong to conclude that "beliefs don't matter." What would be right to conclude is that "beliefs matter very much," but that people hold many beliefs all of which do not produce the same results, which they often try to hold in tension and negotiate toward a more-or-less reasonable balancing of their cognitive commitments and their implied consequences.[117]

Ann Swidler provides a good example. In an argument skeptical about people's "ineffable subjectivity" and "ephemeral subjectivities," Swidler suggests that culture is not about "individual ideas or values" and that "few [people] are presumably moved by deep belief in the principles that lie behind" their behaviors. She claims, for example, that "middle-class Americans *do not 'believe'* in Christmas gift giving," in that they are critical of its commercialism, hassle, and cost (note that "believe" is put in quotation marks, the meaning of which is unclear).[118] Yet people give Christmas gifts anyway. Why? Because, Swidler says,

Christmas gift giving constitutes a semiotic code (that is, a set of relationally defined meanings) in which the relative value of the gifts a person gives [to] others signals the relative importance with which she or he holds those others. Not to give a gift would, independent of the intentions of the giver, be interpreted as a sign that one did not value the (non)recipient. What governs action in this case, then, is not individuals' internalized beliefs, but their knowledge of what meanings their actions have for others.[119]

This does not work. It says that people give Christmas gifts despite "not believing in it" because *they actually believe in it*: people believe they should give gifts as expressions of the value other people have to them, so they do. Just because a belief comes from a larger cultural system of gift giving does not make it *not* a personal belief. Cultural codes and people's beliefs are not mutually exclusive. The assertion that this process operates "independent of the intentions of the giver" and is not about "individuals' internalized beliefs" is manifestly false. The *entire process* is driven by people's "subjective ideas and values," only different ones than Swidler apparently counts as "deep" and causal. How else could being "interpreted," "values," and "knowledge" operate than through people's "subjectivity," "individual values," and "internalized beliefs?" Had Swidler adjusted her notions of how people's subjective beliefs shape their actions, she might have seen the obvious here. But her theoretical agenda forced her to say things that do not make sense. Yet this kind of thinking has been influential in sociology (especially cultural sociology) since 1986.[120]

In short, people's beliefs actually may matter greatly, just not always the ones social scientists happen to identify ahead of time to ask about in surveys and interviews. When that is true, the real problem resides with *us* social scientists and the limits of our methods and measurements, *not* with the people we study and the importance of their beliefs. One could only possibly think otherwise by presupposing the wrong idea that what science is methodologically capable (or not) of doing is what should determine what is real, rather than reality itself determining how science ought to go about trying to understand it. Any good science calibrates itself to properly understand and explain the particular nature of its specific subject of study—rather than working the other way around.[121] How science is conducted needs to be determined by the character of what it is studying, rather than demanding that the subject of study conform itself to some predetermined, abstract model of what science must be. How a science of galaxies best operates is different from the science of human biological reproduction, which is different again from the science of human creativity, social groups, or purposive action. Social scientists operating in the positivist empiricist mode have too routinely demanded that all of social reality fits the capacities of an abstractly standard "Scientific Method," quite narrowly conceived, rather than designing appropriate methods to conform to the human subject being studied. As a result, human persons and social life have often come out looking distorted. Rather than stepping back and rethinking the scientific method in light of those distortions, the dogmas of positivist empiricism drive social scientists instead to push forward with their program. They are thus forced to assert as fact that people really are (science says so) the way they look and act after they have been distorted by the rigid and demanding positivist scientific process, rather than how they actually seem to look and act in ordinary life. Whether that gives us *Homo economicus* or *Homo determinus-geneticus* or whatever other distortion, that outcome is the product of a bad theory of science.[122]

Yet another error some social scientists make in discounting beliefs is failing to see the many ways that beliefs operate in the alternative, allegedly non-belief-based accounts they offer. Take the list of things mentioned above that some say "really" matter to produce action and behavior more than people's beliefs: social network ties, habitus and habituated practices, cultural repertoires of action, immediate social situations, and organizational embeddedness. Could any of these exist or produce causal effects in the absence of people's beliefs about them? How, for example, could there exist social network ties in the first place without people's meaningful beliefs about other people, identities, relationships, communication, information, resources, reciprocity, and so on? The very disposition against beliefs and instead for some other social or structural factors allegedly mattering more importantly itself depends on the belief that beliefs *do* matter. They simply encompass a broader variety of cognitions concerning things people regard to be true, which matter in a broader variety of ways, wider than social scientists often conceive.[123]

Another error some social scientists make in believing that beliefs do not matter is supposing that it is possible for sociology to avoid dealing with human subjectivity. Beliefs, it is often said, are "subjective" and therefore problematic if not impossible to deal with. This view reflects an antimentalist and antisubjectivist presupposition that turns out to be impossible to maintain.[124] It leans strongly in the direction of sociological behaviorism and positivism, which turn out to be impossible to consistently practice.[125] The real problem is not the difficult fact of human subjectivity, although that is difficult in its own way. The problem is some social scientists' empiricist axiom, which insists that only that which can be directly observed may count in an *explanans* in social science. But empiricism is not valid. It is an early-modern epistemological ideology that does not warrant our adherence. Empiricism is also not assumed in most of the natural sciences, which ironically many social scientists seem to be trying to imitate. In fact, at a purely logical level, empiricism is self-defeating in that no observable evidence exists that could possibly validate the truth of empiricism. To be an empiricist, thus, one has to accept things on authority for other reasons that empiricism disallows. Empiricism is also an idea in which some people *believe*, which has real *consequences* for the actions they perform as social scientists. So the presupposition of empiricism that justifies the rejection of human subjectivity as a source of sociological knowledge, which serves as an argument against the relevance of people's beliefs for sociological explanation, contradicts itself. It relies on a belief to justify a rejection that serves an argument against believing in beliefs.

The natural sciences have little problem researching and theorizing realities that cannot be directly empirically observed. That is largely the business in which they are engaged. Science cannot observe neutrinos or quarks or dark matter or black holes or the Big Bang. Nor can it observe the mechanisms by which gravity works or the geological-chemical formation of crude oil. Natural science uses the limited evidence it can observe and experiment upon, in conjunction with its best reasoning abilities and conceptual models of already-understood causal mechanisms, to build general theoretical understandings of what exists in reality and how it works (or worked). And many of those understandings include a lot of entities that no scientist has ever observed. And to the extent to which the natural sciences are concerned with modeling basic causal mechanisms, they are all about studying and theorizing invisibilities, insofar as most causes cannot be observed, only some of their effects. Empiricism as a science-guiding doctrine fails. It should be left behind in the seventeenth, eighteenth, and nineteenth centuries that were its heyday. Yes, human subjectivity is difficult to plumb. Sociologists cannot directly inspect it. And so people's beliefs cannot be identified and measured like years spent in school or age of death can. But that does not mean that human subjectivity and beliefs are not real or do not govern people's actions.[126] It means that the social sciences are highly methodologically challenged disciplines. Beliefs and their effects on actions and behavior are hard to study. What else is new? We just have to deal with that as best we can.[127]

A Comment on Methodological Implications

The complexities involved in the reality of motivated human action present methodological challenges for studying them, sometimes acute ones, which must be met with all the available research and reasoning tools at our disposal (rather than concluding that understanding them is futile or irrelevant).

Connecting actions to the motivations that generated them is not easy. There are often methodological difficulties, some seemingly insurmountable.[128] But that is not because actions are not motivated. It is because the nature of the entities and processes being studied are often not directly observable and are highly complex. We have to face and acknowledge that. Again the nature of the subject of scientific study must determine the nature of the science applied to study it, not the other way around.[129] In principle, any valid social science methodology is capable of contributing to our understanding of people's motivations and how they give rise to action. However, all of the complexities noted above do suggest that certain methods may often be better suited to deal with them than others. Every research design and method must be driven by the particular research question and analysis at hand. But we still must recognize the limitations and advantages of different approaches. For example, surveys of sampled populations that support multivariate quantitative statistical analyses will typically have great difficulty in measuring the range, depth, multiplicity, and other complexities involved in people's motivations. Only very sophisticated and extensive measures will have a chance to capture well the kinds of complexities that define people's motivations. Personal interviews will often be better able to accomplish that. But even interviews, we have noted, often fail to access motivations that are not present to or well formed in people's discursive consciousness.[130]

In many cases, perhaps the most adequate research methodology for studying complex motivated actions will be in-depth, qualitative field studies combining ethnographic observations and personal interviews. Such an approach enhances the researcher's capacity to observe behaviors and interactions (and not merely ask people for verbal reports), to see how different moving parts of a social system work together in various ways and to track social dynamics as they develop over time. Historical methods that enjoy the evidence needed to go into enough depth can also satisfy these interests as well. The latter methodologies, in other words, normally provide for a more sophisticated and complex understanding of the relevant social dynamics than most alternatives. They also normally set up analyses to tell causal stories that follow narrative storylines of developmental unfolding—which is how life actually works—rather than having to rely on the usually thinner method of correlating variables and then subsequently telling quasi-causal stories about how and why they may be associated.[131] As a general rule, then, from a personalist perspective, given the complex nature of human persons and what moves them to action in life, qualitative research conducted over time in natural social settings will often be more appropriate and revealing than variables-based quantitative methods.

Conclusion

Motivations we should understand as causing actions. Human motivations actually *cause* many human actions in the strong sense—they are not epiphenomenal mental states that merely accompany action or post hoc justifications for actions already taken for other reasons. To explain anything social scientifically is to describe its causes, what produced it or brought it about. Since a large swath of human personal and social activities and the social structures that emerge from them are built on motivated actions, social science must understand human motivations. This chapter has offered an account grounded in critical realist personalism of the nature of those human motivations.

3

Against Social Situationism

The account that I developed in chapters 1 and 2 above stands at odds with a number of dominant assumptions and sensibilities in social theory in recent decades. Since these assumptions and sensibilities are not uncommon, I cannot simply pass them by or critique them by mere implication. It is necessary to confront what in some parts of sociological thinking today my approach contradicts. I focus in this chapter on "social situationism."[1] This is not a distinct or official school of theory, but rather a broad and related set of intellectual movements that have shaped the basic terms and sensibilities of much sociological theorizing. My target is not a self-identified, highly coherent, tightly argued school of theory that would merit its own chapter in a theory textbook. Social situationism is more amorphous than that. Despite or perhaps because of that fact, however, its influence has become significant. Although few sociologists today explicitly label themselves "social situationists," many have absorbed much of its outlook. I am not capable of narrating the full history of the development and influence of situationism, nor of offering a fine-grained description of its assumptions, arguments, outlooks, and representatives. For present purposes I will simply provide a sketch of the intellectual genealogy of situationism, draw out its major ideas with illustrative quotes by representatives, and focus on problems in it that are at odds with my personalist view.

The guiding influences on social situationism have been (sometimes the misread or misapplied) ideas of Émile Durkheim, George Herbert Mead, Charles Horton Cooley, W. I. Thomas, C. Wright Mills, Alfred Schutz, Harold Garfinkel, Herbert Blumer, Peter Berger, Erving Goffman, Peter Burke, and Rom Harré. Behind them lay various (again, oftentimes misunderstood, poorly applied, or simply erroneous) philosophical influences of 1920s and

1930s post-Wundtian theories of language, some post-Wittgensteinian theorists (such as Peter Winch), certain existentialist thinkers, poststructuralist and postmodernist theorists, and some midcentury experimental and theoretical social psychologists.[2] Important "schools" shaping social situationism have been symbolic interactionism, dramaturgical sociology, phenomenology, ethnomethodology, social constructionism, social role theory, identity theory, discourse analysis, and parts of cultural sociology.[3] More broadly, the twentieth century's "linguistic turn" has been central in forming situationism. Social situationism we may also understand as a reaction against (usually real problems in) sociological Marxism, Skinnerian behaviorism, Parsonian functionalism, Durkheimian holism, utilitarian rational-choice theory, and metaphysically realist scientistic positivism. Situationism also stakes out a place in psychology.[4] Some situationists view themselves as carrying forward a neo-Weberian "action theory," despite situationism's actual radical redefining and overturning of Weber's original vision (which most situationists fail to realize).[5] Others outright reject Weber as (allegedly) too closely linked to Parsons. Critical realist personalism affirms that many specific claims of social situationism are valid and insightful, especially when reformulated in more realistic terms, but the approach taken as a whole is a problem.

Figure 4 offers a basic depiction of the intellectual genealogy of social situationism as I mean it here, focused on key twentieth-century influences. The main intellectual pieces are placed on a timeline at their roughly appropriate temporal locations. The specific influences of one element on another, represented by the thinner lines in the figure, are sometimes direct and clear, but at other times indirect and only absorbed by another approach later in its development.[6] The figure is full of dense network ties that look messy because the real historical intellectual associations it represents are dense and complex—that is part of the point. The identified schools of thought closest to social situationism on the right side are those most immediately constituting and defining what I mean by situationism.[7] I depict situationism as a "cloud" rather than a clearly bounded box, for a few reasons. First, situationism is somewhat amorphous as an approach in sociological thinking, as real clouds are usually amorphous. Situationism morphs around and can take different shapes, depending on who is assuming or arguing it. I depict social situationism as a cloud also because I believe it can often cloud up our thinking, dimming and blurring our perceptions and understandings of humanity and social life. I also depict situationism's cloud as gray because, when it hovers over sociology for a long time, it tends to create an atmosphere of gloom, as do dark clouds in real life. At first, social situationism seems a nice break from the harsh sunlight of realism, in both its problematic and valid forms.

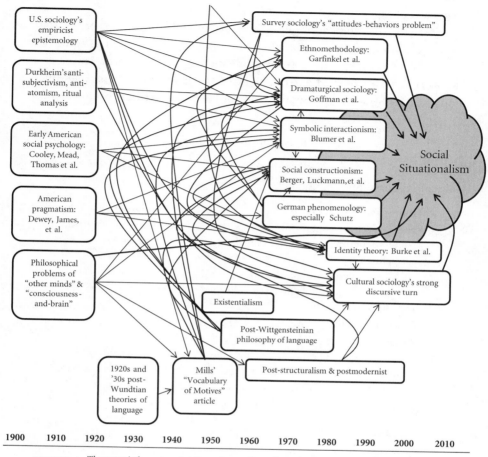

FIGURE 4. The twentieth-century intellectual genealogy of social situationism.

But eventually situationism has the effect of dragging humanity down. My purpose in this chapter is to name the amorphous situationist cloud creating that condition, to try to dispel the cloud, even while condensing what is of value in it in reconstituted form, and thus to help permit more light to shine on humanity and human social life.

How extensive is situationism's influence in sociology today, exactly? I do not know. Determining that is not my purpose. My point is to establish situationism's reality as an approach that more than a few sociologists have embraced and by which more than a few other sociologists have been influenced, whether or not they fully realize it. I am not saying that most sociologists are situationists. I am saying that situationism exists and has come to exert an influence on the thinking of a significant number of sociologists, even many who do not explicitly identify as card-carrying "social situationists." For some sociologists, situationism simply *is* "the sociological perspective" per se, the two are equivalent. For others, situationism names a body of ideas some or many of which they have absorbed. Situationism's complicated genealogy, lack of official public label, and diffuse identity help to obscure some of the influence it has in sociology. But that only means it deserves close examination.

The Situationist Outlook

To focus my assessment of situationism, I proceed by summarizing eight key situationist assumptions and beliefs:

1. People as *people* are the products of the social interactions in which they engage over the course of their lives, the social constructions of the discourses, cultural repertoires, knowledge systems, language games, and formations of self other people imprint upon them.

2. All human doings are *social*—not personal, interior, or private—always informed, defined, and guided by collective processes of social communication and pressure.

3. The central activity in human life is the social *communication* of *cognitive* definitions, meanings, knowledge, rules, vocabularies, and grammars.

4. People's actions are generated as highly local, variable, and contingent responses to *immediate situations* in which they find themselves at any given time, which people continually monitor, interpret, and respond to.

5. People's reported "subjective experiences" are not useful evidence for social science explanations, since people either have no real subjective experiences of the kind that shape actions, or their subjective experiences are vague, inaccessible, and only very loosely coupled to actions and practices.

6. People's actions and practices are *not motivated* by real, internal, subjective entities—such as desires, beliefs, and emotions—that move them to act, since subjectivity is highly problematic, or human activities are simply not the kind of things that are motivated.

7. To the extent that people are pursuing ends in their social interactions, their key goal is to protect their *self-identities* as morally legitimate and respectable, thus placing the matter of identity maintenance at the center of human social existence.

8. The *accounts* that people give to explain their actions and practices are mere post hoc justifications and rationalizations, not reliable explanations of the real causes of their actions and practices.

Readers may see already that social situationism is not internally coherent. How, for example, can the centrality of cognitive knowledge go together with the dismissal of the reality or relevance of subjective experience? How can the denial of motivations fit with the purported basic human interest in identity maintenance? The eight ideas just noted have enough appearance of truth to make them plausible, and enough edginess to make them interesting. But taken as a whole, situationism is false and misleading. These ideas are not merely "wrong from a certain point of view," but wrong as a description of reality as it actually is. Before explaining how and why so, I first illustrate some arguments for each of the eight points above, providing examples of situationist claims from various representatives. I deliberately cite both major and lesser-known theorists from the United States and the United Kingdom to help indicate the breadth and influence of the situationist approach.

Let us begin with the *first* situationist belief, that people are the products of the social interactions in which they engage over the course of their lives, the social constructions of the discourses, cultural repertoires, knowledge systems, language games, and formations of self other people imprint upon them. One could fill an entire chapter with quotes demonstrating the pervasiveness of this viewpoint, but the following suffice. Consider this claim of Sheldon Stryker: "Just as society derives from the social process, *so do persons*. Both take on meanings that emerge in and through social interactions. Since both *derive from the social process*, neither society *nor the individual possess a reality that is prior to or takes precedence* over the other. Society, as a web of interaction, *creates persons*."[8] Randall Collins similarly claims that "radical microsociology means for our own view of ourselves [that] we are all socially constructed; all historically shaped. There is no 'natural' inwardness about our selves," and that "the individual *is* the interaction ritual chain . . . the precipitate of past interactional situations and an ingredient in each new situation. An ingredient, not the determinant"—therefore, "the individual emerges by an apportioning out of *collective* energies and representations."[9] Peter Berger and Thomas Luckmann affirm the same:

> Humanness is socio-culturally variable. In other words, there is *no human nature in the sense of a biologically fixed substratum* determining the variability of socio-cultural formations. . . . While it is possible to say that man has a nature, it is more significant to say that *man constructs his own nature*, or more simply, that *man produces himself*. . . . Man's self-production is always, and of necessity, a *social* enterprise.[10]

Joel Charon says, "the self . . . is an object, *social in origin*, and an object that undergoes change like all other objects: in interaction. . . . It is defined and redefined in interaction. *The self is really a process* like all other social

objects, constantly changing as the individual interacts with others."[11] Erving
Goffman makes the same point, stating that human selves are not the causes
but rather entirely the *products* of social performances:

> A correctly staged and performed scene leads the audience to impute a self to
> a performed character, but this imputation—this self—is a *product* of a scene
> that comes off, and is not a *cause* of it. The self, then, as a performed character,
> is *not an organic thing that has a specific location*, whose fundamental fate is to
> be born, to mature, and to die; it is [instead] *a dramatic effect arising diffusely
> from a scene that is presented*, and the characteristic issue, the crucial concern,
> is whether it will be credited or discredited."[12]

Likewise, Alan Blum and Peter McHugh write: "For any member [of a social
group] to ascribe a motive is thus to do no less than *to generate a person*.
It is to formulate from situated performances a responsibly displayed and
differentiated collection of experiences."[13] A human person is thus merely
a distinct and publicly presented "collection of experiences" formed out of
situated performances.

Human persons per se are therefore generated by the social interactions
in which they engage, which themselves, as we see below, are primarily concerned with affirming the credibility of a self's "character." Most of this is
rooted in older social-situationist theories of the human self that Charles
Horton Cooley and George Herbert Mead advanced.[14] The former, for example, argued that "there is no view of the self that will bear examination
which makes it altogether distinct, in our minds, from other persons. . . . *Self
and other do not exist as mutually exclusive facts*."[15] Human personal selves are
social constructions in our minds. Mead wrote: "*The self . . . is essentially a social structure*, and it *arises in social experience*. . . . It is impossible to conceive
of a self arising outside of social experience."[16]

Such an outlook forces us to abandon traditional understandings of human persons in favor of a highly sociologized view. Randall Collins thus argues, "What we mean by the social actor, the human individual, is a quasi-
enduring, quasi-transient flux in time and space. Although we valorize and
heroize this individual . . . [it] is the product of particular religious, political,
and cultural trends in recent centuries."[17] Barry Barnes also writes that "it is
a mistake . . . to regard [humans] as possessors of stably constituted independent powers and capacities," such as ability to choose, exert causes, or
exercise free will. "Social theorists have no adequate technical rationale for
their references to [human] choice and agency," claims Barnes, and the basis
or reality of their causal power "remains obscure." Distinct human persons
do not even have free will, he says, but only a socially derived "sense" of it:

"Our sense of free will of an agent derives from her susceptibility to others" in social interaction, Barnes insists.[18] Rather than being integrated centers of purpose and action, human beings are highly fragmented and changeable. According to Karin Knorr-Cetina, "The self . . . consists of a multitude of personas which vary with the occasion in which 'the person' is glimpsed . . . observable only in its fragmentation through a series of actions and behaviors." Consequently, "the individual appears as a set of multiple identities which are insulated rather than functionally integrated into just one set of dispositions and beliefs which make up just one individuality."[19] In Barnes's words: "It is useful to remember that no agent is ever regarded as the source of a pure stream of responsible action."[20]

In social situationism, therefore, human persons are entirely dependent upon and defined by *social* life. "If the social person is shaped by interaction," Stryker tells us, "it is social structure that shapes the possibilities for interaction and so, ultimately, the person." Therefore, "there can be no sociological reference to the social person without coordinate reference to at least some aspects of social organization." Much of why this is so is because human life is, according to situationism, organized around knowing the types, definitions, and meanings of things, which all come from society. "Humans respond *not* to the naïve world," Stryker says, "but to the world as [socially] categorized and classified; the physical, biological, and social environment in which they live is a symbolic environment." And because "there exists no ready-made definitions in fully articulated form . . . there will be the need to construct definitions."[21] Knorr-Cetina agrees: "The sociologically relevant person . . . is not a perceptual [that is, directly perceivable single] unit; it can be observed only through a series of actions and behaviors. In these actions, the person manifests a multiplicity of personas which have been linked to social roles . . . or simply to different situations."[22] Being completely dependent for their selves on knowledge of those definitions, persons are thus reliant on and created by social intercourse. Human persons as persons should therefore be understood ontologically as social derivatives, social processes, social products, dramatic effects, and social structures.[23]

Second, social situationism argues that all human doings are essentially *social*—not personal, interior, or private, but always informed, defined, and guided by collective processes of social communication and pressure. This view flows naturally from the first, though it takes a next step. In principle, one might argue that humans are socially constructed, but once socially brought into being, are capable of personal, private, nonsocial activities.[24] But social situationism typically denies that. Everything that humans are, think, and do is social. According to Stryker, "the reality of the self is phenomenological,

and is based on reflexive activity; it has no physical or biological location";
therefore, "self-definitional activity proceeds largely . . . through socially recognized categories." The disconnection of the self from the body or material
environment here is absolute.[25] Consequently, "*self reflects society.*"[26] In short,
"the human organism as an object takes on meaning through the behavior
of those who respond to that organism."[27] Peter Berger agrees, arguing that
the self "is no longer a solid, given entity that moves from one situation to
another. It is rather a process, continuously created and recreated in each
social situation that one enters. . . . Man is not also a social being, but he is
social in every respect of his being."[28] C. Wright Mills similarly wrote that "the
motivational structures of individuals and the patterns of their purposes are
relative to societal frames"; hence, "there is no need to invoke 'psychological'
terms like 'desire' or 'wish" as explanatory, since they themselves must be
explained socially."[29]

These claims again draw upon arguments of older theories. For example,
for William James, the human self is "the sum total of all that an individual
can call his [such as abilities, possessions, relationships, social positions]. . . .
A man has as many social selves as there are individuals who recognize him."[30]
For Mead, what "gives to the individual his unity of self" is "the organized
community or social group," which "can be called 'the generalized other.'"[31]
Therefore, "the locus of mind is not in the individual. Mental processes are
fragments of the complex conduct of the individual in and on his environment. . . . If mind is socially constituted, then . . . [it] must extend as far as the
social activity or apparatus of social relations which constitutes its extent; and
hence that field cannot be bounded by the skin of the individual organism to
which it belongs."[32]

As a result, according to Mills, understanding people's "motives for action
are of no value apart from the delimited societal situations for which they are
the appropriate vocabularies. They must be situated." People are thus always
dominated by other people in social situations whose options determine how
they talk about their own actions: "Variable is the accepted vocabulary of motives, the ultimates of discourse, of each man's dominant group about whose
opinion he cares."[33] Speaking from a German phenomenological rather than
American pragmatist or interactionist perspective, Alfred Schutz similarly
claimed that "living in the world, we live with others and for others, orienting our lives to them," and that "there is only one external world, a *public
world.*"[34] Therefore, for Schutz, "intersubjectivity [between social actors] . . .
is the fundamental ontological category of human existence."[35] Agreeing with
these lines of reasoning, Blumer argued that in "taking the role of the other,"
the individual "is in a position to address or approach himself." From that

observation Blumer immediately deduced that "it follows that we see our-selves through the way in which others see or define us."[36] Collins likewise writes, "The center of micro-sociological explanation is not the individual but the situation. . . . We get more by starting with the situation and devel-oping the individual, than by starting with individuals. . . . Start with the dynamics of situations; from this we can derive almost everything that we want to know about individuals, as a moving precipitate across situations."[37] Charon similarly claims that "a true transcendental self, the 'true, authentic person' is not assumed. . . . [A person's] true self is what he defines as his true self at that point in interaction."[38] And Knorr-Cetina goes so far as to claim flatly that people are far more aware of how other people are acting than they are of themselves, of their own concerns, desires, interests, and intentions: "Participants in an interaction are incomparably better attuned to other par-ticipants than they are to themselves."[39]

Third, social situationists believe that the central activity in human life is the social communication of *cognitive* definitions, meanings, knowledge, rules, vocabularies, and grammars.[40] At first this might seem obvious. But implied in it is the radical discounting of the importance of embodied prac-tices, emotional experience, and volitional desires. Thus Goffman argues that people most essentially have "the motivation to sustain a *definition* of the sit-uation that has been projected before others."[41] Charon claims that "humans do not respond to the world as it exists out there, but to a reality actively *defined* by them."[42] Peter Burke and Jan Stets write: "The self originates in the *mind* of persons and is that which characterizes an individual's *consciousness* of his or her own being or identity. . . . We do not want to give the impres-sion . . . that the self is a little 'person' or *homunculus* residing inside of us that does these things. The self is rather and organized set of *processes* within us that accomplishes these outcomes."[43] Once again, older theories, especially of Mead and Cooley, inform these more recent statements. Mead claimed that "the essence of the self . . . is *cognitive*: it lies in the internalized conversation of gestures which constitute *thinking*, or in terms of which *thought* or *reflec-tion* proceeds."[44] Cooley heavily emphasized the ideational mind's work of imagination, claiming that "the human *mind* is social . . . society is *mental*, and . . . society and the mind are aspects of the same whole."[45] He explained this in greater depth:

> My association with you evidently consists in the relation between my *ideas* of you and the rest of my *mind*. . . . Society . . . is a relation among personal *ideas*. In order to have a society it is evidently necessary that persons should get together somewhere; and they get together only as personal *ideas in the mind*. Where else? What other possible *locus* can be assigned for the real contact of

persons, or in what other form can they come in contact except as impressions or *ideas* formed in this common locus? Society exists in the *mind* as the contact and reciprocal influence of certain *ideas*.[46]

Cooley in fact criticized people adopting the "vaguely material notion" of a person as "a separate material form, inhabited by thoughts and feelings"—that is, embodied persons possessing real subjective states. Instead, he advocated "start[ing] with the idea that the social person is primarily a *fact in the mind*," by which we "find at once that he has no existence apart from a *mental whole* of which all personal ideas are members." As to the "ordinary and traditional" view of humans, which takes seriously their bodies, Cooley considers that to be "fantastic, unreal, and practically pernicious."[47] So strong in fact was this cognitivist, ideational view of Cooley's that he pushed hard to define sociology as a discipline about the study of mental "imaginations."[48] Blumer followed these leads, emphasizing symbolic communication at the heart of his theory: "Interaction in society is characteristically and predominantly on the symbolic level. Human group life is a vast process of such *defining* to others what to do and of interpreting their *definitions*."[49] And Brissett and Edgley claim that "to be motivated . . . is not to be energized by internal or external forces . . . rather it is simply to be in *communication* with others about the sense of one's potentially questionable behavior. . . . Motives . . . are the terms in which the *interpretation* of conduct proceeds, not the causes of it."[50] Thus "despite the beguiling temptation to search for the 'deeper' reason why a person does what he does . . . there is nothing 'deeper' we can infer from verbal (or for that matter nonverbal) phenomena. All we can ever hope to find are other communicative forms."[51]

Following and reflecting the "linguistic turn" in the social sciences, some social situationists have directed this cognitivist interest in social communication in a more linguistic direction, emphasizing people's *talk* and the effect that *discourse* among people has on each other. Barnes thus claims that responsible action is not a capability of distinct persons but a social institution expressed in the social practice of *talking about* intentional action: "Our sociability is expressed in and through the medium of our voluntaristic discourse."[52] Mills also dissolves people's motivations into talk: "Motives are words. . . . They do not denote any elements 'in' individuals. They stand for anticipated situational consequences of questioned conduct [that need explaining]. Intention or purpose . . . is awareness of anticipated consequences." Thus while skeptically discussing "real motives" and "real attitudes" that are "something prior, more genuine, and 'deep' in the individual," Mills rhetorically asks:

Now what could we possibly so infer? Of precisely what is verbalization symptomatic? We cannot infer physiological processes from lingual phenomena. All we can infer and empirically check is another verbalization of the agent's. . . . The only social item that can "lie deeper" are other lingual forms. The "Real Attitude or Motive" is not something different in kind from the verbalization.[53]

Fourth, social situationists believe that people's actions are generated as highly local, variable, and contingent responses to immediate situations in which they find themselves at any given time, which people continually monitor, interpret, and respond to. Quoting Karl Mannheim approvingly, for example, Mills wrote that "both motives and actions very often originate not from within [persons] but from the situation in which individuals find themselves."[54] Cooley contributed to this outlook early in stressing the highly situational and changeable character of human nature, the correct idea about which, he wrote,

departs from the generality of the idea and brings in elements that come from *particular situations* and institutions. Human nature, in any such sense as this, is in the highest degree *changeful,* because the behavior to which it gives rise *varies,* morally and in every other way, *with the influences that act upon it.* . . . *We can make it work in almost any way,* if we understand it, as a clever mechanic can mold to his will the universal laws of mass and motion.[55]

Based on this understanding and the ideas above, people's activities are expected to be determined not by coherent personal life projects but by the influences of particular situations that stimulate different aspects of self-identities. Charon asserts: "What influences the decisions we make in a given situation? The answer is our definition of the situation. . . . What influences our definition? The answer is interaction—with other[s] and with self." Thus personal selves are not entities but acts and interactions: "The self . . . is something that the individual acts toward: We communicate with, analyze, direct, judge, and label the self. *To say that the self changes in interaction with others is to say that these acts change.*"[56] According to Collins, "beliefs . . . situationally fluctuate. . . . What people think they believe at a given moment is dependent upon the kind of interaction ritual taking place in that situation."[57] The way Manford Kuhn's "self theory views the individual, he derives his plans of action from the roles he plays and the statuses he occupies in the groups with which he feels identified—his reference groups."[58] Knorr-Cetina similarly claims that "'subjective' goals continuously depend upon others for their conception and articulation. The same hold true for the subjective reasons that are genuine because-motives."[59] For such reasons, Collins says he is interested in developing "a theory of moment-by-moment motivation, [altering] situation by situation," to explain "what any individual will do, at any moment in time; what he or she will feel, think, and say."[60]

Fifth, social situationists tell us that people's reported "subjective experiences" are not useful evidence for social science explanations, since people either have no real subjective experiences of the kind that shape actions, or their subjective experiences are too amorphous, inaccessible, or loosely coupled to actions and practices to matter.[61] Goffman expresses this antisubjectivistic view with characteristic candor: "[The person] and his body merely provide the peg on which something of collaborative manufacture will be hung for a time. And the means for producing and maintaining selves do not reside inside the peg; in fact these means are often bolted down in social establishments. . . . The self is a product of all of these arrangements, and in all of its parts bears the mark of this genesis."[62] According to Mills, people do not even pay attention to their own subjectivities until some confounding problem arises: "Men live in immediate acts of experience and their attentions are directed outside themselves until acts are in some way frustrated. It is then that awareness of self and of motive occur."[63] The ethnomethodologist Harold Garfinkel wrote that "meaningful events are *entirely and exclusively* events in people's behavioral environment. . . . Hence there is *no reason to look under the skull, since nothing of interest is to be found there but brains.*"[64] According to Burke, people acquire their motivations to action not from subjective processes operating within them but from their social-role identities, which provide social expectations for behavior that reference cultural standards and the action-implications of shared meanings.[65] Barnes dissolves subjectively voluntary action into voluntaristic public discourse: "For all it appears to refer to the internal states of individuals, voluntaristic discourse is actually the vehicle of human sociability, through which its users co-ordinate their actions and cognitions." According to Barnes, then, "internal mental states" are "imputed rather than ascertained," yet "attributions of mental states are always problematic and contestable." So "whilst we make extensive references to internal states, it is not at all clear what the grounds or even the cues for these references are, or what information they convey about the agents referred to"; "just what it is to possess free will, to exercise agency, to be capable of rational conduct . . . are all notoriously problematic questions"; and, "as these states are [empirically] inaccessible [to outsiders], it is hard to see in what way their actual nature can constrain what is said about them," so that "the answer to the problem must lie, not in the private realm, but in the public sphere where states of affairs are accessible to all." Barnes thus concludes that "it is clear that these attributions [of free will, agency, and responsibility] are not inspired by inner states themselves." He says, "it is hard to imagine that attributions [of chosen action] could come to embody 'the truth' about our inner states. Here, as elsewhere, it is better to accept the conceptual relativism implicit in sociological and ethnomethodological work."[66]

The sociology of culture has also been influenced by this skepticism about the reality or accessibility of people's subjective states or conditions. Robert Wuthnow, for example, has argued that "the methodological limitation posed by the subjective approach arises principally from the difficulties associated with making verifiable claims about subjective phenomena," and "underestimating the significance of the social, as opposed to psychological, processes and of attributing too much to the needs and interests of the individual." An approach focused on the subjective, Wuthnow said, suffers "limitations of established methods and, indeed, of clear canons of evidence." Analyzing research interviews taken at face value, for example, assumes they have "evidence of an internal psychological state," whereas by treating them not as containing "meanings but discourse about meanings," we "admit our lack of knowledge about hidden states and examine the discourse itself." Wuthnow thus recommends against "assuming that [people's] commitment is simply an expression of some internal state of the individual" but instead focusing on "the cultural repertoire of utterances and actions" that demonstrate commitment. That means, he said, that "we consciously try to move away from focusing . . . analysis itself on the radically subjective beliefs, attitudes, and meanings of the individual."[67] The cultural sociologist Steve Derné has likewise written that "I locate the . . . force of culture . . . not in internalized ideas but in social practices. . . . The constraint of culture often comes not from the internalized understandings, but from the power of society that is dramatized in social practices."[68]

Sixth, social situationism claims, relatedly, that people's *actions and practices are not motivated* by real, internal, subjective entities—such as human desires, beliefs, and emotions—that move them to act, since subjectivity itself is highly problematic, or human activities are simply not the kind of things that are motivated to begin with.[69] According to Mills, "the verbalized motive is not [to be] used as an index of something in the individual," in part because "there is no way to plumb behind verbalization into an individual and directly check our motive-mongering." Mills declared categorically that "the motives accompanying institutions of war, e.g., are not 'the causes' of war."[70] Collins says simply that "the error to avoid is identifying agency with the individual, even on a micro-level."[71] According to Blum and McHugh, it is a "misconception of motive[s]" to think of them as "concrete, private, and interior 'mainsprings' that reside in people, rather than public and observable courses of [verbal] action." Thus "to locate [a] motive is . . . not to 'find' anything but to describe the necessary and analytically prior [social] understandings and conventions which must be employed in order for a member [of a social group] even to invoke motive as a method for making a social environment orderly and sensible."[72] Peter Winch asserted that "motives can have nothing to do with . . . physiological states."[73] Knorr-Cetina poses this rhetorical question: "What are subjective reasons? Can they be defined and treated as causally efficacious independent of other agents and the situation?" to which her answer is a clear no. Instead, "social action arises from an interlocking of intentionalities in which subjective in-order-to motives are themselves contingent upon the conduct of others."[74] And, according to Charon, to suggest that a subjective motive caused a particular action as an explanation for that action "is almost always an unsatisfactory answer."[75]

Seventh, situationism suggests that to the extent that people *are* pursuing goals in their social interactions their key purpose is to protect their *self-identities* as morally legitimate and respectable, thus placing identity maintenance at the center of human social existence. Much of situationism's case for this is again rooted in the early social psychology of Cooley and Mead. Cooley's idea of the "looking glass self" is particularly influential:

> A social self of this sort might be called the reflected or looking-glass self: "Each to each a looking-glass, Reflects the other that doth pass." . . . In imagination we perceive in another's mind some thought of our appearance, manner, aims, deeds, character, friends, and so on, and are variously affected by it. A self-idea of this sort seems to have three principle elements: the imagination of our appearance of the other person, the imagination of his judgment of that appearance, and some sort of self-feeling, such as pride or mortification. . . . The thing that moves us to pride or shame is . . . an imputed sentiment, the imagined effect of this reflection upon another's mind.[76]

Social situationists have closely followed this lead in emphasizing the protection of one's respectable self-identity as a central concern—even basic motivation—of human life.[77]

Goffman is exemplary in this respect. For him, most social interactions revolve around upholding mutual perceptions of "moral character," a key dimension of any definition of the situation. Any person with recognized claims to moral character "has a moral right to expect others will value and treat him in an appropriate way." That obliges the person also "in fact to be what he claims he is." And that most importantly means *appearing* to be that. Thus "when an individual projects a definition of the situation and thereby makes an implicit or explicit claim to be a person of a particular kind, he automatically exerts a moral demand upon others, obliging them to value and treat him in the matter that persons of this kind have the right to expect." Social life is thus fundamentally about enacting proper public "performances" that succeed in "impression management." And that requires "establish[ing] a framework of appearances that must be maintained, whether or not there is feeling behind the appearances." Social life is about determining, based on "widely embracing implicit conception of what the individual's character must be," "what sort of self and world they are to accept for themselves."[78] As a consequence, Goffman's book, *Asylums*, is highly focused on issues of "personal defacement," "being stripped of one's identity kit," "loss of identity equipment," "prevent[ing] the individual from presenting his usual image of himself," "hold[ing] . . . a humiliating pose," "indignities . . . incompatible with his conception of self," "territories of the self [being] violated," "the embodiments of self profaned," "a violation of one's informational preserve regarding self," "suffer[ing] the permanent mortification of having . . . taken no action," "the terror of feeling radically demoted," "assaults upon the self," "stress and encroachments on the self," "personal failure," and "stigmatization."[79] To avoid such problems, people operate with the shared goal of sustaining a "working consensus" of the meaning of contexts, so agree about "the desirability of avoiding an open conflict of definitions of the situation."[80] Goffman is completely clear that people's actions have *nothing* to do with trying to affirm or enact moral standards, for example, even when the actions clearly concern morality. Action is always *only* about amorally engineering social impressions designed to affirm and protect moral self-identities:

> The individuals who are performers dwell more than we might think in a moral world. But, qua performers, individuals are concerned not with the moral issue of realizing these standards, but with the amoral issue of engineering a convincing impression that these standards are being realized. Our activity . . . is largely concerned with moral matters, but as performers we do not have a moral concern with them. As performers, we are merchants of morality. . . . It may well be that the more attention we give to these goods, then the more distant we feel from them and from those who are believing enough to buy them.[81]

The reductionism here could not be clearer or more cynically antihumanistic. Many people may seem "sincere," according to Goffman, who acknowledges that "there are many individuals who sincerely believe that the definitions of the situation they habitually project is the real reality."[82] But such people are self-deceived by their own convincing performances. The sociologist knows better. It's all only really about the social credibility of self-identity.

This situationist belief is not limited to Goffmanesque dramaturgical sociology, but is assumed and expressed in many other approaches that share the situationist outlook. Take Burke's self-identity theory, for instance. According to him, central in all people's motivation structures is the drive to avoid feelings of distress, disappointment, sadness, embarrassment, shame, anger, rage, annoyance, hostility, anxiety, displeasure, fear, and depression, and the positive drive to enjoy feelings of competence, effectiveness, self-worth, acceptance, and authenticity. How is that accomplished? By having one's role identity verified by other people in social interaction in meaningful situations. Any nonverification of identity causes bad feelings, so social life turns out to be essentially about having others confirm one's self-identity.[83] People are generally interested in "controlling perceived meaning in the situation" and rely on "identity standards . . . as goals for agent-persons to control the perceived sign and symbol meanings." In that, "agents . . . seek to validate existing self-meaning" and "thereby invalidate, to some extent, meanings being maintained by other agents." For Burke, then, *feelings about oneself* are key to "motivational processes," so that social interactions that make people "feel *good* about themselves," "feel *confident* about themselves," and "feel that they are 'real' or *authentic* when their personal identities are being verified" by playing their social roles well are what finally motivates people's actions.[84] All of this reveals the fact that human persons are not coherent centers of action, but rather fragments of self dealing with different social situations and aspects of self-identity. An interaction, Burke writes, is "not between whole persons but between aspects of persons having to do with their roles in the groups or organizations: their identities." This has clear implications for our understanding of what a "person" even is. For Burke, human agency is expressed by pieces of identities, and what we call "the person" serves a mere coordinating function. A "'person' becomes the link between the various agencies that exist within the person. . . . This distinction between person and agent is central to identity theory. In identity theory, *an identity is an agent.* Each person has many identities . . . and each of these identities is an agent."[85]

Other social situationists agree with these arguments. According to Blum and McHugh, for example, "most fundamentally, whatever a motivated actor does will show his methods for affirming himself as a person."[86] According to Stryker, people "incorporate societal definitions of appropriate role behavior into self and . . . internalize salient identities" through "two mechanisms." First, "persons will generally seek confirmation or validation of their identities." Second, "people want to think well of themselves. In brief, self-esteem." The basic motivation of human life and action, in short, is to maintain a positive affirmation of one's self-identity. This view is also implicit in Stryker's discussion of role conflict and role strain, which focuses on the problems of role performance that undercut the consistency of people's self-understandings.[87]

Finally, Knorr-Cetina (quoting Goffman approvingly) suggests that "self . . . is not an entity half-concealed behind events, but a changeable formula for managing oneself during them."[88] If human beings thus have any real "internal" motivation for their actions, it can be reduced to the drive to project and protect their own self-identities as morally legitimate and respectable.[89]

Finally, social situationism believes that accounts that people give to explain their actions and practices are mere post hoc justifications and rationalizations, not reliable explanations of the real causes of their actions and practices. According to Mills, "Rather than fixed elements 'in' an individual, motives are the terms with which interpretation of conduct *by social actors* proceeds. . . . A satisfactory or adequate motive is one that satisfies the questioner of an act or program. . . . Motives are accepted justifications for present, future, or past programs or acts." Thus, "When an agent vocalizes or imputes motives, he is not trying to describe his experienced social action. He is not merely stating 'reasons.' He is influencing others—and himself."[90] Garfinkel asserts that "the person defines *retrospectively* the decisions that have been made. *The outcome comes before the decisions.*"[91] According to Barnes, "motives constitute, as it were, a sense-making system present in the culture that members may use as they will in accounting for actions and coordinating further actions." So when it comes to the role of volition in action, people's "will as we experience it comes *wholly ex post facto* in choosing."[92] "Human beings are neither rational nor irrational," Brissett and Edgley write, "but rather *rationalizers.*"[93] In fact, "since the meaning of any event lies in its consequences, human beings can never be sure of what they are doing until they have done it."[94]

The historical lineage of this approach involves various strands of thought. One perhaps worth noting is Peter Berger and Thomas Luckmann's social constructionism, at least in how others have understood it and put it to use. Take their discussion of "legitimations," for example. Legitimations are not accurate, actual explanations of the hows and whys of things, but retrospective "projections" used post hoc to make social sense of existing facts: "Legitimations produce new meanings. . . . The function of legitimation is to make objectively available and subjectively plausible the . . . objectivations [public social constructions] that have been institutionalized." In discussing alterations of people's definitions of "reality," Berger and Luckmann discuss the need for resocialization and restructured conversation partners ("people and ideas that are discrepant with the new definitions of reality are systematically avoided") for making that effective. That requires a post hoc renarration of one's previous motives: "Frequently this includes the retrojection into the past of present interpretive schemas . . . and motives that were not subjectively present in the past but that are now necessary for the reinterpretation of what took place then (the formula being, 'I *really* did this because . . .'). Prealteration biography is typically nihilated *in toto* by subsuming it under a negative category of occupying a strategic position in the new legitimating apparatus."[95] It would be simplistic to identify Berger and Luckmann as the only source of social situationism's belief that people's accounts are post hoc rationalizations for behaviors pursued for other reasons (or perhaps no reason). Yet their social constructionism illustrates the kind of influence that sundry theories have had in the developing brew of social situationism.

Following in this tradition, Charon claims that "motives are important . . . for understanding [not how and why people act but] how people come to *explain* and *rationalize* each other's acts and their own acts in a relatively simple way." He asserts: "Whatever the actual role of motives (and in most cases that role is probably minor), humans impute motives—we explain each other's actions by assigning motives. Motives are the stated reasons for an act, the verbalized causes of human action that assumes intentions on the part of the actor." Therefore, "whatever the many complex actual reasons for our action taking a certain direction, the explanation we find easiest to give involves deep-seated motives. Motives, however, are oversimplified explanations."[96] More bluntly, Knorr-Cetina asserts that "we tend to 'explain' a particular activity by reference to dispositions [developed in the past]. . . . This type of meaning [however] . . . consists of post hoc interpretations . . . contingent upon the situation. . . . Every such interpretation is determined by the Here and Now from which it is made. Which past experiences are selected as genuine reasons for an action and how they are highlighted and put into perspective is a function of the specific situation."[97]

What Situationists Could Have Said That Would Have Been Right

If social situationism were pure rubbish, it would be easy to dismiss—it never would have gained traction in the first place. But the actual case is more complicated. Social situationism is a complex amalgam of some fundamentally true and insightful ideas (when properly understood and framed), some partially true ideas (which have to be understood along with a variety of other also-true, balancing ideas), some possibly true ideas (depending on how they are defined and applied or in what situations they are deployed), and some inane ideas (no matter how they are taken). Before analyzing what is wrong in social situationism and why, let us begin with a more appreciative accounting. A hermeneutics of suspicion must always be balanced by a hermeneutics of appreciation. Viewing social situationism in a most positive light, how might we reformulate its approach and claims into realistic, insightful, and useful ideas? Here I think is what situationism could and should have said from the start that would have been correct and helpful:

1. People are profoundly influenced by the social interactions in which they engage over the course of their lives, such that the discourses, cultural repertoires, knowledge systems, and language games that (among other things) help comprise human social life profoundly affect the ways that people's natural personal capacities and life projects are developed, expressed, and directed.

2. Human doings involve both personal (including interior, subjective, and private) and social dimensions, such that people's actions must be understood in part as significantly informed, defined, and guided by collective processes of social communication and pressure.

3. One crucial activity in human life (among others) is the social communication of cognitive definitions, meanings, knowledge, rules, vocabularies, and grammars.

4. People's actions are often highly responsive to the local, variable, and contingent influences of immediate situations in which they find themselves at any given time, which they routinely monitor, interpret, and respond to as they go about pursuing their interests and larger life projects.

5. Reliance on people's subjective experiences as evidence for social science explanations is possible and often necessary but also often challenging and fallible, since subjective experiences are not directly observable by second parties, are often not entirely transparent to those experiencing them firsthand, must be represented to others through symbolic communications, and are only sometimes directive of people's actions and practices in straightforward ways.

6. Although people's actions and practices are in fact motivated by subjective realities such as desires, beliefs, and emotions, the nature and operation of motivations for action are complicated and so must be approached and analyzed with care and sophistication.

7. One (among other) basic goal or goods that people pursue in their social interactions and life projects is their own identity coherence and affirmation.

8. The accounts that people give to explain their actions and practices can sometimes and in varying degrees (though not always and in all ways) reflect post hoc justifications and rationalizations rather than reliable explanations of the real causes of their actions and practices.

These claims stated in these ways are not only compatible with critical realist personalism but are also essential insights and cautions about human persons and social life that must be incorporated into any realistic theory. The alterations made may seem subtle, but their implications are enormous. Had advocates of social situationism pushed for this more humble version of their arguments, rather than the more extreme claims further above, they would have made a helpful contribution to our social scientific knowledge. By insisting on their more extreme claims, however, situationism has muddled the air with a theoretical cloud of overstatement, half-truths, and confusion. My reformulation of situationism's actual insights is intended to help dispel that cloud and move us forward with greater clarity and realism.

Where Social Situationism Goes Wrong

The difference between social situationism's problematic eight claims (described near the start of this chapter) and my reformulation of them in legitimate terms (just above) highlights some of the specific ways that situationism has gone wrong. Situationism overstates and misunderstands the ways in which persons are shaped by their societies. Situationism fails to see that human personal life has an important and necessary interior, subjective, private dimension. It compresses the many kinds of human life interests and activities into the one concern of communication of definitions and meanings. It fails to understand how actions are not shaped only by immediate situations but also by long-term identities, life projects, and moral commitments. It too-easily dismisses the idea of actions performed to achieve subjectively motivated ends. Situationism also problematically compacts the variety of human interests into the single concern with socially respectable self-identity. It denies without warrant the possibility and frequent actuality that the accounts people give for their actions may and sometimes do actually reflect the real reasons behind actions.[98] Situationism also often relies for validation on the results of social-psychology experiments that are inappropriate and artificial tests of the situationist behaviors in question.[99] In all of this, social situationism recurrently takes initially helpful but limited and conditional sociological insights into human doings and illegitimately inflates them into comprehensive, totalizing, exclusivist decrees. It is as if situationists cannot be content merely to contribute some valuable-but-incomplete insights. They instead have to take their ideas to the *n*th degree and put themselves in charge of an all-embracing, reductionistic sociological worldview. In doing so, social situationism crosses the line from legitimate sociology into untenable sociolo*gism.*

Worth unpacking further is the fact that social situationism wrongly and impossibly denies the reality of genuinely motivated human action. This is the position that situationism would like to stake out—that human action is not genuinely motivated as ordinarily believed. But the impossibility of this position becomes evident when situationists are forced in the exposition of their own arguments to provide what turn out to be accounts of people's "real" motivations for actions.[100] That plainly admits that action is motivated, even if not as often ordinarily believed. People really do engage in motivated actions, it turns out. It is just that, by the situationist account, people's motivations are different from what we often believe them to be. But that is an entirely different claim altogether than the initial denial of motivated actions per se. This claim simply changes the motivation explaining action. And by admitting that actions are motivated, situationists also necessarily submit their view about the motivational primacy of respectable self-identity to critical evaluation, under which it does not fare well.

Going back to situationist writings and rereading them in light of this critique, it becomes evident that all situationists must and do operate with their own model of purposive, motivated human action in order for their arguments to even seem to work. And the motivations that are attributed to actors turn out to be more various and complex than simply protecting self-identity. For example, in good situationist fashion, Mills attacks and denies the "model of purposive conduct" as a "naked utilitarian scheme" and so "inadequate" for any good sociological analysis.[101] Yet in the very same article, Mills turns out to disclose that people *do* act with motivated purposes. Which? According to Mills, people are generally motivated to "undo snarls," "integrate social action," "resolving conflicts," "integrate one man's action with another's," and "line up conduct with norms."[102] We see then that far from eliminating motivated action—how could that ever be done?—Mills has simply substituted one particular set of motivations for another. As Steve Bruce and Roy Wallis point out, such an argument "presupposes what it is being used explicitly to deny, namely that it is possible to penetrate to the 'real' motives and reasons for action."[103] The real argument turns out not to be about motivations versus not motivations, but the more realistic question of *which* motivations?

Consider too the claims of Barnes, which play out along similar lines. He argues against our ability to understand and explain people's actions as motivated. Yet in order to develop his case, Barnes ends up having to rely on the fact that people's actions actually *are* motived. Like Mills, Barnes simply substitutes his preferred list of motivations for those others might believe. These include people's motivations "to coordinate their understandings," "to sustain a shared sense of what they are likely to do in the future," and to achieve a "coherent ordering around collectively agreed goals."[104] So human actions are indeed motivated, it turns out, only, Barnes believes, motivated to achieve purposes different from what most ordinary people think. Perhaps that is right. But, again, that is a question to be answered with reference to the real world, not as an a priori declaration of a theoretical position.

Furthermore, social situationism's radical skepticism about "subjective states" that serves as the basis for its rejection of standard accounts of motivations is also unjustified and impossible. Without a belief that humans operate in life with reliance on some real subjective states or capacities that are genuinely causally related to their actions—beliefs, ideas, feelings, desires, intentions, and so on—social science becomes a meaningless and hopeless enterprise. What could social science in the absence of such subjective states even look like? How could it function? What would be going on in the minds of the social scientists as they do their work? Why would they even be motivated to want to understand human social life and communicate their findings to others in books and articles? All of science presupposes and relies upon the existence and function of a variety of "subjective states" in human beings to ever get off the ground. And that itself tells us that situationism's skepticism is off.[105] I will not repeat my argument stated in previous chapters, but simply note again that the appeal to empiric*ism* as grounds for dismissing internal states is badly misguided.

Six months before C. Wright Mills published his problematic though highly influential article "Situated Actions and Vocabularies of Motives" in the *American Sociological Review* (in December 1940), the Columbia University sociologist Robert MacIver published an extremely reasonable article on the same topic in the *American Journal of Sociology*, titled "The Imputation of Motives" (in July 1940).[106] MacIver's argument cut the legs out from under Mills's argument even before Mills published his piece. Had Mills read MacIver and had the sense to see the cogency of his case, Mills's article might never have seen the light of day without major revision. Comparing the two, it is clear that Mills's case is more daring, provocative, and unsettling, while MacIver's is more reasonable and balanced. But Mills's argument is flawed and MacIver's correct and helpful. MacIver clearly has the better-grounded philosophical outlook. "Causal knowledge," he observed, "is always inferential, never immediate." Therefore:

> The causal nexus, like every other relationship between data, is not itself a datum. It can never be vindicated by perception or by any of the devices that come to the aid of perception. The assertion of any relationship . . . involves the appeal to reason, and its establishment is a scientific construction.

Motivations that give rise to action therefore may be and in fact are entirely real, even though they can in any direct sense "never be vindicated by perception." Thus "the postulate is not the existence of motives [per se] but the presence of a particular motive within the scheme of a particular situation." In other words, there is no doubt that motivations are real; the only matter in question is *which* specific motivations are important in any given situation. One of the ways we know motivations are real, MacIver says, is through *our own directly, phenomenological human experience* of their presence and operation *inside ourselves*:

> That motives . . . belong to the world of reality is established by the best of all evidences—that of immediate experience. We are all aware that we have motives. . . . To the agent himself these subjective urges are important as conditions and explanations of his act. For him they constitute its why.

Here MacIver makes the same kind of move I advocate—namely, taking fully seriously our personal phenomenological experiences as one source of evidence informing what may be and sometimes must be real.[107] In this case, to deny the reality of motivations of persons is to falsify our own basic experiences of ourselves as we operate existentially in life.[108] In this case, too, MacIver says, allowing empiricism to drive our conclusions is dangerous: "If motives and goals exist as data of [firsthand] experience, the claim [of adherents of "materialistic or mechanistic metaphysics" that motives do not exist] comes perilously close to being a blind dogma. It would exclude from reality something indubitably present in human behavior." In short, empiricism, operating as a supposedly hardheaded scientific principle, ends up functioning, in the face of a reality in which not everything important can be directly observed, as a *dogmatic* ideology. MacIver further rejects the idea that sociologists have absolutely no access to other people's motivations as a way to help explain their actions: "There is no demonstration [by skeptics] that access to [motives] is impossible, but only that it is difficult. . . . Obviously, [we] can read motives only through their manifestations. Sometimes the signs are obscure and baffling, sometimes they are relatively clear." So the fact that accessing other people's motivations is difficult does not excuse sociologists from studying them. In similar ways, most sciences encounter analogous difficulties in their own spheres of study:

> Why should it be unscientific to read the signs as carefully as possible, to develop the logic of evidence and apply it to situations, even though it yields not absolute certainty but only some kind of probability? We may surely advance toward truth by repeated approximations, each based on partial evidence. . . . Some very important types of knowledge, some aspects of all knowledge, we can attain only in [this] way.

But what, we might ask, about the problem of people misunderstanding or misreporting their own motivations? MacIver admits that that can and does happen. So what? What alternative do we have than to do our best, given the tools we have to understand reality as well as we are able? "The misrepresentation of motives is a difficulty, not a total impasse." Besides, MacIver rightly notes, the condition of the possibility of *mis*understanding people's real motivations is the more basic possibility that we can and do actually understand them. Thus the claim that "the agent frequently mistakes and misinterprets his own motives" as an argument against sociologists taking motives seriously "has validity only in so far as motives are knowable." So despite the difficulties in understanding people's motivations and relating them causally to their actions, we simply cannot give up or do otherwise. "It is obvious enough that the investigation of motives is a task beset by particular hazards. . . . But surely the moral is not that we may abandon the endeavor." As with every other science, we can put together the evidence of empirical observation with our best-reasoned understandings and interpretations to come to fallible but nonetheless often reliable and truthful knowledge. As Guy Swanson more recently said, "If all motivational phenomena entail subjective processes, then the 'evidence' for them will always involve inference as well as observation. . . . The consequences are not fatal."[109]

In sum, the refusal to deal with people's real motivations as the grounds of their actions cannot be defended, just as the empiricist dogma that drives such an attitude cannot be defended. Of course sorting out people's motivations is not easy. Dealing with people's motivations as best as we can access and understand them will be fraught with potential error. So what else is new in social science?[110] Social situationism's pretending that it can dismiss or ignore people's motivations at first may sound like an imaginative sociological quest being conducted on the pinnacle of hard scientific realism. In fact it turns out to be a delusional outlook that has taken leave of reality. Just because we cannot directly inspect people's motivations under a magnifying glass with our own eyes—as if motives and everything else real should be just like quartz or an insect—does not mean they are not real and do not exert powerful causal powers that make the human world go around. They are and do. And the fact that studying them is difficult and complicated is *our* social-scientific problem, *not* the problem of reality. Merely because something is difficult to study does not entitle us to simply declare that is must not exist and ignore it.

This critical discussion so far has knocked a number of blocks out from under the social situationist program. I could offer numerous other criticisms of situationism, but I will limit myself to examining one more: its slippery use and often-outright confusion of key terms and concepts. A thorough cataloging of such confusions in situationism would take more words than worth spending here, so I will focus on one telling example: Herbert Blumer's ongoing confusion of reality *itself* and people's meaningful beliefs *about* reality, which many social situationists repeat. The fundamental trap into which Blumer and many other situationists fall is conflating reality per se into mere human perceptions of or beliefs about reality. They are not the same. The first consists of a real object or set of objects. The second concerns subjective human mental interpretations or representations *of* those objects. These are ontologically different things.[111] My meaningful beliefs about the Atlantic Ocean are not the Atlantic Ocean itself, nor do they create the Atlantic Ocean. The Atlantic Ocean exists ontologically independent of any meanings it holds for me or any human consciousness of it. Nonetheless, many social situationists confuse reality with our mental constructions about it.

Blumer, for example, says, "Symbolic Interactionism sees meanings as social products, as creations that are formed in and through the defining activities of people as they interact."[112] So far so good, since Blumer is focused only on meanings, which are indeed socially constructed. But then he continues. One "noteworthy consequence" of this view is that it "gives us a different picture of the environment or milieu of human beings":

> The environment consists only of the objects that the given human beings recognize and know. The nature of the environment is set by the meaning that the objects composing it have for those human beings. Individuals, also groups, occupying or living in the same spatial location may have, accordingly, very different environments; as we say, people may be living side by side yet be living in very different worlds.

Blumer is mixed up. At best he has very poorly stated some crucial points. At worst he has lost touch with reality. Contra Blumer, people's environments can and usually *do* consist of many more and other things than they "recognize and know." That is because the existence of most things in the human environment does *not* depend ontologically on other people recognizing and knowing them. Radon may have existed in Blumer's own home, for instance, without him recognizing or knowing it. Exploitative social structures may well exist in reality and create real effects whether or not anyone involved adequately understands that fact. Also contra Blumer, the nature of the environment is *not* "set" by the meanings that its objects have for people in it. Real human environments are not established by meanings, or at most only some aspects of them are partly so. For example, just because some entire communities have been completely convinced that some women among them are witches did not in fact mean that they really were witches—and even if the social pressure of the communities somehow temporarily convinced those women themselves that they were witches, that would not even have made them witches in fact. Instead, the believed meanings of the communities were simply wrong; the environment, in those cases, had its own realities, net of people's meaningful convictions about them. Furthermore, contra Blumer, individuals and groups living in the same environment in fact do *not* actually occupy different environments. They occupy nearly the same[113] environment, not "very different worlds," as Blumer would have it. The only thing that is very different—and of course very importantly so, as far as it goes—is their potentially varying subjective perceptions, beliefs, and evaluations about their environments. But that is a different, more limited matter. Now we might give Blumer the benefit of the doubt and say that he was merely engaging in a bit of odd rhetorical hyperbole. Perhaps. But even so, the problem is that many other sociologists and scholars in other disciplines do not have the good sense to realize that, but instead read such statements literally and go running off promoting problematically radical social-constructionist theories.[114]

Blumer's argument continues and is worth following. His view, he says, denies the "traditional position of 'realism' in philosophy—a position that is widely held and deeply entrenched in the social and psychological sciences." So Blumer is an explicit antirealist. Yet his understanding of realism is way off base, again confusing real objects and the meanings people hold with regard to those objects. To be a realist, he says, is "to regard meaning as being intrinsic to the thing that has it, as being a natural part of the objective makeup of the thing. Thus [according to realism], a chair is clearly a chair in itself, a cow a cow, a cloud a cloud."[115] Now, whether a cow is a cow in itself, which it is in fact, is quite a different matter than whether the beliefs and meanings we hold about cows emanate directly from the nature of cow-ness per se. They usually do not.[116] Beliefs and meanings are personal and cultural constructions *about* other things. But Blumer is fundamentally confused on this distinction. So he rejects the following "realist" view, which of course no serious realist would ever propose: "Being inherent in the thing that has it, meaning needs merely to be disengaged by observing the objective thing that has the meaning. The meaning emanates, so to speak, from the thing and as such there is no [interpretive] process involved in its formation." Against this imaginary view of "realism," Blumer says that symbolic interactionism "sees meaning as arising in the process of interaction between people." Well, that makes sense. But there is nothing in this last claim that is not fully compatible with real realism—in fact, Blumer's claim requires that realism be correct for the claim to even be possible (that is, real people engaged in real interactions generating real causal dynamics give rise to meanings they adopt). Blumer has gotten himself caught up in a false either/or choice here, which does not actually exist. Having cut himself loose from realism broadly, Blumer then drifts back off into his version of social constructionism:

> The "worlds" that exist for human beings and for their groups are composed of "objects" and . . . these objects are the product of symbolic interaction. An object is anything that can be indicated [including physical, social, and abstract objects]. . . . The nature of an object—of any and every object— consists of the meaning that it has for the person for whom it is an object. . . . Out of a process of mutual indications [through social interactions] common objects emerge.[117]

Blumer here is just being silly. Some objects (those that are mind-dependent, institutional facts) *are* constructed through symbolic interactions. But many other objects (those that are mind-independent, brute facts) are *not* existent as the products of symbolic interaction. And in no way is the "nature" of the latter kind of objects constituted by the meanings it has for people. The nature of mind-independent, brute-fact objects is rather constituted by the objective nature of reality as it happens to be and operate when it comes to such particular objects. Physical and material objects, moreover, do *not* "emerge" out of "a process of mutual indication." If that were so, we could all spin hair into gold and turn bathwater into beer simply by agreeing and acting in our social interactions as if they *were* gold and beer. Blumer is confused. And his confusion had the regrettable effect of confusing a lot of others who have been influenced by him, particularly many social situationists.

My critical analysis of situationism could continue. I could discuss how situationism disregards the embodied nature of human life, often simply ignoring the realities of bodies and especially brains as we understand them today in neuroscience. I could discuss the elisions situationists recurrently make in their discussions of the "socially relevant self," "on the level of symbolic interaction," and "from a sociological perspective"—which admit a clearly partial perspective—and the discussions of human beings per se, in toto, ontologically. At times situationists talk as if they are merely offering one quite incomplete perspective; at other times they talk in grand metaphysical statements about what "is." I could discuss how social situationism—although originally generated in part by a smart rejection of social behaviorism—can end up sounding like a neo-behaviorism in which people simply react to the situational stimuli presented to them at any situated moment, according to very simple response mechanisms.[118] And I could ask how social science could ever possibly be conducted epistemologically in the first place if social situationism were correct, observing that—unless social scientists themselves are able somehow to transcend the human condition by discovering a privileged position of superhuman perspective and knowledge—the human sociological observers would be inextricably caught within the same social situationist web of pressure and determination as all of those they are studying and supposedly explaining. These are major problems for situationism. In the interest of space, however, I will simply name those and move on.

Conclusion

An unreconstructed social situationism contrasts with the personalist theory of motivated human action. But situationism is in fact fraught with numerous defects and inconsistencies. More than a few sociologists are de facto social situationists, nonetheless, whether they know it or identify as such. Situationism is edgy and intriguing. It throws our commonsense understanding off balance. It also places the sociological observer in an epistemologically and analytically privileged position, as the enlightened one who knows what is *really* going on in life. It projects a sense of stark realism by seemingly uncovering what is *really* happening in the social world. And for that reason it can be attractive. But in the end, situationism proves not very realistic. We can do better.

This chapter has critically examined a form of sociological theorizing influential in recent decades. Before moving forward with my constructive personalist argument, the next chapter digs a few generations deeper into the genealogy of sociological theory to examine the discipline's deeper intellectual roots concerning human nature, *Homo duplex,* and the human motivations for action.

Human Nature and Motivation in Classical Theory

I am arguing for a theory of human motivations for action that is grounded in human nature. Lest readers think this is a novel approach for sociology, this chapter examines the work of the discipline's founding fathers—Durkheim, Marx, and Weber—on human nature and motivations. We see that they all believed in particular views of human nature from which they developed their larger theories about motivated action and its relation to society. Each held explicit notions—rooted in relevant philosophical traditions and directly connected to their sociological projects—of what human beings are like by nature and what implications followed for the question of motivations. If contemporary sociologists have lost interest in thinking about human nature and motivations as the microfoundations of social life and sociological explanation,[1] they have forgotten about something that was important to the discipline's classical founders, at least, and that has had consequences for sociological theory since their day. This chapter also provides a springboard for me to continue my argument about human nature and motivations. By highlighting the philosophical anthropologies that were critical for defining and justifying their projects, we can consider further what kind of assumptions and beliefs about human nature and motivations we may need to hold in order for us to conduct the best, most realistic sociology possible.

Émile Durkheim

Of the three theorists examined here, Durkheim believed in what was perhaps the simplest view of human nature. We know what Durkheim thought about human nature not by having to "read between the lines" of his work and making inferences. He wrote explicitly on the subject in a variety of works on education, morality, religion, and knowledge. Durkheim's view of human nature is also clearly presupposed and referenced in his better-known works, including *Suicide*, *The Division of Labor in Society*, and *The Elementary Forms of Religious Life*. His view was informed by Jean-Jacques Rousseau and Immanuel Kant, as mediated by Charles Renouvier and Octave Hamelin, although he saw himself as moving beyond their views. His views, and those of Marx and Weber below (and Freud and many others), were also framed by the anthropocentric revolution concerning religion dating to Ludwig Feuerbach's *The Essence of Christianity*[2] and its associated "projection theory" of religion, which provoked a new kind of intellectual crisis concerning humanity and its nature and place in the social order and universe.

Durkheim is well known for arguing against atomistic, utilitarian, and individualistic explanations of human social life on behalf of the then fledgling discipline of sociology. He was insistent that sociology not be reduced to psychology and that it break from methodological individualism. However, pursuing his *socio*logical agenda did not drive Durkheim away from specifying a theory of human ontology. To the contrary, Durkheim directly depended upon his view of human nature to validate his strongly sociological approach. Sociology, Durkheim believed, *must* address the nature of individual humans, which are the basic element of which social groups are comprised. He wrote that sociology cannot avoid "eventually touching on the individual who is the basic element of which . . . [social] groups are composed. . . . It is impossible to attempt to explain the whole without explaining the part." Therefore, Durkheim insisted, sociologists need to "seek out . . . the causes and conditions of what is most specifically human in man."[3] In fact, Durkheim thought that one of the goals of sociology was to "develop a well-founded, realistic, and comprehensive theory of human nature."[4]

The Dualism of Human Nature. Central to Durkheim's understanding of human being is the idea of the "constitutional duality of human nature" or *Homo duplex*. He believed that all humans embody and experience a double nature, which expresses itself in a dual consciousness. Humans sense themselves, he observed, as being composed of body and soul. We experience corporeal sensations but also concepts in conscious awareness. We know sensual appetites but also feel moral rules impinging upon those appetites. We have individual psychologies but also live as social beings. This persistent dualism is not, Durkheim argued, an invention of philosophers or the ideological imposition of religions. There is a genuine reason, he thought, why humans experience themselves to be, as he quotes Pascal, "both 'angel and beast,'" having "two classes of states of consciousness." The reason "man feels himself to be double," Durkheim wrote, is that "he actually is double. There are in him two classes of states of consciousness that differ from each other in origin and nature" and "two radically heterogeneous beings."[5]

The two sides of this dual human nature are the *individual*, embodied, "organico-psychic" aspect of human being, on the one hand, and the *socially-* determined fact of human existence, on the other. These two parts, Durkheim claimed, are in important ways at odds with each other. There is, he wrote, a "true antagonism between them. They mutually contradict and deny each other."[6] This is why "[man] has been disquiet and malcontent. He has always felt that he is pulled apart, divided against himself."[7] And yet at a higher level, Durkheim wanted to say, especially earlier in his career, the two parts of human nature are actually compatible with and dependent upon each other.

Durkheim's first part of human nature is the embodied, individual human being, what we might think of as the human in a quasi-Rousseauian "state of nature."[8] That part of the human he described as being "spontaneous, private, and egoistic" by virtue of having "sensibilities . . . incline[d] . . . toward individual, egoistic, irrational, and immoral ends."[9] This conceptually presocial individual merely "expresses [his or her] organism"—the "body in which [individuality] is based"—and so is primarily oriented toward the enjoyment of sensory experiences of pleasure. His or her objects of appetite are entirely egoistic, having their own individual satisfaction as their sole desire. Thus, Durkheim argued, it is from "our individual constitutions" that "passions and egoistic tendencies derive."[10] This part of human being therefore tends toward unrestrained self-indulgence and anarchy.

The second aspect of human nature, the socially defined and governed part, is, by contrast, according to Durkheim, what gives rise to conscious mental states, rational activity, the transcendence of self-interest, moral conscience, and life goals shared in common with other people. This part of human being, Durkheim said, is "nothing but an extension of society."[11] This is the aspect of human being that transcends and governs the individual, embodied, psychic self, reining in its unrestrained passion, egoism, and anarchic tendencies. It protects humans from anomie and enables them to act altruistically. It is that aspect, Durkheim suggests, that gives humans the experience of possessing not only bodies but also "souls."[12]

Durkheim's view of the tension between the two parts of human nature seems to have shifted somewhat over time. Anne Warfield observes: "For Durkheim, persons are both rational/social moral beings and a-moral beings of sensation at the same time. The needs and experiences of the two beings within us are inherently in conflict, but not unavailable to one another. Social beings do exist in indirect contact with natural phenomena through the individual being within them."[13] But exactly how the two parts of human nature are both in conflict but "not unavailable to one another" is somewhat ambiguous and apparently shifting in Durkheim's thinking over time.

On the one hand, earlier in his career Durkheim appeared to believe that the two parts of the human dualism—the presocial individual and the socially formed person—existed in a state of mutual complementarity.[14] The individual self needs society to socialize it for its own natural well-being. And the socially influenced self needs the kind of incomplete and socially "needy" individual self to form. The socially unformed individual self is exactly what society needs in order to compose itself, by socializing it into a social self. And society and the kind of human self that society shapes is exactly what the "organico-psychic" individual self needs to realize its own highest good. While sharing much of Rousseau's general framework of thought, Durkheim nevertheless wished to distinguish himself from Rousseau's notions that individuals in a state of nature are self-sufficient, that society is artificial, and that human perfection is lost when the state of nature gives way to the social contract. Instead, Durkheim wanted to insist on the naturalness of society, the good that society does for the individual human, and the true human happiness and flourishing that results from integration into the social body. In this sense, Durkheim believed that the social influence upon humans and their true inherent nature are mutually beneficial and reinforcing.

On the other hand, later in his life—perhaps, some have suggested, as a result of the personally and nationally crushing experience of World War I—Durkheim expressed a more pessimistic view of the relationship between the two sides of the human dualism.[15] In one of the last lectures given in his life, Durkheim's view of the dualistic individual and social self took on an antagonistic and tragic outlook. The dualism of human nature has, Durkheim noted, "a painful character," admitting that society's "requirements are quite different from those of our nature as individuals. . . . Therefore, society cannot be formed or maintained without our being required to make perpetual and costly sacrifices. . . . We must do violence to certain of our strongest inclinations."[16] In a note of near despair, Durkheim conceded in another lecture near the end of his life that "to change man and at the same time to respect his nature is indeed a task that may well exceed human power."[17] Steven Lukes goes so far as to suggest that Durkheim's last thoughts in life are reminiscent of Freud's pessimistic ideas concerning the superego and the id.[18]

The Centrality of Dual Human Nature in Durkheim's Thought. Far from being a minor side interest, Durkheim justified and argued for his larger sociological project by building upon this presupposed dualism of human nature. This theory provided the microfoundation necessary to make sense of his sociological theory of suicide. It helped define the problem Durkheim addressed in his theory of the division of labor. And his twofold view of human nature directly mapped onto the dualism of sacred and profane, which defined his sociology of religion. "The duality of our nature," he claimed, "is thus only a particular case of that division of things into the sacred and the profane that is the foundation of all religions."[19] Durkheim's view of human nature as dualistic was thus not an extraneous interest that showed up only in minor lectures and essays. It was presupposed in all of his works. In *Suicide*, for instance, Durkheim wrote:

> If . . . as has often been said, *man is double*, that is because social man superimposes himself on physical man. Social man necessarily presupposes a society which he expresses and serves. If this dissolves . . . whatever is social in us is deprived of all objective foundation. . . . [We are left with] nothing that can be a goal of our action. Thus we are bereft of reasons for existence.[20]

Durkheim also wrote about the "collective tendency exterior to the individual" as "not in the least surprising for anyone who knows the difference between individual and social states of consciousness." The latter, he wrote, "do not flow from our personal predispositions" but "consist of elements foreign to us."[21] Therefore:

> So far as we have a distinct personality of our own we rebel against and try to escape them. Since *everyone leads this sort of double existence simultaneously, each of us has a double impulse.* We are drawn in a social direction and tend to follow the inclinations of our own nature. . . . Two antagonistic forces confront each other. One, the collective force, tries to take possession of the individual; the other, the individual force, repulses it.[22]

Likewise, Durkheim wrote in *The Elementary Forms of Religious Life* that "man is twofold. Within him are two beings: an individual being that originates in the organism and whose sphere of action is strictly limited by this fact; and a social being that represents within us the higher reality of the intellectual and moral order that we know through observation—by which I mean society."[23] Again, Durkheim links this twofold being directly to the distinction between sacred and profane, on which he thought all religion is based.

In the preface of his earlier book, *The Division of Labor in Society*, Durkheim made clear that the basis of his analysis is his view of the dualism of human nature: "The starting point for our study [is] the connection between individual personality and social solidarity. How does it come about that the individual, whilst becoming more autonomous, depends ever more closely upon society?"[24] Durkheim relied upon this fundamental dualism of human being to develop the book's argument, explaining:

> Two consciousnesses exist within us: the one comprises only states that are personal to each one of us, characteristic of us as individuals, whilst the other comprises states that are common to the whole of society. The former represents only our individual personality, which it constitutes; the latter represents the collective type and consequently the society without which it would not exist.[25]

Durkheim then connected his theory of human being to processes involved in the division of labor:

> Social life is derived from a dual source, the similarity of the individual consciousness and the division of labor. In the first case the individual is socialized because, lacking any individuality of his own, he is mixed up with his fellows in the same collective type. In the second case, it is because, whilst his physiognomy and his activities are personal to him, distinguishing him from others, he depends upon then . . . and consequently upon the society that is the result of their combining together.[26]

In Durkheim's moral sociology, the civilizing of the self of the individual organism by the socially influenced self explains the origins of morality. Morality springs, he claimed, from the social suppression and retraining of individual egoism, passion, and self-interest. The same, in Durkheim's sociology of knowledge, explained the basic categorical concepts that humans need epistemologically to negotiate the world—such as space, time, causation, and so on. These, he argued, are not derived from human experience, as philosophical empiricists such as David Hume claimed; nor are they simply given as a priori features of the human mind, as Kant suggested.[27] Rather, Durkheim said, these basic categories are products of the *social* formation of individual human beings. Finally, Durkheim's theory of education was justified by his view of human nature, for education had, in his mind, to play the crucial civilizing role of taming the egoistic individual human being.

Omar Lizardo thus observes that while Durkheim's important 1914 essay on human nature was written toward the end of his life, his "basic position on the 'dual constitution' of the human mind is not a product of any late shift in his thinking but can be found in its entirety in *Division of Labor*."[28] Lukes correctly states that the dichotomy between the individual and society that expresses itself in Durkheim's theory of human nature defines "the conceptual structure of Durkheim's entire system of thought" and "lies at the basis of the entire system and is reproduced in different forms throughout it. . . . It forms the central and persistent *problématique* of Durkheim's theorizing from beginning to end."[29] In short, although Durkheim was an anti-individualistic thinker, he did not shy away from defining a theory of human nature. To the contrary, he embraced and expressed one and built his entire approach to sociology upon it.

An Ontology of Social Determination. How might we summarize Durkheim's theory of the ontological nature of human being? Humans do have a real ontological nature. But the character of human being, apart from society's salutary influence upon it, is primitive, egoistic, spontaneous, irrational, amoral, anarchic, and driven by the senses, not the mind. Individual humans are not merely empty vessels to be filled by society's content. They possess natural bodies, feelings, desires, and impulses to action. But until society forms those rudimentary capacities in positive, humane directions, the human self will tend toward anomic, deviant, and antisocial behavior. Durkheim used a variety of images and metaphors to describe his view of the individual human. "Individual natures," he wrote in *The Rules of Sociological Method*, are "simply the *indeterminate material* which the social factor fashions and transforms," the contribution of which toward fully developed persons "is made up exclusively in very general states, *vague* and thus *malleable predispositions.*"[30] If, Durkheim said, we could eliminate the influence of society on people and examine "the residue left," the individual would be "reduced to something vague and schematic."[31] Individual humans, Durkheim observed elsewhere, before they are morally educated by society, possess only a "vague, embryonic form."[32] "Man is man only because he lives in society," Durkheim claimed elsewhere, "Take away from man all that has a social origin and nothing is left but an animal on par with other animals."[33] In other writings Durkheim stated, "Deprive man of all that society has given him and he is reduced to his sensations. He becomes a being more or less indistinct from an animal."[34] Throughout his work, Durkheim also relied on organismic images to portray individuals as mere *biological cells* in relation to the complex organism they help compose (society), and without which the cells would have no independent life or purpose. Durkheim also wrote similarly that "the ego cannot be entirely and exclusively itself, for, if it were, it would be emptied of all content."[35] Again, without external social forces to create real human personality, he declared, "there would remain nothing more than a mathematical point, and empty place."[36] These are claims that prefigure similar views that showed up in micro-Durkheimian theorists like Goffman and Collins decades later, as we saw in the previous chapter.

With the "natural individual human" contributing so little to the constitution and formation of the developed, functional people we see in real life, the fact that such people do exist means that it had to have been society that created them. That, of course, was Durkheim's central point. Arguing against individualistic thinkers like Herbert Spencer, who sought to derive social realities from individual human nature, Durkheim insisted that the vast majority of what we take to be human nature was instead derived from social facts.[37] Stating it simply, he wrote: "Human nature is in large part a product of society."[38] Still, society does not extinguish the natural individual human. The primitive, egoistic, spontaneous, irrational, amoral, anarchic, sensation-driven self of individual nature does not go away after society imposes its influence. Society rather *super*imposes upon that individual self the kind of socially determined humanity it demands: "The aim of education," he said, "far from being simply to develop man as he is fashioned by nature, is to graft onto him an entirely new man."[39]

At this point, as we saw above, Durkheim exhibited a certain tension in his thinking. On the one hand, he believed that humans are by nature social creatures and that culture and society are themselves entirely natural—society's disciplined molding of the individual human into its image, therefore, is natural and should be accepted and desired by any person who understands the true human condition.[40] On the other hand, Durkheim noted that the natural individual human resists and sometimes is at war with society's influences, which uncomfortably constrain and discipline its natural tendencies. "Education," Durkheim thus stated, "teaches us to control and resist ourselves."[41] This means that while human beings do possess a true ontological nature, nearly everything we take to be human from our normal experience—that is, our experience of socialized human beings—is historically and culturally variable. Since societies, cultures, and education systems that generate human personality are variable across space and time, the apparently natural humans that are fostered by them will therefore also be variable.[42] To understand the human being properly, therefore, sociology must be historical, comparative, and thoroughly culturally relativistic: "It is civilization that has made man what he is; man is man only because he is civilized. . . . It is only by historical analysis that we can discover what makes up man, since it is only in the course of history that he is formed."[43] Mark Cladis summarizes this line of reasoning well: "With historicism as his starting point, Durkheim combated essentialist views of human nature. History shapes humans, and to take them out of history is to deprive them of their humanity. . . . Humans are contingent historical creatures from beginning to end."[44]

Is Modern Individualism an Exception? One wrinkle in all of this is that another significant theme in Durkheim's work—the emergence of the free individual in modern society—might appear to contradict the account of human nature described above. This modern individual is not the primitive, egoistic, spontaneous, irrational, amoral, anarchic human of nature described above. This free individual is the partially autonomous and self-determining person who emerges as a real social type in modern societies—men and women who possess what Durkheim called a distinctive "personality." Durkheim recognized and appreciated this progressive modern individualism, which results, he thought, from the causal interactions of human bodies, the growth of society, and the increased complexity of the division of labor:[45]

> To be a person means to be an autonomous source of action. Thus man only attains this state to the degree that there is something within him that is his and his alone, that makes him an individual. . . . The stuff of which his consciousness is made must have a personal character.[46]

But if Durkheim's view of human nature described above is correct, how could that free modern individual exist? The answer is that although Durkheim was serious about the partial autonomy and self-determination of the modern individual, he also viewed that self as a dependent and determined product of modern society. The social determination is twofold. First, it requires the preconditions of modern society for this individualism to even be possible. No person brought it about. Social change in the division of labor did:

> Free will . . . and freedom [are] not this impersonal, invariable, metaphysical attribute[s] that can serve as the sole basis for the . . . personality of individuals. . . . That is an outcome that occurs progressively as the division of labor itself progresses. . . . The advance of the individual personality and that of the division of labor depend on one another and the same cause.[47]

Second, living as a modern individualist is itself an act of complete conformity to the dictates of modern society. The individualistic modern human self is not in fact genuinely or fully self-directing, but only appears to be. In the end, modern individualists are merely "the individualized forms of collective forces."[48] Thus "nowadays no one questions the *obligatory* nature of the rule that ordains that we should exist as a person, and this increasingly so."[49] Modern individualism as a social fact is thus embedded within, dependent upon, and determined by modern society. Human "liberty," Durkheim wrote, "can become a reality only in and through society."[50] Freedom and reason, he said, are always based on *conformity* to social control: "When we try to rebel against [social regulation], we are harshly recalled to the necessity of the rule. When we conform to it, [regulation] liberates us from this subservience by allowing reason to govern the same rule that constrains us."[51] Thus "to be free," he wrote elsewhere, "is not to do what one pleases; it is to be master of oneself, it is to know how to act with reason and to do one's duty."[52]

In short, individuals are "free" to act, but only because they first "agree" to act exactly as the governing social order tells them to act. Such a freedom is, in fact, only apparent—at least when understood in traditional humanistic terms. The reality in Durkheim always instead turns out to be an overriding social determinism.[53] Hence, modern individualism by Durkheim's account proves not to contradict the model of human nature described above but offers another piece of evidence verifying it.

Implications for Human Motivations. If human beings are as Durkheim has described them, then what are the implications for human motivations for action? Why do humans act as they do? What causes that action? Is there anything like a "motive," conventionally understood, involved in human actions and behaviors? On these questions, Durkheim followed out the natural logic of his theory. Although human beings are actors in social life, the causes of human actions are normally the force of *society* acting upon and within them. Society is the efficient cause of individual actions and behaviors. Individuals are the means by which society exerts its influence. In their actions and behaviors, individuals channel the influence of society. Society itself is the prime mover. At most, individuals exert causal force in the world by *participating in* society's governing influence over other individuals: "The rest of society weighs upon us as a restraint to our centrifugal tendencies, and we for our part share in this weight upon others for the purpose of neutralizing theirs. We ourselves undergo the pressure we help to exert upon others."[54]

Durkheim used different concepts to describe how these motive influences work. Rarely if ever was "motivation," in the sense of people being self-directed in (nonpathological) action, one of them. Sometimes Durkheim spoke of society as "stimulating" humans into action, as for example, when he said that "something else besides ourselves [that is, society] stimulates us to act." Sometimes Durkheim wrote about "requirements" and "interests" that may propel action. For example: "Society has its own nature, and, consequently, its requirements are quite different from those of our nature as individuals: the interests of the whole are not necessarily those of the part."[55] Other times, Durkheim talked about natural human "needs" and "cravings." So humans, because they are embodied, "need material supplies necessary to the physical maintenance of a human life." Besides this "instinctive" and "indispensible minimum," which is driven by bodily needs, however, "a more awakened reflection suggests better conditions, seemingly desirable ends craving fulfillment." The sentient person, in other words, can imagine and come to crave "an insatiable and bottomless abyss" of "passions" and desires. Durkheim also wrote of action being motivated by "pleasure," as when he stated, "All man's pleasure in acting, moving, and exercising himself implies the sense that his efforts are not in vain and that by walking he has advanced."⁵⁶ Other words Durkheim used to discuss these wants that "have constantly increased since the beginnings of history" are "appetites," "unlimited desires," and "goals."⁵⁷ Durkheim is often not averse to using the word "goal" to describe that which moves people to action. In a complex division of labor, for example, each person can "reach his goal without preventing others from reaching theirs."⁵⁸

Durkheim's main point concerning all of these possible kinds of drives to action, however, was that society needs to control and regulate them. Because natural humans can come to desire an infinite number of passions and wants, which inevitably lead to the unhappiness of perpetual dissatisfaction, people need society to constrain them, if they are to be happy. "The passions must first be limited. . . . But since the individual has no way of limiting them, this must be done by some force exterior to him." That, of course, is society. If a person "respects regulations and is docile to collective authority . . . an end and goal are set to the passions."⁵⁹ That then leads to happiness. By contrast, a man "having too keen a feeling for himself and his own value, [so that] he wishes to be his own only goal" may actually lead to "egoistic" suicide.⁶⁰ What then does it take, according to Durkheim, for the suicidal egoist to "see that he is not without significance" so that "life will resume meaning in his eyes" and "recover its natural aim and orientation?" "He must feel himself in more solidarity with a collective existence. . . . If this occurs, [producing an] . . . understanding that he is the instrument of a purpose greater than himself, he will see that he is not without significance."⁶¹

Rather than human persons as subjects being active instruments achieving their own purposes, humans are instead "instruments *of* a purpose," the purpose of society. Humans need society to tell them what their proper motivations for action should be. "If this [society] dissolves," Durkheim insisted, "all that remains is an artificial combination of illusory images, a phantasmagoria vanishing at the least reflection; that is, *nothing which can be a goal for our action*."⁶² The ends that might motivate any action must therefore be provided by society, not human persons. In Lukes's words, "The social order has primacy over individually motivated actions."⁶³

Durkheim's *Suicide* is a telling study of his view of the irrelevance of personal human motives to action.⁶⁴ In setting up his argument, Durkheim spent many pages questioning the value of explanations of suicide that appeal to the motivations of those who killed themselves. He argued that it is impossible to rely on motives even to define which deaths are suicides and which are not. He pointed out that intentions and motives are "not easily observed. How [can we ever] discover the agent's motive? . . . Intent is too intimate a thing to be more than approximately interpreted by another." What people call the motives of suicide really only turn out to be "the opinions [of others, such as police] concerning such motives," not the actual motives themselves. In one place Durkheim wrote derisively of an "irritated scorpion" being capable of the "motive energy" causing it to sting itself. As to humans, the motives of some suicides, he noted, are nonexistent, imaginary. Those of others he called "futile." Durkheim also spoke of people who are suffering "hallucinations and delirious thoughts" as being motivated by a "purpose" to commit suicide. Having interrogated the general value of motives and found them wanting, Durkheim concluded that "the motives thus attributed to the suicides . . . are not their true causes." Therefore, Durkheim explained, "disregarding the individual as such, his motives and his ideas, we shall [instead] seek directly the state of the various *social environments* . . . in terms of which the various suicides occur" as the real source of explanation. Later, having conducted his own sociological study, Durkheim returned to the question of "the role of individual factors" in suicide, where he again denied that personal conditions and states, such as a neuropathic nervousness or alcoholism, cause suicide. "In a general sense this motive does not cause people to kill themselves. . . . The productive cause of the phenomenon naturally escapes the observer of individuals only; for it lies outside individuals." Again, the real causal agent producing suicide is society.

In *The Division of Labor*, Durkheim made a similar, though briefer, argument against human motivations for personal happiness, interests, or pleasure motivating action resulting in "progress" in the division of labor. That view he associated with utilitarianism, which he rejected. Between individual motives and interests and the division of labor, he asserted, "there is no connection." About the motivation to happiness, he claimed, "it is not that influence which has brought [social transformations] about." Assessing things like people's pleasures and interests is impossible, he said, since they "are necessarily subjective," lacking "all objective criteria" of measurement, and so need to be "ruled out." Likewise, Durkheim claimed that the benefits of civilization to their people and the teleological motivations of people to achieve those benefits are not what have prodded people to develop civilization. It is rather the simple social fact of population size:

> Civilization [is] not . . . a goal that motivates people through the attraction it exerts upon them, not as some good they dimly perceive and desire beforehand, of which they seek by every means to possess the larger possible share. Rather, it is the *effect* of a cause, the necessary resultant of a given state. . . . Men go forward because they must. What determines the speed of their advance is the more or less strong pressure they exert upon each other, depending upon their [demographic population] numbers.[65]

More broadly, Durkheim asserted, "social science must resolutely renounce" explanations that rely on individual characteristics and motivations. People who try to "explain the development of the division of labor by a set of entirely individual motivations [such as to increase pleasure] without adducing the intervention of any social cause" must realize that "however real these variations in pleasure may be, they cannot play the role attributed to them."[66]

Durkheim was consistent in his thinking about motivations and action across his works. In *The Rules of Sociological Method*, he raised the epistemological problem of knowing what motives give rise to actions, even when they are our own motives and actions:

> We know very inaccurately the relatively simple motives that govern us. We believe ourselves disinterested, whereas our actions are egoistic; we think that we are commanded by hatred whereas we are giving way to love, that we are obedient to reason whereas we are the slaves of irrational prejudices, etc. How therefore could we possess the ability to discern more clearly the causes . . . which inspire the measures taken?[67]

That being the case, Durkheim pressed, how can the social scientist know which of *other* people's motives produced which actions and social facts? It is impossible, he thought. Furthermore, human motivations to action, even if they could be identified, never in the end explain anything properly, because appeals to them rely on a teleological logic, which Durkheim believed to be illegitimate. "If social evolution really had its origin in the psychological make-up of man," he wrote, "one fails to see how this could have come about. For then we would have to admit that its driving force is some internal motivation within human nature. But what might such a motivation be?" Durkheim listed three motives—an instinct to realize human nature, a need for progress, and a need for greater happiness—all of which he considered implausible. They all provide "purely teleological" explanations, he objected. "Social facts . . . are not explained when we have demonstrated that they serve a purpose. . . . The fact that they were useful does not reveal to us what brought them into existence." By such an argument Durkheim arrived at one of his basic rules for sociological method: "The determining cause of a social fact must be sought among antecedent social facts and not among the states of individual consciousness."[68] Personal motivations for action are irrelevant in any explanation of outcomes of human life.

Durkheim sustained the same approach to disregarding people's motivations for action in his *Elementary Forms of Religious Life*. There he observed that "the most bizarre or barbarous [religious] rites and the strangest myths translate some human need and some aspect of life, whether social or indi-

vidual. The *reasons the faithful settle for in justifying* those rites and myths may
be mistaken, and most often are; but the true reasons exist nonetheless, and
it is the business of science to uncover them."[69] In short, people engaged in
religious actions do not really know why they are acting as they do—their
own stated reasons and motivations are most often erroneous. But social science is nonetheless capable of identifying their actions' true causes. We have
already seen in the same work that Durkheim had explicitly stated his "dualism of human nature" theory. The lesson that Durkheim then drew out from
that theory was "the irreducibility of the moral ideal to the utilitarian motive;
[and] in the realm of thought . . . the irreducibility of reason to individual
experiences. As part of society, the individual naturally transcends himself."[70]
In other words, society's moral forces transcending individuals' teleological
motivations and reason are more powerful than people's experiences that
give rise to their reasons for action.

To show how consistent Durkheim was in his thinking, we may note that
he repeated the same ideas in an essay on history and sociology published
twenty-five years earlier: "Normally the historian perceives only the most
superficial part of social life." That superficial part is the motivations and accounts of individuals. "It is these motives and reasons," he observes, "that the
historian considers as having effectively been the determining causes of historical development." But, Durkheim judged, "these subjective explanations
are worthless, for men never do perceive the true motives which cause them
to act. Even when our behavior is determined by private interests which . . .
are more easily perceptible, we discern only a very small part of the forces
that impel us, and these are not the most important ones." Our motives and
reasons, he wrote, "stem most frequently from organic states, from inherited tendencies and ingrained habits of which we are unaware. This is . . .
even more true when we act under the influence of social causes." Therefore,
Durkheim concluded, "if we wish to understand the real way in which facts
are linked together, we must give up on this ideological method" of paying attention to people's motivations for action. The correct alternative, Durkheim
thought, was his explanation that directly links macrosociological facts to
other macrosociological facts, leaving individual motives and reasons aside.[71]

Even though individual goals are not what lead to human action, Durkheim nevertheless thought that it is important for life to *seem* to work that
way: "Not only occasionally but continually the individual must be able to
realize that his activity has a goal. For his existence not to seem empty to him,
he must constantly see it serving an end of immediate concern to him."[72]
But such goals of course come from society. Therefore, built into the normally functioning lives of sociologically unenlightened people is the need

for a kind of misrecognition of the sociological truth about personal goals and motivations—they will experience their goals and motives to be their own, when in reality they will have been determined by society. However, sociologically enlightened people will be in the position to realize and happily accept that what they formerly believed to be their own personal goals and motivations are really only determined for them by society—and for their own good, of course.

This is not to say that the natural, individual parts of people never perform motivated actions. They sometimes do. But those actions Durkheim saw as abnormal and pathological, in need of regulation and correction. That is because actions that erupt out of the life of the natural individual self result from their having been inadequately socialized or not being socially controlled well. What forms of action does this take? Anomie, deviance, anarchy, egoism, rebellion, unbridled passion, and other expressions of antisocial behavior. These, of course, Durkheim also studied sociologically, in order to reinforce his point about the godlike quality of society for creating, controlling, and correcting human life. Such behaviors are thus what happen when social regulation weakens, as a result of "society's insufficient presence in individuals."[73] In short, all good human action is driven by social interests and goals, and all action propelled by individual motives is bad, deviant, malformed. As a matter of professional self-reflection, Durkheim viewed it as sociology's role to reeducate people who live in societies held together by "organic solidarity" and who are threatened by anomie and egoism about the essential role of social discipline for promoting normal behavior and discouraging pathological behavior. That was, in his view, a major part of sociology's moral mission. To accomplish it well, sociology needed to demonstrate to people their absolute dependence upon society and their need to happily submit to its governance.[74] Promoting that was a major thrust of Durkheim's sociological project.

Summary and Assessment. Durkheim held a specific view about human nature that saw few native capacities for healthy, motivated action in natural human personhood. Individual motives, driven primarily by the body, give rise to deviance, anarchy, egoism, rebellion, uncontrolled passions, and other expressions of anomic and antisocial behavior. The primitive motivations of individuals therefore need to be regulated and governed by society. Such a view of human nature was reiterated in all of Durkheim's work. Its consequence for the question of human motivations was that it directed sociologists to ignore people's professed and apparent motivations for actions and instead to focus on macrosocial facts that explain social outcomes of interest. The question of human motivations for action was sidelined by Durkheim's presupposed dualistic theory of human nature.

Durkheim was largely correct, personalism believes, in his opposition to atomistic, rationalistic, and utilitarian approaches to social explanation.[75] Social facts and structures are, in truth, emergently sui generis, not reducible to aggregates of individual states or actions. Durkheim's emphasis on the power of genuinely *social* situations and structures exerting forces of downward causation to shape human experience and outcomes was fully justified theoretically and contributed importantly to the development of sociology as a discipline.[76] But on at least three points concerning human nature and motivations, critical realist personalism contradicts Durkheim. The first is that his view of the natural human being is inadequate. Durkheim grossly underestimated the extent and power of natural human capacities, interests, and motivations. If humans "before society gets to them" were really as ontologically emaciated as Durkheim described, then society could simply not be as causally robust as Durkheim insisted. Since Durkheim was not wrong about the formative power of society, he must have been wrong about "individual" human nature. For society to possess the powers that Durkheim rightly observed, human beings must naturally possess more capacities and powers than Durkheim admitted.

Second and related, Durkheim failed to understand that "macrosocial" forces must always exert their downward causal influences *through* the real actions and practices of human agents living at the "micro" (personal) level. This in turn can produce new macrosocial facts and structures. But the causal chain never runs directly from one macrolevel fact to another macrosocial fact. They are always mediated in processes of downward causation through the actions and practices of real, motivated human persons.[77] Lukes explains this point well:

> Durkheim supposed that a sharp demarcation line could be drawn between the social and individual levels of reality. . . . This strange and rigid view lay behind Durkheim's battles for sociology against strong methodological individualism. . . . But the view makes little sense as a positive methodological principle. Every macro-theory presupposes, whether implicitly or explicitly, a micro-theory to back up its explanations: in Durkheim's terms, social causes can only produce [particular] social effects if individuals act and react in these ways rather than those. . . . Durkheimian sociology . . . is notable for its lack of such an explicit micro-theory. Unlike Max Weber, Durkheim never explored the forms of rational action under specific social situations; unlike Freud, he never worked out a model of the psyche. . . . He never realized that even a macro-theory of suicide involves, and must involve, explaining why people commit it. There is, of course, an implicit 'theory of the subject' to be found there. . . . But this theory remains unexplored.[78]

Because Durkheim did not understand this fact, he made the crucial mistake of discounting individual-level factors that he believed were irrelevant to explanation but that in reality are essential for it. In particular, he ignored personal motivations for action. Durkheim thought he was able to get by in his theory of sociological explanation with a thin, primitive understanding of natural human persons. Critical realist personalism, however, says it is wrong to think of human persons (aside from their social influences) as merely "indeterminate material" of "vague, embryonic form," or as "residues" entailing only "vague and schematic" and "malleable predispositions." Persons are naturally much more than this and must be so for any sociological understanding and explanation to make sense.

The third problem with Durkheim's view of human nature—viewed from a personalist perspective—is that it provides no grounds for explaining how or why people possess anything like *innate* human dignity or could be the bearers of *inalienable* human rights. It provides no resources for resisting a broader morally skeptical argument on behalf of absolute moral relativism or skepticism. Contemporary sociologists *qua sociologists* may not care about such matters. But personalism says they are wrong in that position. Personalism *does* care about human dignity and rights and morality. It seeks an academic, scholarly, scientific theory that is compatible with and intelligible for the humanistic moral and political commitments that many academics, scholars, and scientists as persons embrace.[79]

Durkheim did not profess moral relativism, or at least not moral skepticism.[80] He valued and believed in the goodness of social order, human solidarity, altruism, law, education, duty, and so on. But he took too much for granted. He was intellectually inconsistent. In fact, little to nothing in his theoretical description of humanity and social life would lead to or be logically compatible with *rational belief in* the existence of real and objective moral facts of the kind that can transcend the dictates of particular cultures and societies (such as, for example, that slavery is universally morally wrong). Of course, if one *already takes for granted* the existence of and commitment to the kinds of moral facts that Durkheim endorsed, if those can already be *presupposed*, then his theoretical approach might be harnessed to justify instilling those beliefs and values into people through education and socialization. But it is credulous to think that morally committed humanists living in this world can simply take for granted the obviousness of their values, morals, and convictions. Those must be continually justified and defended with good reasons. Although Durkheim did not realize it, his theory could never generate the moral beliefs and values to which he was committed. If anything, his theory tends to work in the opposite direction. For Durkheim, society is everything, and individual people (apart from society) are virtually nothing. Such a view does not naturally underwrite the kind of social order that humanists find attractive. From a consistent Durkheimian perspective, if we are to believe that human persons possess dignity or bear inalienable human rights, that could (and should) only be because society has declared those moral "truths" to be so. In which case, those are part of the "collective consciousness." But if a society were to so happen not to believe, declare, and teach those things—as very many in history have and some today do—then people in those circumstances would have no reason to believe in human dignity and rights. Critical realist personalism claims that people do possess dignity and do bear inalienable rights whether or not their culture and society say so. But Durkheim's view of human nature offers us no grounds upon which to be able with good reason to make such a claim. That is a major problem.

Karl Marx

Karl Marx also held a particular theory about human nature that was central to his sociological analysis. His view was fundamental to motivating, ordering, and making sense of his entire intellectual project. Lacking his account of human nature, neither Marx's social analysis nor his moral convictions would have made sense. Marx's view of the human being was more substantively developed than Durkheim's, firmly rooted in his understanding of material reality and biological life. It echoed an Aristotelian understanding of humanity, which focused on the development and realization of natural needs and capacities. The German word Marx used to refer to human nature was *Gattungswesen,* normally translated into English as "species being" or "species essence."[81] Marx believed that his view of human nature was founded on the "real basis of history," on "nature both as it exists outside man and as man's nature."[82] Human nature is thus truly based on nature more broadly, not on human invention. He thus wrote:

> The first premise of all human history is, of course, the existence of living human individuals. Thus the first fact to be established is the physical organization of these individuals and their consequent relation to the rest of nature. . . . All historical writing must set out from these natural bases.[83]

Therefore, "to know what is useful for a dog, one must investigate the nature of dogs," Marx reasoned. "Applying this to man," he said, in order to understand "human acts, movements, relations, etc.," one "first ha[s] to deal with human nature in general, and then with human nature as historically modified in each epoch."⁸⁴ The language of this last point is crucial to understand. Marx wrote about human nature as something that is fixed by the reality of nature, and therefore permanent—"human nature in general." But at times he also wrote about human nature as something that develops over time—"human nature as historically modified." It is essential for understanding Marx on human nature to realize that the latter meaning presupposes and is based upon the former: change in human nature is simply the development in capacities and potentialities that naturally reside in what is fixed and permanent about human nature. That development can only happen because that which is universal and unchanging makes it possible. And the unchanging is more fundamental than the changing. Thus while it is part of the essence of human nature to develop natural human powers over time, Marx did not believe that human nature, in its most fundamental essence, was variable.

Humanity's "Species Essence." Marx's view of human nature can be summarized as follows. All human beings have a set of natural needs as well as the natural capacities and powers to meet those needs. These needs, capacities, and power are not defined or conferred by society, but are determined by the given material and biological facts of nature. Human beings' embodied, sensuous, and biological constitution and place in the larger material world are thus crucial for understanding human being. Certain natural human capacities give rise to higher forms of experience, particularly consciousness of self, of social relations, and of the human species. That consciousness then generates new social and psychological needs—for companionship, self-affirmation, evaluative reflection, and so on. High-order consciousness also equips humans to engage in complex and creative means to survive and potentially thrive in life. This includes the continual development of new technological and institutional forms to meet their needs. Human nature also entails the capacity for planning for the future and acting to achieve chosen purposes.

Central in all of this needs-satisfying activity is the defining human capacity to engage and transform the *material* world. To be human is crucially to exercise native powers and skills of productive capacity, to become material producers, and to directly reap the benefits of material production. Engaging in the work of material production is thus not a regrettable necessity for creating the preconditions for what matters in human life. For Marx, material production is the central means for developing and realizing the fullness of true human nature, of achieving the human telos. When human social relations, technologies, and institutions function together to promote human survival and flourishing in the material world, then human nature is able to develop and enjoy its full potentialities. Regrettably, however, most of human history has been the story of certain people materially exploiting other people, resulting in the stunting and crushing of human nature. By harnessing the natural human capacities for conscious self-understanding, evaluation, planning, and purposive action, however, Marx believed, humans can transform their practices of material production, meet the needs of all humans, and so achieve the complete realization of the full potentials of human nature.

Let us examine more closely some of the key elements of this view. First, human beings have natural, constant, universal, biological *needs* that must be met in order to survive, much less to thrive. These needs are not social or cultural constructions, not variable by-products of social institutional influences, but rather natural, ubiquitous facts of reality. Marx's writings show that he considered, by implication and statement, these to include the need for food, water, fresh air, clothing, shelter, rest, sleep, sunlight, hygiene, other conditions favorable to health, and ongoing social relationships with other human beings, including sexual relations.[85] Marx took it to be axiomatic that these are simply natural, universal, and ineliminable needs of human nature.[86] In addition, Marx believed that for humans not only to merely survive but also to flourish, they also need to engage in a diversity of educational, recreational, cultural, and other activities that promote their human development. These he referred to as "all-round activity," "free development of individuals," "all-round development of individuals," and "the means of cultivating gifts in all directions."[87] Thus the starting point of Marx's theory of human nature—human needs—is, in his view, grounded in the facts of the material, biological, and social world that humans inhabit. Connected in Marx's mind were people's "*needs, consequently their nature,* and the methods of satisfying their needs."[88] Elsewhere Marx wrote, "The objects of man's drives exist outside him, as objects independent of him. But these objects are objects of his need, objects which are indispensible and essential to the exercise and confirmation of his essential powers."[89] These needs are thus objective and universal, not subjective or socially variable. They therefore give rise, he said, to "desires which exist under *all* relations, and only change their *form* and *direction* under different social relations."[90] All that is wrong with the world, and what should be made right about it, Marx believed, must therefore deal with the "realm of necessity," with what is rooted in nature and is therefore natural.[91]

A second key element in Marx's theory of human nature is the natural human fact of consciousness and self-consciousness. Humans do not merely subsist. Humans are consciously aware creatures, sentient about not only their material environments but also their fellow humans in social relations and themselves as reflective animals. Making humanity the object of conscious reflection is a crucial part of what makes people human. "Man is a species-being," Marx wrote, "not only because he practically and theoretically makes the species—both his own and those of other things—his object, but also . . . because he looks upon himself as the present, living species, because he looks upon himself as a universal and therefore free being."[92] Self-reflexivity and its consequences, Marx argued, are unique to humans. "The [nonhuman] animal is immediately one with its life activity. It is not distracted from that activity; it is that activity," he observed. By contrast,

> Man makes his life activity itself an object of his will and consciousness. He has conscious life activity. It is not a determination with which he directly merges. Conscious life activity directly distinguishes man from animal life activity. Only because of that is he a species-being. Or, rather, he is a conscious being—i.e., his own life is an object for him, only because he is a species-being. Only because of that is his activity free activity.[93]

At the same time, Marx insisted, human consciousness and self-consciousness are not matters of idealism's autonomous or determinative spirit, but rather are "interwoven in the material activity of men"—consciousness is always a dimension of real, embodied human practice, an expression of "actual life process."[94] In fact, it is the very act of engaging in material production that leads to the rise of consciousness and self-consciousness: "People can be distinguished from animals by consciousness, by religion, or by anything else you please. They themselves begin to render themselves different from animals as soon as they being to *produce* their means of subsistence."[95]

A third key aspect of Marx's view of human nature is that humans are endowed with certain powerful capacities to engage and transform their material world. Humans are not only objects upon which the surrounding world acts. They are also subjects and agents of their own lives, of material production, and of history. "The productive power of social labor," Marx wrote, "strips off the fetters of his individuality, and develops the capacities of his species."[96] These involve "the labor-power possessed in his bodily organism by every ordinary man" and "the natural forces which belong to his own body, his arms, legs, head, and hands."[97] All of this, in both its enabling and constraining dimensions, is a simple fact of nature:

> Man is directly a natural being. As a . . . living natural being he is on the one hand endowed with natural powers, vital powers—he is an active natural being. These forces exist in him as tendencies and abilities—as instincts. On the other hand, as a natural, corporeal, sensuous, objective being he is a suffering, conditioned, and limited creature.[98]

The human condition is thus one requiring people's powerful and creative but bounded, natural capacities working to transform material nature to limit human suffering and to realizing the full development of human nature. Marx's "philosophical anthropology says that humans are essentially creative beings. . . . Man is an essentially creative being, most at home with himself when he is developing and exercising his talents and powers."[99] "Innovative and creative activity is natural for man."[100] Such creativity is also closely related to the human capacities to anticipate, plan, and act purposively.

> What distinguishes the worst architect from the best of bees is this, that the architect raises his structure in imagination before he erects it in reality. At the end of every labor-process, we get a result that already existed in the imagination of the laborer at its commencement. He not only effects a change of form in the material on which he works, but he also realizes a purpose of his own.[101]

G. A. Cohen summarizes Marx with three points that capture Marx's thinking on this point: "Men are . . . somewhat rational. The historical situation of men is one of scarcity. Men possess intelligence of a kind and degree which enables them to improve their situation."[102]

Crucial to Marx's thought on this matter is the idea that humans significantly develop the capacities innate in their essential constitution simply by exercising them and engaging them with the material world. In the course of historical social change, he wrote, material producers "bring out new qualities in themselves, develop themselves in production, transform themselves, develop new power and ideas, new modes of intercourse, new needs and new languages."[103] Elsewhere he wrote, "While man works on nature and changes it, he simultaneously changes his own nature. He develops the potencies slumbering in it, and subjects the play of its powers to his own sway."[104] I noted above, Marx is not reflecting a fundamentally formal or variable view of human nature. The essence of human nature is unchanging. But key dimensions of that fixed nature, which are universally and inalienably embedded in it, do indeed emerge, develop, grow, and elaborate in the course of human activity in history. Again, humans act as purposive agents of material production, as creative fabricators of material goods. This is not a mere obligatory prerequisite for physical survival that subsequently puts people in a position to pursue something else that "really matters" about human life. Being material producers is the *essence* of what it means to be human, a defining activity in human nature. To materially "produce as a human being," wrote Marx, is "to have immediately confirmed and actualized in my individual activity my true essence, my human, my communal essence."[105] By exercising their natural capacities for world transformation humans "affirm," "confirm," and "actualize" themselves. The more they do so, the more the "human being as species being . . . has become himself and grasped himself" and "the human essence feels itself satisfied."[106] Therefore, the full development of the essence of human nature through material production is what defines for humanity its true, ultimate purpose in life: "The calling, vocation, and task of human beings is to develop themselves and all their capacities in a manifold way."[107] Following a general Aristotelian teleological logic,[108] Marx thus justifies a key normative element of this larger theory, drawing a conclusion about what the human good is from a purely descriptive account of human nature.

Another point: human persons achieving the fullness of their essential being, by developing their natural capacities, is a responsibility that falls squarely on living, acting people. The achievement of humanity's natural destiny will not be achieved by "society" or an abstract "history," but only by active human agents taking charge of their own lives, of social institutions, and so of history itself. On this Marx was clear:

> History does nothing, it "possesses no immense wealth," it "wages no battles."
> It is man, real, living man who does all that, who possesses and fights; "his-
> tory" is not, as it were, a person apart, using man as a means to achieve its own
> aims; history is nothing but the activity of man pursuing his aims.[109]

Human beings are thus understood by Marx to be active, powerful, responsible agents of their own lives, histories, and destinies who are—in a material world of challenge and scarcity that requires mastering and creative transformation—struggling together to exercise their natural capacities for engaging the world toward the full realization of their own essential nature. Having established that view of humanity, the rest of Marx's work seeks to demonstrate how capitalism obstructs that natural human endeavor, while communism would ensure its achievement.

Why Marx Needs a Human Nature. Many Marxists and interpreters of Marx have come to deny that Marx believed in a definite human nature.[110] This denial has no defensible basis in Marx himself. It is primarily an overreaction against conservative anti-Marxist claims about a universal human nature that they say make socialism impossible. It is then justified by appeal to a few apparently supportive passages in Marx, particularly his sixth thesis on Feuerbach, which, however, are poorly interpreted.[111] This more recent Marxist tradition of denying an essential, fixed, universal human nature makes no sense, as other Marxist theorists have shown.[112] It does not take much effort to see how integral to Marx's larger project his theory of human nature was. If one could somehow delete his views of human nature from this larger work, much of it would become groundless, since most of it flows as natural implications of his beliefs about the essence of human being. A full exposition of how and why this is so is not needed for present purposes. But a few indications may help to reinforce the point.

Take the problem of "alienation," for instance, which is an excellent entryway into Marx's thinking. Marx critiques capitalism as inherently alienating and describes people living in a capitalist system as inevitably alienated. But the meaningfulness of the very notion of alienation depends necessarily upon a contrast with a condition that is *not* alienated. And that in turn requires having some larger referencing idea of what a normal or good human life or condition looks like, in terms of which the state of alienation can be identified. To diagnose something as a sickness presupposes knowing the contrasting state of health. And since alienation is a real human experience, then Marx must have been operating with a definite theory of non-alienated human nature in relation to which alienation would make sense. "Alienation," for Marx, consists of human experience in the world estranged from true human nature, when for people their lived "being does not correspond to their essence," so that people in their existential experience are not "in harmony" with their true selves, thereby denying the possibility that "the human essence feels itself satisfied."[113] Thus, take away his theory of human nature and Marx's "alienation" becomes an empty slogan.

The same is true for Marx's moral claims. It is only because humans really do have such a given, universal, ineliminable nature that Marx can rationally demand that exploited people—all morally sensitive people, in fact—should feel a moral "indignation" about the violation of their natural being. Such moral outrage, Marx pointed out, is "necessarily driven by the contradiction between *human nature* and [actual] conditions of life."[114] All humans have natural basic needs. But certain social conditions prevent those needs from being met, resulting in "suffering, . . . illness or disability, malnutrition, physical pain, relentless monotony and exhaustion, unhappiness, [and] despair."[115] Moral indignation at the unnecessary but destructive social conditions is, in Marx's mind, the natural and obviously correct response to those conditions. Again, take away Marx's theory of human nature, and his moral critique becomes groundless. As a parallel, Marx's vision for economic and social justice also depended upon his theory of human nature. The conditions of justice and freedom that Marx envisioned the proletariat constructing after the communist revolution will have to be achieved, he insisted, "under conditions most favorable to, and worthy of, their human nature."[116] In short, it is real human nature that must dictate what a good society looks like. Communism, for Marx, is about the just meeting of real human needs. But any claims about human needs inescapably presuppose some larger understanding of the human condition, of human nature. To rationally commend the pursuit of some historical project, including revolution and communism, demands first having embraced a theory of human nature for which that project makes sense. Marx knew that. He thus wrote that had he been able to live in a communist system, "I would have directly confirmed and realized my true nature, my human nature, my communal nature."[117]

Finally, Marx's larger presupposed analytical framework of historical materialism, without which Marxism would not be Marxist, is intimately connected to his theory of human nature. According to Marx's materialist conception of history, Allen Wood rightly observes, "the basic determinant of social life and historical development is the relentless tendency of human beings to develop and exercise their capacities to dominate nature and creatively shape it to satisfy human wants and express human aspirations. Marx proposed to render intelligible the structures of human societies, the nature of their institutions, the forms of their art and culture, ideas and values, by tracing all these things back to the character of the productive powers human beings possess."[118] Marx's philosophy of history and social change also depends upon the veracity of a particular view of human being. As Norman Geras notes, "*Historical materialism itself, this whole distinctive approach to society that originates with Marx, rests squarely upon the idea of a human nature.* It highlights that specific nexus of universal needs and capacities which explains the human production process and man's organized transformation of the material environment."[119]

An Assessment. From the point of view of critical realist personalism, Marx offers a more adequate theory of human nature and its implications than Durkheim, even if Marx's view has serious problems. The ontological realism concerning nature, human being, and society presupposed in Marx's thinking is essential. His emphasis on the natural powers, capacities, and limits of entities existing in reality is exactly right. His insistence on centering the embodied condition of humanity for properly understanding of human nature—and more generally on taking materiality seriously and so not slipping into naive idealism—is a salutary move. His understanding of human life being embedded in real practices in time and space, in a way that requires the taking of history and narrative seriously, is valuable. His ability to distinguish between fixed features or conditions of human nature and developmentally variable aspects of that fixed nature is important. Furthermore, Marx's refusal to embrace modernity's standard fact/value divorce—the is-ought divide—which strips science of its moral responsibilities, is commendable. His neo-Aristotelian teleological outlook on the good inherent in the development of human capacities, in undistorted ways that lead to human flourishing, is excellent. His recognition of the brokenness of the world and human existence—of pervasive alienation, exploitation, suffering, and injustice—is crucial. Critical realist personalism also affirms Marx's interest in identifying social causal mechanisms that produce observable historical outcomes. In these and other ways, Marx's theory of human nature is helpful, certainly more adequate than Durkheim's.

Even so, despite these strengths, Marx's view of humanity's species-being is flawed in some crucial, even fatal, ways. Most of those flaws come back to one central problem: Marx's view of human nature lacked enough complexity to account for the fullness of real human ontology and experience. Marx is impossibly simplistic. In the end, he gets human beings partly right. But the other parts that he misses or theorizes poorly are crucial, and so the theory he presents us is problematic. The analytical Marxist Cohen realized that Marx's theory of human nature was flawed, "severely one-sided." By this Cohen meant that Marx, in his effort to resist Hegelian idealism, ignored human interests in and motivations driven by *personal and group identities*. In Cohen's words:

> My charge against Marxist philosophical anthropology is that, in its exclusive emphasis on the creative side of human nature, it neglects a whole domain of human need and aspiration, which is prominent in the philosophy of Hegel. . . . Marx went too far in the materialist direction. . . . He came to neglect the subject's relationship to itself. . . . He failed to do justice to the self's irreducible interest in a definition of itself, and to the social manifestations of that interest.[120]

Hegel and Hegelians emphasized the self's relationship to the self, of the subject to the subject. Marx pushed back hard on this idealism with his historical materialism, which stressed the self's relationship to the world, of the subject to the object. Marx rejected Hegel's description of the world as an expression of self, of the externalization of *Geist*. Consequently, Marx tied everything subjective and "spiritual" back to the material alone and, in so doing, badly ignored questions of self and group identity. Cohen explains the problem: "A person does not only need to develop and enjoy his powers. He [also] needs to know who he is, and how his identity connects him with particular others."[121] Marx believed that people should see, understand, and recognize themselves primarily in the tangible result of their material production, in what they have made with their productive powers. But expecting self-knowledge to derive primarily from the outcomes of material production was inadequate to real human nature and experience, Cohen argues. People also must and do know themselves in terms of social relations and other objects outside of themselves that they did not create, as Hegel had claimed. Central to such a concern is personal and social identity. And that, Cohen says, expands the bases of human motivations for actions. He says, "not that people are motivated by their *need* for identity, but that they are motivated by their *identity*, for which they have a strong need, and the motivating power of the identity reflects the strength of the need identity fulfills."[122] Thus, Cohen concludes:

> There is a human need to which Marxist observation is commonly blind, one different from and as deep as the need to cultivate one's talents. It is the need to be able to say not what I can do, but who I am, [the] satisfaction of which has historically been found in identification with others in a shared culture based on nationality, or race, or religion, or some slice or amalgam thereof. . . . What I am calling divisions of identity are as deep as those of class, and . . . they cannot be explained in the usual Marxist way.[123]

Cohen is absolutely correct. I only fault him for not taking his logic further. For Marx's exclusive emphasis on material productive powers not only caused him to ignore crucially important motivations related to personal and group identity. It also caused him to neglect other irreducibly basic human motivations (which I explain in chapter 5).

Allen Wood has observed that "Marx gives no real argument for identifying labor or production as the most basic or essential human function." Marx simply assumed that as a necessary element of his presupposed materialist conception of history.[124] Everyone begins with some presuppositions, so Marx is not to be faulted for developing a theory based upon presuppositions. But he *is* to be faulted for making the *particular* presupposition about materially productive capacities the most basic and essential human function, for presupposing that specific element of his theory as foundational. That presupposition is incomplete and simplistic at best. If taken to be the fullness of truth on the matter, it is wrong. Productive material work is a basic and essential human function. But it is not necessarily *the* basic and certainly not the *exclusively* essential human function or good. If we want to adequately understand human nature and motivations for action, personalism tells us that we need a more complex picture that is adequate to reality.

Max Weber

Like Durkheim and Marx, Max Weber held a view of human nature that clearly informed his sociology. However, Weber's image of human nature is not expressed quite as straightforwardly as the views of Durkheim and Marx.

Weber never laid out a direct, systematic philosophical anthropology. But it is clear in his writings that a view of human nature did stand as the backdrop of his thinking about what sociology is and how it is done well. The following draws out some of the more important themes in Weber's view of human nature, particularly as they relate to our present concern about motivations for action.[125] We can begin with some of the more familiar Weberian themes.

Purposive, Motivated Human Actors. Weber is well known as a methodological individualist. This means that he believed that human beings, not social structures or organizations, are the ultimate true agents of action in social life. In principle, then, every collective human activity and social outcome should be able to be analytically reduced to individual actions. "Action in the sense of subjectively understandable orientation of behavior exists only as the behavior of one or more *individual* human beings," Weber asserted. Even when sociologists view "social collectivities . . . as if they were individual persons," he wrote, "the collectivities must be treated as solely the resultants and modes of organizations of the particular acts of individual persons, since these alone can be treated as agents in a course of subjectively understandable action."[126] Similarly, Weber wrote that "the individual is . . . the upper limit and the sole carrier of meaningful conduct."[127] Stephen Kalberg thus notes: "With [Weber's] sociology, a new position for the human species crystallized, one steadfastly opposed to the notion that history possesses an independent meaning: *persons* now existed as the unequivocal makers of their destinies, as the center and cause of their activities."[128] In short, Weber elevated and centered individual human actors as the key unit of social life and so the starting point of social analysis.

Furthermore, Weber believed that many of the actions of human beings are both purposive and motivated. Actions are not ultimately "driven" from the outside or determined by society, but are rather subjectively *intentional* in being carried out by people desiring ends that they take action to achieve. Actions are often propelled by people with *purposes* to act in certain ways and not in others. "'Purpose,'" wrote Weber, "is the conception of an *effect* which becomes a *cause* of an action."[129] Purpose is teleological from the point of view of the actor, who purposes to achieve some end. Moreover, in many (though not all) cases, people's purposes are intelligible to themselves and to others. "Since we [social scientists] take into account every cause which produces or can produce a significant effect, we also consider [people's purpose]. Its specific significance consists only in the fact that we not only *observe* human conduct but can . . . understand it."[130] "Man can 'understand' or attempt to 'understand' his own intentions."[131]

Because humans act purposely, they can be properly understood as having *motives* for their actions. People's actions, therefore, can be understood and explained in part by discovering their motivations. Weber wrote that "a motive is a complex of subjective meaning which seems to the actor himself or to the observer an adequate ground for the conduct in question."[132] Similarly, Weber stated that a "motive" is "the meaning an actor attaches to [something in the world, enabling others to] understand what makes him do this at precisely this moment and under these circumstances." Understanding motives, therefore, "consists in placing the act in an intelligible and more inclusive context of meaning."[133] Weber argued that human motives can come in many types. But as a methodological approach, he said, it is best to *begin* by assuming that the motive for any given action—including what seems to be a strange action—is purposively rational. By rational Weber meant calculating means to efficiently or effectively achieve ends:

> The acting person weighs, insofar as he acts rationally . . . the "conditions" of the future development which interests him, which conditions are "external" to him and are objectively given as far as his knowledge of reality goes. He mentally rearranges into a causal complex the various "possible modes" of his own conduct and the consequences which these could be *expected* to have in connection with the "external" conditions. He does this in order to decide, in accordance with the (mentally) disclosed "possible" results, in favor of one or another mode of action as the one appropriate to his "goal."[134]

In short, a great deal of (but not all) human action follows a means-ends reasoning that generates motivations to achieve desired ends by way of best means.

Unlike Durkheim, Weber does not hold an antimentalist and antisubjectivist view of human beings. He believes that what goes on "inside" people's minds matters for causing and explaining their actions. "Thinking and calculating," he stated flatly, "can constitute *causal* factors of the course of . . . action."[135] Of course, Weber's *The Protestant Ethic and the Spirit of Capitalism* is essentially an extended discussion about human motivations for a particular kind of action. But this presupposition about the ontological reality of motivated human action is not limited to only one of Weber's books. It operates in the background and sometimes foreground of all of his sociology. In Weber's thinking, humans simply could not live life without this belief in and existential experience of purposive, motivated, free, ends-oriented action: "The historical human being . . . has an attitude and will of his own and . . . would never 'act' if his own action appeared to him as 'necessary' [that is, socially determined] and not only as 'possible.'"[136] Elsewhere he wrote: "Every single important activity and ultimately life as a whole, if it is not to be permitted to run on as an event in nature [that is, externally determined] but is instead to be consciously guided, is a series of ultimate decisions through which the soul . . . chooses its own fate, i.e., the meaning of its activity and existence."[137] In Weber's view, this is not only a mistaken perception—a misattribution of agency—that people psychologically need to believe. It is at least partially based in reality, in the truth of things as they really are. According to H. H. Gerth and C. Wright Mills, such an outlook was motivated in part by Weber's political commitments:

> Weber's liberal heritage and urge prevented him from taking a determinist position. He felt that freedom consists not in realizing alleged historical necessities but rather in making deliberate choices between open alternatives. The future is a field for strategy rather than a mere repetition or unfolding of the past. Yet the possibilities of the future are not infinite, nor are they clay in the hands of the willful man.[138]

This meant, among other things, that Weber opposed the notion that human action was or could be controlled or determined by any of scientific positivism's "laws of social life."[139] Weber explicitly rejected a positivist approach to social science, which he understood as seeking to discover "'regular' occurrences of certain causal relationships." He insisted instead that "the reality [of social actions and patterns] to which the laws apply always remains equally *individual*, equally *undeductible* from laws."[140]

The Centrality of Cultural Meaning. Human beings behave at least sometimes as purposive, intentional, motivated actors, Weber thought. That means that the causes of their actions derive at least in part from the "inside" of human subjectivity, from their mental states, beliefs, desires, ideas, feelings, and so on. And this means that in order to properly understand human action, one had to take very seriously the meanings entailed in human cultures. Differences in patterns of human action can be explained in large measure by variance in human cultures, because different values, beliefs, and meanings motivate diverse behaviors and actions. Human life, in short, is powerfully shaped by cultural meaning systems and the particular beliefs, values, significance, and intentions they generate. "The fact," Weber wrote, is "that we are *cultural beings*, endowed with the capacity and the will to take a deliberate attitude toward the world and to lend it *significance*."[141] In that situation, people act in relation to "subjective meanings of actions," which are set within "complex[es] of meanings" and "intended meanings." In fact, meaning itself differentiates purposive actions from mere behavior: "We shall speak of 'action,'" as Weber famously defined the matter, "insofar as the acting individual attaches a subjective meaning to his behavior—be it overt or covert, omission or acquiescence."[142] Human beings are thus understood as creatures for whom the cultural meanings of life and the world are crucial.

This is not to say that Weber ignored the force of material reality, human self-interest, or institutional imperatives. He saw those exerting strong influences in human affairs too, as we will see below. Still, he always kept open the possibility that those material, egoistic, and collective forces could be redirected, if not sometimes overridden, by the influence of subjectively meaningful cultural ideas and values. In one of his most well known passages, Weber said: "Not ideas, but material and ideal interests, directly govern men's conduct. Yet very frequently the 'world images' that have been created by 'ideas' have, like switchmen, determined the tracks upon which action has been pushed by the dynamic of interest." Thus what people wish for and can accomplish have always "depended upon one's image of the world."[143]

Weber's general approach is based upon a clear distinction between the natural sciences and the "cultural" or social sciences, a difference insisted upon in Weber's day by thinkers like Wilhelm Dilthey and which Weber himself embraced. The natural sciences concern the nonhuman, material world. The cultural and social sciences, by contrast, investigate human sociocultural life. Because all things human involve a cultural dimension, Weber argued, every study of human life requires an interpretive or hermeneutical component. "The *qualitative* aspect of phenomena concerns us in the social sciences," he wrote. "In the social sciences we are concerned with psychological and intellectual (*geistig*) phenomena, the empathetic understanding of which is naturally a problem of a specifically different type from those which the schemes of the exact natural sciences in general can or seek to solve."[144] Weber viewed this difference as opening up a dimension of understanding only available to social science: "We can accomplish something which is never attainable in the natural sciences, namely the subjective understanding of the action of the component individuals. . . . Subjective understanding is the specific characteristic of sociological knowledge."[145] And this kind of approach requires sociologists to take seriously cultural meanings and values: The "cultural sciences" Weber wrote, are,

> those disciplines which analyze the phenomena of life in terms of their cultural significance. The *significance* of a configuration of cultural phenomena and the basis of this significance cannot . . . be derived and rendered intelligible by a system of analytical laws . . . since the significance of a cultural event presupposes a *value-orientation* toward these events. The concept of culture is a *value-concept.* Empirical reality becomes "culture" to us because and insofar as we relate it to value ideas.[146]

Because he saw something about human beings that crucially distinguishes them from the natural world, in a way that had direct implications for understanding and explaining their actions and lives—namely, subjectivity, purpose, meaning, and intention—Weber insisted on distinguishing the natural sciences from the cultural sciences. He was adamant that crucial in the social sciences was the interpretation and understanding of cultural meanings, even though those were irrelevant in the natural sciences. Nevertheless, despite these differences, Weber believed that the purpose of *both* the natural and the cultural sciences is to identify the *causes* of outcomes of interest.

Some (mostly antipositivist, hermeneutically inclined) thinkers radically divide the natural and social sciences, claiming that human subjectivity and freedom mean that observers can ever only *understand* the meaning of human action, but *never* can identify its *causes*. Protecting human freedom and agency from determinism, they believe, requires renouncing the effort to identify causality in human life. Weber was not one of those thinkers. His sociology was a causal sociology. But it was one that believed that human purposes, reasons, beliefs, and desires could be causes. Thus, for Weber, to come to a proper interpretive understanding of action is to identify its causes: "Sociology," he wrote, "is a science concerning itself with the *interpretive understanding* of social action and *thereby* with a *causal* explanation of its course and consequences."[147] Therefore, Weber was able to write of sociology, for instance, that "we wish to understand, on the one hand, the relationships and the cultural significance of individual events . . . and, on the other, the *causes* of their being historically *so* and not *otherwise*.[148] For our present inquiry about human nature and motivations as Weber saw those, this means that human beings can be and often are the efficient causes of their own actions. Humans are not merely "pushed around" by the determining influences of "social forces." People operate at least sometimes as the agents of their own lives. People are often conscious of their own beliefs, values, and intentions. And they are regularly capable of choosing actions that they believe will achieve their purposes.[149]

Selfish Individuals in Need of Social Discipline. The above is already well known about Weber. Yet it does not tell us enough about his view of the *substantive content* of human nature. Weber's methodological emphasis on the existence and analytical importance of purposive individual actors, motives, and cultural meanings, beliefs, and values all concern primarily *formal* properties of human existence and activity. It essentially tells us: "Here are the dimensions and modes of human being and action that the sociologist must attend to." But did Weber view human nature as entailing any more substantive content?

Yes. First, like Durkheim, Weber considered the *natural* human being—the person as he or she would be apart from socialization—to be selfish and tending toward antisocial attitudes and behaviors. He wrote, for instance, about "particular desires and emotions of raw human nature," such as "cowardice, brutality, selfishness, sensuality, or some other natural drive." Weber recurrently referred to human "impulses" and "drives" (*antriebe*, sometimes translated "instincts") that usually derive from basic human psychology and natural self-interest. For instance, he wrote about human "impulses to conflict," of "anti-normative impulses which form part of the 'mental attitude,'" which "moral commandments . . . are aimed at overcoming," and of religion "subjugating all creaturely impulses to a rational and methodological plan of conduct."[150] He spoke of "the power of irrational impulses" that are part of "the *status naturae*," which religious asceticism seeks to overcome, of the "'acquisitive instinct' . . . of speculators who 'operate on the fringes of criminality,'" and of some religions condemning "uncontrolled instincts," the "irrational desire to gamble," and the "instinctual enjoyment of life."[151] Weber considered sexual drives to be another fundamental human impulse, referring to "sexuality, the drive that most firmly binds man to the animal level" and to the "sex drives [which many think] are absolutely irresistible for the average man."[152] Summing up these "impulses," he wrote that "among the most fundamental and universal components of the actual course of interpersonal behavior" are "sexual love . . . economic interest, and the social drives toward power and prestige."[153] Walter Wallace is thus correct in writing:

> Weber quite unmistakably regards personal self-interest as innate and universal among humans. . . . Personal self-interest is already fixed by genetic inheritance in all human individuals and needs no further fixing there by external imposition. Weber . . . regarded personal self-interest as motivationally prior to "ideas"—i.e., learned values such as duty, honor, the pursuit of beauty, a religious call, etc.—although the latter play important contributory causal roles in value-added process.[154]

Much like Durkheim, Weber viewed the natural individual self as needing society's socialization and discipline if it is to be turned in more sociable, self-controlled, civilized directions. Here is where ethics, and particularly religion, comes in. Cultures generally and religions specifically exert strong forces upon the natural individual self to suppress and retrain the drives and instincts of the *status naturae*. Weber wrote, "discipline appeals to firm motives of an 'ethical' character, it presupposes a 'sense of duty' and 'conscientiousness.'"[155] Furthermore, because religions believe that a human's natural impulses "divert the individual" from their ideal character, controlling those impulses "belongs among the most important substantive characteristics of any particular religion." Religious "sanctification," Weber explains, is thus about "transcending human nature."[156]

The Need for Legitimacy. One implication of the above, which provides an insight into another dimension of Weber's view of human nature, is the universal human need to believe, and to have others believe, that their lives and actions are legitimate. People, Weber said, naturally and everywhere need to believe that their ways of living are justified by good and valid reasons, that they are credible, reasonable, in the right. "Everyday experience," Weber wrote, "proves that there exists . . . a need for psychic comfort about the legitimacy or deservedness of one's happiness, whether this involves political success, superior economic status, bodily health, success in the game of love, or anything else."[157] For example, Weber observed, "Rarely will you find that a man whose love turns from one woman to another who feels no need to legitimate this before himself by saying: she was not worthy of my love, or, she has disappointed me, or whatever other like 'reasons' exist."[158] This need for legitimation also extends from individuals to social systems. Weber wrote: "Action, especially social action, which involves a social relationship, may be guided by the belief in the existence of a legitimate order," what he also calls "the validity of the order." Social orders may be considered legitimate by people on grounds that are affectual, value-rational, religious, or legal.[159] Peter Baehr thus notes:

> Weber not only takes it for granted that human beings have psychological drives, or "impulses," with social consequences; he also believes that the need to justify one's standing in life—as privileged or dispossessed—is among the most basic psychological requirements of the human situation. Chaos, indeterminacy, and uncertainty are existential conditions [that are] too . . . senseless for most people to entertain willingly. As a result, humans seek reassurance that their fate in life is not arbitrary but meaningful.[160]

The Unconscious, Habitual, Confused, and Conflicted. Some interpreters of Weber—perhaps especially those who read him through the lens of Talcott Parsons's "voluntaristic" theory of action—describe Weber almost as a simple-minded advocate of conscious and deliberative means-ends action. Reading these interpretations, one might think that Weber taught that all people consciously hold certain values and purposes and then engage in actions that achieve them best. But Weber is more complicated and realistic than that. For one thing, though not often recognized, Weber had a real appreciation for *unconscious* motives—those operating below the level of accessible consciousness—that govern people's actions. He wrote:

In the great majority of cases, actual action goes on in a state of inarticulate half-consciousness or actual unconsciousness of its subjective meaning. The actor is more likely to be "aware" of it in a vague sense than he is to "know" what he is doing or be explicitly self-conscious about it. In most cases his action is governed by impulse or habit. Only occasionally and . . . often only in the case of a few individuals is the subjective meaning of the action, whether rational or irrational, brought clearly into consciousness.[161]

Similarly, Weber elsewhere argued that "the orientation to the behavior of others and the meaning which can be imputed by the actor himself are by no means always capable of clear determination and are often altogether *unconscious* and *seldom fully self-conscious*." He wrote too about certain religious beliefs and feelings that serve as "a device for compensating for a conscious or *unconscious* desire for vengeance." And he was interested in "the relationship of religion to sexuality," which he views as "partly conscious and partly *unconscious* . . . indirect as well as direct."[162]

Weber also recognizes the reality of *repressed* feelings and motivations: "In the first place the 'conscious motives' may well, even to the actor himself, conceal the various 'motives' and 'repressions' which constitute the real driving force of his action. Thus in such cases even subjectively honest self-analysis has only a relative value."[163] Moreover, Weber knows that people often forget the original reasons motivating actions and so may act in mindless, habitual ways. "Fundamental main principles and postulates," he wrote, may "no longer survive in the minds of those individuals who are still dominated by the ideas which were logically or associatively derived from them, because the 'idea' which was historically and originally fundamental has either died out or has in general achieved wide diffusion only for its broadest implications." Such an idea may have "not at all been raised to the level of explicit consciousness or at least have taken the form of explicitly elaborated complexes of ideas."[164] Fritz Ringer is thus correct in writing: "Weber's account of human action provides for a wide spectrum of motives and behaviors. . . . Behaviors may be not only irrational or habitual, but also largely unconscious—and productive of outcomes that bear little relationship to the motives and beliefs of the agents involved."[165]

Furthermore, Weber is clear that human interests and motives are usually not coherent and harmonious in any given case, but rather complicated and *conflicting*. At a basic level, Weber's view of human action recognized a variety of motivational types. Some action is instrumentally rational, some is value rational, some is affective, some is traditional, and, Weber stated, there may be other modes of action besides those four types.[166] Each of these types of action can and often do clash with the others. When it comes to affective types of action, acting on strong emotions, for example, people are, Weber wrote, "susceptible to such emotional reactions as anxiety, anger, ambition, envy, jealousy, love, enthusiasm, pride, vengeance, loyalty, devotion, and appetites of all sorts, and to the 'irrational' conduct which grows out of them."[167] These actions can clearly clash with one of the other forms of action. In addition, people are capable of "substantive" and not merely "formal" rationality. Action under the latter is based on means-ends calculations that choose the technically most efficient available methods. But in substantive rationality, judgments, decisions, and actions are "shaped by . . . some criterion (past, present, or potential) of ultimate values, regardless of the nature of these ends. These may be of a great variety." The ultimate ends that substantive rationality may apply could be "ethical, political, utilitarian, hedonistic, feudal, egalitarian, or whatever. . . . There is an infinite number of possible value scales for this type of [substantive] rationality."[168] Moreover, different spheres of human social life also entail their own concerns, purposes, and meaning systems—oftentimes putting them at odds and creating conflicts in people whose lives bridge them.[169] Adding more complexity, because human social relationships in any of these spheres of social life are defined primarily by subjective meanings and mutual expectations, they may take many kinds of definitions and forms. These definitions and forms might include convention, agreement, law, conflict, competition, communal, associative, open, closed, voluntary, imposed, administrative, regulative, formal, informal, power, domination, discipline, and much more.[170]

Besides this, the interests and motives that real historical *individual* actors hold "within" themselves at any given time are complex, frequently in tension, and sometimes opaque to both the actors and outside observers. "The actors in any given situation are often subject to opposing and conflicting impulses," Weber wrote. Sometimes "it is not possible to arrive at even an approximate estimate of the relative strength of conflicting motives."[171] Weber believed that it was "blindingly obvious" that "psychological links exist between all . . . kinds of inner relationships" between interests and motives, that any one motive is "combined with others," that this "probably applies to every possible motive of human action."[172] Thus, Weber wrote, "Neither religion nor men are open books. They have been historical [constructions] rather than logical or even psychological constructions without contradiction. Often they have borne themselves a series of motives, each of which, if separately and consistently followed through, would have stood in the way of the others and run against them head-on."[173]

Part of what is going on here, according to Weber, is the fact that individual actors, even when they are accurately and consciously aware of their own interests and motives, often do not process them in a strictly or consistently logical way. Those interests and motives, and the ideas that inform them, are rather processed in historically and psychologically conditioned ways. "Empirical-historical events occurring in men's minds," he wrote, "must be understood as primarily *psychologically* and not logically conditioned."[174] Therefore, Gerth and Mills observed of Weber's view, "there is no pre-established correspondence between the content of an idea and the interests of those who follow from the first hour."[175] In short, human motives for action are many, mixed, often conflicting, and sometimes inaccessible to conscious inspection.

Social Constraints on Action. Notwithstanding all of his methodological emphasis on the centrality of purposive individual action, Weber also clearly recognized that in many cases the imperatives and logic of various institutions and organizations—particularly modern capitalism and bureaucracy—simply *override* the interests, values, and purposes of individuals. At times Weber sounded almost like Marx on this point. "The belief in 'freedom of the will,'" he wrote, wryly, for example, "is of precious little value to the manufacturer in the competitive struggle or to the broker on the stock exchange."[176] Again, sounding nearly Marxist in his emphasis on the objectivity of social structures that govern individual behavior, Weber wrote that "economic laws . . . cannot be deduced from a psychological analysis of the individual but rather from . . . the competitive price mechanism of the *objective situation.*"[177] In situations, such as corporate capitalism, for instance, when "actors" are not persons but social institutions, the inexorable logic of systems tends to override any values or moral influences. Thus, Weber wrote, capitalism "cannot be ethically regulated, because of its impersonal character. Most of the time this domination appears in such an indirect form that one cannot identify any concrete master and hence cannot make any ethical demands upon it." Weber gives the example of "the director of the joint stock company, who is obliged to represent the interests of the stockholders as the masters proper" and "the director of the bank that finances the joint-stock company." He continued: "Decisive are the need for competitive survival . . . hence matter-of-fact considerations that are simply non-ethical determine individual behavior and interpose impersonal forces between the persons involved." In such a "'masterless slavery' to which capitalism subjects the worker," Weber says, "economic behavior has the quality of a *service* toward an *impersonal* purpose."[178] In such instances, the value-governed, purposive actions of individual persons are indeed "of precious little value."[179]

These observations can be generalized as an appreciation in Weber's view of the human condition for individual human limitations, given the realities of scarcity and humanity's total dependence on social relations for life. On this, Weber wrote:

> The basic element in all those phenomena which we call . . . "social-economic" is constituted by the fact that our physical existence and the satisfaction of our most ideal needs are everywhere confronted with the quantitative limits and the qualitative inadequacy of the necessary external means, so that their satisfaction requires planful provision and work, struggle with nature and the association of human beings. . . . By a social science problem, we mean a task for a discipline the object of which is to throw some light on the ramifications of the fundamental social-economic phenomenon: the scarcity of means.[180]

Walter Wallace sums up some of the implications of people's limits, understood in a Weberian framework, for their dependence upon society:

> The human individual, in Weber's eyes, is by nature (1) constitutionally *able* to conceptualize alternative means to a given end but *unable* reliably and precisely to compare and choose among these alternatives . . . without help from fellow humans; (2) constitutionally able to conceptualize alternative ends that a given means might serve but unable to compare and choose among those ends without the help of fellow humans; and (3) constitutionally able to bring about small physical changes in the world but unable to bring about large physical changes in the world without help from fellow humans. It is on this foundation of combined abilities and inabilities of human nature that Weber's theory of . . . "society" is constructed.

Therefore, "human society compensates for the inabilities of human nature" in that "political and religious social institutions [act] as the primary winnowers of all the logically possible value scales, permitting only a few of them to be actually conceived of, and even fewer adhered to, by the billions of human individuals."[181] Under such conditions, it is not surprising that the interests, values, and logic of social institutions and organizations would be able to override those of individuals.

An Assessment. Personalism finds much in Weber's account with which to agree. Weber's insistence on taking seriously distinct persons as the final sources and drivers of action and history is correct. His emphasis on human action as purposive, motivated, and shaped by cultural meanings is right. His opposition to antimentalist and antisubjective assumptions and theories, and his resistance to positivism's nomothetic vision of sociology as discovering the supposed universal laws of social life, are also good. Weber was profoundly right in noting the multiplicity of types and modes of motivation and action. He was similarly correct about the importance of the ineliminable hermeneutical dimension of all sciences of human life, and good about not losing sight of the centrality of causal analysis for sociology. Weber's stress on the drive for legitimacy as an aspect of human motivations and social relations also belongs in an adequate account of human nature and action. Personalism also agrees with Weber's acknowledgment of the sometimes unconscious, confused, habitual, and conflicted aspects of human motivations. And personalism affirms Weber's interest in trying to theorize a limited but genuine freedom in human life and action, in resistance to determinism. All of this personalism affirms.

But critical realist personalism also finds some of Weber's thinking to be problematic. For example, Weber's view that apart from socialization, humans in their "raw nature" are driven by impulses that are selfish, antisocial, irrational, and antinormative is not categorically wrong but is misleadingly incomplete. It is true that empirical humanity involves plenty of cowardice, brutality, selfishness, sensuality, conflict, egoistic acquisitiveness, and other such "creaturely impulses." But those, personalism says, are not the whole of the matter or the most basic and important facts to know about human nature. An adequate account of human nature requires a fuller, more complex understanding. In fact, personalism questions the very idea of positing a presocial, state-of-nature human being. The rare cases of unsocialized human beings (badly neglected and feral children) tell us very little of substance about the true nature of our personhood (other than that persons absolutely require nurturing environments to develop properly). Such an approach wrongly abstracts fictional "individuals" from humanity's real natural being, which is innately social and morally oriented from the start. The idea of an absolutely presocial human, "apart from socialization," is an unhelpful, unreal hypothetical, since such a human could never survive past the first hours or days of life. Critical realist personalism also sees a multiplicity of basic human interests that have both prosocial and, when pursued badly, antisocial potentials. The model, shared by both Durkheim and Weber, that natural humanity is in essence selfish and antisocial, and so in desperate need of society's civilizing control, is at best one-sided, a half-truth that mis-frames the basic human condition. Humans are most fundamentally oriented toward the realization of their own personhood, toward the achievement of goods. Selfishness is not the most basic human condition, but the condition, personalism, says, that pertains when people pursue goods badly.

A second point in Weber's view with which critical realist personalism differs concerns the nature of human freedom. Weber's political liberalism led him to conceive of individual freedom and external social causation as opposite, competing, zero-sum forces. Freedom, Weber assumed, equates with individual human autonomy. Freedom is realized when self-governing, self-directed individuals make unconstrained choices as they wish—which defines matters in a way that pits individual freedom against social constraint and influence. In that framework, the more sociology succeeds in demonstrating the social shaping of human life, the more human freedom recedes. Weber thus had to look to recurrent expressions of charisma, which challenge and overturn established social orders, to rescue some human freedom from the overbearing modern forces of rationalization, capitalist industry, and bureaucracy. No wonder Weber was so melancholy. Personalism, by contrast, proposes an alternative vision of human freedom—one centered not on the unconstrained, autonomous, choice-making, liberal Individual Self, but instead on the character of material, social, and institutional contexts that foster the realization and flourishing of the personhood of real human persons according to their natural being. Freedom is not being able to do whatever one wants. Freedom is enjoying what is necessary to thrive as a person.

Conclusion

This chapter has examined the views of three founding sociological theorists on the matter of human nature and motivations for action. They clearly did not believe those issues were possible to ignore, but all held and argued explicitly for particular views of human nature and motivations for action. And those views were essential for justifying and animating their sociological projects. Durkheim, Marx, and Weber were also not unusual in that. No sociology can proceed without some at least implicit assumptions about human nature and motivations. When sociologists ignore those questions, they are not in fact bypassing them but simply operating with some taken-for-granted, default views. We will do better social science if we do not neglect questions of human nature and motivations but instead bring them to the fore, for explicit examination, debate, and theorizing.

On Basic Human Goods, Interests, and Motivations

Social science must take human motivations seriously in order to understand and explain social life well. So another key question presents itself: among the innumerable real motivations that cause humans to engage in actions, are there any that can rightly be said to be *basic*? Are some motivations more fundamental or original, in relation to which others are derivative or secondary? Can human motivations be arranged in a hierarchy according to how central or primary they are? And if so, which specific motivations are most central or basic?

Basicality

We first need to define what "basic" means. A *basic* motivation is, for present purposes, one that generates actions intended to produce a result that is valued for its *own* sake. The ends of basic motivations are taken to be goods of intrinsic and fundamental value, not merely instrumental goods that serve some other more primary purpose or benefit.[1] Basic motivations generate actions that are not strategic or tactical in serving the purposes of some other interests. They serve their own direct purposes, beneath or behind which nothing more fundamental is sought. Basic motivations are thus those that produce actions expected to achieve results that are ultimately valued for their own worth, value, or benefit.

About any person's motivation, we might ask, "Why be motivated as M to action X?" Most replies will take the form, "In order that Y." In which case, motive M causes action X, which is expected to produce an end or outcome Y. When a motivation is *not* basic, Y is something that will serve to achieve the desire involved in some *other* motivation. But when a motivation *is* basic,

Y achieves an intrinsic good valued for its own sake and not justified or desired in order to realize some other purpose or benefit. When the "in-order-
that" explanations about motives come to an end, one has likely identified
a basic motivation. For instance, some people might be motivated to regularly work out on the treadmill in their local gym. They may not actually like
working out or being in the gym. But they do it anyway. If someone asked
them why, they may say that they work out in order to regularly exercise.
One may then ask what motivates their regular exercise. They may mention
a family history of heart disease and explain that they want to maintain their
cardiovascular health. If asked why again, they may say that cardiovascular
health is essential to staying alive. Then if pressed further, no additional explanation may be forthcoming. That is simply what they most basically want
in this case: to stay alive. Remaining alive will be their final end in this case,
the most elementary benefit, the intrinsically valued good.

The idea that some motivations are more basic than others seems plausible in light of our ordinary experience. Much of what we do seems obviously
instrumental, high up in a chain of means-ends practices. We are motivated
to do these things not because we value what they accomplish in and of themselves but because they help us achieve other, more important ends. Then
again, we also do certain other things simply and only to enjoy the goods
they produce. They are ends in and of themselves that serve no other ends.
Examples may include enjoying certain physical pleasures, the joy of playing
a loved sport, or doing the morally right thing merely because it is morally
right. Our own phenomenological experience thus tells us that a distinction
exists between motivations that are basic and those that are not. We have every reason to believe that this distinction is real and valid. But is it possible to
specify which human motivations are and are not basic?

Existing Accounts

Let us begin with empirical and theoretical work already accomplished in this
area. Psychologists, sociologists, economists, philosophers, and other social
theorists and scholars especially in the last century have advanced different
approaches to the most basic needs, drives, interests, desires, goods, and other
claimed bases of human motivations for action. The following examines a variety of those approaches, seeking to consider their background assumptions
and to explore the extent of agreement among them.[2] Most of these theories
claim to be grounded in the best empirical scientific evidence and conceptual
reflection of their day. But they also clearly assume, more or less consciously,
various background philosophical assumptions, being reliant on thinkers as

diverse as Aristotle, Thomas Aquinas, Thomas Hobbes, David Hume, Adam Smith, Charles Darwin, George Herbert Mead, Émile Durkheim, and Sigmund Freud. In sorting out the diversity of what follows, we should not focus exclusively on the test of empirical evidence, which proves to be of somewhat limited value, but we should also notice the philosophical lineages that inform them and consider how adequate they are to the reality of motivated action we seek to understand.

Approaches emphasizing *needs* tend to work from a biological, materialist, evolutionary outlook. Some needs-oriented theories focus especially on bodily needs. Others also incorporate the importance of psychological needs and social relationships. Theories focused on *drives* (or anxieties or instincts[3]) are often more consistently psychological, frequently adopting a psychodynamic view of human existence. In them, people feel various kinds of pressures—something like hydraulic forces—that their actions are intended to relieve.[4] An alternative image of drives is the drive to settle the disruption of personal disequilibria by reestablishing equilibrium or the discharging of felt tensions.[5] Theories of basic *desires* or *interests* that motivate human behavior, by comparison, can assume different background notions of human nature and behavior. Most emphasize the self-interested, self-fulfilling, yearning, craving, acquiring aspects of human interests and actions. These theories generally tend to recognize physical, psychological, and social desires as distinct and needing conceptual differentiation. They also tend to see more complexity in human motivations and so generate longer lists of basic desires. Accounts that emphasize human *goods* usually emphasize the centrality of human potentials and powers under the right conditions to flourish and achieve excellence through their development. This approach usually operates out of a broad Aristotelian or natural-law tradition. Human action is understood not simply to be a reaction to an innate need or drive, nor an effort to fulfill certain felt desires, but rather the pursuit of conditions and achievements that are believed to be good for human persons.

The discipline of psychology has produced many theories emphasizing *one* basic human need or drive that supposedly generates most or all of human behavior. These mono-motivational accounts have emphasized, variously, the needs for physical survival, ontological security, stable interpersonal relationships, categorizations for order in social situations, social identity and loyalty, self-esteem and valued self-image, cognitive consistency, coherence among beliefs, feelings, and actions, a sense of coherent objective reality, socially shared reality, closure and certainty, and anxiety about mortality or the fear and denial of death.[6] Personalism, however, observes and argues that no mono-motivational account is adequate to the complex reality of human motivations for action. Each view may contribute an important insight or piece of knowledge to the larger problem. But we can proceed believing that an adequate, realistic account will have to entail multiple motivations. Therefore, I focus below on theories that develop three or more distinct proposed needs, drives, desires, interests, capabilities, or goods that motivate action.[7]

Basic Needs and Drives. In his book *Explorations in Personality*, H. A. Murray in 1938 advanced an early, psychological, multiple-motivations account of basic human needs that motivate behavior.[8] Murray distinguished bodily from psychosocial needs. The first he called "viscerogenic." These include the need, he wrote, for air, food, water, sex, lactation, urination, defecation, avoidance of danger, unpleasant stimuli, excessive heat and cold, gratification of the senses, and rest and sleep. The second Murray called "psychogenic," which are not essential biological needs but are nonetheless fundamental to human life. These include the following six:

1. The need for prestige and self-enhancement, superiority, achievement, recognition, respect, and self-exhibition.
2. The need for status-defense and avoiding humiliation, defensiveness, averting defeat.
3. The need to exercise power and dealing with the power of others, independence, aggression, avoiding blame, dominance and submissiveness, submission and resignation.
4. The need for affection, affiliation, friendliness, cooperation, support, nurture, and dealing with rejection.
5. The need to acquire, conserve, order, retain, and construct with inanimate, material objects.
6. The need for cognition, to explore, inquire, know, and satisfy curiosity.[9]

Here we see operating the motivating force of physical, psychological, and social requirements for sustained human life. Human behavior is theorized as driven to meet these basic needs.

The contemporary Danish sociologist Jacob Alsted offers an alternative needs-based account of human motivations.[10] Drawing on existentialist psychology, Alsted grounds motivations in the most basic human need to address "psychic pleasure and anxiety," which he claims have four sources in four distinct domains of life. "Man's existence, living," Alsted writes, "is connected with intense anxiety. It seems that this anxiety takes on four different forms that are experienced by all people. This anxiety and our defense against it express themselves both on an individual and societal level."[11] Alsted also stresses the common human desire to develop and grow. According to Alsted, human motivations derive from the following four universal existential anxieties and corresponding "joys," which may be conscious or unconscious:

1. The anxiety of *isolation*, overcome by integrative social relationships and the joy of belonging.
2. The anxiety of *dependence* and absorption, overcome by self-assertion in social relationships, the joy of recognition.
3. The anxiety of *insecurity* regarding relational change, fragility, and loss, overcome by strong affective relations, the joy of comfort, safety, warmth, care.
4. The anxiety of *stagnation* or stasis, overcome by the joys of life competence, understanding, agency, mastery, risk for gain.

According to Alsted, the basic human need to address these four psychic anxieties and pleasures or joys is the basis of both (micro) human motivated action and the origins of (macro) social structures, which, he writes, "must be seen as collective psychic defenses of their constituents . . . against a chaotic world."[12] His theory thus attempts to explain how the human psyche influences social organization.

The German social psychologist, psychoanalyst, and humanist philosopher Erich Fromm claimed that all people have eight basic human needs, which are uniquely human in that they transcend simple animal needs.[13] They are, he wrote:

1. *Relatedness*: relationships with others, care, respect, knowledge.
2. *Transcendence*: surpassing their own nature by creating things and people about which they care (or, pathologically, destroying people and things through aggression and killing).
3. *Rootedness*: establishing roots and feeling at home in the world, developing past natural maternal security and establishing ties with the larger world (or, pathologically, becoming fixated and afraid to move beyond maternal security or mother substitutes).
4. *Sense of Identity*: establishing one's own individuality (or, pathologically, engaging in group conformity).
5. *Frame of orientation*: understanding the world and our rightful place in it.
6. *Excitation and Stimulation*: striving for goals actively, rather than simply passively responding to the world as it happens to us.
7. *Unity*: developing a sense of oneness with the human and natural environment.
8. *Effectiveness*: being and feeling accomplished.

All humans, Fromm argued, are alienated from their primordial union with nature and yet have difficulty adapting to a changing world due to their lack of natural instincts. That situation is made worse by humanity's self-reflexivity, which makes people aware of their alienation, a general situation Fromm called the "human dilemma." Only by realizing the uniquely human needs listed above, Fromm believed, can people solve this human dilemma.

The American sociological theorist Jonathan Turner is a scientific (as distinct from critical) realist who does believe in the reality of motivations for action. He draws upon a wide range of sociological schools and theories (exchange theory, interactionism, ethnomethodology, phenomenology, structuration theory, and interaction-ritual theory) to identify what he proposes to be the seven "basic needs" of human beings that generate their doings in life.[14] They are, Turner says, the needs for:

1. Group inclusion
2. Trust (in the social and material environment)
3. Ontological security
4. Material/symbolic gratification
5. Avoidance of anxiety
6. Confirmation of self (identity)
7. The sense of facticity (of surrounding world)

These basic motivations, Turner says, are that which gives rise to mental deliberations and calculations, reliance on means of culturally legitimate communications ("ethnomethods"), the presentation of self, and negotiations and exchanges with others.[15] The social psychologist Susan Fiske has identified five similar basic social motives, which are belonging, understanding, controlling, enhancing self, and trusting others.[16]

The humanist psychologist Abraham Maslow has likewise posited a well-known theory of basic human needs, which he numbers at five. Maslow viewed the quest to fulfill these five needs as the source of human motivated action.[17] Maslow's account is progressive, in that the more basic needs must be met through appropriate behavior before higher needs can be addressed and satisfied. The five basic needs, by Maslow's account, are these:

1. *Physiological*: air, water, food, clothing, shelter, sex, sleep, excretion, and such.
2. *Safety*: physical security, resource security, health, wellbeing, avoidance of illness and accidents.
3. *Love and Belongingness*: family, friendship, intimacy, group participation.
4. *Esteem*: self-respect, being valued, status, recognition, attention, confidence.
5. *Self-Actualization*: realizing full personal potential, fulfilling promise and capabilities.

Maslow's account thus spans and links the most elementary Darwinian needs of species biological survival, the Durkheimian social needs of belonging and participation, and up to the higher Aristotelian concern for flourishing through the full realization of natural, innate capacities and powers. Clayton Alderfer later developed Maslow's theory into an Existence-Relatedness-Growth (ERG) theory of motivations that did not require a strict progression in the meeting of needs in the hierarchy and was more cross-culturally flexible.[18]

Edward Deci and Richard Ryan have advanced a theory of three basic human needs that give rise to motivations for action in their highly developed "self-determination theory."[19] Despite being a theory of human needs, not human goods or purposes, Deci and Ryan frame their theory in larger, Aristotelian terms of proper human development. They write that "all individuals have natural, innate, and constructive tendencies to develop an ever more elaborated and unified sense of self. That is, we assume that people have a primary propensity to forge interconnections among aspects of their own psyches as well as with other individuals and groups in their social worlds."[20] They characterize this tendency toward integration as involving inner organization and self-regulation as well as connection with other people. Achieving this integration requires a nurturing social environment to facilitate growth. The three basic or fundamental psychological needs that must be met in interactions between the individual and his or her social environment, if the individual is to develop and achieve integration, are these:

1. *Competence*: feeling effective in ongoing interactions with the social environment and experiencing opportunities to exercise and express one's capacities.
2. *Relatedness*: feeling connected to others, caring for and being cared for by others, having a sense of belonging with other individuals and one's community.
3. *Autonomy*: perceiving oneself as the origin or source of one's own behavior, acting from interests and integrated values (not to be confused with the "negative freedom" of liberalism's self to do what it wishes without obstruction by others).

Deci and Ryan are clear that merely setting and realizing any personal goals is not enough to achieve personal integration. Only realizing those goals that meet the three most basic needs of competence, relatedness, and autonomy foster authentic human development and integration. People's motives may thus derive from purposes other than those seeking to satisfy these needs. In this concern for *proper* development, this needs-based theory more generally resonates with Aristotelian goods-based accounts. However, because the theory's explicit focus is on "needs" that must be met, not on goods or ends to be realized, I locate the theory here.

The University of Leeds political theorist Maureen Ramsay maintains the existence of six basic human needs are as follows:

1. Physical survival
2. Sexual needs
3. Security
4. Love and relatedness
5. Esteem and identity
6. Self-realization

These needs, she argues, are humanly universal, objective, and fundamental in human life.[21]

Manfred Max-Neef, a Chilean economist and developmental theorist, has proposed nine "axial categories," or basic needs, based on his empirical research in Latin America and the United Kingdom.[22] He lists them as these:

1. Subsistence
2. Protection
3. Affection
4. Understanding
5. Participation
6. Leisure
7. Creation
8. Identity
9. Freedom

Max-Neef claims that this list of basic human needs is exhaustive, universal, and so, when not satisfied, uncovers some important aspect of human poverty.

The Canadian social and political philosopher Kai Nielsen has also proposed what he believes to be the central elements of human needs, which he numbers at fourteen.[23] They are:

1. Love
2. Companionship
3. Security
4. Protection
5. Sense of community
6. Meaningful work
7. Adequate sustenance
8. Shelter
9. Sexual gratification
10. Amusement
11. Rest
12. Recreation

13. Recognition
14. Respect of person

And the psychologist Ervin Staub has posited seven basic needs. They are the need for (1) security, (2) effectiveness and control, (3) a positive identity, (4) connection, (5) comprehension of reality, (6) transcendence, and (7) long-term satisfaction.[24]

Finally, some related theories frame their accounts not in terms of needs but instead of basic human "drives." The image of drives, compared to needs, suggests actions being forcefully pushed by innate compulsions or forces within actors. Sometimes human drives are theorized as simply the subjective experience of tensions or discomforts felt when needs are not satisfied. Often drives accounts were expressed in theories of behaviorism. J. B. Watson's behaviorist theory, although more concerned with the nature of learning than with motivations per se, posited a basic drive of animals, including humans, to enjoy the rewards of pleasurable stimuli and avoid painful stimuli.[25] This approach was later picked up and advanced by other behaviorists, including B. F. Skinner. Similarly, E. L. Thorndike proposed that human learning is motivated and succeeds when it produced a "satisfying effect" or facilitated the avoidance of discomfort.[26] Humans thus possess natural interests in enjoying the rewards of positive effects, this approach assumes, which gives rise to motivations for action. W. H. Thorpe also theorized human behavior as animated by drives for biological survival.[27] Environmental conditions producing unmet needs (for air, food, water, and such) stimulate the brain, Thorpe explained, to generate felt drives that activate behavior directed at meeting those needs and so maintaining homeostatic balance that ensures organism survival. Finally, Harvard Business School professor Paul Lawrence claims in his "Renewed Darwinian Theory of Behavior" that humans are driven by four basic motivations: the drives to acquire (to obtain things that enhance reproductive success), to defend (to protect that which is acquired), to comprehend (to understand the surrounding world), and to bond (to connect and relate to fellow human beings).[28]

Basic Desires or Interests. An alternative conceptual approach to human motivations for action than "needs" is that of basic desires. Whereas needs conceptually entail satisfying already-fixed requisites, the idea of desires connotes a more forward-looking, ends-oriented, volition-driven outlook. Desires are said to generate and direct action not in order to meet recurrently felt insufficiencies or life requirements. Desires motivate action by providing the energy of wanting, yearning, craving, longing, or aspiring. Thus desires both specify the objects toward which actions are taken and the energy that requires expending to achieve them. Some theorists who emphasize desires tend to conceptualize them in terms of human interests. Ambiguity sometimes troubles their work, however, around whether by interests they mean real, objective human interests, in the strong sense, or simply those things that so happen to recurrently appeal to or draw the attention of many people.

In 1967, the British psychologist Michael Argyle hypothesized what he believed were seven basic human desires that motivate action, one physical and six social.[29] They are:

1. *Biological Needs*: eating, drinking, and bodily comfort.
2. *Dependency*: help, support, protection, and guidance from parents and people in authority.
3. *Affiliation*: warm and friendly responses from and acceptance by peers.
4. *Dominance*: leading in group tasks, dominating talk, making decisions, enjoying deference.
5. *Sex*: physical proximity and bodily and eye contact, attractions to and intimate interactions with (normally) the opposite sex.
6. *Aggression*: harming other people physically, verbally, emotionally, and so on.
7. *Self-Esteem and Ego-Identity*: receiving approval from and acceptance by other people.

This approach illustrates the sometimes-unclear boundaries between needs-based and desires-based theories. Here basic human needs give rise to basic desires, which propel actions.

More recently, the UCLA psychologist Steven Reiss has enumerated "16 basic desires and values that drive nearly everything we do," as he claims.[30] By "basic" Reiss means that they are things nearly everyone wants that are common to the human species. These core desires, he argues, are both genetically rooted and culturally influenced. "Our basic desires have an evolutionary origin, but they are significantly modified by culture, beliefs, and individual experiences in ways that are still not well understood. What we desire is largely determined by our genes, but how we fulfill our desires is largely determined by culture and experience."[31] According to Reiss, all people have particular "desire profiles" that rank order the sixteen basic desires in a personal hierarchy of value. But all human beings normally desire all of the sixteen items in one way or another. They are:

1. *Power*: the desire to influence others.
2. *Independence*: the desire for self-reliance.
3. *Curiosity*: the desire for knowledge.
4. *Acceptance*: the desire for inclusion.
5. *Order*: the desire for organization.

6. *Saving*: the desire to collect things.
7. *Honor*: the desire for loyalty to parents and heritage.
8. *Idealism*: the desire for social justice.
9. *Social Contact*: the desire for companionship.
10. *Family*: the desire to raise one's own children.
11. *Status*: the desire for social standing.
12. *Vengeance*: the desire to get even.
13. *Romance*: the desire for sex and beauty.
14. *Eating*: the desire to consume food.
15. *Physical Exercise*: the desire to exercise muscles.
16. *Tranquility*: the desire for emotional calm.

With Reiss's theory, the list of basic needs, drives, interests, and desires has grown from three, four, five, six or seven to sixteen. We might be skeptical that some of these (for example, saving) are "basic" desires. I also hope that readers have begun to recognize some thematic overlap across the lists we have reviewed thus far.

Not to be outdone by Reiss, though similar to his list of basic desires, Florida State University psychologist Roy Baumeister has advanced his own theory of seventeen basic desires.[32] Baumeister's basic idea is similar to Reiss's, although he differentiates three subtypes of basic desires: those concerned with physical survival and inherited from and shared with the animal world, those concerning human social relationships, and those generated by human culture. While conceptually distinct, these three subtypes are not unrelated, since many social desires serve physical-survival needs and since "the human psyche is an animal that has been retooled for culture."[33] The seventeen basic human desires, according to Baumeister (which he names and discusses but does not often define, although he apparently means much the same as these terms are defined above), are:

Animal Desires
1. Food
2. Pleasure (avoid pain)
3. Self-preservation (avoid injury/death)
4. Curiosity and Understanding
5. Control
6. Money
7. Power
8. Possessions and Territory

Social Desires
9. Belonging
10. Sex

11. Aggression
12. Nurturance, Generativity, Helping

Cultural Created Desires
13. Language use
14. Self-esteem
15. Guilt, Morality, Virtue
16. Success, Wealth, Fame
17. A Meaningful Life

These basic desires are, according to this theory, answers to the question: What do people want? In Baumeister's account, to have desires or wants *is* to be motivated to act, since motivations essentially consist of desires.

Basic Goals. The psychologist Martin Ford, who is the leading advocate of motivational systems theory, has argued along similar lines with many of the above theorists that human action is purposive and motivated by a set of basic ends to achieve.[34] According to Ford, "motivation provides the foundation for learning, skill development, and behavior change by determining how, where, and to what end people will invest their capabilities for behavioral self-construction." In Ford's view, motivations have centrally to do *not* with needs, drives, or desires, but rather with goals. "Goals," he says, "are thoughts about desired (or undesired) states or outcomes that one would like to achieve (or avoid)."[35] The number of basic, substantive human goals that Ford believes generate purposive action is no less than twenty-four. Half of these basic goals concern within-person consequences, their being about affective, cognitive, and self-organization issues. The other half are about person-environment consequences that concern self-assertive social relationships, integrative social relationships, and task goals. Ford then proposes a small number of specific basic goals under each of these subheadings, as follows:

Affective
1. *Entertainment*: Experiencing excitement or heightened arousal; avoiding boredom and stressful inactivity.
2. *Tranquility*: Feeling relaxed and at east; avoiding stressful overarousal.
3. *Happiness*: Experiencing feelings of joy, satisfaction, or well-being; avoiding emotional stress or dissatisfaction.
4. *Bodily Sensations*: Experiencing pleasure associated with physical sensation, movement, or bodily contact; avoiding unpleasant or uncomfortable bodily sensations.
5. *Physical Well-Being*: Feeling healthy, energetic, or physically robust; avoiding lethargy, weakness, or ill health.

Cognitive

6. *Exploration*: Satisfying one's curiosity about personally meaningful events; avoiding a sense of being uninformed or not knowing what is going on.
7. *Understanding*: Gaining knowledge or making sense out of something; avoiding misconceptions, erroneous beliefs, or feelings of confusion.
8. *Intellectual Creativity*: Engaging in activities involving original thinking or novel or interesting ideas; avoiding mindless or familiar ways of thinking.
9. *Positive Self-Evaluations*: Maintaining a sense of self-confidence, pride, or self-worth; avoiding feelings of failure, guilt, or incompetence.

Subjective Organization

10. *Unity*: Experiencing a profound or spiritual sense of connectedness, harmony, or oneness with people, nature, or a greater power; avoiding feelings of psychological disunity or disorganization.
11. *Transcendence*: Experiencing optimal or extraordinary states of functioning; avoiding feeling trapped within the boundaries of ordinary experience.

Self-Assertive Social Relationship

12. *Individuality*: Feeling unique, special, different; avoiding similarity or conformity with others.
13. *Self-Determination*: Experiencing a sense of freedom to act or make choices; avoiding the feeling of being pressured, constrained, or coerced.
14. *Superiority*: Comparing favorably to others in terms of winning, status, or success; avoiding unfavorable comparisons with others.
15. *Resource Acquisition*: Obtaining approval, support, assistance, advice, or validation from others; avoiding social disapproval or rejection.

Integrative Social Relationship

16. *Belongingness*: Building or maintaining attachments, friendships, intimacy, or a sense of community; avoiding feelings of social isolation or separateness.
17. *Social Responsibility*: Keeping interpersonal commitments, meeting social role obligations, and conforming to social and moral rules; avoiding social transgressions and unethical or illegal conduct.
18. *Equity*: Promoting fairness, justice, reciprocity, or equality; avoiding unfair or unjust actions.
19. *Resource Provision*: Giving approval, support, assistance, advice, or validation to others; avoiding selfish or uncaring behavior.

Task Goals

20. *Mastery*: Meeting a challenging standard of achievement or improvement; avoiding incompetence, mediocrity, or decrements in performance.
21. *Task Creativity*: Engaging in activities involving artistic expression or creativity; avoiding tasks that do not provide opportunities for creative action.

22. *Management*: Maintaining order, organization, or productivity in daily life tasks; avoiding sloppiness, inefficiency, or disorganization.

23. *Material Gain*: Increasing the amount of money or tangible goods one has; avoiding the loss of money or material possessions.

24. *Safety*: Being unharmed, physically secure, and free of risk; avoiding threatening, depriving, or harmful circumstances.

If we are to understand human behavior, according to Ford, we must view it as ultimately driven by motivations to achieve these twenty-four basic goals (or instrumental derivatives of them). Such motivated action is influenced by the capacities and constraints of human biological structures and functions, particular social environments, and repertoires of available personal skills in any given case in question.[36] But beneath all cases of human action stand these twenty-four motivation-generating basic goals, which all normal people aspire to achieve.

Basic Capabilities. The neo-Aristotelian University of Chicago philosopher and political and social-development theorist Martha Nussbaum has contributed significantly to our understanding of basic human needs and interests, which she defines in terms of "central human capacities." She argues that all human life involves ten basic capabilities that people are motivated to act to develop and that a good society works to facilitate.[37] They are:

1. Life
2. Bodily health
3. Bodily integration
4. Senses, thought, imagination
5. Emotions
6. Practical reason
7. Affiliation
8. Other species
9. Play
10. Control over one's environment

These, Nussbaum claims, define in a naturalistic, objective way what it means for people to live a good life and what it means for a society to enjoy prosperity. Insofar as they are basic capabilities that normal, healthy people universally possess and seek to develop, we should consider them as informing well our growing list of basic desires, goals, and goods.

The University of Wisconsin at Madison psychologist Carol Ryff has suggested, based on a review of empirical research, that human beings possess six basic interests that they are motivated to achieve, which she calls basic "dimensions of well-being."[38] In order for people to be enjoying basic welfare and happiness in life, she suggests, these six items must be satisfied or realized:

1. *Self-acceptance*: having a positive attitude toward oneself and one's past life.
2. *Purpose in life*: having goals and objectives that give life meaning.
3. *Environmental mastery*: being able to manage complex demands of daily life.
4. *Personal growth*: having a sense of continued development and self-realization.
5. *Positive relations with others*: having caring and trusting ties with others.
6. *Autonomy*: being able to follow one's own convictions.

Ryff and colleagues have empirically tested these basic features of well-being and report finding them to be valid and supported by the data.

Basic Goods. Mozaffar Qizilbash, a professor of economics at the University of York, United Kingdom, has proposed a list of what he calls "prudential values," which he describes as a basic list of "everything that makes a person's life go better." Qizilbash proposes nine of what he believes are consensual, universal ("culturally nonrelative") values, which we might well consider to be basic human goods, which people are motivated to achieve or experience.[39] They are:

1. Health, nutrition, sanitation, rest, shelter, security
2. Literacy, basic intellectual and physical capacities
3. Self-respect and aspiration
4. Positive freedom, autonomy or self-determination
5. Negative freedom or liberty
6. Enjoyment
7. Understanding or knowledge
8. Significant relations with others and some participation in social life
9. Accomplishment (of the sort that gives life a point or weight)

The Oxford University moral philosopher James Griffin argues that humanity naturally has nine of what he calls "prudential values," by which he means goods that are generally intelligible as valuable for any normal human person, and so define basic interests related to a humanly good life.[40] Five of the nine, as Griffin describes it, can be labeled together as "components of human existence." The nine values and goods, Griffin says, that people are motivated to achieve, are the following:

1. *Accomplishment*: real achievement.
2. *Deciding for oneself*: agency (a "component of human existence").
3. *Minimal material goods*: physical survival (a "component of human existence").
4. *Senses and limbs that work*: bodily functioning (a "component of human existence").

5. *Freedom from pain and anxiety* (a "component of human existence").
6. *Liberty*: to read, consider others' ideas, to worship, of speech and association (a "component of human existence").
7. *Understanding*: knowing about oneself and one's place in the world.
8. *Enjoyment*: pleasure, perceptions of beauty, enjoyment of daily life.
9. *Deep personal relations*: mutual relations of friendship and love.

Griffin's concern is to establish the groundwork for thinking about how humans can improve their ethical judgments and beliefs. But this part of his account fits well the present concern, as it posits a specific list of basic human values and goods.

Finally, Oxford and Notre Dame legal philosopher John Finnis has advanced a somewhat different kind of account of what people live for and why they act.[41] His theory is grounded in the Aristotelian and Thomist natural law tradition. Finnis thus does not focus on things like people's needs for survival, empirically common desires, or goals that most people seem to pursue. Instead, he proceeds by exploring basic human goods that are, he observes, universally and necessarily valued by all normal people.[42] Such basic goods, Finnis suggests, can be identified on the basis of "practical understanding in which we grasp the basic values of human existence and thus, too, the basic principles of all practical reasoning." At this level of analysis, a human good is not (yet) a matter of morality, but simply an object of fundamental value in human life, without which nobody could live anything like a flourishing life. Finnis derives from this general approach seven "basic goods." By "basic" he means that "each is equally self-evidently a form of good," "none can be analytically reduced to being merely an aspect of any of the others," and "each one, when we want to focus on it, can be reasonably regarded as the most important. Hence, there is no objective hierarchy amongst them."[43] The seven basic goods, according to Finnis, are these:

1. *Life* (self-preservation)
2. *Knowledge* (finding out, understanding truth, curiosity)
3. *Play* (intrinsically enjoyable performances)
4. *Aesthetic Experience* (beauty)
5. *Sociability* (friendship, peace, harmony)
6. *Practical Reasonableness* (using intelligence to face problems, choose actions, lifestyles, character)
7. *"Religion"*[44] (origins and order of the cosmos, authority over human freedom)

Finnis argues that these basic goods are "self-evident, obvious" and "not demonstrable, for they are *presupposed or deployed in anything that we would count as demonstration.* . . . Although they cannot be verified by opening one's eyes and taking a look, they are obvious—obviously valid—to anyone who has experience of inquiry into matters of fact or of theoretical judgment."[45] One thus does not start somewhere else more certain and argue for the validity of these basic goods. They are the fundamental basis that the justification of anything else must presuppose. The basic good of knowledge, for instance, simply cannot be proven or argued but is obviously assumed from the very start by any reasonable discussion about any goods, values, or anything else.

Finnis's account is different from most of those above in various ways. According to him, for example, the "basic goods" of humanity are not needs, desires, or goals—they "are not like the definitive objectives of particular projects." Rather, they are simply "*participated in.*"[46] The good is not so much accomplished as something in or of which is shared or partaken. Furthermore, basic goods cannot be "maximized" by calculation (as desires or the ends of goals might be), since, being "basic" (in Finnis's sense), they are incommensurate, and since the action alternatives indicated by any one good are nearly infinite, rendering rational calculations impossible.[47] Moreover, unlike many of the descriptive theories above—Nussbaum, Qizilbash, and Griffin being exceptions—Finnis's account (eventually) generates a normative orientation to action, commending certain behaviors (and, implicitly, their motivations) as good and others as bad. For example, Finnis suggests, "one should not choose to do any act which *of itself does nothing but* damage or impede a realization of participation of any one or more of the basic forms of human good."[48]

A Thematic Synthesis

What sense ought we to make of these various accounts of basic human needs, drives, desires, interests, values, and goods? One possible response is sheer skepticism. How, readers may ask, can we determine among so many competing theories which one is most adequate? At least some of these accounts seem simply to be generalizations projected from scholars' personal values or experiences of life. And some seem biased toward a liberal, therapeutic, individualistic culture. Are any of these really basic or universal or fundamental sources of motivations and action for all humans? I think this skeptical reaction is understandable. I, too, am dubious of some of the theories noted above. But that does not decide whether some kind of good account of basic human motivations might be possible and useful. If we take a more synthetic approach, I believe we can notice—despite the diversity across these lists and the evident historical locations of their theories—*numerous substantive agreements and thematic repetitions across them.* Table 1 displays the commonalities

TABLE 1. Elementary analytical categories of basic goods nesting the common elements of existing theories about basic human needs, drives, desires, interests, values, capacities, and goods

	Body: physical survival, security, and pleasure	Knowledge: conscious, reflexive, self-transcending experience and understanding	Identity: developed and sustained incommunicable selfhood	Agency: centers of purpose, causation, and action	Morality: moral commitment and practice	Sociality: intersubjectivity, communication, and loving relationships
H. A. Murray	air, food, water, sex, lactation, urination, defecation, avoidance of danger, unpleasant stimuli, excessive heat and cold, gratification of the senses, and rest and sleep	cognition, exploration, inquiry, knowing, satisfying curiosity	status defense, avoiding humiliation; defensiveness, averting defeat	to acquire, conserve, order, retain, construct with material objects; prestige and self-enhancement, superiority; achievement, recognition, respect, self-exhibition; exercising power, dealing with others' power, independence, aggression; avoiding blame, dominance, submissiveness, resignation		affection, affiliation, friendliness, cooperation, support, nurture, dealing with rejection
Jacob Alsted	security, comfort, safety, warmth, care (anxiety of insecurity)		independence, self-assertion, recognition (anxiety of dependence)	competence, understanding, agency, mastery, risk for gain (anxiety of stagnation)		joy of belonging (anxiety of isolation)
Erich Fromm	basic animal needs	frame of orientation, rootedness	sense of identity	effectiveness, excitation and stimulation, rootedness	unity, transcendence	relatedness, rootedness, unity
Jonathan Turner	material/symbolic gratification	sense of facticity, ontological security, trust, reduce anxiety	sustain self-conception			group inclusion

		understanding	enhancing self	controlling	enhancing self	belonging, trusting
Susan Fiske		understanding	enhancing self	controlling	enhancing self	belonging, trusting
Abraham Maslow	physiological (air, water, food, clothing, shelter, sex, excretion), safety (physical security, resource security, health, wellbeing, avoidance of illness and accidents)		esteem (self-respect, being valued, status, recognition, attention, confidence)	self-actualization (realizing full personal potential, fulfilling promise and capabilities)	self-actualization (realizing full personal potential, fulfilling promise and capabilities)	love and belonging (family, friendship, intimacy, group participation)
Edward Deci and Richard Ryan				competence, autonomy		relatedness
Maureen Ramsay	physical survival, sexual needs, security		esteem and identity	self-realization		love and relatedness, sexual needs
Manfred Max-Neef	subsistence, protection, leisure	understanding	identity	creation, freedom		affection, participation, leisure
Kai Nielsen	adequate sustenance, shelter, security, protection, sexual gratification, rest, recreation		respect of person, recognition	meaningful work, amusement, recreation		love, companionship, sense of community
Ervin Staub	security, long-term satisfaction	comprehension of reality, transcendence	positive identity	effectiveness and control		connection
Paul Lawrence	acquire and defend	comprehend		acquire and defend		bond

(continued)

TABLE 1. (*continued*)

	Body: physical survival, security, and pleasure	Knowledge: conscious, reflexive, self-transcending experience and understanding	Identity: developed and sustained incommunicable selfhood	Agency: centers of purpose, causation, and action	Morality: moral commitment and practice	Sociality: intersubjectivity, communication, and loving relationships
Michael Argyle	biological needs, sex, dependency (help from elders)		self-esteem and ego identity	dominance, aggression		affiliation
Steven Reiss	eating, romance, (emotional) tranquility	order, curiosity		physical exercise, power, independence, saving	idealism, honor, vengeance	social contact, acceptance, status, family
Roy Baumeister	food, pleasure (avoid pain), self-preservation (avoid injury, death), sex	curiosity, understanding, language use	self-esteem, fame	control, money, power, possessions, territory, aggression, success, wealth	guilt, morality, virtue, a meaningful life	belonging, nurturance / generativity / helping
Martin Ford	entertainment, tranquility, happiness, bodily sensations, physical wellbeing, safety	exploration, understanding, intellectual creativity,	positive self-evaluations, unity, transcendence	individuality, self-determination, superiority, resource acquisition, mastery, task creativity, management, material gain		belongingness, social responsibility, equity, resource provision
Martha Nussbaum	life, bodily health, bodily integrity, play	sense, thought, imagination, emotions		control over one's environment, practical reason		affiliation, play, other species

Carol Ryff			self-acceptance, personal growth, purpose in life	environmental mastery, autonomy	purpose in life	positive relations with others
Mozaffar Qizilbash	health, nutrition, sanitation, rest, shelter, security, enjoyment	understanding or knowledge, literacy and basic intellectual and physical capacities	self-respect and aspiration	accomplishment, positive freedom, autonomy or self-determination, negative freedom or liberty		significant relations with others and some participation in social life, enjoyment
James Griffin	minimum material goods, Senses and limbs that work, enjoyment, freedom from pain	understanding, senses and limbs that work, freedom from anxiety	deciding for oneself	accomplishment, liberty, senses and limbs that work, deciding for oneself/ agency	understanding (moral)	deep personal relations, enjoyment
John Finnis	life (self-preservation), play (intrinsically enjoyable performances),	knowledge (finding out, understanding truth, curiosity), aesthetic experience (beauty)		practical reasonableness (using intelligence to face problems, choose actions, lifestyles, character)	"religion" (origins and order of the cosmos, authority over human freedom)	sociability (friendship, peace, harmony)

Sources: See notes for each theorist above.

Note: Some items are placed in two cells when, according to their theorist's descriptions, they seem to satisfy more than one basic good named.

that I see across the accounts noted above by thematic categories. By following a procedure of (1) aligning common themes and (2) compressing what seem to be nonbasic ideas into more basic concepts, we can combine and reduce the many theories described above into what I suggest is a highly reasonable list of potentially basic motivations for action. None of the items mentioned above needs to be eliminated, all properly fit within one of the six organizing thematic columns. And most cells are filled. Doing this suggests that the widely shared beliefs by many scholars in different fields can be reasonably reorganized for our purposes into six basic human interests or motivations for action.

Of course, simply because these six items represent the outcome of a sorting through the theoretical accounts of needs, desires, interests, and goods reviewed above does not make them the best or correct list. However, with the weight of the synthesis of these many scholarly accounts standing behind this proposed list, I think the burden increasingly shifts to skeptics to advance a better alternative or an entirely different framing of the matter.

Basic Human Goods and Interests

At this point my argument turns an important corner. Until now in this chapter I have simply reviewed what other scholars have observed and argued about basic human needs, desires, interests, or goods that motivate human action. I am now prepared to embrace what we have learned from these existing accounts and advance my own approach. I just observed that the variety of ideas, numbers, and proposals in the theories reviewed above actually—upon a closer inspection of the patterns involved—sort and sift themselves down to a more limited number of highly common themes. I count six in number.[49] This procedure I believe produces a reliable inventory of basic human motivations. Identifying the common themes running across all of the existing accounts offered by various fields of study above I think renders a highly workable starting point for further developing a theory of basic human goods, interests, and motivations for action.[50] To this point, however, I have been moving laterally across various descriptive accounts to get to this point of departure. I now turn the corner and head more directly toward the goal of this book.

My argument runs as follows. Basic human motivations for action do indeed exist in a finite set, which thoughtful inquiry can adequately identify and name. Those motivations are "basic" because they are oriented toward achieving basic human goods. Human motivations are thus closely tied to human goods, *and*, I suggest, to human interests, as follows. Human being involves certain natural, universal, basic *goods*. Some specific things are by nature simply good for human persons, what constitute "the good" for them. The basic *interest* of human persons is to realize those basic goods. Humans have the natural, real interest in achieving what for them is good. And these basic human interests are what produce our basic human *motivations*. Humans are motivated most basically to realize their basic interests, and every other motivation and purpose springs from this elementary fact. In short, we human persons are most basically motivated to achieve our basic human interests, to enjoy what we think are our basic human goods.[51] My procedure for identifying the six basic goods follows this method: to count as truly basic goods, the candidates must be (1) *basic*, that is, a good that is not instrumental for achieving yet another good but that achieves a value desired for its own sake; (2) *irreducible*, that is, incapable of being further subclassified under another category; (3) *motivational*, that is, a potential basis for a good reason or motivation for action; and (4) *sufficient* as a potential motivator, that is, representing a complete and adequate reason for acting even in the absence of additional relevant motivations.[52]

Having sifted through the varying theoretical accounts above and considered them through retroductive reasoning in light of a personalist view of persons in this way, I propose that human persons are ultimately motivated to all action by six, distinct, basic, natural human goods and interests, as follows:

1. *Bodily Survival, Security, and Pleasure*: avoiding bodily death, injury, sickness, disease, and sustained vulnerability to harm; maintaining physical and bodily health and safety; sensual enjoyment, satisfaction, delight, or gratification of appetitive and perceptual desires of the body; and the absence of physical pain and suffering.

2. *Knowledge of Reality:* learning about the world and one's place and potential in it; increasing awareness and understanding of material and social realities; developing or embracing believed-in truths about what exists and how it works that provide order, continuity, and practical know-how to life experience.

3. *Identity Coherence and Affirmation*: developing and maintaining continuity and positive self-regard in one's sense of personal selfhood over time and in different contexts and situations.

4. *Exercising Purposive Agency*: exerting influence or power (broadly understood as transformative capacity) in the social and material worlds, through the application of personal capabilities for perception, reflection, care, evaluation, self-direction, decision, and action, which causes desired (and unanticipated) effects in one's environment.

5. *Moral Affirmation*: believing that one is in the right or is living a morally commendable life, by being, doing, serving, thinking, and feeling what is

good, correct, just, and admirable; avoiding moral fault, blame, guilt, or culpability.

6. *Social Belonging and Love*: enjoying recognition by, inclusion and membership in, and identification with significant social groups; loving and being loved by others in significant relationships.

These six, to employ a chemistry metaphor, compose something like the sociological "periodic table" defining the basic elements of human interests and motivations. All other interest and motivational configurations are compounds or mixtures that are grounded in and so can be traced back to one or more of these six. Those basic goods and interests can and do give rise to myriad secondary, intermediate, proximate, instrumental interests and motivations. And the entire process is mediated and influenced by the particularities of personality, cultural, and social structures and institutions, as described below. But these six basic human goods and interests are what constitute the deep wellsprings of all human motivations, including all secondary purposes, interests, and activities that result and follow.

Theorists of human motivations, we have seen, have tried many ways to frame them in terms that they are believed to be most basically oriented— needs, drives, desires, goals, pleasures, capacities, values, and other related concepts. I believe the best way to understand the *fundamental* orientation of basic human motivations is in relation to what people experience and understand to be *good*, what is their personal good, which always also references a larger understanding of the human good.[53] People's basic life energies and processes are finally oriented toward what they believe to be good for themselves as persons, which is inevitably embedded in more expansive notions about what is good for human beings generally.[54] This approach links a social scientific concern with human motivations with the *eudaimonian*, virtues-based approach to moral life most often associated with the neo-Aristotelian tradition of ethics,[55] and so is most closely aligned with those of Finnis, Griffin, Qizilbash, Ryff, and Nussbaum above.

Goods Grounded in Personal Ontology

The point must be made again that these basic goods and interests are *not* ultimately socially constructed, variable, and relative. They are natural, stable, and universal. Of course, exactly *how* basic human goods, interests, and motivations are specifically understood and empirically pursued *is* culturally variable. But that is an entirely different fact than the common constructionist belief that they are culturally constructed and relative per se. Human persons and cultures do *not* independently determine their own basic goods, interests, and motivations. Those are given by the nature of reality. Humans only determine how their basic goods, interests, and motivations are interpreted (within feasible bounds) and acted upon. My argument is naturalistic, in that sense. Yet since personalism understands all human knowledge as conceptually mediated and subjectively experienced, my account builds in a necessary active human participation in the transformation of basic goods, interests, and motivations into actual actions and practices. And that, as we will see, introduces a complicating, yet tractable, wrinkle we will need to make sense of.

Meanwhile, the basic point here needs driving home. The real ontology of human personhood is what defines natural, basic, human goods and interests, and these natural interests give rise to natural motivations to action. The social world plays the subsequent but important role of mediating and governing the expression, direction, and character of those person-generated motivations as they are directed toward and worked out in action. The influence of the social thus comes in at an analytically and temporally second stage in the process of nature giving rise to motivated action. Human persons are not "blank slates" upon which social orders simply inscribe their marching orders, which persons then responsively follow. Human persons come to social life equipped with a definable set of natural interests, by virtue of their natural ontological constitution and place in the totality of reality and the goods that involves. And those interests naturally generate a particular set of basic motivations to action. Only once those natural, interest-generated motivations have been put into play does any social order direct, mediate, and inform how, when, why, and where they are to be expressed and satisfied.

I mean that "only once" (in the previous sentence) both analytically and with empirical temporality. Analytically, the influence of the social comes to bear on an interest and motivational structure that already exists and operates at the more basic level of persons ontologically. According to personalism, persons exist and operate at a lower or more basic level of reality than do social and cultural orders. The latter are emergent from acting persons, and so personal interests and motivations cannot and do not create motivations, understood analytically. Basic human interests and motivations also precede social orders in empirical temporality. We know that social orders begin to interact with new human persons even before they are born—through social-structurally generated differences in nutrition, maternal health, household stress, prenatal care, and so on. But those social orders are not influencing inert or motivationally unspecified biological organisms. New human persons, both before they are born and after, are by their ontological nature densely packed bundles of innate, bodily grounded capacities and tendencies, which immediately specify their natural interests, given their place in the larger order of reality. And those interests, in turn, immediately define those new persons' basic motivations. The social does not generate that reality, but subsequently responds to, works with, and influences and directs it. The latter process, of course, is immensely important for understanding social life. But it should not be confused with the creation of basic human interests and motivations. Again, persons are not ontologically but *developmentally* dependent on the social world.

It is possible to identify in a sociological analysis a set of social causal mechanisms that explain some event or outcome of sociological concern without pushing all the way down to unpacking the underlying ontology of human personhood and basic interests and motivations that makes those mechanisms possible. It is usually adequate for sociologists to point to ideas like institutional isomorphism, resource mobilization, social-network density, market competition, or some other causal mechanisms that explain a particular case. However, if we want the sociological project *more broadly* to do the work of *science*, then somewhere in our theorizing we do need to explicate the underlying conditions and processes that make our social casual mechanisms work. Among all of the tasks of sociology as a social science belongs the work of describing the underlying human *personal* reality that makes possible and deploys (intentionally and unintentionally) the social causal mechanisms that we offer to explain social life.

The ontological nature of reality is what makes that possible. It is because basic human motivations are not random or absolutely relative but rather ultimately grounded in and generated by the stable, universal nature of human personhood that it is possible to identify a useful and reliable account of basic human goods and interests that give rise to basic motivations for action. Because of this, the broad agreement observed across the many theories examined above is not surprising. That agreement comes from the fact that different observers in different disciplines are ultimately accounting for the same natural fact of human personhood that they observe and experience. Once organized in a way that reveals the genuine commonalities and agreements, it is possible to reduce the differences across the rival theories into a reasonable list of six basic human motivations. And that list comports well with the account of the nature of personhood and human interests advanced here.

Because these human goods are natural, they are also objective to human existence, in that they are goods independent of any person's subjective awareness of them as such—they remain true human goods even when someone does not know or accept them as goods. Very rarely does the latter ever happen, however. Those six natural human interests normally give rise in human experience to six basic human *motivations*. To be clear, those motives are felt, triggered, and expressed *in* phenomenological experience, but they are not ultimately generated *by* experience—their existence is grounded outside of and prior to experience, in the ontology of personhood, not in the particularities of subjective perception and behavior. Further, it is those six basic human motivations that activate, animate, or propel human *action* of all kinds. And human action provides the energy for the existence and operation of all social causal mechanisms.

Unpacking Some Complexity

One important feature of this personalist approach is the irreducible *multiplicity* of goods, interests, and motivations. Basic human goods cannot for the sake of parsimony be further compacted into less than six without doing unacceptable violence to them. This has implications for standard social science theories. Consider, for example, utilitarianism and its hedonic reference point. The nature of personhood is such that purely materialistic or hedonistic accounts of motivations cannot suffice to explain the range of important human motives and actions, since personhood naturally entails other and "higher" goods than merely material acquisition or hedonic satisfaction. Those kinds of materialistic and hedonic grounds of motives do not exhaust the full range of basic human goods and interests that generate people's motivations for action.[56] Hedonic materialism presents too "flat" a view of human nature, goods, and interests—which is why full-blown utilitarian-based analyses that rely on hedonic materialism always turn out to be flat too. Human personhood entails natural goods and interests that are nonmaterial and nonhedonic in the narrow senses.[57]

The irreducible multiplicity and incommensurability of goods and interests also often involves interaction. The six basic interests and the basic motivations they generate do not run on their own parallel sets of "tracks," independent in direction and effect from the others.[58] All of the basic interest-driven motivations can and usually do interact with each other in complex ways in particular situations and contexts to produce different effects and outcomes. Sometimes different basic motivations interact to reinforce each other to overdetermine particular actions. Other times they may generate competing causal forces that complicate, weaken, intensify, or multiply actions. In some cases, different motivations produce different lines of action that can combine in one unit of personal or social life in coherent ways. Other times the differing actions that the distinct combinations of motivations generate conflict and perhaps even neutralize each other. These kinds of interactive complexities are what force most people at the personal level to spend

large amounts of thought, desires-management, and emotions-work to negotiate the basic intended and unintended pushes and pulls of the purposive
goals and means in their lives. It takes most people spending a lot of mental,
affective, and volitional effort to manage the flows of consequences generated
by the complexities of multiple, interacting human interests and motivations
involved their life projects. These complexities are also what generate at the
social level the need for people to develop and rely upon the cultural and institutional recipes, schemas, routines, practices, and structures that organize
most of social life. Finally, these complexities are also what create the complicated and sometimes difficult life conditions that form people's unconscious
structures, which also shape their actions. So a great deal of personal and
social life is necessitated and driven by the fact that our multiple basic human
interests and motivations interact in complex ways that produce complicated
outcomes that vary along multiple lines, depending on their combinations
and situations. If human action were instead motivated by the kind of single
motivations that mono-motive theorists routinely posit as explaining social
life generally, then real personal and social life would be a lot simpler than it
actually is.

My argument so far does not imply that all human motivations are basic.
Most people's motivations concern the realization or achievement of what we
can call intermediate, proximate, or instrumental goods—valuable because
they help to achieve some other goods. The human good is never realized
in one single moment, achievement, or experience. Achieving the true good
is a lifelong quest. What is genuinely humanly good involves complex sub-
dimensions in causally related sequences that link up together in time-space
into coherent life projects in pursuit of the good. Living toward the human
good generally and in any specific personal life always involves the pursuit
of nonbasic as well as basic goods. Crucial in the pursuit of the human good
are complicated, ongoing series of monitoring, evaluations, perceptions,
judgments, choices, and actions giving rise to plans, strategies, and tactics
for living toward basic goods. Discernment, prudence, and other virtues are
required to sort out hosts of possibly compelling beliefs, desires, and emotions, their relations to each other, and the alternative courses of action and
practice to which they might give rise.[59] Therefore, a difference exists between
final, "ends-in-themselves" goods and interests and proximate, "in-order-to"
goods and interests. Of the vast array of human ends, the achieving of which
their related motivations give rise to actions, most are of the latter kind. But
they are oriented toward larger, longer-run, basic, final, or ultimate human
goods.

Motivations oriented toward nonbasic human goods are myriad and

variable, being influenced by the variations of culture and only broadly constrained by the nature of human personhood. Humans possess innumerable
instrumental means by which they may achieve the same final, basic human
goods, not to mention other, proximate, intermediate, instrumental goods.
Only basic human goods are fixed by the stable, universal nature of human
personhood existing in the environment persons live within. Only the basic
motivations to achieve those goods are ineradicable from human existence.
Beyond them, intermediate, nonbasic, proximate, and instrumental interests and motivations are open-ended and countless, limited only by human
imagination and the trajectory of final goods set by the nature of human
personhood.[60]

Real human goods define what are people's real interests, that is, exactly
what is in their interest to achieve, realize, or participate in—which can then
govern their desires, beliefs, purposes, goals, and actions. My account takes
interests to be central in defining human personal and social life. By comparison, some sociological accounts of human life that emphasize meaning,
culture, normative goods, subjective understanding, and personal motivations for action are often conceptualized as different from, or even opposed
to, those emphasizing interest-driven behaviors. The former are associated
with hermeneutical, cultural, interpretive approaches, the latter usually with
materialist theories of production, power, exploitation, and social conflicts
of interest, security, and status.[61] But this distinction and opposition is unnecessary and counterproductive. Human actions are fundamentally interest driven. But real, natural human interests are not properly limited simply to matters of material abundance, power, and security. Human interests
concern the basic goods of personhood, which inescapably include matters
entailing meanings, normative commitments, moral orientations, belief understandings, and even loving relationships. By grounding a realist theory
of motivations and interests in understandings of the human good—rather
than in narrow, materialist assumptions about needs, self-interest, power,
or whatever—personalism is able to develop a normatively oriented theory
that explains human interests *and* an interest-based theory that accounts for
normativity, morality, meaning, culture, and other higher forms of human
interest.

Multiple Mediations

Along with these complexities, we must add the fact that persons' basic and
nonbasic motivations for action are never directly applied from nature to
action, but rather are mediated through multiple modes of human particu-

larity. First, people's natural motivations are always *meditated through cul-ture*.[62] Whatever is stable and universal across human nature and the human condition—which is a lot—is also always worked out in time-space in and through particular cultural contexts.[63] The structures of beliefs, desires, and emotions that give rise to complex human motivations are powerfully influenced by culturally meaningful, enabling, and constraining basic cognitive categories, conceptualizations of reality, definitions of situations, and normative directions.[64] Human motivations are in part defined, formed, and energized culturally by the particular meanings, categories, schemas, concepts, trends, ideas, norms, expectations, currents, concerns, problems, moralities, and other aspects of intelligibility and significance that human cultures provide and sustain.[65] Different human cultures therefore orient, constitute, and propel somewhat different structures of human motivation and, therefore, action. And those contexts powerfully influence the conceivable content, boundaries, textures, directions, and other qualities of the motivations involved. Therefore, particular social scientific accounts of human motivations and actions will necessarily have to engage, describe, and interpret the specific character of the culture or cultures that provided the context of those motivated actions.[66]

Motivated human actions are always facilitated, governed, and constrained by the ordering causal powers of *social institutions and structures*. To observe that human action is motivated in no way denies that human action is also powerfully organized, constrained, and directed by the causal capacities of social institutions and structures.[67] In fact, motivated action, on the one hand, and social institutions and structures, on the other, presuppose and depend upon each other. Neither could exist and operate without the other.[68] Both are dialectically engaged with and implicated in each other. Everything that the social sciences have learned about the power and importance of social institutions and structures in the shaping of human behavior and action can be fully acknowledged and embraced as consonant with a theory of motivated action. Likewise, every institutional and social-structural theory of human social relations must also recognize and account for the reality and centrality of motivated human action for generating and sustaining human social life.[69]

Finally, human motivations for action are also always *mediated at the level of personality* through specific structures of personal beliefs, desires, and emotions. Motivations for action at the level of the person—however ultimately grounded in nature and at a basic level shared across humanity they actually are—never are played out in a generic or uniform way that can ignore the reality of individual embodiment, autobiography, or personality. People act on motivations not as interchangeable or standard specimens of some general human species or class of entity. They do so rather as unique personal beings who not only share a common humanity but also instantiate that humanity in distinct personal lives involving particular structures of beliefs, desires, and emotions. People are never merely the neutral energy and physical material by which natural human goods are realized through the triggering of motivations for action, but rather persons operating with agency. The agency that persons exercise in the pursuit of their naturally defined human good always operates in and through structures of belief, desire, and emotion that are particular at the level of individual personality. The basic goods of human life are indeed shared across humanity. However, they must nevertheless always be pursued by specific persons in historically and culturally specific circumstances through structured processes of cognition, volition, and affect of those particular persons. Stated differently, each person's beliefs, desires, and emotions provide the medium by which their specific motivations are mobilized, and each person's particular structure of cognition, volition, and affect influences the character and content of their motivations for action.

Analytically, social scientists may in various circumstances be required and entitled for methodological reasons to bracket out of their analyses such personal differences in beliefs, desires, and emotions (and often they are focused instead on group averages of attitudes, beliefs, opinions, and so on). That is frequently necessary and legitimate for particular kinds of investigations (even if other investigations definitely require understanding persons' beliefs, desires, and emotions). Even so, in principle, at the level of general social-scientific theory seeking to describe in the social world what exists and how it works, it is necessary to identify, recognize, and take seriously real, acting human persons whose motivations are mediated through structures of beliefs, desires, and emotions, social structures and institutions, and cultural meanings.

The Proposed Model

The ideas I have described so far (and some that I have not yet explained) are depicted in the abstract in figure 5. Reading up from the bottom, we see that the goods, interests, motivations, and resulting actions of human life are most deeply rooted and determined by the given ontological nature of human persons. What persons *are* ultimately governs what they want, think, feel, and do. The first step up notes that the ultimate human telos or purpose of life is the flourishing of personhood. That natural human ontology and telos give rise to the six basic human goods and interests of human life

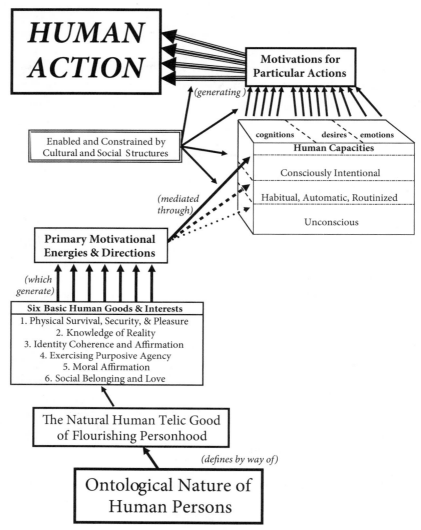

FIGURE 5. A personalist model of human goods, interests, motivations, and actions.

named above. Pursuing and realizing the six basic goods constitutes a life that is flourishing. Those goods and interests in turn generate the primary motivational energies and directions of human activity, which give human life its particular dynamism and orientations toward action. Importantly, however, those primary motivational energies and directions do not directly produce particular motivations and actions. They are always mediated through structures of personality and social life. Thus the primary motivational energies and directions work through the particular consciously intentional, habitual-automatic-routinized, and unconscious capacities of human persons, operating through cognitions, desires, and emotions. In this way, natural human motivational energies and directions that are generated by basic human goods and interests are mediated through a host of personal and social particularities in ways that produce very specific motivations for particular actions. All of that, too, is enabled, constrained, and otherwise conditioned in myriad ways by the downwardly causal influences of cultural and social structures. Human persons then act (or not) upon those motivations to produce their actions and associated activities, such as social practices.

Figure 5 can be read backward for a different direction of analysis. Why do people do what they do? What causes and guides human activity? People's actions are often motivated. Particular constellations of beliefs, desires, and emotions form to produce motives to act in various ways. Those beliefs, desires, and emotions operate at complexly multiple levels of the person, from the most consciously aware and intentional through the habitual and automatic down to the fully unconscious. Furthermore, all of those operations at the level of distinct human persons are normally profoundly shaped by the influences of many cultural and social structures that impinge in various ways on the subjective and material lives of persons.[70] But from where comes the force, drive, and direction that organizes and energizes people's particular cognitions, desires, and emotions that produce specific motivations? Beneath and generating the myriad specific motivations that cause people's particular actions surge up the more primary motivational energies and directions that represent the core vitality and orientation of human life. And these are produced by the basic human motivations to realize the six basic human interests, which are defined by the six basic human goods. Humans by nature seek to accomplish these goods, ultimately in order to realize the final human end of personal flourishing. And all of that is so not because "society" defines it as such. "Society" operates at a much higher level through the enabling and constraining, contextual, developmental influences it exerts on persons and their motivations. Humans by nature seek to accomplish these goods, instead, because of the given ontological nature of their human personhood.

That is simply the sorts of animals humans are—persons—and the proper kinds of goods and interests particular to human personhood.

Social science is familiar and generally comfortable with the top half of this model, everything above the primary motivational energies and directions part. Some of the social sciences, such as economics, are even comfortable with the idea of basic human interests, the step below. They simply theorize those interests differently, more simplistically. Where most in social science part ways with my account is the readiness to specify the multiplicity of basic human goods, to conceive of human life as caught up in the pursuit of a natural teleological good of flourishing, and ultimately to acknowledge the reality of an ontology of human personhood. But in trying to avoid such matters, people in the social sciences create a problem for themselves. For if social science starts only with enabling and constraining cultural and social structures and with people's capacities to think, want, and feel, then it lacks an account explaining where the motivational *interests, energy,* and *direction* for action come from. Macrolevel theories—whether normative or materialist—locate the source of energy and direction somehow in the cultural or social structures of "society." Microlevel theories—whether acquisitive or meaning driven—locate the source of the energy and direction in some feature of the individual agent. (And advocates of the evolve-neuro-genetic-biochemically-behavers view locate the energy and direction in genes, neurons, hormones, and the like.) But the macrolevel strategy does not work, unless one is prepared to posit the existence of a real social-level person-like *agent* existing not emergently from but independently of and over human activity. But that is wrong. Behind every successful macrosocial explanation stand some assumptions about the microfoundations and dynamics of action. And so we come back to persons. None of the major microlevel theories currently on offer suffice either. None are outright wrong, but all are incomplete and therefore unacceptable. Grounding all of human activity in either hedonic rationality or definition-and-meaning-establishing interactions as the micro model, for example, is woefully deficient. Those are far too incomplete views of reality.

We need a better account. We have to explain the interests, energy, and direction of and for human activity in a way that is more realistic, that best comports with all we know about ourselves as human persons living in the world. We need an account with adequate complexity. We need an account that fixes an anchor somewhere in the bedrock of the nature of reality. That is what personalism offers. Before moving on, we will do well to ponder the kind of alternative approach that we are forced to accept if we reject the kind of account I have proposed here.

Considering the Alternatives

A skeptic of the idea that these are in fact natural, basic goods and interests of human persons would presumably argue that one or more of the goods I have theorized are not goods, or are not basic, or are not natural. The first argument would be difficult to make stick, for it would have to convince people that the proposed six goods are not good for people or in people's interests to realize. But which of the six is a likely candidate for that argument? Everything we know about human beings undermines that view. The second skeptical argument is also difficult to make work, for it requires showing that one or more of these goods is actually not really basic but a subcomponent of another one. But which among these are contenders for that argument? Accomplishing some of these goods can also help accomplish others. But that is different from saying one is a mere subsidiary of another. These six seem to be irreducible to each other. Another way to make this second skeptical argument work would be to show that one or more of these six goods does not achieve ends that are of value or worth in and of themselves, but instead are secondary and instrumental for achieving other goods. But can we say that? It is hard to see how we can about any of them. Sometimes some of these can be pursued for instrumental reasons—such as gaining knowledge of reality, say, about how to stay afloat in water so as not to drown, in order to survive under certain conditions. But that itself does not make knowledge about reality a not-basic good. Not all knowledge about reality is sought by people as mere instrumental means to achieve some more basic interest. Humans, lo and behold, consider gaining knowledge about reality as a good in and of itself, and the failure to achieve knowledge about reality would be devastating. The same, I contend, is true for all six of these goods. That means that they are all basic goods.

The third skeptical argument, that these six may be basic goods but are not natural, is also unworkable. I have defined "natural" to mean the stably characteristic features of any entity by virtue of its ontological character. To show that these six goods are not natural, a skeptic might argue that these goods and interests are actually unstable and uncharacteristic among human beings. Alternatively, the skeptic might admit that they are stable characteristics of human being, yet have nothing to do with the ontology of human personhood, but are instead entirely culturally constructed and variable. Neither contention succeeds. No skeptic can find any human culture or society where these six goods are not recognized and prized. Different cultures go about expressing them in different ways, but what they are going about expressing is itself still at bottom the same. Furthermore, human social groups are not volatile or unpredictable when it comes to these goods. No skeptic can show human cultures or societies where sometimes these six goods are valued and other times they are not. The six goods and interests, in short, are durable, universal features of human life. Only in clearly pathological cases of persons—the suicidal, the psychopathic, the schizophrenic, the catatonic— and never in entire social orders, do we find deviations from that fact. All we know about human beings and all of our own personal experiences tells us that these are not simply contingently, artificially, or variably human goods and interests. They are naturally so.

But suppose I am wrong. Suppose that human actions and motivations have no grounding in reality. Imagine that there exist no natural basic human goods, that people's interests are not grounded in an objective condition. Assume that human beings have no real nature or basically constituting organization or orientation toward valued ends. Suppose, in short, that the bottom half of figure 5 is a fiction. Imagine that only the top half of figure 5—the empirical ideas, desires, and emotions operating at various levels of human consciousness and influenced by various cultural and social structures—are real. What then?

Not many social scientists may have thought this scenario all the way through. For the alternatives are inconsistent with most of the worlds in which I assume most social scientists would want to live, understanding what was at stake. Here again, we cannot segregate off the moral and political from the theoretical, even though they are distinct. We all live in a single reality in which the moral, political, and theoretical hang together. Personalist theory explains why a realistic humanism is both possible and necessary. Human persons are the primal causes of their own actions. They are neither autonomously free nor deterministically controlled. They are highly structured, defined, mediated, influenced, and oriented by many ontological, personal, material, and social forces and factors. Yet each human person is finally the active agent—personalism's "center with purpose"—of his or her subjective processes, decisions, and external actions. People do not construct themselves, their interests, or their core motivations in life out of thin air or on their own, as they wish. The primary elements of those features are given by nature. But persons do actively participate in the pursuit of their own natural goods, in the teleological realization of their interests and ends as persons as members of the human species. In this sense, persons are the real, capacitated, and responsible agents of their own lives—even if those lives are significantly enabled, constrained, and mediated by extrapersonal factors. That is the vision of human beings that gives rise to, is consistent with, and ultimately sustains a realistic humanism in personal and social life.

And what of the alternatives? What if humans have no genuine basic goods grounded in reality? What if humans have no ends that are proper to the nature of their being? Or what if they do but human nature turns out to be very different from what personalism describes? Suppose, for example, that utilitarianism's postulate of hedonic rationality is true, or that the advocates of the evolved neuro-genetic-biochemically behavers model are correct. What then? I think the honest answer is the dissolution of the human person possessing dignity and the loss of any rational basis for a humanistic social order. That sounds drastic. How might it be so?

If in reality there are no real, identifiable, objective human goods, then there exists no good, coherent, justifiable reason why *all* things that humans may conceive or desire are not legitimate options as "goods." If nothing is a true natural good, then anything might potentially be (thought of as a) good. In fact, we have to jettison a substantive notion of "good" itself. For without any natural human good, all that is left are perceived or constructed states or objects that people might call "good." But in reality none is actually better, a greater good, than any other. They just are what they are. But they also exist as the potential objects of human desires. What would remain as a very powerful force would be the human *will*. And those desires, if there really is not natural human good, have every right to be arbitrary. People want what they want. If some people—let us say people like the Marquis de Sade—so happen to think that sexually torturing young women is good, then it is good (for them). Others may disagree, even vehemently, but they have nothing objectively valid to which to appeal in order to explain why torturing young women is not good. Those who desire the latter have every right so say, "You enjoy your 'good' and we'll enjoy our 'good.'" The end of that discussion is ultimately reduced to the will and power—and the strongest volition will prevail, ultimately, whatever their wishes, and can do so without valid moral judgment on them. Nietzsche was not wrong about this (assuming his premises are granted). Nor was Pascal.[71] The normative and moral dissolve into the empirical. Things simply are what they are. Rational references to true or natural goods by which to judge them are fictions. Evaluations about just and unjust, good and bad, and so on are groundless and empty—except as emotivist expressions of (arbitrary) desires and reactions.[72]

In short, strong cultural relativists and constructionists have to face the consequences of relativism, which are not pretty, from a humanistic perspective (which still hopes to judge between the pretty and the ugly). We cannot have both relativism and humanism—they are ultimately mutually exclusive.[73] If "all is really relative," then rational judgments to evaluate the normative merits of any of the parts of that "all" in ways that build humanistic practices of life are futile. Anything goes, literally. Relativists then either need to be honest and put their serious moral commitments in a lead box and drop them overboard, or else they might be cunning and manipulate other gullible people to their own arbitrary, emotivist ends by asserting over them "moral" claims as justified that they know in fact to be baseless. The loss of a natural human good thus produces not humanistic persons and social orders, but rather (note my morally fraught adjectives of judgment legitimated by personalism) cynical, capricious, manipulative persons and social relations governed only by desire and power. If that is the kind of people and social orders we want, then, yes, we should deny the reality of a natural human good.

Or what if humanity *does* entail "goods" rooted in the nature of reality, but human nature in particular is in fact very different from what personalism describes? Persons may in reality be out simply to maximize pleasure and minimize pain, or to create and sustain shared definitions and meanings through symbolic interactions. People may be about simply acquiring as much material wealth, power, security, and social status as possible. Or they may be out to fulfill the social expectations of their socialized social roles as well as they are able in order to help meet the functional requisites of society. Those have been major assumptions of various sociological theories. What happens if those ultimately define the natural human "good?" Much the same as described above. If humans are by nature like this, then what is for them "good" is simply more pleasure and less pain, shared and stable definitions and meanings, stockpiles of material goods and domination, or well-oiled role followers and social orders. None of that commends realistic humanism as fitting. Many pleasures can be obtained in ways that violate humanism. Shared and stable definitions and meanings can be upheld through symbolic interaction in the most oppressive, horrific social conditions imaginable. Stockpiles of material goods and power are often gained and defended at other people's real expense, through exploitation, dehumanization, and exclusion. And obedience to the imperatives of social roles toward smooth functioning social orders is as or more consistent with antihumanist collectivism and totalitarianism as with humanism. I am not saying that actual symbolic interactionists, conflict theorists, structural functionalists, and rational-choice thinkers are covert moral relativists and nihilists. Often they are quite the contrary—though mostly because they live with inconsistencies between their scholarship and real life. I *am* saying that if we take seriously the assumptions about human nature, goods, interests, and motivations that are posited by these other theoretical approaches, we end up severely constrained, if not compartmentalized and incoherent, when it comes to rationally explaining and defending realistic humanism. Such a humanism thus has to be imported from outside or smuggled in the back door for reasons having nothing to do with one's social science and its interpretive explanations of the human social world. Personalism provides an alternative.

Toward a Good Life Well Lived

My argument is heading toward a teleological account of human life purpose. People do not act for random reasons. People's actions are grounded motivationally in some basic human interests and goods. But what is the point of those goods and interests? Are they the terminus of the matter, the end of the investigation? No. The basic human goods together point us to and help constitute their own proper end: personal flourishing, deep happiness, thriving, well-being, *eudaimonia*, a good life well lived. Although we humans possess many (I think six) basic goods, that multiplicity does not leave our lives in a jumble, torn between incoherent values or purposes. The six basic human goods themselves constitute, and not simply lead to, a single end. That is our human flourishing as persons. Each of the basic goods is a necessary but insufficient condition for personal flourishing. They provide the major highways by which the single end of human thriving or happiness is reached. Flourishing consists of driving those highways. Achieving any one of the six basic goods alone does contribute to or bring happiness or well-being. But considering any personal life as a whole, all six of the basic goods matter together. The proper human telos of flourishing as persons requires the significant realization of all six basic goods, since they constitute flourishing itself. The failure to achieve any one of the goods severely limits the prospects for realizing personal flourishing. Exactly how much and what kind of realization of our basic human goods is necessary to flourish as persons is a vital issue to sort out, and one that will require serious empirical investigation. Meanwhile, it is helpful to arrange all the conceptual pieces on the table in relation to each other so that the overall pattern of theoretical logic is clear.

Depicting what I have argued in this chapter and how that relates to the final matter of human flourishing is figure 6. In it we see represented the motivated human person, as described by critical realist personalism, acting in a definite direction in order to realize in various ways his or her six basic goods. The person's actions and the prospects of their success are heavily conditioned by two larger contextual forces. One is the social and institutional influences developmentally shaping the achieving person through their highly variable

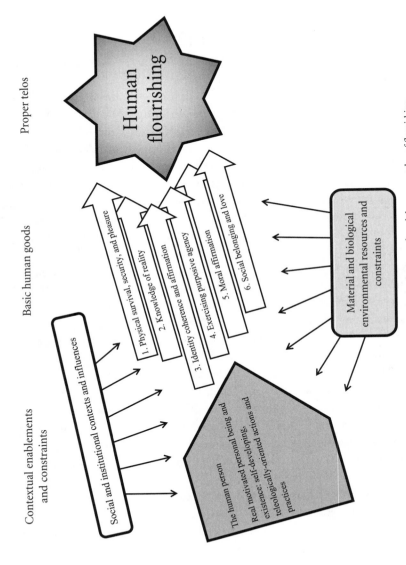

FIGURE 6. The teleologically motivated human person pursuing basic goods and the proper telos of flourishing.

Proper telos

Basic human goods

Contextual enablements
and constraints

Human
flourishing

Social and institutional contexts and influences

1. Physical survival, security, and pleasure
2. Knowledge of reality
3. Identity coherence and affirmation
4. Exercising purposive agency
5. Moral affirmation
6. Social belonging and love

The human person
Real motivated personal being and
existence: self-developing and
teleologically-oriented actions and
practices

Material and biological
environmental resources and
constraints

supply and quality of resources, opportunities, constraints, and so on. The other is the environmental influences of the varying material and biological resources and constraints within which persons live. Most (though not all) of and about the influences of both of those contextual forces remain outside of the immediate control of motivated persons. What acting persons can somewhat control, however, is how they respond to and work with those influencing resources, enablements, opportunities, and constraints. Some people end up doing a lot with a little. Others waste the abundance they enjoy. Good and bad fortune or luck also plays a role in how these dynamics play out. In any case, the personal pursuit of the six basic human goods attempts to coordinate them in relation to each other, so that they are not mutually negating and interactively compromising. Doing that is a major task in human life. And all of that has a proper end: the realization of human personal flourishing, of a good life well lived. That is the natural, proper human personal telos, the end toward which human action is directed, whether poorly or well.[74] The final answer to our original question, then—*What does anyone do with their lives when they wake up from sleep and why do they do that?*—is this: *eudaimonia*, personal flourishing, a good life well lived. And that is constituted and achieved by realizing the six basic human goods.

Conclusion

This chapter has explored the idea of the existence of *basic* human motivations for action—those oriented toward ends that are valued for their own sake. I have argued that we can identify six basic human motivations. They are not constructed by human cultures but determined by the natural interests that persons have in realizing six basic goods of human life. To help identify the six goods, interests, and motivations, I have relied on the ideas, proposals, and theories of numerous prominent scholars in different fields of inquiry who have studied and written about basic human motivations across a century. The knowledge base behind my account here is broad, and the ideas of the best of them, when compared against each other, reveal a clear alignment of common themes. Despite these differences, we discovered a series of parallel themes suggesting common and repeated insights. They point, I proposed, to irreducible and incommensurate basic human goods, interests, and motivations. These six, I argued, are not accidental or variable concerns but rather basic, universal, natural goods, interests, and motivations grounded in the ontological nature of human personhood and the given human condition in this world. They are facts of human nature, common to all but the most pathological cases, which cannot be constructed away. In short,

human activities are indeed ultimately propelled by a finite set of basic motivations generated by the human goods and interests that are proper to human personal being by virtue of the real ontologies that human persons are.
That tells us a lot about human persons, human nature, the human condition, and human life. And it sets us up to explore the next step of the ultimate
human telos, human flourishing itself.

6

Toward a Theory of Flourishing

What does it mean for a human person to live a good life? Can people find direction outside of their immediate desires for genuinely reliable guidance on how to live well? Does life have any real purpose anyway? Or is one way of life no better or worse than any other? How could anyone know? These are some of the most important questions we can ask in life. Their answers determine the kinds of lives people lead and societies people build and defend. But can they be answered? I believe so. This chapter develops personalism on the question of the purpose of human life (note, however, that it also must be read in conjunction with the following chapter). Personalism provides insight into what is genuinely good in human life for practical reasoning in ethics and morality. The idea of a true human good may be difficult for people today to take on. Yet we must if we wish to know the truth about ourselves, understand our actions, and wish to do better social science. But to succeed in this, we have to rise above centuries of thinking that have attempted (and failed) to make sense of life and the world in the absence of any notion of a natural human good. We have to retrieve and renew a more ancient view of thought and life, one that goes back at least to Aristotle,[1] which in recent decades has enjoyed a revival in the academy.[2] I mean the *eudaimonian* or virtues-based tradition of thought and ethics. We do not need to become card-carrying Aristotelians, but we will benefit by learning from neo-Aristotelian theory. Exposure to Aristotle sparked enormously innovative and fruitful thinking in medieval universities, the first universities. It can do the same for us today.

What Is Flourishing?

Let us begin where we ended the last chapter and ask ourselves: how do the six irreducible basic motivations, interests, and goods discussed there relate to each other? I said that they cannot be compressed into one single, all-encompassing good, interest, or master motivation. Where does that leave us? Is life about struggling to realize *six* different goods that may or may not coordinate in their demands or implications? Personalism says there is a larger framework or purpose within which those six basic goods make sense and are coordinated: the flourishing of human personhood. Basic human goods serve the ultimate human purpose. The basic goods are elementary, fundamental, primal. But they are not the end of the matter. Beyond the basic goods stands one telos that frames them and which they serve and constitute.[3] A good way to convey the character of this final end and purpose in life is to name it *flourishing*, also sometimes called here "thriving" or "a good life well lived." All of the six basic human goods serve and comprise this larger end of flourishing. To have a good life is to live in a way that one flourishes as a person. To find reliable guidance beyond ourselves for truly living well is to learn how to practice virtues that are required to flourish. The starting point, rooted in the nature of reality from which all thinking about and living of human life should proceed, concerns the proper human telos: to flourish as the kind of beings that we are, *as persons*. We are not to flourish as apes or gods or something else that we are not. The sky is not the limit. Everything does not go. It is ultimately not up to us to determine what it means to flourish. The features, capacities, and limitations of our naturally given personhood determine that. (Post)modern people may resist or deny this fact. But that does not make it not a fact. It simply means that many (post)modern people have ridden off the rails on some important matters. Reality is what it is, however otherwise we may wish to think about it.

Etymologically, to flourish means "to blossom," to grow and bloom in mature, fruitful, beautiful ways. To thrive, etymologically, means "to seize," to grasp and capture the fullness of life, to live life well to the fullest. All living organisms naturally strive to live, grow, and bloom, to robustly achieve the fullness of their natural capacities. All living organisms work against death, disease, and weakness. The physical functioning of our human bodies works this way. Other natural human capacities are the same. The life of persons is by nature oriented toward learning, becoming, developing, growing, expanding, and maturing.[4] Humans are naturally interested in learning how reality works and what is good. Humans by nature want to exercise their capacities and powers and to master skills. Humans cannot escape making evaluations of better and worse, good and bad, attractive and ugly, just and unjust, praise-worthy and reprehensible. And humans are naturally attracted to what they believe to be higher, better, more appealing. A world in which humans did not seek to learn, grow, and thrive would be quite unlike our world.

Aristotle called the kind of happiness and flourishing I describe here *eudaimonia*. That comes from the Greek words "eu" (good) and "daimōn" (a type of benevolent guardian spirit or minor deity in ancient and Hellenistic Greek religions, mythologies, and philosophy). *Eudaimonia* literally means enjoying the care of a benevolent deity or guardian spirit, which the Greeks considered highly desirable. Philosophical uses of the word by Aristotle and others, however, involve no divine or supernatural references. *Eudaimonia* for Aristotle meant "doing and living well." The word is often translated into English as "happiness," although our impoverished contemporary ideas about happiness and what produces it makes that not the best translation. *Eudaimonia* does not mean simply enjoying a pleasurable condition or experience, being content with one's state of life, or savoring subjective gratification or contentment, as "happiness" usually means today.[5] *Eudaimonia* suggests meanings and conditions that are richer and more profound. Aristotle noted that happiness conceived as pleasure, cheerfulness, or contentment can often be produced for a time by immorality and perversity, while *eudaimonia* is the result of virtue, never immorality. *Eudaimonia* refers not to a moment in time but to an entire life well lived. It references not only a subjective state of consciousness but objective conditions, such as having genuine friends, being virtuous, and enjoying the love of others.[6] The purpose of human life in this sense also involves not only living well but to some extent having life *go* well, expressing right conduct and prosperity. Even so, people may encounter real difficulties that make life unhappy (in the shallow sense) for a time, yet which can promote *eudaimonia* for people if they respond to the difficulties well. So this idea is not about a temporary feeling, but about a good life objectively well lived—the fact that one has with one's life moved toward one's proper telos by living a worthy, proper, and happy life of virtue.[7] I will thus generally use the word flourishing and sometimes thriving and well-being rather than happiness to suggest the rich, complex meanings of *eudaimonia*. That will always mean not simply thriving biologically or emotionally but flourishing in all dimensions of human personhood.[8]

How can anyone know or have good reason to believe that flourishing is the proper telos of human life? That, Aristotle observed, is *self-evident*. Ask people why they do whatever they do (given constraints) and *ultimately* one will hear some version of the answer, "Because I want a life that is happy, flourishing, enjoying well-being." Although many people are not actually flourishing or happy (which I address the next chapter), nobody makes or accepts the purpose of life to be their own demise or wretchedness or living a "bad spirit." Normal people want to be as happy, fulfilled, flourishing, and achieving their potential as well as they understand it and how to achieve it.[9] Aristotle asked, "What is the good for man? It must be the ultimate end or object of human life, something that is in itself completely satisfying. Happiness (*eudaimonia*) fits this description. . . . Surely it is that for the sake of which everything else is done." He argues that the ultimate purpose of life, its final end, must be a supreme good, and "*eudaimonia* more than anything else is . . . just such an end, because we always choose it for itself, and never for any other reason." The perfect good, he claims, must be something "we take to be one which by itself makes life desirable and in no way deficient." That, he says, is *eudaimonia*. "Happiness, then, is found to be something perfect and self-sufficient [i.e., itself making life desirable], being the end to which our actions are directed."[10] In short, *eudaimonia* is life's final goal in itself, the end toward which other actions are engaged (whether well or poorly), that which in and of itself makes life desirable. No larger or higher purpose beyond human flourishing exists in this world. Other goals and activities in life exist to serve the purpose of flourishing.[11]

But how does one achieve a flourishing life? The answer at a personal level is, by becoming as fully as possible in actual *experience* that which one *is* ontologically, namely, a human person. People flourish, thrive, and are most genuinely happy when they develop and actualize what they by nature *are*. Persons are not inert objects. They are living, growing, dynamic beings defined by potentials, powers, and capacities (and limitations). People have a natural disposition to grow, learn, develop, and realize their inherent capacities and powers. We are always in motion, moving (either effectively or badly) toward our telos. Human motivations are *oriented toward* (which is not the same thing as effective in realizing) the natural interests in achieving and participating in those basic goods.[12] Human life thus has a true purpose, not to do whatever one wants or to meld into the collective, but rather to develop the fullness of flourishing personhood. That of course requires human freedom and agency as well as social solidarity and participation. It also requires the right kind of social structures and environmental conditions. This displaces individual autonomy and self-assertion as well as collectivist absorption and obedience as life's proper end. That "flourishing is the final human good" is simply a true, descriptive statement. It is an ineradicable fact that it is good to live in ways that promote and embody personal flourishing, however difficult and unsuccessful that may be.[13]

This approach does not mean that movement toward one's personal good is essentially selfish, since people *must* define their genuine good as also necessarily entailing seeking and serving the well-being of others. But such other-regarding, loving actions are pursued at least in part because people believe them to be leading toward and reflective of what is good, including validly for themselves as persons. "There is no reason in principle why an ethical theory which starts from the perspective of the agent's final end should not allow that the interests of another [person] matter to the agent for their own sake."[14] One cannot thrive without truly and genuinely seeking the thriving of other persons. That is just the way reality is. Again, people normally act to enhance the good in and of their lives.[15] As long as people understand their true good to necessarily entail seeking the well-being of others, that "self-seeking" cultivates love and is morally legitimate.

To make sense of this approach, we must always operate with a substantive understanding of what human persons ontologically *are*. No theory of motivated action can avoid taking, even if implicitly, a substantive position on the ontology of personhood. All theories of motivation flow from tacit or explicit models of the nature of human actors. Without a clear idea of what human persons are, we cannot develop an account of what motivates their action. By my account of human personhood,[16] personal flourishing means at heart being and living as a "self in loving relationships with other personal selves and with the non-personal world." What we are *properly* motivated for action to achieve and how we *ought* to live morally are thus connected in one coherent whole to what is real and how it works. And both entail personal, interpersonal, and social-structural aspects.

Personal Becoming

Living human beings are ontologically 100 percent persons, but they are variable in the *realization in existential experience* of the capacities and tendencies of their personal being. Personhood is a 0/1 fact for humans—there are no fractions or percentages of personhood. All living humans are 1 = person, nothing less. However, the ontology of personhood has *in existential experience* to be developed, grown, and brought to fulfillment. That part varies. Particular persons differ greatly in the extent to which their ontologically real personhood is unfolded and realized in actual existence and experience. Some are only nascent in their development and actualization. Others are impressively mature and developed. Still others are past their primes and declining in various ways. Variation in the empirical expression of the powers and capacities of personhood is obvious. But that must not obscure the ontological fact that all living human beings are 100 percent persons.

Human life is in essence a quest, the proper end of which is to achieve the full existential development and exercise of the powers, capacities, and tendencies of personhood—toward the realization of the six basic goods. I am not saying that this is easily or often achieved, but it is a basic human orientation defining how humans ought to live and in fact how we do live more or less well or badly. Life is about becoming, the realization of personal being, the enjoyment of the six basic goods of human personhood.[17] It is not essentially about experiencing pleasure and avoiding suffering, or acquiring material goods and power. Those may be means to ends, if properly approached. Nor is life about fulfilling the obligations of social roles into which one has been socialized, or reproducing the habitus of one's social order, or generating and maintaining social definitions and meanings through symbolic interactions. Those too may serve the proper telos of personal flourishing. But they are at best partial and subsidiary goods and processes, not the main event. At worst they can become oppressive, manipulative, and dehumanizing, diminishing the expression and enjoyment of personhood. In short, none of the visions of the gist of human life implied by the main alternative sociological accounts capture what human life is really about. Personalism does.

Essential to grasp is the ineradicably *teleological* character of human personal life. Being a person is not about stasis or equilibrium. It is about going somewhere, pursuing an end. Life must entail personal growth, unfolding, and development that moves in right directions (and so also has the potential to move in wrong directions). For human persons, existence is not a happening to simply take in, but an active journey, a movement toward a proper destination. That inherently implies that the present, the status quo, where one is now, is not good enough, not the right place, not the final destination. One needs to move, to change, to get somewhere. To stay put would be to stagnate, to fail to realize one's true end. One has to get on the roads of life, to move toward the goal, to achieve a purpose that is presently unfulfilled. It is not adequate to demand not to be judged as deficient just as one is at present. All persons are incomplete and inadequate just as they are. Everyone needs to progress toward their telos. To be a person requires moving ever nearer toward the goal, toward a fully developed expression of personhood. This is to pursue what the Greeks called *arete*, "excellence." Mere being, surviving, or existing is eventually to slip backward, to move away from the destination. To realize the teleological end requires continually moving forward, developing, striving. (Entailed in that, too, are also appropriate rest, reflection, and appreciation of goods achieved.)

The central question that imposes itself on all persons journeying toward their personal telos is: What means can persons employ to achieve their proper end? What will help people toward excellence of personhood, en route to living up to the fullest potentials of their particular personhood? These are not abstract, technical, or scientific questions, but matters of "practical reasoning"—what Greeks thinkers in the tradition I follow here called *phronesis*, "practical or moral wisdom." These are concrete how-to queries. The answer is that many tried-and-true means exist that persons can and must learn. Aristotle called these "virtues," using the same word *arete*, suggesting the idea of learned moral excellence. Modern people often snicker at virtue-talk, associating it with Victorian prudishness, puritanical repression, or individualistic self-righteousness. But virtues in the *eudaimonian* tradition are different. Virtues are hard-won dispositions and practices of excellence that lead to a flourishing, truly happy life.[18] Virtues are not naive or innocent or smug. They are difficult and experienced and satisfying. Learning and practicing virtues demands discipline and practice, which pays off in human excellence.[19]

Aristotle conceived of the virtues as "golden means," prudently determined middle positions between the extremes of excess and deficiency. Between the extremes of cowardice and rashness is the virtue of courage. Between insensibility and intemperance is the virtue of temperance. Liberality stands as the virtue between the immoderations of illiberality and prodigality, just as munificence stands between pettiness and vulgarity. And so on.[20] Other thinkers have proposed other virtues. Plato named the four "cardinal virtues" as temperance, prudence, courage, and justice. Other classical Greek and Roman virtues include humor, mercy, dignity, tenacity, concord, nobility, endurance, modesty, and equity. The Christian tradition teaches the "cardinal" and "heavenly" virtues of faith, hope, love, temperance, charity, diligence, patience, kindness, humility, and chastity. Islam, Judaism, Buddhism, and many other religious and certain other ethical traditions propose their own list of virtues. For present purposes, specific virtues received from various traditions are not the main point. What matters is grasping the concept that human experience and accumulated wisdom identify specific sets of learned dispositions and practices that tend strongly to produce and comprise lives of human excellence, flourishing, and well-being. Learning and practicing them constitutes the proper telos. Exercising them helps constitute the realization of flourishing. Ignoring them and perhaps practicing vices instead moves people away from their telos.[21] Personal virtues do not describe the beginning and end of human flourishing; as I will note below, enjoying the right kind of social structures and environmental conditions are absolutely crucial too. But virtues are necessary as well.

What good for thinking about the end of personal wellbeing is this focus on *arete*? Personalism says we need always to return to the ontology of personhood to think about virtues. The telos of human life is to realize most fully in existential actuality the ontologically real potentialities and capacities of personhood. To flourish is to cultivate, strengthen, and robustly express the various dimensions of personal being. That entails developing human capacities for consciousness, reflexivity, bodily health and presence, self-transcendence, coherence of experience, personal identity, moral commitment, social communication, responsibility in causing action, participation in social interactions, personal agency, experience of intersubjectivity, and, to crown it all, being and living as a particular kind of self who is engaged in loving relationships with other personal selves and the nonpersonal world. With such a substantive description of what persons are we can work backward and forward to think through a personalist understanding of what the telos looks like and what virtues help achieve and constitute that end. The process is actually empirical and practical, though it is also heavily reliant on what humanity has learned through life experience and can pass on in the form of true wisdom and life-giving tradition.

A genuinely good, flourishing human life of well-being is thus not defined by a "flat" view of human existence, purpose, or ends. Human being by its very nature is built for the progressive development, exercise, and actualization of increasingly higher human powers, capacities, and relations, toward the greater realization of human thriving. Human life is fundamentally teleological in a sense that the proper, ultimate human end transcends mere survival, drives, needs, desires, or any static view of the purposes of human activity. The final human good of flourishing of personhood is an achievement that requires a lifetime of the progressive development and realization of human goods. Physical survival and the meeting of many needs and desires are preconditions for and indeed part of human flourishing, since all human persons are embodied creatures, and a healthy body living in a material world is essential to personhood. But human life is not simply about meeting bodily needs and sating appetitive desires, for humans are not merely bodies with animal desires. Human persons are embodied spirits, and so also have "spiritual" interests, goods, and motives. Meeting animal needs and desires in certain ways is thus a necessary but insufficient condition for the realization of genuine final human ends. The authentic human good is oriented toward the meeting of many animal needs and desires, within appropriate limits and directed toward proper ends, but also, very importantly, the going beyond, the transcendence of those needs and desires. The meeting and transcending of those needs and desires necessarily moves persons in their natural teleological quests for the greater flourishing of their personhood to *higher* goods and interests. What begins with a genuine human interest in physical survival, safety, and pleasure naturally moves progressively upward to more complex and immaterial concerns with knowledge, self-identity, and agency for action. Having realized, if not mastered, those higher interests, however, the human good is still not yet adequately realized. For persons in pursuit of flourishing must still progress to higher levels of realization of their own natural human capacities toward the achievement of their final good. Those capacities entail matters of moral commitments and practices, and communion and love in social relationships. In short, the authentic realization of human personhood naturally involves a *hierarchy* of capacities to be progressively achieved or actualized.

One implication is that personal living in pursuit of the ultimate good of human flourishing is best organized into something like a "life project."[22] I mean by this adequately *coherent life plans* consisting of adequately integrated strategies and means for achieving the good that are well fitted for the particular person in question's opportunities, constraints, resources, talents, and callings.[23] Life's goods cannot be successfully sought after randomly, serially, or in a disconnected, uncoordinated, or haphazard way. Good lives need to be lived as adequately coherent wholes. Life plans can include multiple, disparate pursuits, but good ones cannot be fundamentally incoherent. Persons themselves are relatively coherent "centers with purpose." Realizing human goods and ends requires reflecting upon what is truly good and organizing purposes, actions, and virtuous practices that will help achieve what is good. That requires discernment, prioritizing, prudent decisions, observation, learning, discipline, and the coordination and self-directing of goals, actions, and habits. Without that kind of reflection, deliberation, choosing, and self-governing, the chances of personal flourishing are greatly reduced.

Happily, features of the kind of conditions or environments that promote human flourishing can be empirically identified.[24] They include certain necessary material resources, social-structural contexts, educational experiences, and personal commitments. Given our discussion so far, we can identify certain *universal human preconditions* and *proximate ends* that help to constitute and make the proper final end of life possible. Stated in terms of the ontology of personhood, these universal conditions and provisional ends include physical, bodily self-preservation; safety, health, and maturation; the exercise and development of subjective consciousness and experience; self-reflexivity and self-transcendence; social communication and intersubjective understanding with other persons; the exercise of personal agency as the responsible efficient cause of one's actions; establishing and maintaining durable, unique identity as embedded in but not enveloped by social groups; forming and acting upon moral commitments; and coordinating the above by sustaining a purposive "center of" personal self for life. (Below I will clarify a more precise list of necessary preconditions for realizing the six basic human goods and flourishing.)

The meeting of those conditions of flourishing can be realized to different extents and to varying degrees. That is dependent on the presence of particular kinds of environments that nurture (or not) proper human development toward flourishing. Oftentimes people fail to enjoy the kinds of environmental conditions needed for their development toward flourishing. When that results in the systematic developmental stunting of persons, we may call that social-structural evil. Specific material, relational, and social-institutional contexts matter hugely for the kind of thriving that can be realized in any given personal life or group of persons. Material and social-structural conditions must exist that promote bodily survival, safety, health, and maturation. Relationships must exist that train, educate, model, and reward choices and practices that promote flourishing. Social institutions must be developed and sustained that encourage the proper kinds of activities, participation, education, experiences, and habits that foster authentic human flourishing. Persons must be shaped to make prudent commitments and choices that promote rather than compromise their own flourishing. In the absence of these kinds of material, relational, and institutional contexts, persons will likely not flourish. In their presence, however, persons enjoy environments that nourish, though not guarantee, their flourishing. That has big implications for moral philosophy and political theory. Aristotle thus understood that humans are inherently political animals, meaning that the development and flourishing of our very nature absolutely requires participation in good and virtuous social orders.[25] Flourishing, in other words, is never merely a personal accomplishment, but is radically developmentally dependent upon good social orders, on the right kind of social structures, for is realization. Furthermore, reciprocally, promoting good social orders is inescapably entailed in the pursuit of personal flourishing; seeking the common good is constitutionally part of seeking one's own personal good.

There are few precise rules or obligations in all of this, the fulfilling of which would specify clearly what the living of a good life would look like for any given person. A *eudaimonian* approach is not much interested in fixed rules—that tends more to be a Kantian concern.[26] The approach here instead seeks to grasp what is good in light of the reality of human personhood; imagine what a specific life in pursuit of the good could, would, and should look like; learn virtues that promote and instantiate that good in actual life; and put all of that together in a coherent life story and project in ways that pursue personal thriving. Prudence, self-understanding, insight, discernment, and readiness are essential to continually learn. With these distinctions we can provide an account of our telos that is both general and specific enough to include all people appropriately. There actually is one master telos for all persons. But it allows for a variety of paths and expressions in pursuing it. At the same time—because of the given nature of human personhood—it provides real content that can guide the disciplines and choices every person makes in moving toward (or away) from their proper end.

This all means that a person living a good life is more like becoming a master artist or player in some sport or complex game, such as chess. It requires dedication, learning, discipline, and practice to move toward excellence. A life well lived is not something like watching television, answering phone calls, or recreational shopping. One does not have it happen to oneself, simply respond to the initiative of others, or engage in life for amusement. One is not a consumer of experience as it comes but a producer of genuine goods and achiever of ends worth attaining. A life well lived requires being proactive, learning from role models, being oriented to change, and striving toward proper ends. This is the posture of a life of *arete* lived in a quest for *eudaimonia*, the way of learned practical virtues toward the telos of personal flourishing.

But, one may insist on asking, how do we *know* this? It is a misguided question. Our inescapable epistemic condition as human persons is that we do not *know* many things in any definite, indubitable sense. We always first *believe* certain things for better or worse reasons, and only then can we begin to have good grounds for further believing certain things about reality. In short, like it or not, we are all epistemological presuppositionalists—that is our one and only human option.[27] The task then is to see through "practical adequacy" and other means how well our presuppositions and their implications fit reality. So the right question is not, "how do we *know* this?" but, "Do we have good reason to believe this to be true?" and "Are the reasons that commend this view better than those commending rival views?" Still, it might be understandable if some readers find this hard to believe. Looking at the world around us, instead of observing people and societies mastering virtues in pursuit of well-being we see much evidence of selfishness, stupidity, indifference, vice, arrogance, laziness, evasion of accountability, and dehumanization. Explaining how and why that is so in view of the discussion thus far will be the task of the next chapter.

Contingency and Variability

To adequately understand personal flourishing and to explain its failure, it is necessary to grasp the contingencies and variability involved. We must understand that personal flourishing is not automatically given; it must be achieved in spite of many obstacles and distractions working against it. Flourishing is not an entitlement in the sense that every person born into the world is guaranteed it. Human flourishing is a goal that must be achieved, accomplished, or realized against sometimes-difficult odds and obstructions. Tragically, not all humans flourish in their personhood. Many die young, are neglected and abused, or compromise and stagnate. Many are unjustly deprived, suffer debilitating misfortunes, or fail to overcome obstacles and distractions. These are tragic and sometimes dreadful facts. But the fact that not all persons flourish does nothing to negate the reality that flourishing is indeed the purpose and drive of human life. Members of some kinds of liberal societies—who tend to believe that certain entitlements must be made to everyone—may be especially tempted to think that if the most basic human good and end are not achieved by everyone, then it must not be the most basic human good or end. The idea of equal opportunity and possibly equal outcomes defines most human and civil rights and social entitlements. And some version of this does define a personalist view of human rights. But nothing can *guarantee* that all persons realize their own flourishing. That *is* the proper goal of human life and society. Human relations and institutions should be constructed to foster flourishing. And everyone and everything ought to work toward the ever-expanding achievement of human thriving. The promotion of personal flourishing toward the common good is the criterion by which all societies must be judged, the central standard of any social ethic.[28] But the empirical fact is that not all persons do flourish. The moral significance of that fact must not be minimized, as some naturalistic theories do. Nor must the tragedy or injustice of it compel us to reject the notion of flourishing as humanity's purpose and motivating energy.

Personal flourishing is, I have said, dependent upon a set of necessary personal and social-structural conditions that make it possible. These conditions are necessary in the sense that the elimination of any one of them is sufficient to compromise flourishing. Some of them are more instrumental means for flourishing; others help constitute flourishing itself as they develop.[29] The necessary conditions include at least the following:

Bodily Sustenance + Material Resources + Avoiding Misfortune + Being Loved + Training + Learning Virtues + Commitment to Growth + Social Participation + Loving Others → *Realizing Six Basic Human Goods* = FLOURISHING

Bodily sustenance means that to flourish, persons need the proper nutrition, water, shelter from the elements, and clean air to sustain healthy bodily life. By material resources I mean access to sufficient possessions, property, land, tools, forms of transport, raw materials, and so on by which to fabricate the material world in ways to transform it for the better, earn a living, and learn about reality. Avoiding misfortune denotes persons not falling victim to debilitating accidents, diseases, disasters, violence, and other unexpected turns of fate that seriously compromise health and life. Being loved means being the object of one or more other significant person's self-giving care, affection, and commitment to one's well-being motivated centrally to promote one's genuine good, not for instrumental reasons. The primary source of love is normally parents and family, but can include kin, parent surrogates, friends, and others.[30] By training I mean teaching, instruction, and education in a variety of life skills—practical, rational, emotional, relational, technical, and so on—by teachers, guides, instructors, and role models. Learning virtues signifies acquiring and practicing the habituated character dispositions, traits, and practices that tend to lead to the living of a good life—such as prudence, truthfulness, courage, justice, temperance, generosity, patience, endurance, wit, and so on. Commitment to growth means the basic disposition and dedication of persons to continue to work throughout life toward the proper telos of flourishing, including resisting or overcoming failures, obstacles, compromise, diversions, sloth, despair, and other threats to ongoing teleological movement toward thriving. Social participation means enjoying and taking advantage of access to a variety of associations, communities, and institutions in one's society, by which one benefits from and contributes to the variety of goods entailed in those memberships, involvements, and activities.[31] Loving others is the final necessary condition *and* experience of personal flourishing. That means giving of oneself for the genuine good of others in the form of care, affection, and commitment to their well-being, motivated not for self-regarding or instrumental reasons, but primarily to promote the true welfare and happiness of the other, and often to enjoy interpersonal communion with them.[32]

Human persons cannot in this world fully flourish who are seriously deprived of any one or more of these nine social-structural and personal preconditions, because they are necessary for realizing the six basic human goods. The grave deprivation of even one may severely diminish or abort the potential for flourishing. At the same time, the enjoyment of these nine conditions does not itself equal the realization of the six basic goods or flourishing. That is only expected to *lead* to them. Realizing the six basic human goods and so flourishing are larger, more coherent experiences and facts than simply the sum of these nine requirements. Enjoying these preconditions does not guarantee personal flourishing. We are talking about complex, human experiences here, not laws or mathematical equations. Some persons who seem to "have it all" nonetheless wash out or fail in life for inexplicable reasons. So the above are clearly necessary but not automatically sufficient conditions for accomplishing the six basic human goods or personal thriving.[33]

The first five of the nine necessary conditions named above involve requirements or enjoyments that are primarily beyond the control of persons. They must be provided to each person, particularly early in life, by other persons and social environments in ways that are largely beyond the influence of the recipients. All persons are thus crucially developmentally dependent upon the surrounding social-structural world in a variety of ways to even have a chance at personal thriving. That is why good social relationships, institutions, and practices are so important. Individualists who try to explain life outcomes primarily in terms of the personalities, efforts, and luck of individuals ignore these crucial social-structural influences on failure and success in personal thriving. This analysis is meant to be a corrective against individualism. By contrast, however, the last four of the nine necessary conditions fall significantly, though not entirely, within the control of persons. Nobody but the persons in question themselves can learn and practice virtues, remain committed to personal growth and overcoming, actively participate in social life, and genuinely love other persons. People are not autonomous in any of this, in complete control of these matters. Learning virtues, for example, requires the presence and investment of more virtuous, mature, accomplished persons to model, teach, reinforce, interpret, and reward them. And social participation requires not only a readiness to become involved in community and institutional life, but opportunities for such participation, which must be afforded by other actors and social arrangements. Lastly, to repeat, we must never forget that personal flourishing requires learning to love and actually loving other persons. Love is probably one of the words social scientists use least, despite its common usage by ordinary people.[34] Yet my definition of human personhood and everyone's existential experience makes love an inherent and necessary feature of human flourishing. No person can fail to love other persons and still flourish.[35] Part of what it means to *be* an actualized human person is to engage in loving relationships with others. But since this view is not common in the social sciences, it must be persistently restated. Love stands at the heart of humanity's being, purpose, and teleological end, social science theories ignoring love notwithstanding. These four conditions, which are at least somewhat in the control of persons, ought to serve as a corrective for any "sociologism" that believes that persons are not responsible for their life outcomes, since it is all determined by "society."

Viewed negatively, harmful social-structural and personal conditions and experiences possess the causal capacity to impair, damage, and possibly terminate personal flourishing. These we might call "damagers." Some are within and others are beyond the control or influence of any given person. For instance, developmental trauma during the infant, childhood, and adolescent years—including physical or emotional neglect, abuse, stress, molestation, or violence—tends to short circuit personal thriving, even when the nine necessary conditions of flourishing noted above are otherwise met. Inheriting bad genes can seriously impair the advancement of persons toward greater flourishing in a variety of ways, by making certain persons susceptible to fatal diseases, risk-taking, or alcoholism, for example. Material deprivations caused by severe poverty, group discrimination, or economic oppression undermine access to the basic resources necessary for personal thriving. Social exclusion similarly undermines movement toward thriving. Some of these "damagers" are essentially the deprivation of the necessary conditions for thriving named above. Others exert causal powers exogenous to those nine conditions.

To complicate matters, however, we must note that persons can within certain bounds genuinely flourish in terms defined relative to their opportunities, enjoyment of necessary preconditions, and the impairments of damagers and other external constraints. As a baseline rule, by the nature of things, persons cannot flourish in a vacuum, in states of severe deprivation, apart from the right kinds of nurturance, formation, and support of many different kinds. At the same time, to qualify the argument above, what it means for persons to flourish may be in part defined not only by the nature of human personhood and materiality generally, but by the particular circumstances within which any given person's life is set. The exact expression and achievement of flourishing are always in some sense *relative* to the *potential* to flourish in any given case.[36] What it means for any given person to flourish in part needs to be "indexed" to their "starting conditions." What real flourishing means for disabled athletes in the Special Olympics can look different from what flourishing means for completely capacitated and healthy athletes in the regular Olympic games. Yet both can genuinely flourish. For some persons of limited mental ability to overcome daunting obstacles through determination and hard work to simply graduate from high school may represent a much higher state of achieved personal thriving than another person in possession of a very different set of gifts, resources, and opportunities graduating with a master's degree. In part the difference is made by what is achieved relative to the opportunities and resources to realize the achievement. The more any person has been given, the more we generally expect of them, as we evaluate whether they have thrived in life or not. And in part the difference is made by how the achievement was accomplished, how much of a learning and exercise of virtue was needed for its realization—with more virtue exercised and the more obstacles overcome contributing to a more significant sense of flourishing. We generally do not consider people who have had everything "handed to them on a silver platter" to be flourishing, however nicely their lives may be going. And we often admire people who have overcome hardship and long odds to realize difficult goals. For many people, flourishing is accomplished through resilience amid pain and brokenness, perseverance through pain and suffering, and triumph over hardship—such that their thriving is not in spite of but because of and through the brokenness of the world. Even the severely disabled can flourish relative to the conditions they have been "given" with which to work.

In this sense, even persons in desperate conditions can recalibrate what it means to flourish in a relative sense or to approximate something like flourishing. It may not look like what flourishing might otherwise have entailed in more fortunate or just situations. But the recalibrated version of thriving can involve genuine aspects or representative pieces of flourishing. In wretched circumstances, human persons can sometimes nonetheless strive to carry on with expressions of dignity and love, sometimes merely symbolic, that powerfully express at least a shard of the form of thriving that would robustly flourish under different circumstances. Despite some of the most dangerous, horrific, and dehumanizing conditions, persons nonetheless have found ways to be humane, kind, forgiving, truthful, generous, and tender. And those can be powerful expressions of a kind of personal thriving in the face of indescribable deprivation and evil. For instance, testimonies of remarkable expressions of kindness and courage in Nazi concentration camps that were otherwise overwhelmed by unspeakable cruelty and fear express an assertion of the personal good that affirms a determination to not abandon the proper human telos. One cannot speak directly, without engaging in a kind of blasphemy, about "flourishing" when it comes to the Nazi Holocaust. But we also cannot ignore these glimmers of personal flourishing offered at least as protests against such a vicious machine of death. Simply to have been kind to another in that extreme context of inhumane cruelty we might consider, in some sense, a drastically recalibrated form of real movement toward personal thriving. Similarly, we see in Aleksandr Solzhenitsyn's novel, *One Day in the*

Life of Ivan Denisovich, how human dignity and loyalty in the face of un-speakable cruelty of the Soviet gulag prison system can express a drastically altered but nonetheless genuine assertion of a determination to protect and uphold a fragment of human personal thriving—even the way Ivan Deniso-vich properly holds his spoon to bring his soup up to his mouth, rather than hunching over, bespeaks a radically relativized insistence on flourishing.[37]

The same can happen in less drastic conditions. Persons face a range of potential degrees of thriving existing between the most optimal conditions for flourishing, on the one hand, and its complete impossibility, on the other. Pov-erty seriously limits the ability of the impoverished to flourish as persons. But within the constraints poverty poses, impoverished persons sometimes can still pursue and achieve relative expressions of personal thriving, as they are able. The poor can be and often are—sometimes more so than the wealthy—generous, caring, and personally happy. That is not an excuse for poverty—it must never be used to justify poverty. But it is true. Realistically, the existential forms and expression of flourishing in the context of poverty will be different and most likely diminished compared to what it might be otherwise. Yet we must also recognize different kinds of deprivation and poverty. Some of the most materially prosperous households can suffer severe relational and emo-tional deprivation. Some of the wealthiest young people in centers of the most prosperous nations in the world are genuinely impoverished when it comes to human goods like learning virtues, social participation, being loved, and knowing and pursuing a real life purpose. Personal flourishing in any given case is thus somewhat relative to the particular configurations of weakness, lack, and difficulties present. I am not positing a "moral equivalence" across all forms of scarcity, obstruction, and damagers affecting human thriving. Some privations and deficits are more serious and morally condemnable than others. But we need not believe that only those humans who enjoy all of the best resources, endowments, and opportunities stand a chance of flourishing.

Furthermore, flourishing is not a 0/1 condition, but is progressively (and sometimes regressively) realized (or eroded) in matters of degrees, usually developmentally across one's entire life. *Eudaimonia* is not like reaching nir-vana, where one works toward it for a long time and at some distinct point achieves it. Persons normally exist in variable states of real but incomplete flourishing (or perhaps stagnation or failure). From a *eudaimonian* point of view, what matters more than where one stands at any given time is the direc-tion in which one is headed and the pace of one's movement. A good life is one characterized by movement *toward*, rather than away from, one's proper human *telos*; and the more resolutely one moves toward it, rather than lan-guishing, the greater thriving one will enjoy. This also means that one may be viewed, at the end of one's life, as having lived a rich, full, happy life without that meaning one had reached a state of perfect flourishing. The complete realization of human thriving in this world is elusive, perhaps impossible. Even so, significant growth and movement in the right direction—even when falling short of perfection—helps to constitute thriving.[38] Real advance on the journey is a major part of happiness and thriving.

Despite being a human universal, personal flourishing as the proper telos of humanity is never expressed in a uniform manner but is always existentially defined and worked out in its particulars in specific historical and cultural contexts. Existentially, flourishing is never realized in an ahistorical or supercultural way, because persons are inescapably historically and culturally specific beings. While all humans face a common telos of personal flourishing, exactly what is possible, what that might look like, and how it will be expressed in time and space will vary a great deal (though not absolutely) across time and cultures. There is more than one way for human persons to flourish; in fact, there are many ways. That does not mean that *every* possible way a person might construct a life will cultivate flourishing. Many do not, as we know from human experience. Still, flourishing can be realized in human existence in a variety of possible ways, depending on the particulars of history and culture. All human thriving need not conform to one uniform version but can take a variety of cultural forms and experiences. What it might look like to flourish as a human person in a particular pre-Columbian, Native American civilization would be somewhat (though not absolutely) different from what it would look like in a Polynesian island culture during the same era. And those would look different again from thriving in Beijing or Denmark today or for humans centuries in the future. The differences are not absolute. Because all humans share a nature grounded in a specific *ontology*, what it means for any person to flourish will always share certain core features, no matter where and when. But the possible ways that those features are expressed in human *existence* across time and space will vary, within the larger, common boundaries of the human possibilities. Indeed, part of the task of the teleological quest of any person to realize their own flourishing is figuring out how that can and should be achieved, given their own particular place in history and culture.

Nested within this historical and cultural variability, the expression of personal flourishing in the life of any given distinct person also can involve an even greater diversity of existential possibilities. If the particularities of history and culture bound the possible expressions of personal flourishing for people, the range of possible valid expressions or experiences of personal flourishing of distinct persons within those histories and cultures is even greater. What flourishing may look like for any given person depends a great deal on the particularities of the person. Different personal histories, interests, gifts, loves, callings, and contingent experiences will rightly move different persons to pursue flourishing in different ways. Some will be artists, others scientists. Some will be manual laborers; others will earn a living with ideas. Some will get married and have large families, others will not. And so on. Neither personalism nor its *eudaimonian* ethics requires uniformity when it comes to a good life well lived. In fact, within certain naturally given boundaries, flourishing demands a diversity of expressions, experiences, and enjoyments. In taking seriously the particularity of persons, personalism naturally expects that existential flourishing will work its way out in a variety of ways. And that, when properly shared and enjoyed, contributes to the making of a good society. Personalism thus well balances what all humans share, on the one hand, and how they vary, on the other. It describes a broad trajectory within which any human thriving must find itself, yet it allows for a broad range within that trajectory for the diverse cultural and personal expressions of flourishing. In this, again, the one and the many, the common and the distinct, the unity and the diversity of humanity are named, honored, and promoted.

It helps to make sense of all of this if we distinguish between three levels of ends: the shared human telos, a personal telos, and a life plan. The shared *human* telos is the general end toward which all humans ought properly to move, given the nature of what they as persons are, and which helps to define the right boundaries within which all humans should move forward toward their natural end. The word "the" intends to suggest that there is only one human telos in virtue of there being one human personhood.[39] A *personal* telos, by contrast, concerns the more particular ends that are good and fitting for specific persons, given their unique biographies, interests, gifts, and social conditions. The word "a" here (instead of "the") says that because each person has his or her own distinctive personal telos, there are many personal *teloi* across many people. Finally, a life plan as I mean it here consists of a set of specific intentions and commitments about relationships, activities, education, vocations, locations, and other practical matters that together comprise much of the actual long-term content of any given person's life as he or she intends to live it. Most elements of people's life plans are not morally good or bad in and of themselves, but they can become morally significant by way of promoting or undermining flourishing. These three ends-related concepts thus range in character from expansive-though-not-absolute generality (the shared human telos) to biographically specific ranges of possible life ends (a personal telos) to highly particular intentions and choices by which specific people's lives are carried out (life plans). A person's life plans must be appropriately nested within their personal telos, which in turn must be contained within the bounds of the shared human telos. Different life plans may fit one person's personal telos. Furthermore, very many different personal *teloi* can fit well within the expansive, single, shared human telos. But every person's life plan must fit within the parameters of their personal telos, just as every personal telos must fit within the trajectories and ends of the shared human telos. No life plan can be authentically good if it does not work toward achieving a personal telos, just as no telos can be personally good and proper if it is humanly bad or improper. By making these distinctions between the shared human telos, a personal telos, and life projects, we are able to make sense of the challenge of specificity and generality in proper ends. All persons ought to live in a way that pursues the human telos in one way or another, because they are persons. Every person ought also to be living so as to pursue their own personal telos, for that defines the right direction and end of their lives as distinct persons. And every person ought to carry out specific life plans that suit their own highly particular interests, talents, needs, opportunities, and constraints. Evident here is an inverse relationship between scope of generality and range of options. The human telos entails the greatest scope of generality and yet the smallest range of proper options, namely, one. Life plans concern the most specific scope of identity and behavior possibilities, and yet the largest range of potential choices that might count as good and proper for any given person's life.

History must be brought to bear on this discussion in yet another way, I believe, by recognizing that the natural, proper "project" of the human race as a whole—to express existentially what it is ontologically by realizing personal flourishing—is arguably also at a broadly temporal level an unfolding, collective historical achievement. The natural, organic, ontological, and biological unity bonding together the human race means that we human persons (whether we know or accept it or not) are participating in and advancing at a grand-historical level an ongoing process of collective learning about ourselves, about our nature as a species, and about the proper end and means for achieving our real purpose. Flourishing is, of course, ultimately always a personal accomplishment for (or failure of) each human being. But flourishing *also* should be and in some ways arguably is a collective project of humanity as a whole, pushed forward by our accumulated understanding and long-term growing potential for realization through historical experience, developments, and learning across millennia and centuries of human history. Negatively, flourishing as a collective historical project is also advanced and clarified by the failures and violations of it in human historical experience, by which humanity sometimes learns more about flourishing, at least in certain ways—even when we are poor at putting what learning we accumulate to good use.[40]

We gain by thus historicizing human understanding and the end of personal flourishing. It will not do to theorize human flourishing as a static good, as a question of biological or cultural homeostasis or the mere repeated accomplishment (or failure) occurring within distinct personal lives. An ahistorical view of human flourishing, or one that casts teleology as relevant only for the biological lifespans of distinct persons, fails to appreciate the larger temporal, transpersonal dimensions of the matter. What every person inherits as culture from the accumulated human experience contributes to (as well as perhaps detracts from) his or her prospects for personal flourishing. Further, the particular expressions of flourishing that persons at different points of history can conceivably realize and achieve is dependent upon what has happened and been learned by humanity before. Included in that are not only new cultural ideas about flourishing but also newly invented technological means that help promote flourishing, such as improvements in food production and medicine. This is partly why what genuine flourishing may look like in one time and place may be different from another. This need not produce a naive, nineteenth-century-like belief in the inevitable evolutionary advance of Progress and Reason. But it does hold open the possibility that humanity can get and actually has gotten somewhere constructive in self-understanding and the promotion of flourishing.

This also allows us to affirm that personal flourishing is indeed the natural, real, and proper teleological end of human life, even if and when whole peoples in previous times and places in history did not understand, believe, or enact that. People and cultures can be mistaken about what is true and real. The fact that personal flourishing is the proper telos of human life is therefore not dependent upon all peoples and cultures throughout history knowing and affirming it—any more than bacteria and viruses caused illnesses among people who did not even know they existed. Even so, we should not underestimate humanity's at least intuitive awareness of the purpose of life being *eudaimonia*. Historicizing the human understanding of and increasing capacity to achieve new dimensions of personal flourishing helps us see *both* how thriving has been the constant telos of humanity for all of history *and* how the recognition and role of thriving could vary across time and space.

Conclusion

There is obviously more one might say about flourishing, but space does not permit that here. It will have to wait for future development. Meanwhile, this chapter has focused on the "bright" side of personal being—that humans enjoy the capacity, tendency, and often experience of developing their myriad real powers of personhood to maturity and expression in existence, toward flourishing. My account has emphasized the need for both personal and social-structural conditions as necessary for human thriving. But a theory of flourishing is only part of the story, one often also twisted and broken by another, related story that often seems to dominate the brighter side. That is, the facts of failure, error, ignorance, indifference, pathology, malice, and evil. A *eudaimonian* account that emphasizes natural human goods, virtues, and flourishing must also explain these darker realities. That is the task of the next chapter.

Understanding Failure, Destruction, and Evil

Human life is a quest toward something good. Yet this quest often does not succeed. Life is beset with obstructions, diversions, and dangers. Some of what waylays people in this quest is beyond human cause and control. But much that troubles and thwarts us is all too human, caused by ourselves, other people, and social institutions. Experience in life and the world tells us that something is deeply wrong with people and society. The final task of this book is to show how a theory of motivations based on understanding humans as *natural-goods-seekers* can account for how and why people so often desire and act toward *the bad*, what is not good. My purpose in this chapter is not to plumb the deepest metaphysical depths of the ultimate cosmic origins of evil. My analysis takes for granted that something like brokenness and evil find a place in our world. My query instead addresses this question: in a *eudaimonian* reality, in which human life is properly oriented toward goods, virtues, and flourishing, why do failure, destruction, and evil happen? The short answer to these questions is as follows. Flourishing is not automatic or guaranteed, but contingent. It must be purposively accomplished against resistance and obstacles, both internal and external. Achieving human flourishing requires a specific set of resources, experiences, and efforts provided by other persons and social institutions, and capitalized upon by persons seeking to flourish. People who benefit from and take advantage of the requisites of flourishing stand a good chance of thriving. But the default outcome for those who do not enjoy and capitalize upon these resources, experiences, and efforts is personal failure, stagnation, and degeneration. In some cases, people become evil. This chapter unpacks these ideas. In it, I pay disproportionate attention to human evil, since it seems to pose a most problematic challenge for my teleological personalism.

Six Types of Personal Telic Failure

The failure to flourish in human life can be analytically categorized into six broad types:

1. Environmental Deprivation
2. Stagnation
3. Avoidant Destructiveness
4. Negligent Evil
5. Instrumental Evil
6. Sadistic Evil

Most failures to flourish consist of the first three types. The first kind of failure to flourish—environmental deprivation—is produced primarily by persons *being failed* by their material and social environments and relationships in ways that are largely beyond their control (though often not beyond the control of other responsible people and social institutions). For example, persons die of illness in childhood—or of starvation, thirst, or exposure in famine, drought, or extreme weather. They are stillborn or born with radically malformed bodies or brains. They are stricken young in life by horrible diseases. They are grossly neglected or abused by parents or guardians who are inept, evil, or mentally ill. Some suffer severely debilitating cognitive, emotional, or physical disorders caused by bad genes, dysfunctional neurology, or some other bodily pathologies. Others are killed or gravely damaged in wars, by battering spouses, wild animals, or bad accidents. Yet others are casualties of natural disasters, such as earthquakes, landslides, and tsunamis.[1] Some people are born into crushing poverty from which there is no escape. Others are horribly persecuted and exterminated for racial, religious, or ideological reasons. And so on. In such cases and all like them, these persons fail to flourish not primarily because of anything they could control or for which they are responsible. They are the victims of tragic, unjust, or evil forces and circumstances—the heartrending casualties of a broken, unfair, sometimes cruel world. Through no fault of their own, these persons cannot and do not realize in existential existence the fullness of their natural personhood.[2] They remain fully persons ontologically as long as they live but are deprived of the opportunity existentially to achieve anything like the flourishing of their unique personal being. In some cases, there is little consoling that can be said to help. Their reality is tragic, dreadful, heartbreaking. In some such cases, their failure to flourish could not be prevented by any human means. In others, however, failure to flourish could have been prevented but was not—which seems to make their fate even worse. In these latter cases, we are very likely speaking about social institutions and conditions that are unjust, exploitative, or oppressive, perhaps even social-structurally evil. This first category of failing to flourish—more accurately, *being deprived of the chance to flourish*—often raises weighty moral questions and concerns in social and political ethics.[3]

Unlike the first type of failure to flourish, important in the remaining five types is the role played by the bad choices and inadequate, misguided, or malignant efforts and actions of the persons involved and other persons and institutions. These types usually also entail deprivations of vital, nurturing resources, relationships, and experiences. But some of the explanation for these failures comes back to problems in the personal agency of some of the people involved. The most benign of these (the second general type of failure) is personal *stagnation*, a "stalling" of people's quest to flourish. Here persons get "stuck" in life, stop exerting virtuous effort, and wind down new personal growth. The world is full of such people, especially perhaps among the middle-aged and older. Most of them are decent and functional. But they are not achieving much new that is good in their lives. Other people who live or work closely with them are often aware of their functional lack of interest in personal growth and sometimes have to bear some of the disagreeable consequences. People in stagnation can be difficult for others, but they are usually manageable. Stated differently, these stagnating people have given up on optimizing flourishing and have settled for mere "satisficing." They have stalled at a point in life that is not ideal, but which they think is sufficient, and they are satisfied to stay there. They remain content with a mere acceptable threshold of growth and happiness. If stagnant people indulge a characteristic vice, it is *sloth*. (Speaking of virtues and vice, however, should not cause us to forget that all personal choices are made within social contexts of powerful downward causation that influence them, even when personal choice remains at play.)

Such an approach is represented in figure 7 (by position *b*). There we see the general trend that the more virtuous effort persons exert, all else being equal, the more flourishing they enjoy. At a basic level, I suggest, learning and practicing virtuous efforts produce significant payoffs in flourishing (position *a*). But that positive slope often plateaus somewhat in the mid-range of virtuous effort, so that the return-on-flourishing-to-effort ratio is reduced. Here (position *b*) is where many people stagnate. To continue to move toward greater flourishing requires additional expenditures of virtuous effort (position *c*), which these stalled, satisficing, stuck persons are not interested in doing.

The third type of personal failure to flourish moves beyond mere stagna-

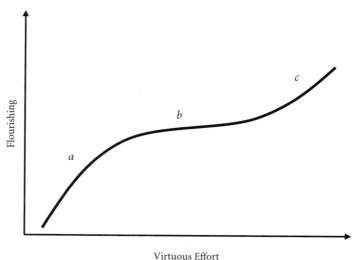

FIGURE 7. Effort-to-flourishing curve with stagnation plateau.

tion into a mode of *avoidant destructiveness*.[4] Such cases are not merely un-interested in new personal growth and movement toward their proper telos. They are positively, actively, stubbornly resistant to it—even if they are not consciously aware of that fact. What would be required of and for them to grow and move toward greater flourishing confronts them as more difficult, more threatening than they are willing or able to deal with. So the basic posture of such lives is to resist the challenges of growth. Having already adapted to a life of stagnation, it is easy to take this next step away from flourishing toward destructiveness. But there is a cost. The seeming protections and avoidances destructive persons seek do not come for free. To *force* a life of avoidant destructiveness to work—in the context of our actual personal, interpersonal, and social reality—requires various forms of denial, distortion, falsification, resistance, and manipulation. When the force of objective reality pushes against destructive people in ways that demand adjustment, change, growth, or movement, resistance to those forces means they have to push back on reality—to struggle *against* its natural grain. And that always results in some combination of absorbing certain costs in their own personal being and imposing costs on other people.

Living against reality inevitably brings friction, collisions, splinters. Avoiding the healthy pains and losses that are required for proper personal growth inescapably imposes different, less generative pains and losses.[5] Nobody escapes pain and loss—the only question is whether they are the kinds that lead to flourishing or destruction. Moreover, sustaining the posture of destructiveness over time requires upping the ante. There is no static equilibrium here. Reality presses increasingly hard over time on those who refuse it, and so—when proper growth is avoided—reality must be resisted all the more determinedly. Larger costs must be personally absorbed and imposed on other people. And since the basic posture here is one of avoiding pain and loss, destructive persons usually increasingly impose the pain and loss on other people.[6] They must progressively make others pay for their unwillingness or inability to suffer the pain and losses required for them to properly grow. This moves them away from being merely difficult to other people (as the stagnant are) to being positively damaging. If avoidant-destructive people indulge a characteristic vice, it is self-centered *cowardice* (*deilia*, to use Aristotle's term), which is worse than mere sloth. More important to these than the well-being of others, including those they may love, is the determination to avoid the pain and loss that their own proper growth would require. The telic quest toward genuine flourishing is not simply stalled out. It is actively avoided, denied, and subverted. And the fact that genuine personal flourishing always also entails promoting the flourishing of other persons becomes perversely mirrored in the negative here, in that the sustained avoidance of one's personal flourishing inevitably requires diminishing the flourishing of other persons. (Here too we must remember about the downwardly causal powers of social contexts for shaping such personal choices and outcomes.)

The last three types of human failures to flourish bring us to *evil*, the extreme opposite of flourishing. There are three kinds of evil to distinguish. One results from inexcusable negligence or recklessness, not purposeful maliciousness. This I call *negligent evil*. The second concerns the evil necessity or consequence of actions pursued instrumentally for other reasons, not directly to enjoy the damage of the evil itself. This we can call *instrumental evil*. The third springs from the malicious sadism of the evil person. This I call *sadistic evil*. All three are common in the world and produce real, destructive evil*doing*, although not all require the agency of evil *people*. Evil deeds, in other words, are not always committed by evil persons, although they sometimes are. *Ongoing* evildoing of any kind, however, including negligent evil, does eventually produce evil persons.

By "evil" generally I mean *foreseeable intolerable harms produced by culpable wrongdoing*.[7] This definition requires three basic elements: intolerable harm, foreseeability, and culpable wrongdoing. Wrongs are only genuinely evil when (a) the evildoers who committed them have good reasons (which any reasonable person should be aware of) not to commit them, so which they are personally responsible and blameworthy for ignoring, (b) when the harm caused could have been seen beforehand, *and* when (c) their actions or inactions damage other people in ways that are intolerable, atrocious, catastrophic, or monstrous.[8] "Severe and unremitting pain or humiliation, debilitating and disfiguring diseases, starvation, extreme [disempowerment], and severely enforced isolation are evils," for example, "when they are brought about or supported by culpable wrongdoing."[9] Bad outcomes are thus *not* evil when their perpetrators genuinely had no good reason to think their actions would produce intolerable harm or when the harms done are not severe.[10] They may still be very wrong, but they are not evil. This approach helps us to distinguish not only evil deeds from evil persons but also evil motives from evil intentions. The former (motives) concern people's desires (and related beliefs and emotions) to commit evil; they are the inclinations that dispose people to do evil deeds. The latter (intentions), by contrast, involve willful *decisions* to *act upon* evil motives, the *volitional purposing* to commit evil. Not all evil motives develop into evil intentions—some people with evil motives exercise virtues to resist them, or are too frightened or socially constrained to act upon them. And not all evil intentions become evil deeds—sometimes intentions are thwarted, as with cold-blooded terrorists whose bombs fail to detonate. So, people with evil motives (perhaps many of us, at different times) need not be evil people. But people with persistently evil intentions *are* evil, whether or not they are able to fulfill their malicious intentions. This general approach enables us to distinguish the potential evil involved in deeds, persons, motives, and intentions in a way that is not simplistic but complex and nuanced.[11] It also helps us to identify and analyze evil institutions, practices, and laws.

With that framework in hand, let us now turn back to the three specific types of evil mentioned above. Evil, I have said, is foreseeable intolerable harms produced by culpable wrongdoing. Yet some evils that ruin other people's lives are produced not by sadistic monsters but by otherwise ordinary people who so happen to act recklessly or negligently. Here we confront *negligent evil*, the fourth general type of failure to flourish. To illustrate it autobiographically, when I was a toddler (I am told), I very nearly drowned in a two-foot-deep children's pool at my family's swimming club, because the babysitter supposedly watching me was instead embroiled in a poolside conversation with her friend—happily, someone else saw me face down at the bottom and I was resuscitated. Three years later (I vaguely remember), while riding my tricycle across the street in front of my house, I was struck by a fast-speeding car driven by a sixteen-year-old boy who had just received his driver's license. My tricycle was flattened, but fortunately I was thrown away from the car and, with some hospitalization, survived the accident without long-term damage. Now, I assume that neither my babysitter nor the speeding boy was an evil person, but they *were* badly negligent and culpably reck-less. And had I actually drowned or been killed by the car, their *deeds* in fact would have been evil, since in those circumstances the potential harm caused to me and my family was in fact foreseeable (to any reasonable person) and the damage caused would have been severe, intense, and irreversible, in short, intolerable. Events like these that result in less fortunate outcomes than mine represent the first kind of evil—not an instrumental or sadistic evil, but real evil nonetheless, caused by gross negligence and inexcusable recklessness. If there is a characteristic vice associated with the cause of this form of evil, it is *flagrant irresponsibility*. In many cases, evil of this sort may relate to the first kind of failure to flourish named above, that is, persons *being failed* by their relationships and environments in ways largely beyond their control. Negli-gent evil is also not always interpersonal—it also often happens institution-ally, with outcomes like toxic industry pollution, bad investments of other people's fortunes, failure to install the proper safety and warning devices in dangerous environments, and so on. The subjects of such failures are the victims of events beyond their control, while the perpetrators of such events are the causes of evildoing resulting from unconscionable risk-taking, negli-gence, and recklessness.

A second form of evil, *instrumental evil*, is, I think, more morally rep-rehensible than the first, but less so than the third. It consists of intolerable harm produced as the recognized necessity, risk, or result of actions under-taken to achieve different ends than the evil itself. The evildoing here is some-thing like "collateral damage" expected, occasioned, or required in order to realize another overriding goal. Persons and social institutions committing this kind of evil do not do so primarily in order to enjoy the horrific damage they produce. Instead, they simply tolerate or ignore that damage (however unbearable it may be to their victims), since they believe it to be justified or necessary to realize more important (to them) purposes.[12] The underlying logic is, "the ends justify the means"—success is worth the risks and costs (to others).[13] Examples of instrumental evil include the following. An army officer tortures a war captive, not because he enjoys torturing people (some who torture actually do not enjoy their work) but in order to elicit vital in-formation that may help win the war. A married man seduces the naive wife of another man simply because he wants to enjoy the triumph of conquest and pleasure of sex with her, and when they are discovered (as he had every reason to know they might be), it destroys both marriages and the long-term emotional well-being of the wife and her husband—in which case, the se-ducing man's goal was not to cause that intolerable harm, although he was (culpably) prepared to inflict it upon others in order to realize his immediate goal. Examples could be multiplied, but the point is clear. Also clear should be the fact that the perpetrators of instrumental evil are not merely irresponsible people who inadvertently commit evil deeds, but are actually evil *people*—not necessarily thoroughly, but evil at least in some ways. And the characteristic vice of their evil is *callousness*—not ignorance, not negligence, but cold indifference to the feelings, well-being, and futures of others who suffer as casualties of their wickedness.[14] The social equivalent of instrumentally evil people can be named as instrumentally evil social institutions, which promulgate evil not purposively but readily as a by-product of some purpose they pursue, such as the accumulation of wealth, power, or status. Such callousness often involves the *active* psychological "silencing" by persons and institutional leaders of good reasons that argue against committing evil—reasons that compel most people and social groups not to act on their possible evil motives.[15] Related to this problem is the matter of moral indifference by both persons and social institutions—something like "sins of omission," as some religious people call it, as opposed to actively committed sins—by passively allowing evil to be committed by simply not acting against it. For related reasons, most perpetrators of instrumental (and sadistic) evil tend not to view their acts as particularly bad; many view them as reasonable or justified.[16]

Finally, we must observe a third form of evil, *sadistic evil*.[17] This is evildoing for the purpose of causing destructive suffering on others.[18] Sadistic evil always involves evil deeds committed by evil persons. Its perpetrators reflect fairly stable dispositions and intentions to instigate evil acts that cause intolerable destructive suffering to others, precisely for the sake of seeing the suffering caused. The pleasures gained by sadistically evil people committing evil deeds are enjoyed as a direct result of the intolerable destruction itself. It may be the pleasure of pure sadism, a malignant neural reward system that "lights up" when observing others suffering. It may be the satisfied pleasures of narcissistic dominance and control over others, which is more purely realized by the capacity to render them helpless through suffering. Or it may be the pleasure of an internal terror relieved by witnessing it imposed on the bodies of other people instead of oneself.[19] In any case, such people "destroy for the sake of destruction and . . . hate for the sake of hate."[20] The characteristic vice-cum-pathology of this kind of evil is, not surprisingly, *sadism*. Evil persons of this sort want to see others suffer—a condition associated with the inability to feel empathy with other people.[21] Again, this evildoer silences any good reasons against evildoing. There are more than a few real cases of such sadistic people driving country roads, walking city streets, and sometimes sitting in chambers of political power. Many if not most psychopathic kidnappers and torturers, mass murderers, serial rapists, perpetrators of school shootings, intentional spreaders of sexually transmitted infections, and political and military instigators of genocide are sadistically evil (although in certain cases, some are instrumentally evil). As a reminder again, while my categories tend to focus our attention on persons, we must remember that the restraint or facilitating of these kinds of evil are highly conditioned by the social structures and political situations in which persons find themselves—once again, the personal and the social-structural cannot be isolated or exclusive.

Both instrumental and sadistic evil can be carried out personally or else indirectly through authorized agents—for example, by commanding others to commit evil deeds, such as torture or genocide. Suffering can also be imposed on others in different forms and through different methods. For instance, a sadistically evil adult can (directly) torture a child by inflicting suffering on his or her body, or torture that same child (indirectly) by forcing him or her to watch the slow mutilation of his or her living pet kittens. While I have focused my attention above on evil against persons, evil can be directed against animals as well as people. Human beings are not the only targets of evil. Evil persons can impose their culpable, intolerable harms on nonhuman animals, while avoiding direct malicious acts toward people.

Furthermore, evil can be either massive and obvious, or everyday and hidden. The word "evil" often conjures mental images of colossal, world-historical wickedness, such as the Holocaust or the September 11 World Trade Center terrorist attacks. Notorious serial killers, rapists, and mass murderers, such as Ted Bundy and David Parker Ray, also commit dramatic evil. But this attention to obvious, world-historical evils can distract us from the more prosaic yet also catastrophic evil that is pervasive in human life: *everyday evil*. One does not need to be a Joseph Stalin or Charles Manson to intentionally wreak malicious destruction on the lives of others. Some seemingly ordinary people are also profoundly evil, though they accomplish their evil in more subtle and private ways.[22] Oftentimes, violence and destruction are inflicted upon people not most unlike us, but by those most similar and closely related.[23] They may not murder by the scores or millions, but they do willfully and maliciously torment, humiliate, and destroy others.[24] "Everyday evil" may be more "benign" and pedestrian than serial-rape sprees and war crimes against humanity. But it is also more insidious, difficult to detect, and extensive in society. Its accumulated total impact in damaging human flourishing may therefore be just as devastating as more obvious, dramatic works of evil, only in different and diffuse ways. By acknowledging the real evil found not only in genocides and torture chambers, but also every day in schools, workplaces, families, neighborhoods, cliques, summer camps, romantic relationships, professional associations, religious groups, and beyond, we are compelled to admit and name the extent and malignancy of humanity's too-common pathological rejection of flourishing.[25]

Finally, evil can be personal and institutional. Sometimes distinct persons turn out to be destructive in horrific ways that seem hard to explain based on their socialization and circumstances. But many expressions of personal evil are fostered by deficiencies in any of the nine environmental preconditions discussed in the previous chapter, many of which are a matter of social-structural injustice. Evil can also be institutionalized in social structures that systematically stunt and destroy persons, which often makes the evil processes and effects less detectable and tractable, and usually makes the evil's capacities more systematic and powerful.

The six types of failure to flourish described above are depicted in figure 8.[26] The first (environmental deprivation) is a separate category of failure (being failed), determined by the lack of access to the resources, relationships, and experience needed to flourish, shown in figure 8 below the thick spectrum line. The other five (shown above the thick spectrum line) vary according to deficits in virtuous effort, the intensity of resistance to personal growth, and the severity of their negative consequences. Of those, negligent evil is highly dependent on particular circumstances for its expression, so is shown above the spectrum of more standard forms of failure that vary more directly according to virtuous effort (not) expended.

The Ontology of Badness and Evil

Badness and evil in human life are understood and explained in different ways by different belief systems. One is *dualistic*—believing that good and evil are independent, equal, opposing principles existing and struggling against each other from the beginning or forever, as in Zoroastrianism, Manichaeism, and many forms of Gnosticism. Another is the *samsaric* view—the belief that failure and evil consist in an illusion of individual separateness sustained by misguided desire, attachment, striving, and bad *karma* that drive continuing cycles of reincarnation, which can only be overcome by enlightenment and *dharma* (right living) to achieve *moksha* and *nirvana*, the "snuffing out" of (the illusion of) individual existence and merger into the all-encompassing *Brahma*. Some version of this view is assumed by the main Indus religions of Hinduism, Buddhism, and Jainism. Another version of badness and evil as an illusion we might call the *amoral naturalist* perspective, represented by Friedrich Nietzsche and some neo-Darwinian metaphysical naturalists. This outlook renounces traditional moral and religious meanings of the word

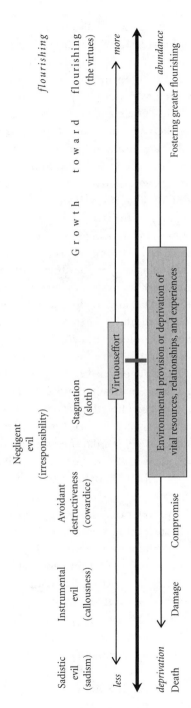

FIGURE 8. The spectrum of movement toward failure and flourishing.

"evil" as moralistic inventions of the weak used to control the strong, and instead means by the word mere natural functional uselessness. A fourth understanding of what is bad and evil we might call the *complementary* view, which suggests that evil is not an enemy of good so much as a corresponding opposite of good, existing, when properly balanced, in a united whole— something like the Taoist view of yin and yang.

In contrast to these beliefs, the approach to what is bad generally and evil specifically that I adopt and apply in the personalist theory here is the *privatio boni* ("privation of good") view.[27] This approach says that badness and evil do not possess their own positive, distinct, independent ontological being in rivalry to good. Ontologically, evil has only a "shadow" existence that is parasitical on the good. Ultimately, only good is independently real, and all of reality is innately good in being. So to try to find the substantive source of what is bad or evil is like trying "to see darkness or hear silence."[28] Badness and evil come into being only in the absence of the good.[29] Evil cannot be creative or life giving; it is always destructive.[30] Evil is "the attempt to regress to the pre-human state, and to eliminate that which is specifically human: reason, love, and freedom."[31] Therefore evil cannot and does not exist independently as a real counterpart to good, but only in negative form, in parasitical dependence upon that which it corrupts, a silhouette of what is good, in the absence, obstruction, or misdirection of the good.

However, when evil does parasitically impose its negative power on the good, through its absence and misdirection, it definitely does take on a malignant existence with massive capacities to distort and destruct. Even so, just as light really does exist on its own, but darkness and shadow do not, except as the absence of light, so good really does exist, but evil and the bad independently do not—what is evil and bad come to exist only in the absence, hindrance, or misdirection of good.[32] Thus when we consider evil and badness in human life, we do not refer to an autonomous ontological substance or self-grounded force. No such thing as evil exists independently as a something. This in no way denies the power of evil in the world, nor its real destructive effects. Evil is not simply an illusion about which we must become unconfused, or the misnaming of mere amoral, natural "dysfunctions," or a balancing complement to goodness. Yet neither is evil a self-subsistent power or being, existing as an eternal rival to the good in a metaphysically dualist universe. Evil and badness are *privatio boni*. With this view, the horrific experience of evil is fully acknowledged, not denied or turned into a misunderstanding, yet the ultimate goodness of being itself is also sustained and affirmed, not doubted, relativized, or refused.

How can evil acts embody the privation or misdirection of what is good?

All it takes for evil to spring into existence, I suggest, is the absence of what is good. Consider some extreme cases. Rape is inexpressibly wicked and morally reprehensible in the extreme—but in a deeply twisted and depraved way it is evil exactly in virtue of the *privation* of the goods of consent, mutuality, and loving communion in sex properly engaged, or a hideously *misdirected* attempt to achieve the true goods of sexual intimacy and the exercise of the power of personal agency. Violent vigilante revenge is morally wrong, yet in essence it represents the *privation* of the good of procedural justice and a *misdirected* seeking of what is a genuine human good, that of proper retributive justice. The physical battery of wives by husbands is also repellently evil, yet precisely so in its *privation* of anything that makes a good marriage good (love, tenderness, self-giving)—importantly, in the very structure of that privation, the battery does not happen in the abstract or between strangers, but within the empty shell of the otherwise-good relations of husband and wife, violated, eviscerated, mocked, and made unreal by the battering. Explaining these as *privatio boni* does in no way trivialize their evils. We speak here about matters of life and death, of violations and ruptures of unspeakably grievous wrong and destruction. So real and rightful is the true good in life, that its privation or misdirection proves to be of shattering consequence. Rather than seeing the absence of the good as negligible, then, this account compels us to recognize it as catastrophic.

Being itself is impossible without the at-least-implicit contrast of that-which-is-not. To affirm a "Yes" implies the possibility of a "No." To desire something is to reject other things. To will a particular good necessarily implies a lesser good that was not willed. To shine light on an object casts a shadow on its far side. To love and be loved raises the possibility of not loving or being loved. To choose rightly necessarily entails the potential to choose wrongly. To affirm a truth risks affirming a falsehood instead. The not-love, the wrong choice, the falsehood affirmed do *not* need to be actualized. They do not *have* to be brought into existence. They could stay in the realm of negation and nothingness. But they cannot *not* be possible.[33] Otherwise, what would be the meaning of love and right choices and truth? So the human negation of the real is always potential, even in a good world, though not inevitable. To want to live in a reality not involving any possible bads necessarily means forgoing living with real goods.

Having been schooled as moderns to believe that moral good and evil are social conventions with no real basis as truth in reality, the proposed view may seem farfetched. But what is actually fanciful is the modern view of evil. It leaves us incapable of making sense of human experience, which is both sodden with blood and an irrepressible human objection to its shedding. We need to jettison modernity's trivializing of morality and become moral realists. And unless we are prepared to become dualists (which we should not), the *privation-boni* view is the best account of evil going. With it, in a *eudaimonian* world, persons really can be oriented toward and motivationally driven by the teleological quest to realize their naturally proper goods, interests, and telos, and yet still be tempted by and fall into malice and destruction. Failure and evil can happen in a personalist world, parasitically on the good and with dreadful consequences. "Good consists of a transforming our existence into an ever increasing approximation to our [personal] essence; evil into an ever increasing estrangement between existence and essence."[34]

This *privatio boni* account helps to explain why persons never escape the fundamental orientation toward and motivation to realize human goods. Human actions and interactions are always conducted to realize goods, whether they are true or false goods, well-understood or misguided goods. Human institutions and social structures are as well. Humans cannot choose between goods and not-goods. They always choose toward apparent goods. But they do not always know what the true goods in any context are, may not exercise the will power to pursue the best good, and may have not learned the virtues necessary to discern and realize the true good. The goods that people pursue can thus easily be and often are the wrong goods. Goods can be wrong by virtue of being *lesser* goods in particular situations, the *wrong amount* of goods (too little or too much), or goods that are *inappropriate* in certain contexts. What in any situation is bad, wrong, or evil, therefore, is ultimately actually some genuine good that is deprived or misguided. Thus persons never act in ways that escape an orientation toward the good.

Biological analogies may be illuminating. Take cancer, for example. Cancer is not the development in a body of an independent and innately destructive organ set in opposition to healthy organs. Cancer is the mal-development and misdirection of healthy bodily processes of cellular reproduction and tissue growth. Cancer is the getting-out-of-control of natural bodily goods. The reproduction and growth of biological cells and tissue are normal, healthy processes of bodily life. The pathology of cancer results through the privation or misdirected overexpression of the normal operations of various oncogenes and tumor-suppressor genes, so that certain cells proliferate pathologically and become destructive. Some of the genetic alterations that cause this result from entirely normal processes of genetic replication, as probabilistically generated mutations. Other genetic anomalies are caused by environmental conditions that distort the healthy development and maintenance of bodies. Human bodies employ natural means to prevent and correct for such cancer-causing genetic errors, including the natural self-destruction of abnormal cells (apoptosis). When such natural processes of cell and tissue development become misdirected and pathological, however, they can become compounding and self-amplifying. Eventually the cancer—which is an evil for the body—can turn deadly. But the cancer itself is not the result of a hostile, self-subsistent biological entity taking over the body from within or without, or an innately unhealthy, distinct organ of the body. It is rather the malfunctioning through privation and misdirection of entirely normal biological processes of cellular and tissue growth. So it is analogously with moral evil in human life.

The Privation of Basic Human Goods

To illustrate, we might ask: How do failure and destruction relate to the privation or misdirection of the six basic human goods proposed in chapter 5?[35] One basic good is to achieve bodily survival, security, and pleasure. This good can easily be turned toward the bad and become the occasion for failure and evil. Their absence and misdirection produce worlds of grief and ruin. The simple absence of bodily life is death. The privation of bodily security for any person means vulnerability to accident, attack, sickness, and disease—an existence of intolerable anxiety and, inevitably, injury, illness, and a high chance of eventual death. The complete absence of physical pleasure in life is hard to conceive, but imagine what it would be like if the receptors of every neuron in one's brain having to do with pleasure were blocked. That would be a dreadful existence of numbness to any perceptual or appetitive enjoyment, an experience on the spectrum of bodily sensations limited completely to the side shading off from sense-neutrality to discomfort and agony. Such a life, knowing no pleasure whatsoever, would be dreary at best, torturous overall. Consider too misdirected pursuits of this good of bodily survival, security, and pleasure. People here, lacking the virtues of prudence and temperance, seek and enjoy what is truly good, but by the wrong methods. "Wrong" here means satisfied in inappropriate ways (the wrong means), incorrect amounts (the wrong extents), or by lesser than appropriate goods (the wrong goals). People may seek to extend the good of living by spending their entire lives obsessing about nutrition and exercise, at the expense of other life goods. They may pursue the good of bodily security by arming themselves to the hilt with lethal weapons or simply never leaving their homes for fear of danger. People may try to enjoy the good of bodily pleasure by potentially proper means (such as food, drink, intoxicants, relaxation, sex, or beauty) yet by various forms of immoderation and excess, as with gluttony, drug addiction, overeating, laziness, sexual promiscuity, obsession with people's physical attractiveness, addiction to shocking (or any) media, and, at a far extreme, sadism. In every case here, people try to realize a good, but do so in mishandled ways and to misdirected extents, all of which undermine and damage the true good.

The second basic human good is knowledge of reality. The privation and misdirection of this good also produces the failure to thrive. Not to understand how the material and social worlds work and how to flourish as persons in them diminishes human health and safety. At the extreme are cases of severe mental disability, childhood isolation, acute neglect in socialization, and certain severe mental illnesses. Simply holding beliefs about reality as true that are in fact false often gets people into big trouble. More insidiously, willingly holding beliefs that are false—living in denial—is often more destructive. The more people refuse to let go of their familiar but inaccurate "road maps to life," the more dead-ends and accidents they get into. In some cases, people can be so fixated on clutching the "ontological security" of an airtight worldview, on maintaining order above all else, that they refuse the kind of openness needed to ponder fresh questions, learn new ideas, and grow as persons. This may lead people into cults, both religious and secular, into "safe" but stunting jobs or relationships, or any other number of social positions that negate flourishing. Such absences of knowledge about reality thus lead to a failure to thrive. The misdirection of knowledge about reality usually leads to worse. Such interests gave us "Nazi science," effective methods of torture, Chernobyl, malevolent computer hacking, Bernie Madoff, mutually assured nuclear destruction, and other horrors and devastations. Again, what exists is the good of knowledge, and in its privation and misdirection we find failure, evil, and destruction.

The same holds true with identity coherence and affirmation. In its absence we find identity crises, dissociative identity disorder, retrograde amnesia, dementia, acute false memory, schizophrenia, and paranoid delusion. Another privation of this good is the failure of affirmation by significant others. Those who endure this suffer insecurity, anxiety, low self-regard, and can be driven to severe disorders. Misguided identity self-affirmation on the overdone side is also detrimental. There we find narcissism, megalomania, acute arrogance, self-entitlement, personal boundary violations, and, in some cases, psychopathology. People's and groups' misdirected attempts to affirm their own identities also easily become compulsive and destructive. Interpersonally, it is reflected in the social exclusion and hypercriticism of others, one-upmanship, hurtful cliques, and domination. Among groups, we see it in hypernationalism, racism, sexism, religious domination, militant secularism, xenophobia, violent political ideologies, and many other forms of destructive group identity assertion. Again, here a genuine good deprived or misguided readily becomes a true bad.

The ways that the privation and misdirection in exercising purposive agency have ill effects are obvious. To be deprived of agency is to be inert, helpless, lifeless. Exercising agency in misdirected ways holds more potential for hurt and destruction. When people do not act with enough of the right agency—for example, as authorities responsible for protecting the weak and vulnerable—they often fail to do good and possibly do harm. When people act with too much agency, they also risk failure and harm—when, for example, people become meddling, overbearing, and intrusive, inappropriately intervening in situations that are not theirs to fix, or creating new problems by acting too strongly or with too much haste. Acting with the right amount of agency, yet in misdirected ways, can be pernicious and destructive. Terrorists act with plenty of purpose in their mass murder. So do totalitarian states, war criminals, con artists, drug cartels, serial killers, pimps, predatory rapists, and white collar criminals in the various malignant activities in which they engage. The evil here is not people exercising personal purposive agency per se, but rather exercising agency in misdirected ways and in the absence of the proper good, given particular circumstances.

Moral affirmation involves believing that one is in the right or is living a morally commendable life. In its absence, we have an amoral or immoral existence, which is bound to be harmful. Persons lacking any motivation for moral affirmation, thus defined, are sociopaths who care nothing about shared normative and moral values. Indifference to moral praise or blame is a pathological state. Indifference can also be socially structured in social institutions, which can prove to be all the more destructive.[36] The misdirection of this good also produces trouble and sometimes evil. Pursued out of fear or denial, the search for moral affirmation easily becomes twisted.[37] Some people become groveling and obsequious to gain moral affirmation. Others become demanding and tyrannical. Some need other people to be or look bad in order for them to feel or look better in comparison. Others do anything possible to evade moral accountability or admit fault. Again, projection, scapegoating, transference are not uncommon pathological mutations of this good, they are *everyday* wrongs and sometimes evils. Groups thus feel good by condemning, dehumanizing, and destroying others. Still other people exaggerate their efforts and so become unrealistically self-condemning, guilt ridden, or self-denigrating. Among collectives, the good of moral affirmation is recurrently hijacked to legitimate immoral wars, movements, genocides, laws, expulsions, occupations, and other activities that wreck the human good.

The sixth basic good is social belonging and love. All manner of damage, grief, and wreckage is produced in the absence of this good. For persons to be rejected, excluded, and isolated, outcast, invisible, untouchable, and irrelevant, leaves them retarded, wounded, or deformed in their personhood. No healthy, happy human person can develop under those conditions. This good is also noxious when pursued in misdirected ways. Belonging and love of some easily develop into the exclusion of and indifference toward others, for instance. The privations and misdirection of this good casts many shadows of negative being, conjuring a wraith of the true goodness, which leaves behind a host of non-goods, anti-interests, not-flourishing in life.

Naturally Determined to Indeterminacy

But *why* in a reality in which natural-goods-seeking people are fundamentally oriented toward *eudaimonia* do stagnation, destruction, and evil ever happen? Before providing the concrete answer, we must add more theoretical backdrop. Achieving the natural human telos of flourishing is not easy, automatic, or guaranteed. Much in human life is given by nature. But reality also entails a natural indeterminacy, openness, and variability in human outcomes. It is not predetermined that persons will always pursue well their natural telos, or that they will succeed when they do. Part of what it means constitutionally to be a person is that no one is forced, guaranteed, or determined to pursue properly and achieve his or her basic goods and ultimately flourish. People must act. And people's actions are oriented toward natural human goods. But when it comes to the ontology of personhood being realized in existential experience, the reality is one of open and contingent variability. That is not post hoc conceptual gerrymandering to salvage shaky personalist ideas, but is built into the basic assumptions, terms, and outlook of personalism. Humans by nature possess capacities, powers, tendencies, and limitations that are marked by openness, indeterminacy, freedom, choice, learning, discipline, development, and movement toward potentially divergent ends. Persons are not preprogrammed machines or animals governed by behavioral impulses beyond deliberation and control. We can reflect on, evaluate, and revise our own beliefs, commitments, practices, goals, and life projects. Persons enjoy (and struggle with) a significant (though not absolute) "world openness" in this way.[38] So while the nature, ontological reality, and telic orientation of human persons are given by nature, what persons do with their lives in existential actuality in response to those fixities is not fated or determined. Quite the contrary—the possibilities are many.

Modern people tend to assume that happiness is readily achievable in this life, sometimes considering happiness to be nearly an inalienable right.[39] But while *eudaimonia* is the end to be achieved by all persons, only some do in fact achieve it. Failure is possible and actual. That possibility is built into the nature of life. A quest in which everyone automatically ended up in the same end would not be a quest. It would be an amusement park ride. A journey that easily took everyone to the same destination would not be a journey, but a group tour package. The natural purpose and proper end of humanity is never simply served up on a platter by the cosmos.[40] Receiving it that way would violate the growing, developing, telic nature of personhood. Flourishing must be actively, personally achieved (as well as social-structurally facilitated). Aristotle took as a starting point that many human beings do not, for various reasons, undertake the difficult journey toward personal flourishing. He observed that "the utter servility of the masses comes out in their preference for a bovine existence"—that is, most people prefer lives of minimal contentment being stupid and sluggish like cattle.[41] "Aristotle is a realist, not an idealist regarding human nature. He knows that clear thinking, if it is not correct thinking, will pardon vice as easily as it will applaud virtue."[42] For Aristotle, flourishing is not easy: "Failure is possible in many ways . . . but success in only one. That is why the one [failure] is easy and the other [success] difficult; it is easy to miss the target and difficult to hit it. . . . Men are bad in countless ways, but good in only one."[43]

Achieving *eudaimonia* takes progressive learning, the acquisition of virtues, the expenditure of effort across a lifetime, and the enjoyment of social-structural and institutional preconditions that make thriving possible, which can be difficult in the face of hardship, misfortune, tragedy, injustice, and oppression. People are often interpersonally and institutionally deprived of the kind of love, education, formation, and nurturing material and social contexts needed to flourish. In various ways, people are forced or choose to settle for achieving lower-level human goods rather than higher ones. People's potentials must be actively realized, and any given potential can lay dormant or be frustrated, damaged, or misdirected. This open-endedness of the personal existential challenge, as precarious though it may be, is what makes life a journey or quest. And along the way, what is good is also defined in part as the very pursuit of the good, so that the quest becomes part of the purpose it pursues. The good cannot be bought or sold, traded or stored. It must be acquired and *participated in* through the living of life in particular ways. It must be continually pursued in time and space, or else the destination is not reached. Achieving the good requires much of persons. It is possible to get wrong, to be misled, to ignore, to settle, to get distracted and sidetracked, to fail.

This indeterminacy of personal actions and outcomes opens up room not to flourish, setting up various failure scenarios.[44] Thus people can for various reasons, including institutional reasons, misunderstand what is humanly good, and so not pursue and realize their telos. These we might call *the ignorant*. People can understand what is good, but, again for various reasons, not learn about or perhaps misunderstand the virtues that help persons to realize the good. These we might call *the untrained*. People may understand the proper human good and theoretically know the right means to it, but to fail personally to exercise in actions the virtues necessary to achieve their telos. These we might call *the undisciplined*. In some unfortunate cases people know the true good and the correct means to it, and do live virtuously, but still for various reasons (often having to do with misfortune and accidents) nonetheless fail to achieve their own thriving. These are *tragic victims of fate* (connected to the first general type of failure named above). Yet other people not only fail to achieve the human good but actively and willfully deny, violate, and attack what at one level they view as the good because they also believe doing so is a higher good. These are *the pathological*. Finally, persons may do everything "right" at the personal level yet still be victims of social-structural injustice, deprivation, and exploitation in a way that causes them to fail to thrive. These we might call *victims of institutional injustice*. So, again, personal thriving is not given, it must be achieved. And oftentimes, in the world-open condition of contingent human existence and given the injustices of so many social institutions, people fail to achieve it.

The Real and the Believed

We need to step aside for a moment and introduce a distinction that has been latent in the discussion so far. That is the difference between people's objectively *real* interests and what people *believe* to be their interests. The difference is between what is real in fact and what persons perceive to be real, whether accurately or not. The facts of reality do not guarantee accurate perceptions of reality in people's experience. Even less so do people's perceptions per se make anything real. Reality is whatever it is, and people's beliefs about reality are something else (although beliefs by virtue of being believed become a new subset of reality). This distinction makes sense of the potential difference between what is *actually* good for people and what people *think* is good for them.[45] Sociologists have long recognized and wrestled with this kind of difference and the theoretical issues it creates. Karl Marx's distinction between "class interests" and "class consciousness," for example, between a "class *in* itself" and a "class *for* itself," reflects this difference. For present purposes, it is enough to recognize that people can misunderstand their own true goods, interests, and ends. People can believe that they are actually living in pursuit of what is good, yet be mistaken, sometimes badly so. The overall intention and impulse may be right but the substantive ends or means are wrong.

This is not merely a theoretical possibility. People often misidentify what is truly good for them. Slippage often happens between what *is* good and what people (want to) *believe* is good. People often think it is good, in their real interest, for example, to dominate other people, to be routinely intoxicated, to make profits at the expense of others' well-being, to always be right, to amass piles of wealth, to work as little as possible, to stuff themselves with junk food, to exercise power for its own sake, to be the most physically attractive person around, to regularly gamble, to own every product and gadget conceivable, to copulate with every mate possible, to bully others, or to be free to do anything they want to do. And such beliefs do not appear in people's heads out of thin air. They are promoted by sundry institutional interests in social life— such as the food, alcohol, media, gaming, vacation, sports, sex, gambling, advertising, and restaurant industries, among others. Powerful forces in human economies and societies lead persons away from, not toward, their true good and end. Complexes of multileveled cultural ideas and social institutions and structures, which may or may not be objectively correct or promote genuine goods, powerfully shape people's understandings of what is good. This means that living a good personal life cannot be easily separated from living in a good society—personal ethics cannot be detached from social ethics.

Potentials for Bad Inherent in Capacities for Good

Every human capacity that facilitates the possible realization of the good also carries with it the *potential* to be *turned* to the bad. Human failure and destruction are not inevitable. In principle, human life could be (or could have been) one of only good. Bad in the human condition is only a *potential*, not a fated destiny. But the real potential for the bad is *innately* and *directly* connected to the human potential for good. Every power that persons possess, which by nature is properly oriented toward the good, also has the inescapable possibility of being used for bad. Every positive affirmation entails a potential rejection. This means that what is wrong in human life does not come from some wholly alien source or power unrelated to what is good. The bad is intimately associated with the good. That is part of what makes it so insidious and intractable. If the human bad had a completely different source, nature, and power than the good, it might be easier to isolate and eradicate. But the potential for bad being directly tied to the capacity for good makes matters more difficult.

Go back to the definition of personhood given in chapter 1 and consider each element of it. Then go back to my account of human personhood in my book *What Is a Person?* and examine the thirty natural capacities from which personhood emerges.[46] Each is naturally turned toward the realization of the human good but also holds the potential to be exercised for bad, at both personal and social-structural levels. The natural human capacity for memory, for example, is necessary for the achievement of good, and much good can come from its proper exercise. But memory also has the ability to be turned to self-destructively obsessing about regrets, holding grudges, or remembering information that can be used to harm other people and passing on group hatreds from one generation to the next. Consider human creativity, an essential power to be exercised in a flourishing personal life. Creativity can be used for the bad, to imagine paralyzing causes of fear, to invent institutional instruments of torture and murder, and to concoct effective ways to manipulate and belittle other people.[47] The same potentially dual function of these natural human capacities applies to every other human power. These natural human capacities entail a kind of indeterminacy, allowing them to be put to use in ways personally and institutionally that not only achieve goods but possibly also obstruct, stunt, violate, attack, and destroy the thriving and even existence of persons.

The Privation of Necessary Facilitating Conditions

Now let us get more concrete. I said in the previous chapter that personal flourishing is developmentally dependent upon a particular set of necessary conditions that make flourishing possible—namely, Bodily Sustenance + Material Resources + Avoiding Misfortune + Being Loved + Training + Learning Virtues + Commitment to Growth + Social Participation + Loving Others. The privation of one or more of these necessary conditions tends to result in the human failure to flourish. In some ways, it is that simple. Persons who enjoy these conditions will be well positioned to flourish. When such factors are present but work incompletely, inconsistently, or at cross-purposes, persons in those situations likely flourish only moderately or incompletely. And when one or more of those conditions are seriously missing in a person's life, they are set up if not almost doomed to fail to flourish. Sometimes it only takes one severe developmental trauma or deficit in one area of life to severely diminish the realization of human personhood. Other times, people are impressively able to overcome bad odds and still achieve a measure of personal thriving, despite the lack of nurturing environmental conditions.[48] In yet other cases, bad combinations of the wrong conditions produce disasters, in which pathological persons encounter world-historical opportunities to wreak colossal destruction on other persons, the earth, and eventually themselves. The failure of some persons to flourish is thus significantly explained by deprivations in crucial environmental conditions, which leads to compromise, pathology, and sometimes death.

The reasons and ways that this happens are easy to understand. Again, persons deprived of essential material resources (access to clean and nutritious food, water, shelter, clothing, medicine, and such) cannot flourish. People lacking the right kind of training in social relationships (love, instruction, and discipline by parents, siblings, kin, mentors, teachers, friends, neighbors, voluntary associations, clergy, and such) will also fail to thrive.[49] Humans deprived of access to life-enhancing institutional contexts (opportunities to participate in the right kinds of education, work, play, the arts, athletics, politics, community life, and such) will likewise be constrained in their quest for personal flourishing. Etcetera. Flourishing is never achieved in autonomous independence. All persons are radically dependent *developmentally* on the material and social world around them for the *existential realization* of the thriving of their personhood. So when that material and social environment fails persons, when humans are deprived of one or more of them, their personal flourishing is compromised.

Before moving on, it is necessary—especially among social scientists, many of whom (perhaps especially sociologists) tend to downplay factors related to personal effort—to underscore one point, about the necessity of persons "learning virtues." An essential part of what is required to flourish as a person is ongoing personal commitment, effort, and growth.[50] The proper end of human life is not achieved easily. The quest to flourish is more like Odysseus's arduous voyage home than a walk in the park. The very idea of a quest suggests the need to get somewhere else, against distances, obstacles, weariness, and other tests of one's ability to reach one's destination. To hope to succeed, all persons must continually rise to the occasion, learn and exercise virtues, overcome obstacles, bypass distractions, transcend lesser goods, and redeem failures. That venture is always more or less difficult, being threatened by diversions, imprudence, compromise, and failure. The nature of reality involves significant "resistance" to the quest for the good. Some social scientists might think that as long as people have the right opportunities, resources, and incentives, they will definitely, maybe nearly automatically thrive as persons. But that is empirically false. Sometimes, we know, people who "have it all" are the least motivated to capitalize upon what they have to develop, grow, and thrive. Other people have only moderate but reasonable opportunities to live toward flourishing, yet nonetheless do little to thrive, but settle instead for surviving, idling, and stagnating. Right human effort has a lot to do with social and institutional constraints, resources, and opportunities. But persons are not entirely socially controlled beings, according to personalism, and the necessary right effort is not fully determined by external resources and opportunities.

Two Potential Objections

Before proceeding, I respond to two possible objections. First, putting the ideas of "natural" and "achieved" together in the same context may seem wrong to some readers. Thinking about something as simultaneously "just the way reality is" and "not automatic" may feel off beam. We tend to think of things that are "natural" as happening automatically, and "just the way reality is" as inevitable and occurring spontaneously and unavoidably. Human digestion being a natural process also means, in part, that it happens even when we sleep, does it not? We need not intend to make our digestion happen. With this assumption operating in the background, it is hard for us to hold together the fact that humans have a natural, universal, proper personal end *and* that this end is not automatic, not guaranteed, but must be achieved in an uncertain quest. But that is the way it is here. What human personhood is and how it works is simply different from digestion. Reality being stratified, complex, and emergent tells us not to be surprised by that. Many parts of nonhuman reality actually operate the way personal thriving does. Nearly everything in nature happens "just the way it does" only under certain sets of conditions that allow and foster it. What at first glance may seem automatic and guaranteed, "just the way it is by nature," turns out to be dependent upon the operation of a combination of enabling causal conditions and can be experienced variously. So human personhood, when it comes to ontologically real goods, interests, and ends, turns out to be not very different from the way much of the rest of nature works.

Another reason some readers may have difficulty accepting my argument is that their moral sensibilities tell them that if something is a basic good for human beings, all people should have access to it, perhaps have a legal right to that good. If the point of living is to lead and enjoy a good life, then should not everybody have the same shot at that as everyone else? Yet my account involves a kind of natural inequality or injustice—some people are for reasons often beyond their control privileged and others deprived, some are "dealt a good hand of cards" while others suffer tragic misfortune, some get to enjoy a rich life of personal well-being while others have the development of their personhood stunted, diminished, compromised, or terminated. That does not seem fair, especially when linked to "just the way things are." What about that?

Personalism strongly affirms these moral instincts and reactions. Yes, all persons should have access to the basic goods of personhood. All of the essentials of basic human goods must be protected and made available for participation by all as basic human rights. To the extent that humans can control it, no person should be deprived or excluded from the opportunity to realize basic human goods, to move forward on a responsible quest toward the flourishing of their own personhood as best as can be realized. Personalism thus gives rise to a "birthright-of-minimal-provisions" principle of personal and social ethics. Every person ought to have a shot at expending the effort to live a life that is good and thriving. Everyone should, so far as it is humanly possible, get to participate, have access, be challenged, and be sustained on his or her journey toward flourishing. The fact that this often does not happen is morally wrong, especially when humans have any control over it. Those moral sensibilities represent the core of personalist ethics and illustrate the way the "is" of reality informs the "oughts" of personalism. That means that such moral sensibilities should *attract* us to personalism, not render its description of reality suspicious. To refuse personalism on this point because the world in full of inequality and injustice does nothing to change those facts, but only reinforces them, by abjuring the most solid moral rationale for attacking and changing them. Instead, we need to grasp the deeply humanistic nature and implications of critical realist personalism. We should recognize and work with the moral truths that are grounded in the nature of reality, including real human personhood, and use our personal and social powers to conform the world to one that better respects the particularity and dignity of all human persons. That will affirm the best of our moral sensibilities and will contribute to the thriving of our own personhood and that of others.

The Existential Conditions of Fear, Denial, and Love

My account so far still lacks a dynamic explanation of what initially triggers and promotes the bad in human life instead of the good. Just because something is possible does not mean that it must become actual. Some potentialities are never realized. Something must cause actualities when they are actualized. So what causes failure? In keeping with critical realism's emphasis on complexity, the answers to this question must obviously be multiple and complex. Given space limitations, I will focus on only one causal force among many—yet one worth considering. Others, of course, ought also to be considered and examined, though doing anything more complex is beyond my capacity here. One answer to the question of what dynamic trigger helps cause failure leads us to the matter of people's primal responses to the objective condition of human vulnerability and the common and powerful emotional response of fear. All humans live in contexts of immense vulnerability to personal harms of many kinds, a condition that commonly evokes the primordial affective response of fear, which typically provokes people to respond and behave toward other persons and the world in ways that tend to inhibit and sometimes terminate progress toward flourishing—and, under certain conditions, give rise to evil and destruction.

In myriad ways, all humans throughout all of their lives are *dependent, vulnerable,* and *needy.* No person at any stage of life is self-sufficient, invincible, or sovereign. No one is the sole source and ground of their own being. Every person, no matter how healthy, powerful, or wealthy is radically dependent on resources, information, and care found or supplied by sources beyond themselves. They are dependent both on other persons in direct relationships and on social institutions for the provision of these goods. On some of these, we humans are *radically* dependent, meaning that our existence would be seriously damaged and perhaps ended without them. On others we are *chronically* dependent, meaning that the need for them never goes away. I refer of course to the human needs for oxygen, water, food, light, spatial orientation, bodily self-control, physical touch, protection from the elements, clothing, avoidance of physical attack, accident, injury, and illness, human love and care, mutual understanding, affirmation, affection, stable meaning, ontological security, and the keeping of overwhelming chaos and insanity at bay. These are basic physical, biological, relational, and psychological requisites for a functional human life. Such needs, dependencies, and vulnerabilities cannot be wished away, or bought off with any amount of money or political influence.

This puts every person in a precarious situation. At almost any moment, something could happen that might suffocate, maim, or kill us. The chances may be large or slim, but they are never zero. People are continually caught off guard by accidents, tragedies, and severe weather. On any day, any person could be diagnosed with a terrible disease. At any moment, anyone could be informed that a loved one has been abducted, killed in an accident, or murdered. On any day, terrorists could attack. In any month, the global economy could begin to collapse. So much can fail: friends, bodies, banks, marriages, jobs, economies. Planes may crash. Houses may burn. Savings may be lost.

Missiles may be launched. Energy sources may be cut. Climates may change. Asteroids may hit. People, cultures, the entire human race may go extinct. Many such things have happened, do happen, and will happen. That is the frightening truth for humanity. We are incredibly vulnerable to harm. And the existential weight of that knowledge when fully confronted can be nearly crushing. What can people do in response? Humans face, as far as I can see, three different options in responding to this vulnerable condition. One is *fear*. The second is *denial*. And the third is *trust*. Fear and denial lean us toward failure when it comes to realizing human goods. Trust, on the other hand, tends to promote an approach to life that fosters flourishing.

First, consider *fear*. Much evidence points to fear as the basis for people choosing against human goods. When personal life is governed by fear, it is inevitably directed by a fundamental mistrust and defensive self-protectiveness. The world beyond the self comes to be viewed fundamentally as a threat that must be evaded, resisted, or beaten. That orients persons toward persistent self-regard that may involve, if necessary, a readiness to deny reality, compromise the telic quest, and inflict the costs of one's self-protectiveness on others, on the material, animal, or social world beyond the self. That posture prepares persons to assert the unreal in various ways, to dehumanize others, to inflict damage, and to refuse trust, virtue, and growth. That derails the teleological quest for flourishing, leading to failure and sometimes malice and evil. Scholars who study emotions say fear is one of a small set of primary emotions (including happiness, sadness, surprise, disgust, and anger).[51] Fear actually has a highly adaptive function, alerting people to potential and real threats to their well-being. But fear rarely operates as a carefully calibrated, well-tuned, highly accurate and discriminating indicator of genuine reasons for fear, to which instincts and reason can then respond well. Fear is also not merely a personal fact but often the result of larger cultural and institutional conditions that promote it.[52]

Fear often takes over as a generalized orientation to life—even sometimes among seemingly confident people—and governs people's primal reactions and decisions. Fear can also retreat far to the background and only emerge powerfully under certain conditions. However fear makes its home in people's existence, living out of fear normally drives people to bad decisions, actions, practices, and lifestyles. The anthropologist Ernest Becker has argued that the universal human fear of death, specifically, is the taproot of most of humanity's incessant cultural activity and great cultural achievements, on the one hand, and of the species' ubiquitous evil and self-destruction, on the other.[53] Erich Fromm argued—perhaps not mutually exclusively—that most human evil springs from a deep human fear of the freedom and openness of life.[54] Some researchers who study evil people, such as socio-pathic serial murderers, argue similarly that the fear of death is a primary reason for humanity's pervasive, morbid fascination with violence, horror, murder, and death, including attraction to the most grotesque and revolting media depictions of torture and carnage.[55] This suggests that something deep in humanity is strangely attracted to that which we also dread, abominate, and find repulsive, terrifying, and horrific.[56]

But fear rarely manifests itself in anything as dramatic as sociopathic serial killings. Its more standard expressions are prosaic. Because of fear, people hoard instead of share, use others instead of love them. They are defensive and aggressive, apathetic and detached. People lie and deceive, steal and cheat because of fear. Fear makes people desperate and, often as a result, stupid. Fear churns up anxiety and distress, which helps people to believe lies and propaganda. Fear also seeks to resolve itself by myriad destructive means, such as aggression, dehumanization, and scapegoating. Fear turns friends and allies into corpses and enemies. It gives us the Stalins and Hitlers of the world, but also the pathetic, shriveled nobodies who ruminate over odium in dimly lit living quarters. Fear turns prison guards and summer campers into sadists, and parents into control freaks. Fear is the wellspring of jeal-ousy, pettiness, compromise, and meanness. Fear is also closely connected to fighting—the initial impulse to flight generated by fear, when obstructed, easily turns into the impulse to fight. Whatever else helps to explain problems in human life, fear seems to be at the bottom of much of it.[57] So to live out of fear—whether felt on the surface or buried deep in the self—is not to move toward personal flourishing.

Consider next *denial*. People live in denial when they confront possibili-ties or actualities they do not want to personally experience and respond by pretending they do not exist. These usually involve needs unfulfilled, vulner-abilities encroached upon, yearnings unmet, and loves lost. Behind much of these stand the specters of suffering and death, which continually circle the edges of life, and sometimes assault its center. Denial can be accomplished in various ways. One is simply to put an idea out of one's mind. "Stop thinking about that," we tell ourselves, deploying our will to change the content of our cognitions. That our child, late in coming home, may have been killed in an automobile accident, for instance, is a real possibility we can refuse to allow ourselves consciously to entertain. Another version of denial responds to threats by forming the belief that they do not actually exist. Sometimes this works as a temporary coping strategy: "No, it simply *can't* be, you are *wrong!*" Denial can also operate at the level of institutions.[58]

Sometimes denial digs in its heels as a desperate refusal to live in reality.

That defiance of reality is more stubborn, more determined to hold the bad-ness at bay, whatever the other costs may be. It may be denying that one's alcoholism is ruining one's life and those of others, or refusing to acknowl-edge that one's sexual practices are likely to give one or others HIV/AIDS. Such denial involves a refusal to accept responsibility and be accountable, or the refusal to suffer pain and experience the real bodily, emotional, and other consequences of loss. In the end, denial is a refusal of reality, to accept and live in and with what is real. And, as noted above (regarding avoidant-destructive people), that exacts huge personal costs. Humans cannot over time refuse reality and get by as if all is well. To continually deny reality is to increasingly live in *un*reality, in a place of *non*being, in an existence of nega-tion that *can not exist*. Ultimately, *nothingness* is the end of that road. And the way to that destination is littered with the destructive accessories and symp-toms of denial: deception, incoherence, delusions, contradictions, duplicity, anxiety, and irrationality. The ultimate end of the severest denial of reality is self-annihilation—and the destruction of many other people and much property along the way.

Here we touch, as another aside, on a basic principle of personalist eth-ics: *always live in reality*. The human good can only be realized within and in response to what is real, not dreams and delusions.[59] Reality is the only way forward toward a good in life. When one lives in reality—accepting it in full-ness as well as it can be understood—one has nothing to hide, no fictions to protect, no secret to keep, no discomforts to finesse. Nobody is pretend-ing otherwise. However, once a person begins to live in denial, even only a bit of it, the denial must spread or stop. There is no equilibrium in reality's denial. The force of reality is so strong that denying it takes huge energy and work to accomplish, even for a time. Because reality is ultimately one unified whole, when even only one part of reality is denied, other parts related to it begin to encroach, to trespass, to unmask the denial as unreal. Reality has so many ways to impose itself upon us that protecting any one part of it from an admission of the truth requires extending the strategy of denial to new parts of life. What starts off with one lie turns into many, simply to maintain the first. When carried out seriously and resolutely, this takes the person down. People's denials do not change reality, only the people who deny and those they know, and not for the good. Living in refusal of reality always distorts, corrupts, disintegrates, and damages.[60]

One psychological mechanism (that arguably also operates at the institu-tional level) by which this destruction occurs we might call the "mental costs of cognitive deception." The human brain is naturally wired to work with our other perceptual organs to learn and know as well as possible what is true about what is real. We may not often do that well, but our biological equipment has been formed to tune us into our real environments so that we may survive and thrive in them. Therefore, to get ourselves to believe something other than reality, the not-reality—that is, self-deceptions—requires working against the natural tendencies of human biology, perception, and psychology. That exacts a drain of energy, a kind of psychic resistance or friction, to devote an unnatural amount of mental resources to sustain the not-reality in belief. People pay significant mental and physical costs to maintain reality-denying beliefs. It may come in the form of fatigue, anxiety, wariness, mental incoherence, disassociation, or some other dysfunction, but some cost is always paid. Another mechanism by which the damage of denial is wrecked involves what psychologists call "projection bias" and "externalization." This happens when people unconsciously deny the influence of their own thoughts, attributes, or emotions and instead (erroneously) ascribe them to objects in the environment, often other people. The effect is to blame anything but themselves when things go wrong, to deflect personal responsibility for one's behaviors or condition. People thus refuse to accept the real causes of and responsibilities for problems (usually themselves or loved ones) and instead project them onto other people or circumstances. Think: "The tree got in the way of my car!" But projection damages the projector and others. It harms the former by enabling the continuation of problems, preventing people from owning up to difficulties that can only be solved when responsibility is owned. It often also harms other people because it places blame on them that is undeserved, involving unfair accusations or insinuations of guilt, which generate conflicts, as falsehoods are stated as accusations in the service of delusional self-protection.

An even more insidious and destructive consequence of people's and institutions' failure to accept and live in reality, and to improve upon it as best as they are able, is this: the tendency for certain negative emotions to be expressed in ways that have nothing to do with the cause of those emotions but instead to be transposed and vented in inhumane and violent ways. For instance, a tragically classic way that people deal with humiliation and shame from past personal violations or abuse is to redirect that emotional energy onto other objects as outlets or compensations. Psychologists call this "transference." People who feel bad about themselves make themselves feel better (for a time) by making others feel bad. The victim becomes the victimizer. Those who have been abused, abuse others. Those who have been belittled, bully others. Sadism compensates for suffering. A related version of this process carried out at the group level is scapegoating. Here the group focuses its diffuse, collective anxiety or guilt on a concrete object, an animal, person, or other group, and punish or sacrifice it as a way to "expiate" its anxiety or guilt.[61]

The possible forms of denial are nearly endless. "Eating this trash food won't hurt my health much." "I know this is not good for me, so I'll begin to stop it tomorrow." "If I do whatever it takes to succeed, I can make myself secure in life." "My life would be perfect if he had not done this to me, so I have to make him pay." "I know it happens to other people but it won't happen to me." "Another shot of heroin (or whatever) will get rid of this horrible feeling inside." "If I just go back and behave myself better this one last time, maybe he won't beat me anymore, but will really love me." Those are the personal examples, which can, of course, be matched with many institutional examples: "If we continue to dump our waste in this river, it should not hurt it too much." "Our selling of fraudulent financial packages won't really hurt anyone or the economy," and so on. What human experience tells us, however, is that the continual denial of reality ultimately helps nothing. Reality always wins. Efforts to escape it recurrently end up creating more trouble, grief, and destruction than honestly dealing with reality ever would have. This is, among other reasons, why Aristotle named courage as a crucial virtue for flourishing, and why cowardice is the characteristic vice of avoidant-destructive people.

The alternative to fear and denial in response to the facts of humanity's radical dependence and vulnerability is a disposition of *trust*. That means the readiness to go forward in life with a realistic confidence that one will survive and be taken care of despite the threats and dangers of life in this world, fostered by the belief that trust is justified and that there are worse things in life than suffering and death. Trust operates importantly at the personal and interpersonal plane, obviously, but also at the level of culture and institutions.[62] Trust acknowledges fully the real difficulties and terrors of human existence. It denies nothing of the helplessness, peril, and horrors of human life in this world. But trust is not overwhelmed by those facts, nor finally driven by them into fear or denial. In trust, people stand up and live their lives in the belief that they are adequately secure despite life's real insecurities. Trust accepts that things have, can, and will go wrong, but that life must and can be lived in the belief that the good and the right will finally overcome the wrong. Trust does not know what will happen next, but it nonetheless steps into the future with a hopeful but realistically prudent confidence. Trust is unwilling to be cowed or defeated by the threats of life. It is determined to overcome, to move forward, and to thrive to the extent that thriving is possible. And if the trustful person is waylaid or even destroyed by tragic *fortuna*, then he or she will do everything possible to still live and die with honor, dignity, and love, encouraging others to also continue living their lives in trust.[63]

That sounds nice, perhaps even pathetically credulous. So how, one might ask, given the needy and vulnerable human condition lived in this precarious and sometimes-treacherous world, can anyone muster and live out of that kind of trust? Why and how in a world of real danger, scarcity, vulnerability, and menace could *any* human trust in life? The answer is simple and difficult. Humans can live lives of trust *when they believe that they are loved*. Love is the only thing that finally makes trust possible (though not necessarily inevitable)—lots of love received from and given back to other persons. By love, again, I mean people's active commitment to enhance and protect the well-being of other persons, motivated simply for the good of other persons and not by exchange considerations of merit or reward. Trust is not conferred by wealth, power, or social status—they can disappear quickly, so are often actually a source of fear and anxiety. Personal trust has one source: believing that one is loved, which requires *actually being* loved (except in cases where people live in the illusion that they are loved when they are not, which usually cannot last long). People who have never been loved—particularly not at an early age—cannot trust and will not flourish. Persons who are loved can trust and flourish.[64] And part of what it means for them to flourish is to become a person who loves others. The activity and experience of love thus arguably stands at the heart of human existence. Around love (or its lack) human life revolves, and either flourishes or destructs. But my more specific point of this section is simply that in the absence of love, humans easily respond to the insecurities and threats of life in this world with fear and denial, and those in turn are often responsible as dynamic triggers for ways of life that lead to failure and sometimes evil.

A Multileveled, Conjunctural Approach

Critical realist personalism tells us that reality is stratified, complex, and causally interactive and contingent. It helps us to see both upward emergence and downward causation operating at all levels of being and influence. It instructs us to get ready for real complexity as we attempt to understand and explain reality. When it comes to human failure, destruction, and evil, therefore, personalism prepares us to see and understand—and therefore to model—complex, multiple, interactive levels of reality operating in upwardly emergent and causally downward directions. We have to bring into our theoretical models possible multiple dimensions of human personal reality—including

biology, existential condition, individual personality, immediate environmental situations, and larger social structural environments. Anything less
will give us myopic and simplistic explanations. Personal outcomes of flourishing (or not) are dependent on complex interactions between the givens
of and developments in human bodies and the variable environmental and
social-structural contexts and experiences with and within which those bodies interact and develop. All human outcomes involve complicated interactions of nature and nurture, body and environment, biology and experience.
And between them, the influences run in both and all directions. Little is
absolutely determinative. Most everything is interactive and responsive. We
therefore cannot understand variance in human failures to flourish by focusing exclusively on genetics or neuroscience or psychology or socialization or
social structures or any other one site of analytic concern. All of those and
more are implicated in any given outcome of personal flourishing. To understand and explain, we need a more complex, comprehensive, coherent approach than any of the academic disciplines alone provide. Table 2 describes
the kinds of factors that multidisciplinary research has shown to contribute
to human failure, violence, destructiveness, and evil.

I cannot here explain each of these factors. Suffice it for present purposes
to note a few particular points. First, many factors that help to cause failure,
destruction, and evil are variable (biology, personality, situations), while others are more constantly part of the baseline human condition (precategori-
cal existential dreads) and can only be mitigated, constructively directed,
or contained (through symbolic, rather than bodily, expression, or through
learned virtues and social control).[65] Second, truly evil acts are possible on
an "everyday scale" even when only a few of the conditions at a few levels (in
table 2) are met, but genuine, full-blown collective evils require more factors
at most levels to combine causally to produce them. Distinct evil persons
can destroy and humiliate, but can do so only in limited amounts as lone
actors. Full-blown evil of the most devastating kind requires the technology and power of social institutions—of coordinated collective action—to
wreak the greatest destructive horrors against persons.[66] The more that distinct people with inclinations to darkness find themselves in evil-fostering
social and institutional contexts, the more their personal dark tendencies are
nourished. Third, human capacities for most kinds of failure, destructiveness, and evil are developmentally formed, starting very early in life.[67] Many
failed and destructive persons suffer from an inability to empathize with the
experiences and feelings of other people, which—since capacities for empathy not only have some stable basis in temperamental personality but are

TABLE 2. Background and proximate causes of human violence and destruction

Background causal factors	Proximate causal factors
Environmental and institutional factors	*Personal factors*
Poor parenting and maladaptive families	Narcissism, robust egotism
Violent residential neighborhood	Threatened high self-esteem
Cultural norms that support violence	Lack of empathy for others, desensitization
Experiences of victimization	Dehumanization of others, deindividuation
Material deprivation	Belief in the acceptability and efficacy of violence, retaliation, aggression
Group conflict	Low tolerance for living with insecure situations and feelings
Fear-inducing events	Hostile attribution, expectation, and perception biases, aggression scripts
Lack of bystander interventions in previous violent encounters	Tendency to displace responsibility
Exposure of violent media	Belief in cultural stereotypes about groups
Association with antisocial peers	Low self-control, lack of inhibiting barriers to evil acts
Separation of authority decision makers from the enactors of evildoing	
Biological predisposers	*Situational facilitators*
Low serotonin	Social stress and provocations
Attention deficit hyperactivity disorder	Alcohol and other drugs involved
Hormone imbalances	Frustration, threat, fear, or anxiety-promoting stimuli
Executive function deficits	Pain or discomfort, being in a bad mood
Monoamine oxidase A (MAO-A) dysfunction	High temperatures
Short SERT allele	Available weapons
Low brain-derived neurotropic factor (BNDF)	Boredom, ambiguity, misinformation
Dysregulated Catechol-O-methyltransferase	Tit-for-tat, escalating vicious-cycle interactions
Existential conditions	*Social structural facilitators*
Reduced capacity to symbolically express pre-categorical dread of existential terrors	Loud noise
Inability to counter an "autistic-contiguous" experience with a "depressive" position	Lack of condemnation or intervention of bystanders

TABLE 2. (*continued*)

Fear of freedom and death	Bureaucracies, technologies, and polities of destruction
	Organizational separation of decision making from implementation, diffusion of responsibility
	Etc.

Sources: Baumeister, *Evil: Inside Human Violence and Cruelty*; Staub, *The Roots of Evil*; Alford, *What Evil Means to Us*; Vetlesen, *Perception, Empathy, and Judgment*; Card, *The Atrocity Paradigm*; Fromm, *The Heart of Man*; Becker, *The Denial of Death, Escape from Evil*; Peck, *People of the Lie*; Kellerman, *Savage Spawn*; Morton, *On Evil*; Oakley, *Evil Genes*; Katz, *Ordinary People and Extraordinary Evil*.

also profoundly shaped by lack of loving socialization by parents and other family and nonfamily members—has deep roots in infant, toddler, and early childhood experiences.[68]

We can take any factor in table 2 and break it down in finer detail to spell out more precise processes by which it works. Consider, for instance, biological factors. Recent research in neuroscience and genetics tells us that different persons embody different genetic and neural bases of tendencies to act in antisocial, aggressive, and violent ways.[69] Variance in vulnerabilities to or proclivities toward (which is different from determination of) destructive and even evil behaviors is thus *partly* rooted in the body.[70] Some of this literature is unacceptably reductionistic.[71] But some is not, at least when properly framed by a critical realist view of the complexity, stratification, and emergence of reality. And responsible scholarship pushes us toward a greater appreciation for the importance of biological bodies in helping to shape subflourishing personal life outcomes. The elemental capacity of human bodies to enjoy pleasures and suffer pains plays a huge role in the failure to flourish. Potent neurological processes involving neurotransmitters such as dopamine and oxytocin can exert intense and sometimes nearly overwhelming powers to direct and at times control human behavior. So some of the very aspects of embodied human life that properly contribute to personal thriving (food, alcohol, sex, rest, visual stimuli, and such) can also easily take over life and undermine personal thriving (through overeating, alcoholism, laziness, promiscuity, and excessive visual-media consumption). All of the body's powers and vulnerabilities are capable of being trained, directed, disciplined,[72] and deployed to contribute to life practices that, with the exercise of virtues, move us resolutely toward the teleological end of thriving. Yet none of this implies biological determinism, because biology itself is interactive with and somewhat shaped by environment and experience. Brains, for example, can be rewired by experiences, such as becoming a parent and childhood trauma and stress. So persons' experience in interpersonal relationships and social institutions interacts with biology to shape life outcomes.

Consider situational factors too. Studies suggest that social situations that do the following are more like to get people to participate in evildoing, whether reluctantly or enthusiastically:

- Present a seemingly reasonable initial justification or rationale for engaging in otherwise undesirable actions.
- Arrange a verbal or written contractual obligation to perform the expected behaviors.
- Provide meaningful social roles for participants to play.
- Present basic rules to follow that would normally seem reasonable but that can later be applied in extreme ways.
- Change the ways actions are semantically described to reorient normal meanings of words that make the evil seem more justified.
- Diffuse responsibility for bad outcomes among multiple actors.
- Begin with small, inconsequential actions and then increase levels of wrongdoing incrementally.
- Begin with the just and rational exercise of authority and gradually shift to an unjust and unreasonable exercise of authority.
- Make the costs for exiting the situation high and the process of exit difficult.
- Disallow standard forms of verbal dissent by stigmatizing them as off limits.[73]

Again, situations are not determining but, among other factors, are important to understand.

Finally, let us consider social-structural and institutional causal mechanisms of human failure, destruction, and evil. These are amenable to empirical investigation and theoretical understanding. The late sociologist Charles Tilly, for instance, has described four basic social causal mechanisms that recurrently generate the kind of durable inequalities of resources necessary for human flourishing—the deprivation of which thus contribute to failures to flourish. These are, according to Tilly:

- *Exploitation*, "when powerful, connected people command resources from which they draw significantly increased returns by coordinating the effort of outsiders whom they exclude from the full value added by that effort."
- *Opportunity Hoarding*, "when members of a categorically bounded network acquire access to a resource that is valuable, renewable, subject to monopoly, supportive of network activities, and enhanced by the network's modus operandi."

- *Emulation*, "the copying of established organizational models and/or the transplanting of existing social relations from one setting to another."
- *Adaptation*, "the elaboration of daily routines . . . on the basis of categorically unequal structures."[74]

Likewise, the psychologists Jim Sidanius and Felicia Pratto have elaborated a comprehensive Social Dominance Theory (SDT) that explains intergroup relations of oppression, domination, destructive discrimination, tyranny, and brutality. Their illuminating theory involves interpersonal, intergroup, intrapersonal, and institutional causal mechanisms that produce and maintain group-based hierarchies of domination. They include personal "social dominance orientations," "aggregated individual discrimination," "aggregated institutional discrimination," "behavioral asymmetry," hierarchy-enhancing "legitimizing myths," and "hierarchy equilibriums and constraints."[75] With more space, I could list other social-science theories describing how various forms of human failures to flourish, including evil, occur through identifiable causal mechanisms.[76] The discussion here has been brief and suggestive. But the basic point should be clear. Because reality is stratified, complex, and contingently causal, our social-scientific understandings and explanations will also have to be multileveled, adequately complex, and accounting of interactive causal contingencies.

Socially and Psychologically Structured Historical Inheritances

Nobody begins life with a blank slate. People inherit the consequences of all the bad and good in human life and society that predates their birth. If we set aside the difficult question of the *ultimate* origins of evil in human existence, a great deal of the actual darkness with which anyone at any place and time lives can be explained with reference to the many broken social institutions, relationships, and cultural beliefs and practices inherited from the past, which shape all the lives they touch. Many problems are also engraved into people's psychological and emotional structures in ways causing them to perpetuate the problems into the next generation. This rough homology of objective and subjective structures makes breaking the propagation of failure, malice, and destruction difficult. Life socialization, practices, patterns of thought, action, and reaction form deeply ingrained habits of assumptions and strategies. Marx was right on this point: "The tradition of all the dead generations weighs like a nightmare on the mind of the living."[77] Once investments are made into certain ways of life and institutional practices, more are usually made to reinforce and protect them. It is easier to sustain a direction than to change. In virtuous lives of telic learning, growth, and overcoming, that dynamic produces upward spirals of achievement and flourishing. In lives short on virtue, the bad, wrong, and possibly evil becomes hardened, reinforced, and defended in downward spirals of error, corruption, and destruction of others.

A major challenge to any person's flourishing, therefore, is that in life all people arrive into an already existing, structured, troubled world full of older people and institutions, many of whom are already stuck in various ways, and of problems deeply embedded in social practices, institutions, and structures. The intergenerational transmission of the "defeators" of personal thriving described in the previous chapter is powerful. The accumulated cultural and institutional inheritance of humanity's lack of love, abuse, exploitation, aggression, selfishness, and indifference perpetuates these problems across generations.[78] All persons are thrown into such a world, which explains the destabilizing "thrownness" (*Geworfenheit*) of this human condition.[79] If each new human was able to start afresh on their quest toward personal flourishing, in a morally virgin world, without any of the weight or pollution of previous history forming their experience and character, their lives might look different. But for real human persons, being radically developmentally dependent upon the existing social and material world to realize the persons they are, such fresh starts are impossible. And no historical attempt to induce that kind of fresh start—through revolutionary transformation or utopian withdrawal—has succeeded in eradicating darkness from human experience. In many cases, these attempts have only produced even greater evils. Any developed account of failure, malice, and destruction in human life must therefore take seriously the reality of deeply embedded, temporally transmitted social, institutional, and psychological structures of brokenness.[80]

Against Social Situationism Again

As an aside, before moving on, we must return on this topic to deal again with social situationism, which I critiqued in chapter 3. Much influential social psychological work over the last decades—building on the famed Milgram experiments on "obedience to authority"[81] and Philip Zimbardo's "Stanford prison experiment"[82]—has promoted the idea that there are no evil people in the world, only "ordinary" (that is, good) people who are compelled to act evilly because of the behavior-distorting situations in which they inadvertently find themselves. This work has served the ideological and political purposes of liberal individualism in two ways: first, by defending the secular Enlightenment notion of innate human goodness (against theological notions of human sinfulness); and, second, by framing humanity's problem as the abuse of social and political authority, not of broken human persons. The implication is that if autonomous individuals were free to behave as they chose, without the warping influences of social and political institutions and systems, then the world would be well. Here we have not only political liberalism but also a particularly antiauthoritarian version of it championing the spirit of the rebellious 1960s. Zygmunt Bauman makes this antiestablishment situationism explicit in his sociological analysis of the Holocaust, claiming that "*inhumanity* is a matter of *social relationships*" and "*cruelty* correlates with certain patterns of *social interaction.*" Thus, Bauman claims, people have a "moral responsibility for *resisting socialization. . . .* Morality may manifest itself in *insubordination toward socially upheld principles*, and in an action *openly defying social solidarity and consensus.*"[83] In short, the problem with darkness and evil is not located in persons but with modern authorities armed with bureaucracy and technology that forces people into bad situations. Despite some valuable insights that this approach provides, I find it to be fantastically naive.[84] For starters, the conclusions of scholars like Milgram, Zimbardo, and Bauman actually do not clearly match or follow from their evidence.[85] The standard conclusions also routinely fail to consider the possibility—almost inconceivable for many Enlightenment liberals—that evil potentials or tendencies actually reside in most "normal" people. Zimbardo has written that "our results are . . . congruent with those of Milgram, who most convincingly demonstrated the proposition that evil acts are not necessarily the deeds of evil men, but may be attributed to the operation of powerful *social* forces. . . . The inherently pathological characteristics of the . . . *situation* itself . . . were a sufficient condition to produce aberrant, anti-social behavior."[86] But psychologist C. Fred Alford rightly objects:

> *Wait just a minute! Milgram did not demonstrate any such thing, he just concluded it.* Only if we *presume* that evil is a situational attribute, not a quality of mind or heart, does this conclusion make sense. . . . What if this [acting in a situation that would absolve them of their sadistic actions] is just what these normal men and women want? . . . Then . . . finding that [they] are just reacting to their environment would miss the point.[87]

The better conclusion, Alford observes, "the most straightforward and obvious explanation of all," is that "the conditions of the study, a drama in which the role of disciplinarian was offered to all, were sufficient to *bring out* the evil in normal men and women, their sadism."[88] Thus even in our examination of human failure and evil—seemingly moral and philosophical issues—we find ourselves confronting the problems of sociological social situationism again. And by taking the same approach to it that I developed in chapter 3, we can avoid some of its simplistic, unrealistic, person-discounting assumptions. For present purposes, that means *centering persons* not only with questions of human goods, but also human failures, destruction, and evil.

The Quest for the Good Energizing the Bad

The fact that the bad is so intimately linked to the good makes it easy to get them confused. This helps explain why humanity's pursuit of the bad can become so determined and zealous. When people pursue what is bad, it is done with the energy naturally intended to achieve the good. When people do bad, they often think they are doing good. Even when they live in ways that they know are bad, the motivational energy that compels them is the same that directs people toward the good. If the bad were a whole different species of being, substantively alien to the good, it would be easier to tell them apart and notice a different motivational structure. But the bad closely maps onto the good, always existing parasitically on it. All of the ways that humans go wrong take exactly the form of basic human goods, only in ways that are pursued badly, distorted, or deprived of the good. So, for example, "people demonize the other not out of ignorance or intolerance but to protect their own threatened goodness."[89] Pursuing the bad easily becomes confused with the quest for the good, and the energy expended toward it comes from the same source as that seeking the good.

Human being is innately being in becoming. Personal and social existence is development, one way or another. Life is moving in a becoming direction. The question is: becoming who and what? Human persons are incomplete in existential expression, though not in ontology. Being teleologically oriented means not yet arrived, not hitherto complete or achieved. The position is one of felt need to fill, to complete, to satisfy. It involves something like a hunger, a desire to get something or somewhere.[90] This provides a dissatisfaction innate to human existence in relation to the good. It also sets people up for possible attempts to fulfill that dissatisfaction with pseudo or lesser or diversionary goods. The good is a difficult good, not easy. And there is a continual temptation to substitute easy, lesser goods for higher goods—to settle, to satisfice. That may lead to temporary satisfaction, but normally it satisfies increasingly less over time. Escalating addiction may become the model. Yet even when the quest for personal flourishing is diverted and distorted by the pathologies of the bad, the natural, inexorable drive for the good *cannot be turned off.* Until death, it pushes humans to advance, to develop life as an active project. Even when the course of lives becomes stuck or disfigured, a restless energy drives it onward. We cannot simply stop short of life's natural telic goal. Nature's compulsion keeps on compelling. We humans do not just go bad and stay put. Our badness is continually driven by a relentless energy to develop, energized as the misdirected pursuit of the good. The vehicle of our lives never halts, but drives forward, whether on a good course or off course. The motive energy naturally given to pursue the good is exactly what people expend to fuel the doing of bad. And that is a powerful force.

Thresholds into Pathology

Why is the mere *possibility* of evil brought by some people into *actuality*, despite the most grievous of effects it brings? Why, with the option of true flourishing standing clearly along life's road and at the end of that road, do people ever instead choose malice and destruction? How could The Nothing compel a human will to act against the good? I have already said that one of the ways that things go wrong in and for humanity is when people and institutions deny reality, become distracted, give in to compromises, and get stuck on obstacles. That leads at first to mere personal stagnation—a benign settling, compromise, and failure to advance. But eventually and inevitably, human energy seeking to achieve the good drives the always-becoming person on and eventually mutates pathologically, becoming misdirected and deprived of good in ways that lead to the genuine destruction of others and, eventually, of the malignant person. The drive toward false goods that denies reality and still seeks to justify itself must increasingly engage in falsehoods, lies, coercion, and eventually destruction of others and self in order to sustain itself. At some point, the mere stagnation and destructiveness turn into full-blown pathology.[91] In this way, the unrelenting pursuit of the good in bad ways eventually becomes highly destructive. The vice that then comes to be is worse than error, sloth, or cowardice. It involves the *will*, the purposive volition to destruct. But what is involved in that process that helps explain the passage of the threshold of failure and stagnation into genuine evil?

Human beings and social institutions seem to find the possibility of darkness to be sorely tempting, however irrational, dysfunctional, and destructive its consequences may be. For seemingly inexplicable reasons, human beings, as the self-directing efficient causes of their own actions, seem to find it nearly impossible not to head into whatever is possible, even when it is darkness. If it is *possible*, at least some humans indulge the temptation. If certain people climb mountains simply because the mountains are there, many also seem drawn to leap into the abyss of nothingness just because it is there. I cannot explain why that is so, but its truth I think is familiar. Have humans in history ever had something about which they said, "We can do it, but we won't"? Rarely.[92] Every possibility seems to at least some humans irresistible—even when it turns out to be a plunge into evil.[93]

Once evil is engaged, escape becomes difficult. This is no moralizing cliché, but a psychologically and sociologically verifiable fact. Once nefarious events have been initiated, a series of vicious psychological, institutional, and social forces circle in to reinforce, consolidate, rationalize, and perpetuate them. One reason is that much of human organizational behavior consists of the determined avoidance of accountability.[94] The human desire and capacity to excuse, legitimate, and justify what is wrong is astounding—driven primarily by the misdirected pursuit of the human good of moral affirmation. Having once stumbled or jumped into darkness, people and institutions find it difficult to bring themselves and their actions out into the light, especially against the urgings of compatriots to remain in the darkness together. Evil embeds itself in habitus, routine practices, social structures, practical consciousness, deep cultural categories, cognitive structures, and socially hard-to-break patterns of behavior. The downward spiral once begun seems easier to sustain than the upward spiral to initiate. Shame, fear, inertia, laziness, and denial keep the cycle of brokenness turning, whereas real disclosure, acknowledgment, remorse, pardon, restitution, reconciliation, and a turn back to the good is painful, difficult, and uncommon—however much they represent the path back to flourishing.

Finally, the more vices and bads a person or institution chooses, the less equipped he, she, or it subsequently becomes to know and to choose the good.[95] Moves away from goodness are *degenerative* in this way; they produce an ultimately necrophilial "syndrome of decay."[96] One does not indulge in the not-good without consequence. Darkness corrupts those who venture into it. Aristotle himself taught this, that just as it takes the accumulation of practiced virtues to move toward *eudaimonia,* the practice of vices only moves one further from an understanding and enjoyment of the good.[97] Perhaps only few humans ever get past the point of no return, over the waterfall of moral oblivion. More social institutions than persons seem to, however. But the closer anyone or any institution gets to it, the stronger the psychological, sociological, and moral currents pulling toward it become and the harder they are to resist.

Conclusion

We can through careful reflection on history and life experience go a long way toward understanding and explaining human personal, institutional, and social-structural failure and evil. I have attempted that in this chapter. But in such an inquiry we may also be wrong to lose complete sight of the deeply irrational and in some ways baffling nature of evil. Failure and evil are violations of reality. They reflect something inexplicably broken, not something intelligibly working. Destructive evil in particular is inherently irrational and antireality. Evil traffics in incomprehensibly destructive deeds, inexplicable wickedness. Thus a common reaction to the Holocaust, the archsymbol of twentieth-century human evil, was uncomprehending silence—appropriately so.[98] In its own negative, malignant way, evil is plainly real and powerful as the privation of the good, but it is not finally clear—despite our too common familiarity with the fact—why humans gravitate to its destructiveness. That may simply be one of the impenetrable mysteries of personhood in this broken world, which even the best science may never finally explain.[99] Admitting this, however, is not a theoretical cop out, not an intellectual bailing from a problem that refutes personalism. To confess our limits of understanding and explanation when it comes to human failure and willful evil is consistent with personalism, given all I have explained above. In any case, what is good makes sense, is rational and explicable. The not-good, the negation, the malicious, the pathological, destruction, The Nothing are what finally make no sense. In the end we must live with the fact that while reason and understanding illuminate the human telic good, there is no good reason in or for destructive evil. Thankfully, the incomprehensibility of evil need not obstruct virtuous personal and institutional living toward the good. The mystery of darkness and evil need not be solved before we can learn, know, live virtuously toward, and (re)construct social structures that promote our proper telos of human personal flourishing.

Conclusion

Social scientists must bring a thick, rich, and realistic notion of what human persons are to their scholarly work in order to do it well and be true to reality. Yet much of social science currently operates with impoverished views of human beings and propagates such views among social-science consumers. To improve our practices, we need to work with a personalist model of human personhood. Personalism best describes and explains our human ontology, condition, and experience—at least better than any available alternative—and so offers a sound basis upon which to theorize the microfoundations of social life. Embracing personalism will mean adopting a *teleological* view of human being, action, and social life. We humans are not simply doing *whatever* with our lives. We are doing something specific, however culturally variable its expression may be, which is defined by our essential human condition and life in the material and social contexts in which we find ourselves. That something we are doing ultimately is pursuing, more or less well, our natural human telos of flourishing, what Aristotle called *eudaimonia*. Furthermore, we must take seriously that human persons live *motivated* lives and engage in motivated actions, although not always consciously so. Persons are *natural-goods-seeking* animals. People pursue basic human interests through particular life projects, whether they fully know it or not. The main question is how well or poorly we pursue and live them. People's motivations are ontologically real subjective entities operating in the depth reality of their personhood. Motivations consist ontologically of complexes of beliefs, desires, and emotions that operate from and through persons to move them to action. The human eye cannot directly observe motivations for scientific inspection, it is true. But that is also true about many things that scientists study.

Most sociologists have from the beginning—including Durkheim, Marx, and Weber—held definite views about human nature and developed their theories of people's motivations and actions based upon them. Yet some of the underlying assumptions, inherited from the *Homo duplex* model of these early theorists and reinforced by our liberal culture and society, have laid conceptual traps that have impeded social science's ability to describe and explain human personal and social life well. Crucial among those problematic inheritances has been the presupposed division of reality into distinct individuals, on the one hand, and the realm of the social, of society and institutions, on the other hand. Much of the history of contemporary sociology theory can be read as the frustrated inability to provide a workable account of the human being or the humanly social, given the individual-*versus*-social categories it presupposes. Many misguided theoretical conflicts have been waged on behalf of the primacy of an individualistic ontology over a social-centered one, championing either The Individual or the Social Self, engaging in impossible upward and downward conflations.[1] As long as we presuppose the basic categories of the *Homo duplex* model, such fruitless conflicts will continue.[2] We have to dispense permanently with The Individual and the Social Self and work instead with a realistic, rich, robust vision of the human *person*. By beginning with the person instead of every other attempted concept, focus, or model, social science will be able to finally let go of the fictitious, autonomous, self-generating, and self-sustaining "individual" of Enlightenment liberalism—yet without falling into a bleak, nihilistic antihumanism or totalizing collectivism or sociologism. Social science will then be able to talk sensibly, instead of daftly, about the real ways that people are and are not "the products of society"—since a good theory of the person helps us to see the crucial distinction that persons are in fact *not ontologically* dependent upon, but *are* profoundly *developmentally* dependent upon the social for life, formation, direction, and expression. That distinction describes the real relationship between the parts and the whole in human life and works wonders to clear up some muddled thinking about humanity in the social sciences.

Essential in the personalist account I have offered is a strong *anti-reductionistic* attitude. It relies squarely on the recognition of the realities of *emergence* and *downward causation* to prevent our differentiated, ordered, complex, and stratified reality from being compressed down into lower and simpler levels of being and operation through invalid reductionistic moves. The social thus cannot be reduced to the mere aggregation of individual effects. The social has a reality and power irreducible to the distinct people at the next level down from which the social emerges. Yet because the social is ontologically emergent from the activities of persons, it cannot be explained apart from their activity. At the same time, as an emergent reality, the social possesses capacities of downward causation that profoundly shape the lives of the persons below it. All of the real entities and their relations are thus properly recognized and preserved in a multidimensional, complex, coherent, dynamic reality. Not only are the social sciences thus rightly protected against illegitimate invasions by the natural sciences (genetics, neuroscience, evolutionary psychology, and such), but every legitimate science—using particular disciplined methods to understand some dimension or level of reality proper to its investigation and theorizing—is protected from illegitimate interlopers. At the same time, the rationale for fruitful interdisciplinary work is explained and justified.

Critical realist personalism also shows how the long-standing positivist divorce of facts and values can be reconciled. Personalism lays the groundwork upon which social science can pursue a morally committed yet disciplined and empirically and rationally accountable body of knowledge about human social life that is relevant for the promotion of human flourishing. It also provides a reality-based approach to considering what it might mean to live a *responsible* human personal and social life. It frames such an outlook in a way that links personal and social ethics and holds in proper tension the light and dark side of human nature. Personalism does not overemphasize the more impressive or the more sinister side of humanity, falsely portraying humans as either near-gods or irrational beasts, perhaps even monsters. With a view that is neither naïvely optimistic nor despairingly bleak, personalism does not bang us back and forth against the opposing walls of credulous confidence and grim despair, as so much modern thought has.

Personalist theory also takes a strong position on the reality and teleological pull of natural, *basic human goods*. An identifiable set of multiple, incommensurate, and irreducible basic goods exists, the realization of which tends to promote human thriving and well-being. As difficult as this may be for modern minds to accept, we actually can, through study, retroductive reasoning, and careful reflection on the long history of human experience and the findings of science, describe specific conditions and ends that are objectively and universally good for human persons. That in turn explains the basis of real human *interests*, and the source of human motivations for action. People's motivations are ultimately traceable back to the basic human goods and interests that define and energize the human teleological quest for flourishing. Human interests are thus finally objective and universal, not simply culturally constructed on an absolute range of variability. That enables us to know and recognize that something like "false consciousness" can be real among human persons, without having to resort to a patronizing or devaluing view of people or a hopeless view of dehumanizing social conditions— since reality will tend to keep not more than a moderately long tether on people's ability to misrecognize their true interests. It also enables us to talk meaningfully about what kinds of social institutions and processes are objectively good for people and what are bad, about what a good society may look like and why bad societies *are* bad.

Consider the alternative. If we humans lack any *natural* goods or ends that are real, then we become undefined and undirected in our motivations, interests, and purposes. Humans then operate with beliefs, desires, and feelings that lack naturally given purposes, direction, or order. What would then determine people's motivations, interests, and actions would be given not by natural human goods and ends, but by culture, society, historical contingency, human creativity, and self-determining decision. In which case we have no good reason to reject the dangerous belief that "anything goes." This approach is actually the orthodox doctrine of much of modern thought since the rejection of Aristotle in the seventeenth century, even if it has taken very long since then to work out the full moral and political implications. It is certainly the reigning dogma in social science today. Personalism, however, denies the reality of that account.

I suggest that the real and most powerful reason why moderns want to reject the idea of a natural, proper human telos, of a naturally given good, and instead believe in ungoverned, undirected, unlimited human self-creation and self-direction is not because good evidence, human experience, and sound reason make that most believable. It is rather because moderns are committed, however unaware, to following a particular modern *spiritual project*, the pursuit of *a sacred good*—namely, throwing off restraint and achieving human happiness through individual autonomy, self-definition, and self-determination. To make everything new, to leave behind the past, to be unbound by any tradition, to enjoy maximum choice, to be free from any constraint, to be able to buy whatever one can afford, to live however one desires—that is the guiding vision of modernity's spiritual project. It is spiritual (not merely ideological or cultural) because it names what is sacrosanct, an ultimate concern, a vision for what is most worthy in a sense that transcends any individual life. It is spiritual because it speaks to people's deepest personal subjectivities, their most transcendent vision of goodness, their definition of ultimate fulfillment. It is spiritual because as a deep cultural structure it occupies a position in the modern West homologous with salvation in God that was prized in the premodern Christendom that modernity broke apart. And it is spiritual because, by being sacred, it is worth protecting, defending, policing, fighting for, perhaps dying for, even killing for. Being such a sacred matter, modernity's spiritual project of unfettered individualism virtually *must* champion the currently orthodox doctrine that denies proper ends and natural goods. This book seeks to profane this modern spiritual project by declaring the unorthodox view that human persons do indeed entail natural goods, interests, motivations, and ends. I do this not simply to profane for its own sake, but because it is *true*, and because the modern spiritual project is deeply misguided, even if it is well intentioned, and therefore has some seriously problematic effects.

The discipline of sociology has generally tried either to remain neutral on an account of human goods and flourishing or has promoted an antinaturalistic cultural and moral relativism. When the idea of a good life or human flourishing does arise in sociological thought, sociologists typically say that flourishing is determined by how any culture variably defines it (relativistic cultural constructivism), as maximizing pleasure (hedonic utilitarianism), or some similarly problematic view. Incongruously, however, most sociologists are also personally motivated in their scholarly work and teaching by visions of and desire to promote particular views of human flourishing in which they really believe. Few sociologists actually suppose that every cultural idea about the human good is as equally valuable or morally worthy as any other. For many, the vision they believe and promote is: the full realization in society of individual, autonomous selves as auto-directing agents, entitled to live as they please without external restraint (while not obstructing others) and be affirmed in that by everyone else. In short: an expressive version of liberal individualism. So it is inconsistent if not disingenuous for sociologists to reject the idea, as I have advocated here, of the discipline being grounded upon a substantive account of a teleological human good.[3] The only question that remains, then, is, *which account is best*. Personalism commends itself as a better account than its rivals. Or so I believe.

The matters discussed in this book thus do not concern questions of only "academic" interest disconnected from the real world. Personalism makes a big, practical difference in many areas of life. If people together lived their lives as personalists, instead of guided by other theories, it would have real, felicitous consequences. Societies organized on personalist premises would take on institutional and cultural forms different from those organized on, say, liberal, libertarian, anarchist, authoritarian, or collectivist principles. Social scientists may discount the role of beliefs and ideas in shaping social life. But such an outlook—itself based on certain believed-in *ideas* about reality and how it works—is self-defeating. Believed-in ideas are deeply embedded in and governing of cultural and institutional structures and, over the long run, powerfully shape the forms and practices of human social life. Whether people are liberals or pragmatists or collectivists or socialists or personalists or whatever else, that makes a big difference over time in how they (we) assume, think, feel, desire, and go about constructing and living personal, social, economic, and political life.

On Good Explanations

Critical realist personalism does not create a full or novel methodological program. Still, it raises larger questions about what a good social science explanation requires. Some specific points of methodology also follow. For starters, a good explanation, most social scientists will agree, answers a specific research question—usually a "why?" or "how?" question—asked about a specific social condition or event, the answer to which is either unknown or the currently accepted answer to which is incomplete or wrong and needs correcting. A good social science explanation will provide new understanding about matters that are important and interesting. It will be satisfyingly rationally intelligible—meaning that, once the explanation is presented, reasonable people will readily recognize and appreciate how and why the condition or event being explained actually exists or happened. And it will in some sense be curiously unexpected.[4] Most social scientists would agree with these standards so far. Critical realist personalism also insists, however, that all explanations be expressed in a *realist* mode—that is, as best-possible descriptions of real entities, systems, structures, and processes operating in actual reality that elucidate how or why a condition or event exists now or existed in the past. Good explanations are also inherently *causal*—they describe the causal conditions and forces that brought about the condition or event being explained. The explication of the complex of causes that produced the result *is* itself the explanation. And in this, human beliefs, meanings, motivations, and other subjective realities are accorded causal status, along with many other kinds of real causes. Good explanations must also reserve a central place for the causal effects of living and acting human *persons*. No social science explanation can succeed without at least an implicit account of the causally efficacious personal agents involved in the process—however much they are variably guided, enabled, and constrained by cultural and social structures. Explanation need not remain at the level of persons (as some methodological individualists have asserted), since arising emergently from persons are ontologically real social realities that possess and exert their own emergently causal powers—an account of the causal effects of which proves necessary in most adequate explanations. Accounts that are missing persons inadvertently or intentionally do not provide good explanations.

Since all explanations are finally causal in logic, all good explanations must also implicitly or explicitly be cast in some *narrative* or quasi-narrative form. Causation operates temporally, in processes across time (and space). So in order to explain how and why causes operated as they did to produce outcomes, the explanation needs to account for that temporal process. Causal explanations, in simplest structure, take this analytical form:

time^1 conditions → relevant causal influences → time^2 consequences

That obviously involves a temporal sequence.[5] The more explicitly a causal narrative is described in its temporally developing terms, the more intelligible and persuasive (and usually interesting) it tends to be. Explanations lacking temporal movement and narrative structure—such as many statistical analyses of cross-sectional data—tend not only to be boring but also explanatorily inconclusive. To be remotely convincing, usually a post hoc quasi-story must be told about how the various snapshot-measured variables work in time, which the data and models themselves do not actually show.

All good social science explanations will usually also tend toward greater *complexity* rather than parsimonious simplicity—not because we want complicating confusion, but because reality *is* complex, and any adequate explanation about some part of it must recognize and represent that complexness. We must allow, in short, for "adequate complexity" in our explanations and be skeptical about accounts that embody the "myth of the average experience."[6] Accounts that are too simple and pared down will not be adequate. Good accounts in social science will also usually involve and be comfortable with some amount of *uncertainty*. The modernist quest for foundationalist certainty has failed. We today have to understand ourselves as finite creatures operating from a particular personal perspective with fallible understandings based on (usually) inadequate evidence. That need not drive us to despair, but it should caution us against overconfidence and unrealistic expectations. We should hold every explanation to the highest reasonable standards. But we must also be prepared to accept explanations that are good, the best, all things considered, but not necessarily airtight and indubitable. Epistemic humility is necessary, as is a readiness to work with our best accounts (the "BA principle"[7]) rather than demanding irrefutable accounts. Said differently, we must be satisfied in each analysis to work toward an "inference to the best explanation" (IBE), rather than hold onto some impossible positivist standard of certain knowledge.[8] Part of making this work will involve intentionally employing the reasoning tool of *retroduction*, and not simply deduction, induction, and inference. We must be willing to trust realist transcendental reasoning operations that ask, for instance, *what must be the case*, even if it is not observable, if reality, as we best observe and understand it, is what it is. Empirical data alone cannot provide us our explanations. We need, within a larger critical realist frame of understanding, to couple our (inadequate) empirical evidence with the very best (fallible) tools of reasoning to produce our best possible explanations—and be content to live with them as true until better evidence and reasoning provide better explanations. And that means at some point overcoming our skepticism to trust our best results, even when we know that down the road they may prove insufficient or even wrong.

Returning to the matter of persons in explanation, personalism also says that social scientists are justified in *relying on the accounts of real persons* in order to understand the reasons involved in what is being explained as well as possible *from their perspective*, at least as a means to get investigations rolling. It is wrong to immediately bypass the accounts of persons in order to jump to an interpretation about which the persons involved would not understand or recognize. We may eventually end up legitimately arguing such an interpretation, but it is not the place to start. The beginning of research must take the accounts of persons involved in the social reality being explained with full seriousness. Only then might the social scientist be entitled to offer as the explanation an interpretation of processes about which the persons involved would not be aware, as a conclusion reached after much investigation. This methodological approach means that we ought always "initially and presumptively" to start by looking for explanations involving first-person "personal intelligibility" (what would be accessible and sensible to the persons actually involved), and move on to explanations involving third-person "extra-personal intelligibility" (understandings about which the persons would not be aware) when the accounts of the persons involved seem inadequate, wrong, or deceptive in some ways.[9] This approach rightly takes persons seriously, without wrongly assuming that persons are fully aware of all the causal forces involved in the social realities in which they are involved.[10] Finally, any good social science explanation will have to take seriously the *interests* and *motivations* that move the relevant persons to act as they do, which—in the context of historical cultural and institutional inheritances and the structure of contemporary circumstances—explain the event, outcome, or condition under consideration. Yet personalism pushes us one step further: the interests and motivations ought to be at least implicitly comprehensible in terms of the *basic goods* of human life and the ways people succeed and fail to realize them, as I described that in the last three chapters.

A good explanation will thus bring together in one coherent narrative the following. It will begin with a clear, focused *research question*, posing a "how?" or "why?" inquiry about a matter that is important and interesting. It will describe the positions, dispositions, and circumstances of the *persons* and groups of persons involved in the matter being explained—including the content and intensity of their particular assumptions, perceptions, beliefs, desires, feelings, interests, and so on, which *motivated* their relevant actions. It will describe the developing *structure of relations* between the persons involved in the situation or event being explained and the causal forces that those relations exerted on the persons involved. That will require telling the *history* behind the matter in question that set up the dynamics of interest. A good explanation will also describe any relevant material, infrastructural, institutional, and cultural resources, enablements, opportunities, obstructions, or constraints in the larger physical and social environment—explaining how they figure into the ongoing causal processes at work.[11] It will describe well the ways that the various operative personal and social *causal mechanisms* at work produced whatever outcomes they produced—expecting these to be complex, interactive, and dynamic. It will also attend to the dynamic temporal interplay between the personal and the social levels of reality, showing both how persons acting and interacting gave rise *emergently* to real social facts possessing emergent causal capacities and how the *downwardly causal* force of social causal mechanisms transformed the positions or dispositions, actions and interactions, of the persons involved. That will draw upon the big *theoretical* bag of social science's known general causal mechanisms that recurrently operate in various social settings, to show how particular mechanisms operated in the particular case in question. A good explanation will thus describe how the various persons, groups, or institutions were *changed in a temporal process* (or prevented from changing) as a result of the causal forces at work. And it will show how the specific condition or event (which the desire to understand motivated the investigation in the first place) *resulted* from the complex and dynamic working out of all of the above. There are many ways that might be done, but those basic elements should be in place in a good explanation.

What should we make of social-science research and scholarship that does less than this, by not including these elements of a good explanation? Not every piece of published social-science research must contain a genuine explanation. A legitimate part of the job of social science is simply to describe the world well, to accurately tell what seems to be happening in social reality. Sheer description when done well is, I think, one of social science's greatest gifts to the world. Of course, before anything in social life can be explained, we need a solid enough descriptive understanding of what is happening in reality that needs explaining. Sometimes sheer description itself is terrifically illuminating, even sometimes self-explaining. In any case, it is important to be clear when we think we are merely describing and when we are explaining. Sometimes what are only descriptions of states of affairs and relationships present themselves in social science as if they were explanations. A great deal of normal-science regression analysis of variables, for examples, purports to provide explanations, when in fact all that ever provides are descriptions of associations—which then *still* need explaining.[12] That does not necessarily diminish their value or contribution. But it does remind us of our need to be clear about the difference between describing something that may yet need to be explained and actually explaining it. Real explanations require describing the specific causal mechanisms at work among motivated personal agents engaged in activity in the world that operate in complex processes that change (or prevent change in) particular social conditions from one point in time to a later point in time.

To accomplish that kind of explanation, social science will need to set aside some common frameworks of thinking and adopt instead critical realism as the metatheory that makes better sense of social-science explanation in this mode. Broadly, social science needs to make a decisive break from the positivist empiricism that has long dominated the discipline. Positivism is shot through with fatal flaws. What is valuable in positivism is retained and better accounted for in critical realism. Social science also needs to reject the program of postmodernist deconstruction. Some of the postmodern critique is valid and important, but taken alone it is silly and destructive. Again, what is good and valuable in postmodernism (and postpositivism generally) is retained and reconstituted in more helpful ways in critical realism. Finally, social scientists would do well to retain the crucial insights of hermeneutical interpretivism concerning, for example, the need for interpretive cultural understanding of meanings, beliefs, and symbols in any explanations. But too many streams of interpretive social science are underachieving—especially those claiming that we can do no more than describe well the meaningful perspective of agents involved in social events. The kind of hermeneutical interpretivism social science needs is Weberian, in the specific sense of taking seriously the goal of providing *causal* explanation as intrinsic to a discipline's purpose.[13] Again, critical realism does the best job of subsuming what is good and necessary in the best of hermeneutical interpretivism within its larger framework of understanding that is more intellectually satisfying and analytically adequate. In short, critical realism is the metatheory that best frames and describes what social science is and ought to be, which draws together and constructively synthesizes the best of historically rival approaches and philosophies.[14]

In addition to these general observations, the argument of this book suggests some specific research agendas of importance. Social science can make renewed efforts to better understand how beliefs, emotions, and desires work together in complex ways to *form* motivations that generate actions. We can better research how and why persons *learn* and *change* their beliefs, emotions, and desires in interactional and institutional settings. We can research more how social factors *interact* with neurological and cognitive dynamics—engaging especially with the cognitive sciences—which produce motivational processes and patterned action outcomes. We can examine more closely not only how people are shaped by the immediate social situations in which they find themselves, but also how they *resist, redefine, and otherwise transform* such situations because of extrasituational features of their personhood. We can pay attention not only to the diversity of human experiences that exists across cultures but also to what humans *share* as a species, what the limits are to human transformation and experimentation, what *universals* bound our lives and shape our cultures and institutions.[15] Social science can do more focused research to better understand the complexities of social conditions that promote and undermine *flourishing* and *failure*. Under what different historical, material, demographic, and environmental conditions, we might ask, do different peoples develop to envision and pursue human flourishing in different ways? What are the empirically knowable features of human life that tend to cultivate human thriving, and which tend to destroy it? We know a good bit of what factors lead to evil actions and form evil persons, as I have defined them. But we have more we could learn about the social conditions that encourage personal stagnation and avoidant destructiveness, for example, as described in chapter 7. For that matter, social science could think and study a lot harder about what exactly human flourishing looks like and how it might be better observed and measured. Also, as I argue below, social science can invest more into the study of *love* and the lack of love, and their crucial role in human flourishing and failure. Social science should rethink the concept of *culture* and approach cultural analyses in the light of the basic human goods and interests proposed above and the human teleological quest for *eudaimonia*. Obviously, many social scientists have already conducted research along some of these lines. But I believe that the personalist agenda can provide a more helpful framework and focus to the meaning and organization of such research programs than many of the current, often disconnected, and not always theoretically properly framed lines of scholarly investigation do.

On Taking Love Seriously

One final word. Virtually no social scientist talks about love in their scholarly work—at least directly. Love is a concept and reality that has been exiled from social science, banished to the hinterland of personal feelings and values.[16] In a post-Kantian world, most seem to believe that those are matters about which we can really know nothing. But of all the mindless social constructions that social science ought to deconstruct, rather than reinforce, that is one of the worst. Love may seem "unscientific" to many social scientists, but that is because they assume the wrong view of science. Let us say it again: the sciences need to conform their concepts, methods, and theories to the realities they seek to understand, allowing specific dimensions of reality to determine how particular sciences are done, rather than forcing that reality to conform to a preconceived, uniform notion about what science is and must be. *The* "scientific method" (singular) is tyrannous nonsense. What we need instead are many appropriate scientific methods, all driven by the actual nature of the various dimensions of reality that a given science studies. Social science has made significant headway in the study of a number of important aspects of life that have an abstract or latent quality, including social trust, social capital, and democracy. There is no reason why social science cannot also seriously study love. Doing so can only improve the realism, insight, and relevance of our scholarship.

The reality is that love is a central fact of human existence. Without love, human beings could and would not exist. They could not survive; they certainly would not thrive.[17] Without love there would be no social world to study or social scientists to study it. Love happens all the time, in fact. It happens among couples, spouses, parents, children, kin, friends, and sometimes relations and institutions beyond. The world of course suffers a miserable deficit of love. But love happens nevertheless. To think that social science cannot study love as a central fact of human life is bizarre. To believe that social science should not speak the word "love" is absurd. It reflects some kind of weird, fearful allergic reaction to the dreadful idea that "hard scientists" might judge social science as not scientific. And it reflects the mind-constraining power of our dominant, misguided social-scientific assumptions and theories about human nature and motivations that blind us to love's reality and power. It is time for social science to grow up and proceed with confidence to study the human social world as it really is and operates. Love not only happens sometimes, it is an essential fact that makes the human world feasible. Love can be studied empirically and theorized intelligently. Categories such as love, good, and evil can function as explanatory concepts.[18] We are derelict in our scholarly responsibilities if we fail to appreciate and study love in human life.

For the argument of this book, love is critical. Human life has a natural teleological end, the realization of which depends on certain necessary conditions, both internal and external to the person. Crucial among those conditions is the experience and exercise of love. The kind of interpersonal relationships needed to help persons pursue the human good require love. The nurturing and protection of embodied human biology requires love. The provision of the material resources that persons need to survive and thrive requires love. The kind of social and institutional contexts that nurture, challenge, and instill the virtues needed to achieve basic human goods involve love, even if it stands in the background. And the kind of right personal effort people need to expend in order to realize their own good requires that they have been loved and that they too love—that they love themselves, the good, and other persons. Human societies without love are bodies without blood. Even when humans survive and somewhat prosper through having received an adequate, though not great, amount of love, the probability still remains of their living out of the fundamental postures of fear or denial. One power that can prevent that is love. Love fosters trust, interpersonally and institutionally, and trust promotes human flourishing. Do we need something more significant to justify taking love seriously?

Notes

Introduction

1. A handful of other social scientists have also observed that social science needs, but does not have, a good, general theory of human motivations. D. Emmet, "Motivation in Sociology and Social Anthropology," *Journal for the Theory of Social Behavior* 6 (1976): 85–104; Walter Gove, "Why We Do What We Do: A Biopsychosocial Theory of Human Motivation," *Social Forces* 73 (1994): 363–94; and Frank Miyamoto, "Self, Motivation, and Symbolic Interaction Theory," in *Human Nature and Collective Behavior*, ed. Tamotsu Shibutani (Upper Saddle River, NJ: Prentice Hall, 1970), 271–85.

2. Herbert Simon, "Human Nature in Politics: The Dialogue of Psychology with Political Science," *American Political Science Review* 79 (1985): 303.

3. By "humanism" I mean nothing highly technical or historically specific, but views of reality and life that place particular value on the distinctive personhood of human beings, that honor the particular dignity and worth of persons, that recognize the moral significance and responsibility of human actions, that seek through education and other means to encourage what is good and noble and to discourage what is regrettable and destructive in humanity, and that seek to construct social institutions that reflect, respect, and enhance human life as understood in such terms. Such humanistic views may be secular or religiously justified. Either way, they are meant to contrast with various antihumanistic views that see little of distinctive importance or value in human beings, that may value humanity as a collective but at the expense of distinct persons, that view human persons in fundamentally instrumental terms, that subordinate the good of persons to the good of the state or the economy, that compromise justice for persons while promoting the narrow interest of dominant groups, that blatantly violate basic human and civil rights with impunity, and so on.

4. See Christian Smith, *What Is a Person? Rethinking Humanity, Social Life, and the Moral Good from the Person Up* (Chicago: University of Chicago Press, 2010), 62–88.

5. Anna Wierzbicka argues that unlike the good, the distinction between right and wrong is actually an artifact of the English language (*English: Meaning and Culture* [New York: Oxford University Press, 2006]); also see Edmund Pincoffs, "Quandary Ethics," *Mind* 80 (1971): 552–71.

6. Philippa Foot, *Natural Goodness* (New York: Oxford University Press, 2001).

7. Andrew Sayer, *Why Things Matter to People: Social Science, Values, and Ethical Life* (Cambridge: Cambridge University Press, 2011).

8. Even basic social science concepts like discrimination, tolerance, violence, bridging capital, prosocial behaviors, inequality, and productivity are morally fraught concepts.

9. This typology partly follows Jeffrey Alexander's exposition in his *Action and Its Environments* (New York: Columbia University Press, 1988), 11–45. It also partially maps onto the four "action concepts" Jürgen Habermas discusses. *The Theory of Communicative Action*, vol. 1, *Reason and the Rationalization of Society* (Boston: Beacon Press, 1981), 75–101.

10. Paul du Gay provides an illuminating historicizing of this tradition's notion of the human self in his 2005 *Sociological Review* article "Which Is the 'Self' in 'Self-Interest'" (53, no. 3: 391–411), an idea that contemporary social science often oversimplifies.

11. This tradition has an even deeper theological genealogy, of which few of its contemporary adherents are aware, in the late medieval nominalism of William of Ockham and his followers, which emphasized the absolute volitional freedom of God as a sovereign, choosing agent—but that is another story. See Michael Gillespie, *The Theological Origins of Modernity* (Chicago: University of Chicago Press, 2008); William Placher, *The Domestication of Transcendence* (Louisville, KY: Westminster John Knox Press, 1996).

12. I will not much engage this fifth approach further in this book, but simply suggest the core of its problems in this note. This account of humanity fails in various ways. Most crucially, it fails to understand the reality of emergence (explained in chapter 1), by which new entities at higher levels come into being that have properties and capacities that cannot be found at the lower level from which they emerged. It therefore fails to understand that the social and the personal cannot be adequately explained by being reduced to the biological. This account also depends on vulgar, scientistic reductionism driven by quixotic visions of a unified science-of-everything commanded by evolutionary biologists and their associated colleagues. However, once one understands emergence and its implications, this entire account collapses. Its approach also makes irrelevant what nearly all humans in known history take to be most certain and important about human life—namely, the reality of human subjective experience and the power of its substantive content to define and mobilize the living of life, which this model judges that as merely an epiphenomenal delusion. What "really" moves and determines life are the natural physical operations of genes, neurons, and chemicals. This of course requires slipshod anthropomorphizing, as in the case of Dawkins's "selfish genes." It is confused nonsense. The result is a hard-core antimentalist commitment that makes inconsequential people's ideas, beliefs, desires, feelings, values, aspirations, commitments, and intentions for understanding humanity. Those subjectivities are only being "used" by biology—the alleged true agents of human life—to accomplish the reproductive imperative, which is the single "will" of biology. Much that is phenomenologically real and important to human beings is pushed aside by the authoritative hand of reductionistic scientism. I believe that the social sciences have more to learn from genetics and neuroscience—to which they (except psychology, if that is still a social science) have been long closed—about the interaction of natural body processes and contingent social experiences. But that is a different matter than pushing a comprehensive model of human beings that aspires to take over the social sciences in toto. The latter must be resisted, and with good justification. See Christian Smith, *Moral, Believing Animals* (New York: Oxford University Press, 2003), 37–43; Smith, *What Is a Person*, 198–206. Also see Mary Midgley, *Science as Salvation* (London: Routledge, 1992); Midgley, *Evolution as a Religion* (New York: Routledge, 2002).

13. For a devastating critique of this paradigm, however, see Raymond Tallis, *Aping Mankind: Neuromania, Darwinitis, and the Misrepresentation of Humanity* (Durham, UK: Acumen, 2011). Also see Steven Rose, *Lifelines: Life beyond the Gene* (New York: Vintage, 2006).

14. Social scientists need not subscribe to only one of these views. Some of the more in-

teresting theories combine aspects of two models. They are interesting because the theoretical combination provides for a greater, more realistic complexity than any single approach. Pierre Bourdieu, for example, merges in his theoretical method both the strong notion of societal determination of people's behaviors found in the dependent norm-followers model (habitus) with the assumption about basic motivations being the drive to increase and protect status and power, the ability to dominate others, found in the rationally acquisitive individuals' account (capital and fields). Hybrids are thus possible, at least in theory, though oftentimes they prove difficult to systematize theoretically. Nevertheless, despite the possibility of combining the basic models, as distinct theoretical paradigms they provide the elementary building blocks of perspectives that have largely governed social scientific thinking about humans. Even when we draw the theoretical map differently, most of the same fundamental issues identified here remain in play. There are only so many plausible permutations of theory describing human beings, action, and social life, so we will inevitably run up against most of the same fundamental issues, presuppositions, and arguments.

15. The psychologists Jack Martin, Jeff Sugarman, and Sarah Hickinbottom (*Persons: Understanding Psychological Selfhood and Agency* [New York: Springer, 2010]) correctly observe that "the concept of the person has all but vanished from psychology" and "while psychologists lavish their attention on the study of personality, they devote surprisingly little to the question of what is a person" (57, back cover).

16. Margaret Archer correctly notes that "sociological imperialists ha[ve] labored long and hard with a vacuum pump on humankind, sucking out the properties and powers of our species-being, to leave a void behind to be filled with social forces" (*Being Human: The Problem of Agency* [Cambridge: Cambridge University Press, 2000], 315–16).

17. Philosophers have advanced significant arguments about these matters, including teleological and realist arguments, from which social scientists ought to learn. See, for example, Scott Sehon, *Teleological Realism: Mind, Agency, and Explanation* (Cambridge, MA: MIT Press, 2005); G. F. Schueler, *Reasons and Purposes: Human Rationality and the Teleological Explanation of Action* (New York: Oxford University Press, 2003); Jesús Aguilar and Andrei Buckareff, eds., *Causing Human Action: New Perspectives on the Causal Theory of Action* (Cambridge, MA: MIT Press, 2010); Alfred Mele, *Motivation and Agency* (New York: Oxford University Press, 2003); Carlos Moya, *The Philosophy of Action: An Introduction* (Cambridge: Polity Press, 1990).

18. I have developed an account of personal ontology and some of its moral and political implications in previous books: *What Is a Person?* (University of Chicago Press, 2010) and *Moral, Believing Animals* (Oxford University Press, 2003), and will not much repeat those arguments here. Readers who have read them will be advantaged in understanding what follows. I do my best to present here a coherent argument that stands on its own. But I also do build upon what I argued in those books, so readers unfamiliar with them and uncertain about my arguments here may need to refer to them for clarity.

19. Consider, for example, the words of the French revolutionaries Abbé Sieyès and Robespierre in this tradition: "The national is prior to everything. It is the source of everything. Its will is always legal; indeed it is the law itself," and "The people is always worth more than individuals. . . . The people is sublime, but individuals are weak." Emmanuel Joseph (Abbé) Sieyès, *Qu'est-ce que le tier état?*, quoted in William Sewell Jr., *A Rhetoric of Bourgeois Revolution* (1979; Durham, NC: Duke University Press, 1989), 46; and Maximilien Robespierre, *Lettres à ses commettans* (Paris, 1792), II: 55, quoted in Gertrude Himmelfarb, *Roads to Modernity* (New York: Vintage, 2004), 184, respectively.

20. Jan Bengtsson, *The Worldview of Personalism: Origins and Early Development* (New York:

Oxford University Press, 2006); J. B. Coates, *The Crisis of the Human Person: Some Personalist Interpretations* (London: Longman, 1949).

21. By phenomenologically serious, I mean placing significant but not absolute epistemological authority in our own best human personal phenomenological experiences after they have been interpreted and interrogated by reason and evaluated in light of collective human experience—related to Charles Taylor's "BA [best account] principle," as described and interpreted by Smith (*What Is A Person?*, 107, 112). By contrast, sociology is often enamored with an elitist, debunking attitude that fundamentally distrusts ordinary human experience and understanding, which it seeks to replace with a gnosis of sociological insight. For instance, Randall Collins writes, "To see the common realities of everyday life sociologically requires a gestalt shift, a reversal of perspectives. Breaking such deeply ingrained *conventional* frames is not easy to do; but the more we can discipline ourselves to think *everything* through the sociology of the situation, the more we will understand why we do what we do" (*Interaction Ritual Chains* [Princeton, NJ: Princeton University Press, 2004], 5, italics added). Barry Barnes also frankly states what many sociologists assume—namely, that the interpretations and explanations of "outsiders" (sociologists) are usually superior to the understandings of "insiders" (ordinary members of society): "Ordinary members of society are not . . . proponents of the [sociological] account advanced here. In proposing that account there is the implication that everyday activity may be described better from the outside than by those who enact it. . . . This is indeed so; it is true of all social practices that for some purposes there are better descriptions of them than those initially used by members themselves." Barnes, *Understanding Agency: Social Theory and Responsible Action* (London: Sage, 2000), 72. For my account of how ordinary human experience plays epistemologically into the process of scientific inquiry, see Smith, *What Is a Person*, especially pp. 104–14.

22. The concept of "action" seems simple enough, but its meaning and value are debated. Action tends to convey a particular sense of discrete, intentional, meaningful, means-ends behavior, as defined particularly by Max Weber. Much human activity in life, however, does not consist of action in this sense. Some social scientists prefer to speak of "behavior" as a form of activity that is not assumed to be so consciously purposive, which humans share with many other animals. Others emphasize the centrality of "practices" among the activities of human life, which more strongly denotes the idea of repetition, habituation, and reduced intentional awareness. Still others propose "repertoires of action" to emphasize the constraints that culture imposes on action. Yet other social scientists emphasize "habitus" or "habits" as the dominant forms they believe human activity takes, which points to the relatively mindless, reiterated, difficult-to-break kinds of activities common among humans. Finally, we may note a variety of bodily activities and behaviors that people usually cannot entirely purposively control, which however sometimes have real personal and social consequences, such as breathing, panic attacks, digestion, snoring, and so on. Naming one concept that encompasses all of these different ideas is difficult. Human "doings" might qualify, although people do not normally talk that way. For present purposes, I do not need an all-encompassing term. To keep the language in this book manageable, I will use the words "action" to indicate not simply the narrower meaning defined by Weber, but the more expansive meaning that encompasses the ideas of means-ends actions, practices, repertoires of action, and many habits and behaviors—the justification of which should become clear as the book unfolds. I do not claim that this book's theory explains all kinds of habits and behaviors or uncontrollable bodily activities and behaviors in an unrealistically comprehensive way, yet it covers a major swath of human activities that matters most to most social scientists.

23. For example, Richard Swedberg's *Principles of Economic Sociology* (Princeton, NJ: Princeton University Press, 2003) emphasizes but does not clearly define interests.

24. Foot, *Natural Goodness*.

25. For compelling arguments for value realism, see Graham Oddie, *Value, Reality, and Desire* (New York: Oxford University Press, 2005); John Rist, *Real Ethics: Rethinking the Foundations of Morality* (Cambridge: Cambridge University Press, 2002); David Enoch, *Taking Morality Seriously: A Defense of Robust Realism* (New York: Oxford University Press, 2013); Russ Shafer Landau, *Moral Realism: A Defence* (New York: Oxford University Press, 2005); Terence Cuneo, *The Moral Web: An Argument for Moral Realism* (New York: Oxford University Press, 2010); also see essays in Geoffrey Sayers-McCord and A. J. Ayer, eds., *Essays on Moral Realism* (Ithaca, NY: Cornell University Press, 1988).

26. Reinhold Niebuhr, *The Nature and Destiny of Man*, vol. 1 (Louisville, KY: Westminster John Knox Press, 1996); also see Charles Lemert, *Why Niebuhr Matters* (New Haven, CT: Yale University Press, 2011).

27. Smith, *What Is a Person?*, 386–94.

28. Roy Bhaskar, *A Realist Concept of Science* (London: Verso, 1997); Bhaskar, *Critical Realism* (New York: Routledge, 1998); Bhaskar, *The Possibility of Naturalism: A Philosophical Critique of Contemporary Human Sciences* (London: Routledge, 1979); Andrew Collier, *Critical Realism: An Introduction to Roy Bhaskar's Philosophy* (London: Verso, 1994); Berth Danermark et al., *Explaining Society: Critical Realism in the Social Sciences* (New York: Routledge, 2002); Andrew Sayer, *Realism and Social Science* (New York: Sage, 2000); Sayer, *Method in Social Science: A Realist Approach* (New York: Routledge, 1992); Margaret Archer, *Realist Social Theory* (Cambridge: Cambridge University Press, 1995). On how novices might learn critical realism, see http://www.nd.edu/~csmith22/criticalrealism.htm.

29. 5B:8, Meng Ke (372–289 BC), quoted in Robert Bellah, *Religion in Human Evolution* (Cambridge, MA: Harvard University Press, 2011), ix.

30. I use the word "proper" in this book to modify various nouns. That may sound suspect (i.e., "judgmental") to many ears today. By "proper," I do not mean in accordance with established social mores, conventions, norms, or etiquette. I mean rationally or morally appropriate to or for the entity referenced. Proper in this sense does not refer to positive law or custom, but rather relations between or treatments of entities that are fitting or correct, given the particular nature of the entities in question.

31. Although, the nonhuman world can also be reasonably conceived as operating teleologically (and some biologists speak as if that were so), but in a way very different from humanly conscious, rational, and intentional ends-seeking—suggesting that the most subtle approach requires a theory with different *kinds* of teleologies at work. But that is not my argument here.

32. From Middle French *moderne*, from Late Latin *modernus*, "modern," from Latin *modo*, "just now, in a (certain) manner," from *modo* "to the measure," ablative of *modus* "manner, measure."

33. Brad Gregory, *The Unintended Reformation: How a Religious Revolution Secularized Society* (Cambridge, MA: Harvard University Press, 2012).

34. While social scientists may not know it, some philosophers are seriously doubting the reasonableness of modern antiessentialism—for example, see Brian Ellis, *The Philosophy of Nature: A Guide to the New Essentialism* (Montreal: McGill-Queen's University Press, 2002); Tuomas Tahko, ed., *Contemporary Aristotelian Metaphysics* (Cambridge: Cambridge University Press, 2012); Edward Feser, ed., *Aristotle on Method and Metaphysics* (New York: Palgrave Macmillan, 2013); Ruth Groff and John Greco, eds., *Powers and Capacities in Philosophy: The New*

Aristotelianism (New York: Routledge, 2013); also see David Baird, Eric Scerri, and Lee McIntyre, eds., *Philosophy of Chemistry* (New York: Springer, 2009).

35. "The notion that we 'have a nature,' far from threatening the concept of freedom, is absolutely essential to it. If we were genuinely plastic and indeterminate at birth, there could be no reason why society should not stamp us into any shape that might suit it." Mary Midgley, *Beast and Man* (New York: Routledge, 1995), xxxvii–xxxviii.

36. My approach to what is "natural" is clearly different from and in some ways opposed to romanticist, "folkist," nationalist theories of what is "natural," which, following Johann Gottfried von Herder and others, wed (mostly specious) ontological claims about cultural, social, and political belonging to "natural" personal and political identities and obligations—see Lloyd Kramer, *Nationalism in Europe and America: Politics, Cultures, and Identities since 1775* (Chapel Hill: University of North Carolina Press, 2011), and recent works by Roger Friedland on religious nationalism.

37. Critical realism's approach actually combines a nondeterministic view with a compatibilist view of human freedom and agency and causality (often considered rival positions), the details of which, however, are beyond my ability here to explain.

38. One possible response to this book's argument is that it is "so Western." Certainly, the geographic location of the origin of the ideas that undergird the book are mostly Western, but that is ultimately irrelevant to the argument. All ideas come from somewhere. The geographic and cultural genesis of ideas says nothing about their truth value. I seek to offer a universal account, not one that is true only in the West.

39. Colin Renfrew and Iain Morley, eds., *Becoming Human: Innovations in Prehistoric Material and Spiritual Culture* (Cambridge: Cambridge University Press, 2009). Whether "radical evolution" or "designer evolution" will sometime change that situation in a "posthuman" future is a question for a separate discussion, though one to which personalists will have a big stake in contributing.

40. Alasdair MacIntyre rightly argues that no sociological analysis escapes philosophy: "The philosopher cannot be merely an external commentator on the social sciences; for philosophical arguments will actually enter into and forge critical links within the sociologist's explanations. The expulsion of philosophy from the social sciences . . . turns out to be another lost positivist cause." MacIntyre, "Rationality and the Explanation of Action," chapter 21 in MacIntyre, *Against the Self-Images of the Age* (London: Duckworth, 1971), 259.

41. For instance, I am aware that my argument engages numerous important debates in ethics, religious studies, political theory, human rights, pragmatism, and other fields and issues, which I am unfortunately not able to address explicitly here.

42. By liberalism I mean the social and political tradition that emphasizes the ontological primacy of individual humans, often theorized in an abstract, universal form, individual autonomy and the self-determinations of their own interests, the importance of negative liberties, the priority of the right over the good, skepticism about ideas such as the common good and human solidarity, and so on. Personalism shares and defends other values and themes in the liberal tradition (though often for different reasons than liberalism), including inviolable personal dignity, participatory politics, liberty of conscience, bounded pluralism, institutional accountability, responsible private property, and so on.

43. See Donald Levine's excellent *Visions of the Sociological Tradition* (Chicago: University of Chicago Press, 1995), 05–51.

44. So does American higher education generally. Many academics not only doubt whether they believe in the modern project, but also are uncertain about the actual nature, status, and future of human beings per se—*ourselves*. Institutionally, higher education seems to suffer an

intensifying crisis of legitimacy and direction. What *good* is academia producing, many ask, that justifies the resources it consumes? But that question often proves difficult to answer, since we seem to lack the capacity even to discuss what *is* good. The humanities seem increasingly dispensable to many, for some very bad reasons. The sciences seem strongly turned toward providing immediate instrumental means for corporate business ends. The vision of a humanistic, liberal-arts education fostering the living of rich, full, good lives is increasingly displaced by one of instrumental education pursued for credits, credentials, and careers. Whether the methodological and metaphysical materialism, positivism, naturalism, constructionism, pragmatism, scientism, and relativism that comprise the jumble of doctrines that governs academia today can sustain a higher-education project worthy of the name and effort is debatable. See, for example, Richard Arum and Josipa Roksa, *Academically Adrift: Limited Learning on College Campuses* (Chicago: University of Chicago Press, 2010); Anthony Kronman, *Education's End: Why Our Colleges and Universities Have Given Up on the Meaning of Life* (New Haven, CT: Yale University Press, 2008); Harry Lewis, *Excellent without a Soul: Does Liberal Education Have a Future?* (New York: Public Affairs, 2007).

45. Smith, *What Is a Person?*; Smith, *Moral, Believing Animals.*

Chapter 1: Critical Realist Personalism—Some Basics

1. Smith, *What Is a Person?*, which those who have already read will find some overlap in this chapter but little in what follows. This chapter selectively draws upon and synthesizes a variety of sources, including Alistair McFadyen, *The Call to Personhood* (Cambridge: Cambridge University Press, 1990); Martin Buber, *I and Thou* (New York: Scribner, 1970); Jacques Maritain, *The Person and the Common Good* (Notre Dame, IN: University of Notre Dame Press, 1966); Eileen Cantin, *Mounier: A Personalist View of History* (New York: Paulist Press, 1973); Jan Bengtsson, *The Worldview of Personalism* (New York: Oxford University Press, 2006); Michael Polanyi, *Personal Knowledge: Toward a Post-Critical Philosophy* (Chicago: University of Chicago Press, 1958); John Crosby, *The Selfhood of the Human Person* (Washington, DC: Catholic University of America Press, 1996); John Crosby, *Personalist Papers* (Washington, DC: Catholic University of America Press, 2003); Robert Spaemann, *Persons: The Difference between "Someone" and "Something"* (New York: Oxford University Press, 2006); Thomas Williams, *Who Is My Neighbor: Personalism and the Foundations of Human Rights* (Washington, DC: Catholic University of America Press, 2005; Karol Wojtyla, *Person and Community* (New York: Peter Lang, 1993); Karol Wojtyla, *The Acting Person* (Dordrecht, Holland: D. Reidel Publishing, 1979); Rufus Burrow Jr., *Personalism: A Critical Introduction* (Saint Louis: Chalice Press, 2003); Leroy Rouner, ed., *Selves, People, and Persons* (Notre Dame, IN: University of Notre Dame Press, 1992); Peter Spader, *Scheler's Ethical Personalism* (New York: Fordham University Press, 2002); Archer, *Being Human: The Problem of Agency*; and Michael Carrithers, Steven Collins, and Steven Lukes, eds., *The Category of the Person* (Cambridge: Cambridge University Press, 1985).

2. The focus of this book regrettably does not allow a satisfactory engagement with Bourdieusian theory; such a detailed exploration of the relation between Bourdieu and personalism awaits future work. The same is true for critical theory more generally.

3. See Tallis, *Aping Mankind.*

4. For present purposes, I make no claim that only human beings are persons. Much of reality as we understand it *is* nonpersonal, but the question of whether some nonhuman persons (such as, for instance, an alien species on a distant planet) may exist I leave unanswered, since that is not important to my argument.

5. I refer in this book both to human beings (plural) and to human being (singular). By the former, I mean to denote *people*, actual human persons who have lived or do live on this earth. By "human being" (singular), in contrast, I mean the very *being* of humanity, the ontological fact of persons.

6. For the present, I sidestep the philosophical question of whether abstract objects that arguably do not have causal powers (such as numbers) are real.

7. Of course, once even thin notions of consciousness and imagination enter, materialism begins to crumble.

8. For personalism's case against the strong social constructionist view, see Smith, *What Is a Person?*, 119–206.

9. See John Searle, *Making the Social World: The Structure of Human Civilization* (New York: Oxford University Press, 2010).

10. Jane McCarthy wrestles with similar issues and distinctions with her notion of "the relational individual," in "The Powerful Relational Language of 'Family': Togetherness, Belonging, and Personhood," *Sociological Review* 60 (2012): 68–90.

11. Joseph Agassi, "Methodological Individualism," *British Journal of Sociology* 11, no. 3 (1960): 244–70; Steven Lukes, "Methodological Individualism Reconsidered," *British Journal of Sociology* 19, no. 2 (1968): 119–29; Milan Zafirovski, "Spencer Is Dead, Long Live Spencer: Individualism, Holism, and the Problem of Norms," *British Journal of Sociology* 51, no. 3 (2000): 553–79; W. W. Sharrock, "Individual and Society," in *Classic Disputes in Sociology*, ed. R. J. Anderson, J. A. Hughes, and W. W. Sharrock (Boston: Allen and Unwin, 1987), 126–56.

12. Douglas Porpora, *The Concept of a Social Structure* (Westport, CT: Praeger, 1987); Smith, *What Is a Person?*, 317–83.

13. Anthony Giddens, *The Constitution of Society* (Berkeley: University of California Press, 1984); James Coleman, *Foundations of Social Theory* (Cambridge, MA: Harvard University Press, 1990).

14. See Terrence Deacon, *Incomplete Nature: How Mind Emerged from Matter* (New York: Norton, 2013).

15. Critical realist personalism's emphasis on natural human capacities in need of existential development invites engagement with Martha Nussbaum and Amartya Sen's arguments about human development as creating capacities (for example, Nussbaum, *Creating Capabilities: A Human Development Approach* [Cambridge, MA: Belknap Press of Harvard University Press, 2011]), given the similarities and differences (for instance, Nussbaum strikes me as too captive to liberal individualism)—but such an engagement is beyond my capacity in this book, unfortunately, so it will have to await future development.

16. Still, to believe in the existence of entities does not require a commitment to some kind of Neoplatonic realism—namely, the belief that every instance of an evident thing represents the embodiment of a more-real universal form or ideal. Some personalists might believe that, but none need to.

17. As will become clear below, not all persons enjoy what it takes to develop the existential unfolding of the full empirical dimensions of the ontology of their personhood, yet that does not reduce or eliminate their personhood, but only means its development in existence is curtailed or aborted.

18. Smith, *What Is a Person?*, 61–88.

19. See Philip Clayton and Paul Davies, eds., *The Re-Emergence of Emergence* (New York: Oxford University Press, 2006).

20. Emergence is antidualistic and antimonistic—it explains the existence of very different

qualities and features in a reality that is understood to be unified, not dualistic, though not a singular monad either. See Geoffrey Hodgson, "The Concept of Emergence in Social Science: Its History and Importance," *Emergence* 2, no. 4 (2000): 65–77. For an argument that emergence was central to Durkheim's theorizing, see R. Keith Sawyer, "Durkheim's Dilemma: Toward a Sociology of Emergence," *Sociological Theory* 20, no. 2 (2002): 227–47.

21. See figures 1, 2, and 3, pp. 33, 57, and 74, of Smith, *What Is a Person?*

22. Theists might say that God is the agent who makes this happen, but for present purposes that is not a determinative issue.

23. See Roy Bhaskar, *Scientific Realism and Human Emancipation* (London: Verso, 1986). The background conditions of society's domination of persons include the temporal preexistence and transcendental necessity of social forms, the removal of powerful institutional sectors from the human regulation of all but the most powerful persons not always pursuing the common good, and the tendency of social structures toward reification (see Smith, *What Is a Person?*, 317–82).

24. See the Transformational Model of Social Action (TMSA), in Roy Bhaskar, *The Possibility of Naturalism* (London: Routledge, 1998); Archer, *Realist Social Theory*.

25. Martin Heidegger, *Being and Time* (New York: Harper, 2008).

26. I am grateful to Roy Bhaskar for helping me better clarify in this paragraph these distinctions.

27. Margaret Archer provides examples of sociological reductionism in her critiques of upward, downward, and central conflations (*Realist Social Theory*).

28. Midgley, too, attacks "a very general notion which is by now deep-rooted among people who want their psychology to be scientific. It is the notion that motives must not be examined and explained *as motives*, but always reduced to something else" (*Beast and Man*, 101).

29. Sebastian Samay, "Affectivity and Moral Behavior," in *Personalist Ethics and Human Subjectivity*, ed. George McLean (Washington, DC: Paideia, 1996), 28–31.

30. Foot, *Natural Goodness*.

31. M. A. Beek and J. Sperna Weiland, *Martin Buber: Personalist and Prophet* (Westminster, MD: Newman Press, 1968), 52–65.

32. Instructive is the central role that personal relationships play in human happiness. Ambrose Leung, Cheryl Kier, Tak Fung, Linda Fung, and Robert Sproule, "Searching for Happiness: The Importance of Social Capital," *Journal of Happiness Studies* 12 (2011): 443–62; Derek Bok, *The Politics of Happiness* (Princeton, NJ: Princeton University Press, 2010); Robert Lane, *The Loss of Happiness in Market Democracies* (New Haven, CT: Yale University Press, 2001).

33. John Stuart Mill is an exemplar: "The only part of conduct of anyone for which he is amenable to society is that which concerns others. In the part which merely concerns himself, his independence is, of right, absolute. Over himself, over his own body and mind, the individual is sovereign"; "individuality is the same thing with development and . . . only the cultivation of individuality . . . produces, or can produce, well-developed human beings"; and "the individual is not accountable to society for his actions in so far as these concern the interests of no person but himself." Mill, *On Liberty* (1859; Indianapolis: Hackett, 1978), 9, 61, 93. Also see Ralph Waldo Emerson's essay on "Self-Reliance" (1841; New York: Empire Books, 2011).

34. See Gregory, *Unintended Reformation*.

35. See John Kekes, *Against Liberalism* (Ithaca, NY: Cornell University Press, 1997).

36. The difference between individuals and persons is also seen in the fact that while individuals can easily be seen as abstractions, persons always have *names*, are named—an idea Brian Brock suggested to me, for which, thanks.

37. Douglas Porpora, "Recovering Causality: Realist Methods in Sociology," in *Realismo Sociologico*, ed. A. Maccarini, E. Morandi, and R. Prandini (Genova-Milano: Marietti, 2008); Douglas Porpora, "Cultural Rules and Material Relations," *Sociological Theory* 11, no. 2 (1993): 212–29; Douglas Porpora, "Sociology's Causal Confusion," in *Revitalizing Causality: Realism about Causality in Philosophy and Social Science*, ed. Ruth Groff (New York: Routledge, 2007); Berth Danermark et al., *Explaining Society: Critical Realism in the Social Sciences* (New York: Routledge, 2002), 52–53, 56, 59, 74; Andrew Sayer, *Method in Social Science: A Realist Approach* (New York: Routledge, 1992); also see Robert Koons, *Realism Regained: An Exact Theory of Causation, Teleology, and the Mind* (New York: Oxford University Press, 2000).

38. See Groff and Greco, *Powers and Capacities in Philosophy*.

39. A well-known account of this position—drawing out, wrongly, in my view, some Wittgensteinian ideas to certain wrong conclusions—is Peter Winch, *The Idea of a Social Science and Its Relation to Philosophy* (London: Routledge, 1958). Also see Phil Hutchinson, Rupert Read, and Wes Sharrock, *There Is No Such Thing as a Social Science* (Surrey, UK: Ashgate, 2008).

40. This approach differs from the standard view of agency as reflecting conditions in which the agent "could have acted otherwise," expressed, among many others, by Anthony Giddens (*New Rules of Sociological Method* [London: Hutchison, 1976], 75). Persons can act with real agency even when they have no choice in actions, for example, by purposefully choosing to affirm and carry out an action when they only have one realistic option, something people do all the time. Such an approach reframes matters in a way that better (than autonomous liberal individualism) addresses problems of causation, determinism, and meaningful affirmations of what is good even when there is not an array of options from which to choose. Agency, thus, can be expressed not only in social situations such as the free consumer choosing between products to purchase—the standard model—but also by persons in highly constrained circumstances. See Colin Campbell, "Distinguishing the Power of Agency from Agentic Power," *Sociological Theory* 27 (2005): 407–18.

41. Hilliard Aronovitch explains this nicely ("Social Explanation and Rational Motivation," *American Philosophical Quarterly* 15 [1978]: 197–204).

42. See Alasdair MacIntyre, "The Idea of a Social Science" and "Rationality and the Explanation of Action," chapters 19 and 21 in MacIntyre, *Against the Self-Images of the Age* (London: Duckworth, 1971), 211–29, 244–59.

43. See Roy Baumeister, Matthew Gaillot, and Dianne Tice, "Free Willpower: A Limited Resource Theory of Volition, Choice, and Self-Regulation," in *Oxford Handbook of Human Action*, ed. Ezequiel Morsella, John Bargh, and Peter Gollwitzer (New York: Oxford University Press, 2009), 487–508.

44. One clarification: I just said that personalism's understanding of causation need not be mechanistic. That is true. A bit confusing, perhaps, then, is the fact that the same approach uses the term "causal mechanism" to describe the operation of the natural powers and capacities of entities that may influence things in the surrounding world. We must distinguish between causes operating "mechan*istically*" (which I deny) and causation operating through causal "mecha*nisms*" (which I affirm). Ideally, scholars would find a better term than *mechanisms* to describe the causal processes at issue. Meanwhile, this distinction should be understood and honored.

45. Peter Hedström and Richard Swedberg, *Social Mechanisms: An Analytical Approach to Social Theory* (Cambridge: Cambridge University Press, 1998).

46. Nor did Peter Hedström and Peter Bearman get social mechanisms exactly right in their *Oxford Handbook of Analytical Sociology* (New York: Oxford University Press, 2011).

47. Phil Gorksi has made this point well and posed a constructive alternative in Gorski,

"Social 'Mechanisms' and Comparative-Historical Sociology: A Critical Realist Proposal," in *The Frontiers of Sociology*, ed. Björn Wittrock and Peter Hedström (Leiden: Brill, 2009). Also see Peter Machamer, Lindley Darden, and Carl Craver, "Thinking about Mechanisms," *Philosophy of Science* 67 (2000): 1–25.

48. Daniel Robinson, *Aristotle's Psychology* (New York: Columbia University Press, 1989), 97–111. More on this in chapters 5–6.

49. Experience with artificial reproductive cloning is inadequate to say anything substantial about its implications for the uniqueness of personal selves. However, even in the natural version of reproductive human cloning—identical twins—each twin always turns out to be his or her own person, not a copy of their twin sibling, despite their having many identifiable physical and personality features in common as genetically identical.

50. The particularity of persons also commends a cultural ethic as good that balances reliable policies and rules with equal justice for all discerning sensitivity on the part of those who administer justice, policies, and rules to the particular conditions, circumstances, and contexts of persons who are affected by them. All good moral, legal, and educational systems recognize the need to tailor treatments and judgments to the particularities of specific cases. Equal justice does not mean one size fits all. Justice, instead, requires prudent judgments that are sensitive to personal particularities. And that requires wisdom on the part of those making judgments. If this were not so, we could replace judges and teachers with computers.

51. See Herschel Baker, *The Image of Man: A Study of the Idea of Human Dignity in Classical Antiquity, the Middle Ages, and the Renaissance* (New York: Harper, 1947).

52. In part because of the long historical religious roots that formed its entrenched categories, which seem to run as deep as Jewish monotheism's transcendent, one God defined against the particulars of created (nondivine) humanity and the cosmos, reproduced as well in Islam, though modified significantly by Christianity's Trinitarian doctrine of God.

53. Archer, *Realist Social Theory*.

54. Some readers might believe that the twentieth century discredited sociopolitical and economic collectivistic systems, but I think that would be naive. Because it resonates with something that is partly, though not entirely true, collectivism will always be a temptation in the construction of human social orders.

Chapter 2: Rethinking Motivations for Action

1. Walter Gove, "Why We Do What We Do: A Biopsychosocial Theory of Human Motivation," *Social Forces* 73, no. 2 (1994): 363–94.

2. Dennis Brissett and Charles Edgley, *Life as Theater: A Dramaturgical Sourcebook* (New Brunswick, NJ: Transaction, 2007), 201–2, 203, 22, 23—which the introduction by Robert Stebbins of the University of Calgary calls "the best single source book on the dramaturgical perspective as applied in the social science" (xi). See John Rex, *Key Problems in Sociological Theory* (New York: Routledge, 2002), 63–65.

3. The words "motivation" and "motive" come etymologically from the Latin word *motus*, which means "to move," by way of the Late Latin *motivus* ("moving") and Middle French *motif* ("a moving reason")—linking the idea of motivations to the capacity to be made to move.

4. Robert Paul, "What Does Anybody Want?: Desire, Purpose, and the Acting Subject in the Study of Culture," *Cultural Anthropology* 5, no. 4 (1990): 431–51.

5. For example, humans "steer our lives one way or another using reasons and purposes not causes and effects." Brissett and Edgely, *Life as Theater*, 203.

6. Dave Elder-Vass, *The Causal Power of Social Structures: Emergence, Structure, and Agency* (Cambridge: Cambridge University Press, 2010); Emmet, "Motivation in Sociology and Social Anthropology," 86.

7. James Coleman is right that analytically the macro always "dips to the level of the individual" (*Foundations of Social Theory*, 8)—in his larger argument about what has come to be called "Coleman's 'boat'"—even if his view of persons as individuals is mistaken.

8. Even if many of the outcomes are not intended, per Thomas Schelling, *Micromotives and Macrobehavior* (New York: Norton, 2006).

9. E. Tory Higgins and Arie Kruglanski, "Motivational Science: The Nature and Function of Wanting," in *Motivational Science: Social and Psychological Perspectives*, ed. Higgins and Kruglanski (Philadelphia: Psychology Press, 2000), 1–20.

10. Roy Baumeister, E. J. Masicampo, and Kathleen Vohs, "Do Conscious Thoughts Cause Behavior?" *Annual Review of Psychology* 62 (2011): 331–61; Aronovitch, "Social Explanation and Rational Motivation." It is worth noting that one reason some social scientists rejected the belief that meaningful reasons can be causes was the inability to assimilate reasons into covering-law explanations, which my account rejects.

11. Roy D'Andrade, *The Development of Cognitive Anthropology* (Cambridge: Cambridge University Press, 1995).

12. See Charles Camic, "The Matter of Habit," *American Journal of Sociology* 91 (1986): 1039–87.

13. Not to mention the fact that in many important ways, talk itself is a significant form of action—per Naomi Quinn and Dorothy Holland, "Culture and Cognition," in *Cultural Models in Language and Thought*, ed. Holland and Quinn (Cambridge: Cambridge University Press, 1987), 9.

14. For example, Howard Schuman and Michael Johnson, "Attitudes and Behavior," *Annual Review of Psychology* 2 (1976): 161–207; Icek Ajzen and Martin Fishbein, "Attitude-Behavior Relations: A Theoretical Analysis and Review of Empirical Research," *Psychological Bulletin* 84, no. 5 (1977): 888–918; Icek Ajzen, "Nature and Operation of Attitudes," *Annual Review of Psychology* 52 (2001): 27–58; Gerd Bohner and Nina Dickel, "Attitudes and Attitude Change," *Annual Review of Psychology* 62 (2010): 391–417; also see Alfred Mele, *Effective Intentions: The Power of Conscious Will* (New York: Oxford University Press, 2009); E. Tory Higgins, "Social Cognition: Learning about What Matters in the Social World," *European Journal of Social Psychology* 30 (2000): 3–39; Icek Ajzen, "The Theory of Planned Behavior," *Organizational Behavior and Human Decision Processes* 50 (1991): 179–211; Wolfgang Prinz, Gisa Aschersleben, and Iring Koch, "Cognition and Action," in Morsella, Bargh, and Gollwitzer, *Oxford Handbook of Human Action*, 35–71. Also see Nancy Snow, *Virtue as Social Intelligence: An Empirically Grounded Theory* (New York: Routledge, 2010).

15. Stephen Vaisey, "What People Want: Rethinking Poverty, Culture, and Educational Attainment," *Annals of the American Academy of Political and Social Science* 629 (2010): 75–101.

16. The psychological science of motivations, which sociologists ignore to their detriment, is massive and complex. See, for example, James Shah and Wendi Gardner, eds., *Handbook of Motivation Science* (New York: Guilford Press, 2008); David Dunning, ed., *Social Motivation* (New York: Psychology Press, 2011).

17. M. D. Vernon, *Human Motivation* (Cambridge: Cambridge University Press, 1969).

18. Higgins and Kruglanski, *Motivational Science: Social and Psychological Perspectives*; E. Tory Higgins and Thane Pittman, "Motives of the Human Animal: Comprehending, Managing, and Sharing Inner States," *Annual Review of Psychology* 59 (2008): 361–85; Peter Gollwit-

zer, "Implementing Intentions: Strong Effects of Simple Plans," *American Psychologist* 54, no. 7 (1999): 493–503.

19. Icek Ajzen, "The Theory of Planned Behavior," *Organizational Behavior and Human Decision Processes* 50 (1991): 179–211.

20. Donald Davidson, *Essays on Action and Events* (New York: Oxford University Press, 2001).

21. Douglas Moo, *Motivation: The Organization of Action* (New York: W. W. Norton, 1996).

22. This is a modified version of theories expressed in Alvin Goldman, *A Theory of Action* (Englewood Cliffs, NJ: Prentice Hall, 1970); Daniel Dennett, "Intentional Systems," *Journal of Philosophy* 68 (1971): 87–106; Douglas Porpora, "On the Post-Wittgensteinian Critique of the Concept of Action in Sociology," *Journal for the Theory of Social Behavior* 13 (1983): 129–46. Accidental actions by my account are thus *not* purposive, but result unintentionally from usually purposive actions (see Davidson, *Essays on Action and Events*).

23. "Normative reasons" are considerations that count in favor of something, which can be offered either before or after the thing the reasons justify; these are also sometimes called "motivating reasons." "Explanatory reasons" by comparison are considerations that explain why things happened, usually offered after the fact. For a more complicated analysis of motivating reasons, see Christian Miller, "Motivation in Agents," *Noûs* 42, no. 2 (2008): 222–66.

24. Philosophical discussions of reasons include T. M. Scanlon, *What We Owe to Each Other* (Cambridge, MA: Harvard University Press, 1998); Derek Parfit, *On What Matters* (New York: Oxford University Press, 2011); Michael Smith, *The Moral Problem* (Oxford: Blackwell, 1994); John Broome, "Reasons," in *Reason and Value*, ed. R. Jay Wallace, Philip Pettit, Samuel Scheffler, and Michael Smith (New York: Oxford University Press, 2006), 28–55; Richard Norman, "Practical Reasons and the Redundancy of Motives," *Ethical Theory and Moral Practice* 4 (2001): 3–22; Eve Garrard and David McNaughton, "Mapping Moral Motivation," *Ethical Theory and Moral Practice* 1 (1998): 45–59.

25. These include the personal powers of conscious awareness; mental representation; volition; practical consciousness; understanding quantity, qualities, space, and time; emotional experience; assigning causal attribution; intersubjective understanding; episodic and long-term memory; interest formation; creativity; innovation; imagination; self-reflexivity; meaning communication; technological invention and use; composition of narratives; language use; symbolization; valuation; anticipation of the future; identity formation; self-transcendence; abstract reasoning; truth seeking; aesthetic judgment; moral awareness; and so on.

26. Some philosophers argue that either beliefs or desires alone can motivate action, though I disagree.

27. Antonio Damasio, *Descartes' Error: Emotion, Reason, and the Human Brain* (New York: Penguin, 1994).

28. Moo, *Motivation*, 19.

29. Matthew Chew, "The Theoretical Quandary of Subjectivity," *Review of European Studies* 1, no. 1 (2009): 23–34; Marc Hauser and Justin Wood, "Evolving the Capacity to Understand Actions, Intentions, and Goals," *Annual Review of Psychology* 61 (2010): 303–24.

30. Peter Lipton, *Inference to the Best Explanation* (New York: Routledge, 2004).

31. The belief per se is the mental attitude of taking a premise or proposition to be true, not the content of the premise or proposition itself.

32. Nathan Brody, *Human Motivation: Commentary on Goal-Directed Action* (New York: Academic Press, 1983).

33. Philosophers are actually divided about the finer points concerning the exact status of

beliefs. My position aligns with views presented by Lynne Rudder Baker, *Saving Belief: A Critique of Physicalism* (Princeton, NJ: Princeton University Press, 1987).

34. Which helps make sense of John Searle's suggestive observation: "I believe that George Washington was the first U.S. president even when I am not thinking about it, indeed, even when I am asleep" (Searle, *Making the Social World: The Structure of Human Civilization* [New York: Oxford University Press, 2010], 26).

35. By some accounts, holding and examining beliefs are crucial markers of personhood per se. Simon Evnine, *Epistemic Dimensions of Personhood* (New York: Oxford University Press, 2008). Also see Carol Dweck, *Mindset* (New York: Random House, 2006).

36. See Fritz Strack, Roland Deutsch, and Regina Krieglmeyer, "The Two Horses of Behavior: Reflection and Impulse," in Morsella, Bargh, and Gollwitzer, *Oxford Handbook of Human Action*, 104–17.

37. Melvin Spiro, *Culture and Human Nature* (New Brunswick, NJ: Transaction, 2003), 162.

38. Stephen Vaisey, "Socrates, Skinner, and Aristotle: Three Ways of Thinking about Culture in Action," *Sociological Forum* 23, no. 3 (2008): 603–13.

39. Giles Pearson, *Aristotle on Desires* (Cambridge: Cambridge University Press, 2012).

40. Henrik Poulsen, *Conations* (Aarhus, Denmark: Aarhus University Press, 1991).

41. William Irvine, *On Desire: Why We Want What We Want* (New York: Oxford University Press, 2006); George Schueler, *Desire: Its Role in Practical Reason and the Explanation of Action* (Cambridge, MA: Bradford, 1995).

42. Timothy Schroeder, *Three Faces of Desire* (New York: Oxford University Press, 2004); Zeki Kawabata, "The Neural Correlates of Desire," *PLoS ONE* 3, no. 8 (2008): e3027. doi: 10.1371/journal.pone.0003027; Morten Kringelbach and Kent Berridge, eds., *Pleasures of the Brain* (New York: Oxford University Press, 2009).

43. Kathleen Lennon, *Explaining Human Action* (La Salle, IL: Open Court, 1990). For two realist, goods-based arguments about the relation between values, desires, and goods, see Graham Oddie, *Value, Reality, and Desire* (New York: Oxford University Press, 2009); and Dennis Stampe, "The Authority of Desire," *Philosophical Review* 96 (1987): 335–81.

44. Theodore Mischel, *Human Action: Conceptual and Empirical Issues* (New York: Academic Press, 1969). See Pearson, *Aristotle on Desires*.

45. Nico Frijda, *Emotions and Beliefs: How Feelings Influence Thoughts* (Cambridge: Cambridge University Press, 2000); Martha Nussbaum, *Upheavals of Thought: The Intelligence of Emotions* (Cambridge: Cambridge University Press, 2003); Anthony Kenny, *Action, Emotion, and Will* (New York: Routledge, 2003).

46. Jon Elster, "Emotion and Action," in *Thinking about Feeling: Contemporary Philosophers on Emotions*, ed. Robert Solomon (New York: Oxford University Press, 2004), 151–62. Solomon argues that emotions are not only a crucial way of persons knowing but also provide motivational orientations toward the world ("Emotions and Choice," in *Explaining Emotions*, ed. Amélie Oksenberg Rorty (Berkeley: University of California Press, 1980), 251–83. Porpora calls emotions "orientations of care" in *Landscapes of the Soul: The Loss of Moral Meaning in American Life* (New York: Oxford University Press, 2001), 17, 59, 319.

47. C. E. Izard, "Four Systems for Emotion Activation: Cognitive and Noncognitive Processes," *Psychological Review* 100 (1993): 68–90; Antonio Damasio, *The Feeling of What Happens: Body and Emotion in the Making of Consciousness* (New York: Mariner Books, 2000).

48. Nico Frijda, *The Emotions* (Cambridge: Cambridge University Press, 1986); David Myers, "Theories of Emotion," *Psychology* (New York: Worth, 2004), 500.

49. Jenefer Robinson, "Emotion: Biological Fact or Social Construction?" and Jessie Prinz, "Embodied Emotions," in Solomon, *Thinking about Feeling*, 28–43 and 44–58, respectively.

50. Joseph Ledoux, *The Emotional Brain* (New York: Simon and Schuster, 1998).

51. Jaak Panksepp, *Affective Neuroscience: The Foundations of Human and Animal Emotions* (New York: Oxford University Press, 1998).

52. Many emotions, however, are simply beyond people's capacity to regulate in socially normative ways, and "many of the greatest emotional experiences in life—good and bad—come as a surprise" (Elster, "Emotion and Action,", in Solomon, *Thinking about Feeling*, 160; also see the chapter by Neu in the same volume).

53. Paul Ekman, "An Argument for Basic Emotions," *Cognition and Emotion* 6 (1992): 169–200.

54. Jonathan Turner, *Human Emotions: A Sociological Theory* (New York: Routledge, 2007).

55. See Johnmarshall Reeve, *Understanding Motivation and Emotion* (Hoboken, NJ: Wiley, 2008); Denys DeCatanzaro, *Motivation and Emotion* (New York: Prentice Hall, 1998); Eva Ferguson, *Motivation: A Biosocial and Cognitive Integration of Motivation and Emotion* (New York: Oxford University Press, 2000); Mark Leary, "Motivational and Emotional Aspects of the Self," *Annual Review of Psychology* 58 (2007): 317–44; Herbert Simon, "Human Nature in Politics: The Dialogue of Psychology with Political Science," *American Political Science Review* 79, no. 2 (1985): 301.

56. The common element being the idea "to move"—the word *emotion* coming from the Old French *emouvoir* ("to stir up"), derived from the Latin *emovere* ("to move out, remove, agitate"), a compound of *ex-* ("out") + *movere* ("to move").

57. Frijda, *The Emotions*, 460. Frijda writes that desires energize motivations while emotion monitor and govern actions "belonging to other goals and other programs than its own. . . . Emotions proper result from monitoring whether events promise, or threaten to interfere with, concern satisfaction. . . . Desires, by contrast, initiate and maintain new courses of action; they establish goals and activate programs for achieving them" (460).

58. Panksepp, *Affective Neuroscience*, 144–63.

59. Ronald de Sousa, "Emotions," in Solomon, *Thinking about Feeling*, 65. Also see Calhoun's discussion of emotions and teleology in the same volume, 117–18.

60. Robert Solomon, "Emotions, Thoughts, and Feelings: Emotions as Engagements with the World," in Solomon, *Thinking about Feeling*, 76–88. Also see chapters by Goldie, Calhoun, Greenspan, Nussbaum, and Baier in the same volume. Also see Hans Jonas, "To Move and to Feel," in Jonas, *The Phenomenology of Life* (Evanston, IL: Northwestern University Press, 2001), 99–107.

61. Michael Stocker, "Some Considerations about Intellectual Desire and Emotions," in Solomon, *Thinking about Feeling*, 139.

62. Jon Elster, "Emotion and Action," in Solomon, *Thinking about Feeling*, 151.

63. Robert Stocker and Elizabeth Hegeman, *Valuing Emotions* (Cambridge: Cambridge University Press, 1996).

64. Frijda, *The Emotions*, 473.

65. On the centrality of emotions in the making of moral judgments, see Arne Johan Vetlesen, *Perception, Empathy, and Judgment: An Inquiry into the Preconditions of Moral Performance* (University Park: Pennsylvania State University Press, 1994).

66. N. J. H. Dent rightly argues, in neo-Aristotelian mode, that emotions, desires, and a reasoned understanding of what makes for a good human life are integrated by the virtues, which

help form an ordered unity of mind and "heart" (*The Moral Psychology of Virtues* [Cambridge: Cambridge University Press, 1984]). Also see Charles Chamberlain, "The Meaning of *Prohairesis* in Aristotle's Ethics," *Transactions of the American Philological Association* 114 (1984): 147–57.

67. See, for instance, Panksepp, *Affective Neuroscience*; Michela Balconi, *Neuropsychology of the Sense of Agency: From Consciousness to Action* (New York: Springer, 2010); Anthony Freeman, Benjamin Libet, and Keith Sutherland, eds., *The Volitional Brain* (Exeter, UK: Imprint Academic, 1999), 1–76; Frank Krueger and Jordon Grafman, eds., *The Neural Basis of Human Belief Systems* (London: Psychology Press, 2013); Richard Lane and Lynn Nadel, *Cognitive Neuroscience of Emotion* (New York: Oxford University Press, 2002); Timothy Schroeder, *Three Faces of Desire* (New York: Oxford University Press, 2004); Joseph Ledoux, *The Emotional Brain* (New York: Simon and Schuster, 1998); Susan Greenfield, *BBC Brain Story: Unlocking the Inner World of Emotions, Memories, Ideas, and Desires* (London: DK Books, 2001); Jay Schulkin, *Roots of Social Sensibility and Neural Function* (Cambridge, MA: MIT Press, 2000); Joseph Ledoux, *Synaptic Self* (New York: Penguin, 2003); Ronald de Sousa, *The Rationality of Emotion* (Cambridge, MA: MIT Press, 1987).

68. Jing Zhu, *The Conative Mind: Volition and Action* (Saarbrücken, Germany: LAP Lambert Academic Publishing, 2012). As far back as the mid-1980s, the neurologist Antonio Damasio wrote that the "anatomical and functional knowledge about the SMA and its vicinity will permit us to model the neuronal substrates of the *will* and thus overcome a persistent objection of those who favor a dualist position regarding mind and brain" (Damasio, "Understanding the Mind's Will," *Behavioral and Brain Sciences* 8 [1985]: 589, italics in original). Stanford University's Richard Snow wrote in 1980 that "both conative and affective aspects of persons and situations influence the details of cognitive processing. . . . A theoretical account of intelligent behavior in the real world requires a synthesis of cognition, conation and affect. We have not really begun to envision this synthesis" (Snow, "Intelligence for the Year 2001," *Intelligence* 4 [1980]: 194). Also see R. Snow, L. Corno, and D. Jackson, "Individual Differences in Affective and Conative Functions," in *Handbook of Psychology*, ed. D. Berliner and R. Calfee (New York: Macmillan, 1996), 243–310; W. Huitt, "Conation as an Important Factor of Mind," *Educational Psychology Interactive* (Valdosta, GA: Valdosta State University, 1999). Also see Tallis, *Aping Mankind*.

69. George Homans, "Bringing Men Back In," *American Sociological Review* 29 (1964): 809–18.

70. See Scott Sehon, "Teleological Explanation," in *A Companion to the Philosophy of Action*, ed. Timothy O'Connor and Constantine Sandis (Malden, MA: Wiley-Blackwell, 2010), 121–28.

71. Habermas thus rightly observed that "the teleological structure is fundamental to *all* concepts of action," including the normatively regulated, dramaturgical, and communicative (*Reason and the Rationalization of Society*, 101). See Ann Mische, "Projects and Possibilities: Researching Futures in Action," *Sociological Forum* 24 (2009): 694–704.

72. Tim Bayne, "Agentive Experiences as Pushmi-Pullyu Representations," in *New Waves in Philosophy of Action*, ed. Jesús Aguilar, Andrei Buckareff, and Keith Frankish (New York: Palgrave Macmillan, 2011), 219–36.

73. For one account trying to build complexity into a theory of meaning, motivation, and action, see Alan Fiske, *Structures of Social Life: The Four Elementary Forms of Human Relations* (New York: Free Press, 1991), especially 99–114.

74. The following explorations could no doubt benefit from engagement with scholarship in legal theory on the nature of motivations for actions and human capacities to discern them, but that too is unfortunately beyond my ability to take on here.

75. By incommensurate, I mean lacking a common quality or standard of measurement

that makes comparison or trade-offs possible. On multiplicity, see George Loewenstein, *Exotic Preferences: Behavioral Economics and Human Motivation* (New York: Oxford University Press, 2007).

76. "There is no such thing as action except as an effort to conform with norms." Talcott Parsons, *The Structure of Social Action* (New York: Free Press 1937), 76–77.

77. Siegwart Lindenberg, "Homo Socio-Economicus: The Emergence of a General Model of Man in the Social Sciences," *Journal of Institutional and Theoretical Economics* 146, no. 4 (1990): 727–48; William Meckling, "Values and Choice of the Model of the Individual in the Social Sciences," *Swiss Review of Political Economy and Statistics* 112, no. 4 (1976): 545–59; Siegwart Lindenberg, "An Assessment of the New Political Economy," *Sociological Theory* 3 (1985): 99–111.

78. Randall Collins: "Human beings are emotional energy seekers. . . . If not emotional energy seekers, what else could human beings be?" (*Interaction Ritual Chains*, 373). Motivationally, he claims, that is because "emotional energy has a powerful motivating effect upon the individual; whoever has experienced this kind of moment wants to repeat it" (39).

79. See Jonathan Turner, "Toward a Sociological Theory of Motivations," *American Sociological Review* 53 (1987): 15–27, who says, "none alone completely captures the full dynamics of motivation" (22).

80. Tom Tyler, *Why People Cooperate: The Role of Social Motivations* (Princeton, NJ: Princeton University Press, 2011); Ernst Fehr and Herbert Gintis, "Human Motivation and Social Cooperation: Experimental and Analytical Foundations," *Annual Review of Sociology* 33 (2007): 43–64; Mehran Thomson, *The Springs of Human Action: A Psychological Study of the Sources, Mechanisms, and Principles of Motivation in Human Behavior* (New York: Appleton, 1927).

81. Steven Reiss, "Multifaceted Nature of Intrinsic Motivation: The Theory of 16 Basic Desires," *Review of General Psychology* 8, no. 3 (2004): 179–93; Siegwart Lindenberg, "Values: What Do They Do for Behavior?," in *Raymond Boudon: A Life in Sociology*, vol. 3, ed. Mohamed Cherkaoui and Peter Hamilton (Oxford: Bardwell Press, 2009), 59–89; Gordon Allport, "The Functional Autonomy of Motives," *American Journal of Psychology* 50 (1937): 141–56.

82. Michael Jensen and William Meckling, "The Nature of Man," *Journal of Applied Corporate Finance* 7, no. 2 (1994): 4–19.

83. Thus, from my perspective, Neil Fligstein and Doug McAdam's recent attempt to formulate a *dual*-motive theory of motivations—emphasizing both "instrumental" and "existential" (need for meaning and identity) motivations as basic and irreducible—is too simplistic (*A Theory of Fields* [New York: Oxford, 2012], especially 18, 22, 43–44, 50, 137–39).

84. Joseph Forgas, Kipling Williams, and Simon Laham, eds., *Social Motivation: Conscious and Unconscious Processes* (Cambridge: Cambridge University Press, 2005).

85. John Bargh and Tanya Chartrand, "Automaticity in Goal Pursuit," in *Handbook of Competence and Motivation*, ed. Andrew Edwards and Carol Dweck (New York: Guilford Publications, 1999), 624–46; John Bargh and Ezequiel Morsella, "The Unconscious Mind," *Perspectives on Psychological Science* 3, no. 1 (2008): 73–79; Malcolm Gladwell, *Blink: The Power of Thinking without Thinking* (New York: Little, Brown, 2005); Fritz Strack and Roland Deutch, "Reflective and Impulsive Determinants of Social Behavior," *Personality and Social Psychology Review* 8, no. 3 (2004): 220–47.

86. See Stuart Hampshire, *Thought and Action* (New York: Viking, 1959).

87. Not that it is by any means unimportant—far from it! See Margaret Archer, *The Reflexive Imperative* (Cambridge: Cambridge University Press, 2012).

88. Henk Aarts and Ap Dijksterhis, "Habits as Knowledge Structures: Automaticity in Goal-Directed Behavior," *Journal of Personality and Social Psychology* 78, no. 1 (2000): 53–63; Ronald

Deutch and Fritz Strack, "Duality Models in Social Psychology: From Dual Process to Interacting System," *Psychological Inquiry* 17, no. 2 (2006): 71–100; Shelly Chaiken and Yaacov Trope, eds., *Dual Process Theories in Social Psychology* (New York: Guilford Press, 1999).

89. Omar Lizardo, "The Cognitive Origins of Bourdieu's *Habitus,*" *Journal for the Theory of Social Behaviour* 34, no. 4 (2009): 375–401; Stephen Vaisey, "Motivation and Justification: A Dual-Process Model of Culture in Action," *American Journal of Sociology* 114 (2009): 1675–715.

90. Bill Pollard, "Identification, Psychology, and Habits," in Aguilar, Buckareff, and Frankish, *New Waves in Philosophy of Action*, 81–98.

91. Charles Camic, "The Matter of Habit"; Timothy Wilson, Samuel Lindsay, and Tonya Schooler, "A Model of Dual Attitudes," *Psychological Review* 107, no. 1 (2000): 101–26.

92. Roy Wallis and Steve Bruce, "Accounting for Action," *Sociology* 17, no. 1 (1983), 105.

93. Colin Campbell, *The Myth of Social Action* (Cambridge: Cambridge University Press, 1996), 57–58.

94. See, for example, Ran Hassin, James Uleman, and John Barch, *The New Unconscious* (New York: Oxford University Press, 2005).

95. Virginia Blankenship, "The Dynamics of Intention," in *Goal Directed Behavior: The Concept of Action in Psychology*, ed. Michael Frese and John Sabini (Hillsdale, NJ: Lawrence Erlbaum, 1985), 169–70.

96. Obviously, a massive psychological literature exists on the unconscious, which I cannot engage here.

97. Roger Schank and Robert Abelson, *Scripts, Plans, Goals, and Understanding* (Hillsdale, NJ: Lawrence Erlbaum, 1977), 119.

98. Steven Heine, Travis Proulx, and Kathleen Vohs, "The Meaning Maintenance Model: On the Coherence of Social Motivation," *Personality and Social Psychology Review* 10, no. 2 (2006): 88–110.

99. Siegwart Lindenberg, "Intrinsic Motivation in a New Light," *Kyklos* 54 (2001): 317–42; Herbert Kelman, "Interests, Relationships, Identities: Three Central Issues for Individuals and Groups in Negotiating Their Social Environments," *Annual Review of Psychology* 57 (2006): 1–26.

100. Edward Deci and Richard Ryan, *Handbook of Self-Determination Research* (Rochester, NY: University of Rochester Press, 2002), 15–18; Kelman, "Interests, Relationships, Identities," 1–26.

101. Martin Ford, *Motivating Humans: Goals, Emotions, and Personal Agency Beliefs* (Newbury Park, CA: Sage, 1992), 115–18; Michael Chapman and Ellen Skinner, "Action in Development—Development in Action," in Frese and Sabini, *Goal Directed Behavior*, 200–213.

102. Heinz Heckhausen and Julius Kuhl, "From Wishes to Action: The Dead Ends and Short Cuts on the Long Way to Action," in Frese and Sabini, *Goal Directed Behavior*, 134–59; Piers Steel and Cornelius König, "Integrating Theories of Motivation," *Academy of Management Review* 31, no. 4 (2006): 889–913.

103. Peter Gollwitzer, "Implementing Intentions: Strong Effects of Simple Plans," *American Psychologist* 54, no. 7 (1999): 493–503; Arthur Markman, C. Miguel Brendl, and Kyungil Kim, "From Goal Activation to Action: How Does Preference and Use of Knowledge Intervene?," in Morsella, Bargh, and Gollwitzer, *Oxford Handbook of Human Action*, 328–49; Arie Kruglanski and Catalina Kopetz, "The Role of Goal Systems in Self-Regulation," in Morsella, Bargh, and Gollwitzer, *Oxford Handbook of Human Action*, 350–67.

104. Ezequiel Morsella, "The Mechanisms of Human Action," in Morsella, Bargh, and Gollwitzer, *Oxford Handbook of Human Action*, 1–32.

105. Some reductionistic philosophers and neuroscientists back them up, too, including, for

example, Stephen Stich, *From Folk Psychology to Cognitive Science: The Case against Belief* (Cambridge, MA: MIT Press, 1985); Patricia Smith Churchland, *Neurophilosophy: Toward a Unified Science of the Mind-Brain* (Cambridge, MA: MIT Press, 1989); Paul Churchland, *Scientific Realism and the Plasticity of Mind* (Cambridge: Cambridge University Press, 1986).

106. Empiric*ism* is a metatheoretical epistemological doctrine, quite distinct from simply being empiric*al*, i.e., referencing observable evidence in arguments.

107. Ruth Marcus, "Some Revisionary Proposals about Belief and Believing," *Philosophy and Phenomenological Research* 50 (1990): 132–53; R. B. Braithwaite, "The Nature of Believing," *Proceedings of the Aristotelian Society* 33 (1932/33): 129–46. Dispositionalism ultimately collapses into behaviorism, and so philosophers have largely abandoned it.

108. Some versions are specimens of the larger species of thought known as antimentalism and antisubjectivism. In sociology, Émile Durkheim was an antimentalist; George H. Mead was a moderate antimentalist. Claude Lévi-Strauss, much of practice theory, Michel Foucault and the poststructuralists, B. F. Skinner and behaviorism, Robert Wuthnow of the 1980s, Pierre Bourdieu, and various streams of postmodernism share a broader skepticism about the existence or sociological relevance of human mental states called beliefs.

109. Richard LaPierre, "Attitudes and Actions," *Social Forces* 13 (1934): 230–37; Irwin Deutscher, *What We Say/ What We Do* (Glenview, IL: Scott, Foresman, 1973); also see H. Frances Pestello, Fred Pestello, and Irwin Deutscher, *Sentiments and Acts* (Piscataway, NJ: Aldine Transaction, 1993). Much of this pertains to moral traits specifically, however, so is also not entirely pertinent to the larger issue.

110. Snow, *Virtue as Social Intelligence*, a very important book.

111. Besides the more general fact that all of human social life and civilization is built up out of people's beliefs, as shown, for example, by John Searle, *Making the Social World* (New York: Oxford University Press, 2010).

112. One might retreat to the weaker position that *some* beliefs *sometimes* do not matter, which only puts us back in the place of taking at least some beliefs quite seriously, forcing us to specify which beliefs matter under what conditions, which is an entirely different approach than the generalized skepticism about beliefs into which some fall.

113. In that some bugs may even hold some kinds of proto-beliefs, such as a spider's possible quasi-cognitive awareness that "a fly is caught in my web."

114. Yet sociological sociobiology, evolutionary psychology, and some neuroscientists, for instance, reduce human beliefs, desires, and motives away and replace them the reproductive-fitness "interest" of genetic material or operations of the physical brain. Daniel Wegner, *The Illusion of Conscious Will* (Cambridge, MA: MIT Press, 2002); also see Herbert Gintis, "A Framework for the Unification of the Behavioral Sciences," *Behavioral and Brain Sciences* 30 (2007): 1–61. But see Baker, *Saving Belief.*

115. Quinn and Holland, "Culture and Cognition," 7.

116. See Vaisey, "Motivation and Justification."

117. An early attempt to account for this problem (focused specifically on attitudes) in survey data analysis was the "contingent consistency" hypothesis—see A. Ackock and M. DeFleur, "A Configurational Approach to Contingent Consistency in the Attitudes-Behavior Relationship," *American Sociological Review* 37 (1972): 714–26; Allen Liska, "Emergent Issues in the Attitude-Behavior Consistency Controversy," *American Sociological Review* 39 (1974): 91–101; Kenneth Andrews and Denise Kandel, "Attitudes and Behavior: A Specification of the Contingency Consistency Hypothesis," *American Sociological Review* 44 (1979): 289–310. Surveys, however, face severe limits in their ability to account for this complexity.

118. Ann Swidler, "Cultural Power and Social Movements," in *Cultural Sociology*, ed. Lyn Spillman (Malden, MA: Blackwell, 2002), 313, 315, 316, italics added.

119. Ibid., 316, italics added—notice the words "interpreted," "value," and "knowledge" in this quotation.

120. Ann Swidler, "Culture in Action," *American Sociological Review* 51 (1986): 273–86. Swidler's larger program in cultural sociology needs more probing in this context. Swidler stands out as one who has been concerned in the field of culture to develop a particular argument about motivations and action. Her 1986 article is one of the most highly cited publications from cultural sociology, and her 2001 book, *Talk of Love: How Culture Matters*, provided Swidler an opportunity to elaborate and defend her view (Chicago: University of Chicago Press). Subsequent debates have also enabled Swidler to clarify her position on some key issues (Swidler, "Comment on Stephen Vaisey's 'Socrates, Skinner, and Aristotle: Three Ways of Thinking about Culture in Action,'" *Sociological Forum* 23, no. 3 [2008]: 614–18). Swidler takes a stand on the larger question of purposive, ends-motivated human action, so she makes a good interlocutor for my personalist position. She opposes the idea—which she identifies as Weberian and Parsonian—that culture provides people with goals or ends organized as values and norms, which they then choose the means to achieve. Instead, she asserts that people first learn or develop cultural repertoires of "strategies of action"—which are "general solutions to the problem of how to organize action over time"—and that these then subsequently determine the ends, goals, and values people hold and profess (*Talk of Love*, 82). Swidler insists, in short, that people's purposes, goals, and valued ends do not shape their strategies of action, but rather that the causal influence works in the opposite direction: "Culture has its effects not by providing the ends actors pursue but by shaping the patterns into which action is routinely organized," and "a person's available strategies of action shape the kind of goals he or she pursues instead of the other way around." Swidler furthermore declares that "what people want is a product of the cultural shaping of their capacities for action," that "the cultural influences individuals and groups carry into new situations are those that form their capacities for action—not their ends or goals," and that "values are not the reason why a person develops one strategy of action rather than another. They are not, so to speak, the originator of the chain of 'reasons' why someone acts as she does" (*Talk of Love*, 82, 83, 84, 86, respectively; see Jason Kaufman, "Endogenous Explanations in the Sociology of Culture," *Annual Review of Sociology* 30 [2004]: 335–57). In this Swidler is antisubjectivist and antiteleological, as I defined the latter above.

Personalism agrees with some of what Swidler argues. Yet her denial of the importance of motivations oriented toward achieving certain valued states of affairs (goals, goods, ends, purposes) for generating human action is at odds with the personalist theory I am advocating. If Swidler is right, then my theoretical project is in trouble—and vice versa. Do we have good reason to accept Swidler's arguments? I think not. A close reading of her case against the reality and importance of ends-motivated, ends-oriented human action reveals multiple problems—many of the same kinds of problems analyzed above. I count at least seven problems in Swidler that I think undermine her theoretical case. To begin, three of Swidler's specific critiques of the "Weberian/Parsonian model" turn out to be attacks on nonexistent opponents, in that she is refuting positions that neither Weber nor Parsons nor any other reasonable social theorist would hold. One is of "human beings choosing their actions *one at a time*, in light of their values and interests," building up "actions *piece by piece*, striving with *each act* to maximize a given outcome," so that "*individual* actions . . . make sense by themselves." The second unreal position Swidler critiques is that motivated, acting people "ha[ve] to *think about* each action they perform." The third concerns Weber or Parsons supposedly telling us to "assume that having the skills or capacities to act in a certain way is *unproblematic*, so that all persons need to ask themselves is, 'What do I really want?'" (*Talk of Love*, 81, 82, italics added). If any real theorists had actually argued these positions, Swidler would be right in attacking them. But neither Weber nor Parsons theorized that people select isolated actions that make sense as individual units to perform in serial order, that people needed to consciously think or deliberate about their actions before they could act, or that sociologists could assume or ignore whether actors possess the capacities to carry out actions.

Second, Swidler provides little evidence to justify another of her strong empirical claims— namely, that values and ends are not as deep and enduring as the Weberian/Parsonian model would have us believe, and that, instead, "what tends to have more continuity is the style or the set of skills and capacities with which people seek whatever objectives they choose." To establish this key point in her book, Swidler cites her own 1986 article, which is the precursor of this very argument in question. The primary evidence for this point, in short, is Swidler repeating herself in print. To illustrate her idea that "people change their ends relatively easily in new circumstances," Swidler does observe that immigrants can shift from valuing family continuity and honor in their home country to wealth and prestige after they have immigrated to a new social context. But that anecdote hardly verifies her larger claim. Shifting up from the level of individuals to societies, Swidler then says (though offers few scholarly references to establish) that comparative analyses of economic development have clearly failed to show that ultimate values or ends influence economic activity or socioeconomic development (*Talk of Love*, 80). But that references what is in fact a far-from-settled debate. Many social scientists continue to provide evidence and arguments that cultural values and norms shape motivations and actions in ways that greatly influence economic development (for example, Lawrence Harrison and Samuel Huntington, eds., *Culture Matters: How Values Shape Human Progress* [New York: Basic Books, 2000]; David Landes, *The Wealth and Poverty of Nations: Why Some Are So Rich and Some So Poor* (New York: W. W. Norton, 1999]; Lawrence Harrison, *Who Prospers: How Cultural Values Shape Economic and Political Success* [New York: Basic Books, 1993]). Swidler has read widely in literatures relevant to her study. If the empirical evidence that people's skills and capacities for action are much more stable and enduring than their goals, values, ends is in fact so definitive, it would have been valuable to lay it out in references and endnotes. But she did not.

A third problem with Swidler's argument is its emphasis on culture affecting action by influencing the "kind of selves" that people become, which raises more conceptual problems for her argument than her theoretical case is able to handle. Central to her argument is the idea that culture imparts capacities to its users, the first of which is "the capacity to be a certain kind of self." Culture, she argues, helps people "learn how to be, or become, particular kinds of persons" and shapes "the sense of self." As a result, "people develop lines of action based on who they already think they are." In this way, culture does not affect action "directly" by motivating actors to achieve ends or goals, but rather indirectly by constructing selves that can adopt certain strategies of action. But to focus on the selves and identities of persons as a means to invalidate the idea of motivated, ends-oriented human action reflects a shallow view of what the identities and selves of persons *are*. Swidler takes a strong constructionist, pragmatist, situationist approach to persons, selves, and identities, claiming (but not justifying) that "personal identity . . . results . . . not from anything inherent in individual personhood" and that the "self" is "constructed very differently in one . . . social situation versus another" (*Talk of Love*, 73, 71, 83, 87, respectively); her view seems influenced by the skeptical "accounts" version of motivations offered by C. Wright Mills, "Situated Actions and Vocabularies of Motives," *American Sociological Review* 5 (1940), and Marvin Scott and Stanford Lyman, "Accounts," *American So-*

ciological Review 33 (1968): 46–62. What Swidler does not grasp about the identities of persons, however, is how inescapably and powerfully linked they are with moral commitments, horizons of value, and teleologically oriented life projects. Charles Taylor has made this case clearly in his masterful work, *The Sources of the Self,* as have others (Cambridge, MA: Harvard University Press, 1989). Here is not the place to go into detail. Suffice it for present purposes to say that a key part of what culture does in the formation of the identities of human selves is to set people's lives in the perspective of broad moral spaces, horizons of sight, and visions of the good, in relation to which selves are necessarily formed and known (Smith, *Moral, Believing Animals*). And that inevitably raises questions about goods, purposes, ends, goals, interests, and values—the very ideas Swidler wants to sideline. In short, the personal identities that Swidler wants to emphasize cannot be formed and sustained in the ways that interest Swidler apart from their engaging the very kind of goods, goals, morals, values, interests, and ends that Swidler also seeks to marginalize.

Fourth, one of Swidler's crucial examples simply does not work. She provides a key case study in the person of the liberal Protestant pastor, Art Townsend, to demonstrate that it is really new social situations and new strategies of action that determine people's ends, values, and norms, and not the other way around. But Art Townsend's case demonstrates no such thing. If anything, Art's story can be read more convincingly as telling us that, through a process of self-reflection and criticism, he came to embrace a new set of goals and values, which then have motivated him to change his self-identity and strategies of action. It takes no editing of Art's story to see that he in fact has many internalized ends, goals, and purposes that seem to be driving his actions and attitudes. These are to become much better at loving himself and loving and accepting other people (be a "professional lover"), to experience personal "growth," to be a more "confident" and "responsible" person, to stop recurrently "beating himself up," to become more in charge of his own decisions and reactions, to lead a "coherent moral life," to better reach "interpsychic agreement" with others, to be a better pastor in helping his church parishioners ("these beautiful special people"), "enlightenment," to better practice an "ethic of integrity and responsibility," and finding "ways to solve problems" and "reach mutually satisfactory understandings" instead of becoming upset about problems and conflicts. These are all, in fact, goals, ends, and purposes oriented by values and embraced norms. There is no way around that. So Swidler here has not demonstrated with Art Townsend that strategies of action clearly determine goals, ends, and values, rather than the reverse. She does claim that the strategies of action came before the new goals, ends, and values. But the problem of causal direction is as ambiguous here as it is in most variables analysis using cross-sectional survey data. To make her case, she would have had to have followed Reverend Townsend as he changed over years, instead of conducting interviews at one period of time. Since she did not, and since his narrative suggests the equally possible validity of motivated, ends-oriented action explaining his case, Swidler has not yet made a convincing case for her proposed theoretical argument.

A fifth problem is that Swidler takes for granted a series of social conditions and situations in order to build her theoretical case, which her own theory seems unable to explain. For example, we hear in and through her exposition about the existence of things like people's "given mode of life" with which different cultural items "fit" more or less well. She does not elucidate clearly in her writing what terms like "given mode of life" mean. But we may nevertheless ask: What about modes of life makes them "given" and what determines their obdurate character if we remove the action-directive power of goals, purposes, values, ends, and norms? Similarly, how should we think about what "modes of thought and action" are in the absence of the analytical terms Swidler wishes to sideline? Are not values, goals, norms, and ends "modes of thought" relatable to action? Swidler's account also assumes a "problem of how to organize action over time." Left unexplained, however, is what creates this "problem." What motivates this need to organize action? Does that really have nothing to do with people pursuing culturally provided ends, values, and purposes? Swidler also describes people who are caught in conundrums in interviews while describing them as "undaunted"—an interesting observation (*Talk of Love*, 30, 107, 82, 40, respectively). Why should people be undaunted when a researcher reveals unsolved problems in their cultural frames of explanation? Why not instead just smile and ask for the next question? Might it be that Swidler's interviewees are in fact driven in their interviews to be people who give intelligible accounts of their lives, and for good reason? And, if so, then were not many instances of motivated, ends-driven actions perhaps staring Swidler in the face even as she conducted her interviews?

Sixth, Swidler's argument seems to presume, problematically, that people naturally choose the *easiest* thing in life to think or to do. For example, she suggests that "culture constrains action because people can most *easily* construct strategies of action for which they already have the cultural equipment" (*Talk of Love*, 86). The idea that people naturally flow with whatever is easiest fits Swidler's larger (pragmatist) argument—that is why she relies upon it. For example, since she thinks it is much easier to change one's goals, values, and norms (which, after all, seem to be "only" abstract cognitive ideas) than to change one's established strategies of action (which, by her account, are embodied, habitual, and profoundly relational), she concludes that strategies of action determine goals, values, and norms rather than the other way around. People allow it to happen that way because it is easier. But this "route of least resistance" assumption is just that: an assumption. Swidler has not argued for it, much less established its validity. I think it is more-than-infrequently empirically falsified. People often do what is easy. But people also often do what is more difficult and challenging. Why? Because that is more invigorating, rewarding, stimulating, fulfilling, or just morally right in their understanding. If we drop the assumption that people can be counted on to do what is easiest in life, then one of the tiny but important threads in Swidler's pattern of argument is pulled out and the fabric of her case begins to fray even more. Assume instead that people sometimes do hard things. Why would they? Because achieving the proper telos of human life is sometimes hard. And that brings us back to action motivated to achieve ends.

The seventh problem is that Swidler's theory seems oddly empty when it comes to explaining why people are ultimately doing anything at all. What is the ultimate purpose or drive of anyone's action? Swidler's account is full of statements reflecting the logic of simple sentences containing subjects, verbs, and objects, such as, "people use culture." Rarely in her account, however, are those sentences elaborated with the preposition "in order" followed by an infinitive ("to _____"). So we are often told that people do things. But we are not often told *why* they are doing them. That may be because providing such an explanation raises issues of motivations, purposes, goals, and the like, which Swidler's argument wants to discount. Of course, the very phrase "in order to" is inherently teleologically oriented, assuming that action is done for a purpose, to achieve a given end or ends. In fact, Swidler herself clearly states at one point that "we must ask what people use their culture *for*." But she is less than clear in answering that inquiry. We know that she says that people mobilize cultural capacities in order to organize lines or strategies of action. But that is not enough. *Why* do they do that? For what purpose, proximally or ultimately? And we know that she says that culture should be conceptualized like a tool kit of "implements" and "skills" (*Talk of Love*, 70, 24, 25, respectively). But, again, *why* should they be implemented and exercised? Swidler analogizes the skills of culture with those of actors, musicians, and dancers. But we know the "in order to" of *their* skills: to accomplish the *goal* of acting, performing music, and dancing well. So what then is the equivalent use of cultural tools, skills, and implements in her cultural tool kit? To simply take what Swidler says in various parts of her writing at face value, people are animated (I refrain from saying "motivated") to perform their actions, including using culture, for the following reasons, interests, or purposes: to find cultural items that "correspond to a situation or explanatory problem," to live a "life [that] seems to be working," to "move among situations," to "orient action within each situation," to "orient themselves," to "ground [their] sense of life meaning," to "make sense of many different scenes or situations of action," to "organize [their] worldview," to "respond to new situations," to "frame and reframe experience," to "rendering . . . situations," to "explain or justify one's life," to "understand [their] own life," to "grasp experience," to "structure . . . experience," to "solv[e] life's difficulties," to "solv[e] problems" (*Talk of Love*, 25, 28, 30, 31, 34, 39, 40, 53, 55, 59, 69, 83, 86, respectively). But what are we to make of this list of things-which-actions-address-if-not-accomplish? From what I can discern, what people are finally "up to" in life, according to this account, are two things. First, they are in the business of *making meaning* in order to orient, understand, and justify their lives and experiences. Second, people are in the business of *solving problems* that arise in life. And it could well be that solving problems is a subset of the first focus, of making meaning, insofar as lack of orientation, understanding, and justification are real problems for meaning-making animals. If Swidler's position is that people are driven by the need to make and maintain meanings, then that is a not-unreasonable view. But it is also at best partial—it fails to capture the fuller, richer range of interests, goods, and purposes that generate human action. If problem solving remains an independent, basic motivator in human life, then that simply returns us to a problem I identified above: in order to explain what counts as a problem and why people are moved to solve them, Swidler has to resort to concepts and arguments that are alien to her own account. We seem stuck here in either or both of an overly narrow view of human interests or a self-referential explanation that proves to be confusing.

The concern with problem solving reminds us of how closely philosophy always lurks in the background of sociology. Swidler is influenced by pragmatism. (She is also influenced by practice theory, which entails additional philosophical commitments.) Swidler never explicitly announces the influence of pragmatism in her thinking (for instance, it is not listed in the book's index), other than to twice (pp. 81, 240) reference the pragmatist social theorist Hans Joas (*The Creativity of Action*, trans. J. Gaines and P. Keast [Chicago: University of Chicago Press, 1996]). Still, pragmatism's influence is evident. Joas's intellectual presence in the book is located squarely at the pivot of her key theoretical chapter (chapter 4), at the turning point between her summary of Geertz, Weber, and Parsons and her richest exposition of her own alternative theory (*Talk of Love*, 81–82). Joas seems to be an important hinge in Swidler's theoretical case. (Swidler does takes Joas's argument one step further than his own, however; whereas she notes that he only claims that "goals and means are in fact chosen reciprocally" [81], she in the next two pages claims that means [available strategies of action] actually *determine* goals.) This illustrates again my contention that sociologists cannot escape philosophy, that some philosophical account or other operates in the background of all sociology.

Swidler's case suffers from other weaknesses worth noting but not elaborating. Her argument collapses certain important conceptual distinctions in confusing ways, such as people's *actions* and *experiences*—which are not the same things and cannot be treated interchangeably. She actually only provides a few concrete examples of "strategies of action," despite that being her central concept, and does not spell out in detail how strategies of action work as a *process*, over time. This is in part because an analysis of people's talk is a poor means of showing temporal processes at work. Swidler also tends simply to assume, rather than actually to argue, that the way culture shapes human action, how culture "makes a difference in human action," is most evident in how people "use" culture, when in fact culture might influence action in many ways other than people's using it (*Talk of Love*, 71).

Much of what Swidler argues in her book (that I have not focused on here) is insightful and valuable. But accepting what is good in her argument does not require also rejecting the fundamental notion that action is motivated, that people's activities are teleologically oriented to realize goods and interests. When it comes to her key theoretical criticism of motivated human action, her case is unconvincing. Her strong argument that culturally informed ends, values, and goals do not motivate action but rather are determined by the constraints of particular strategies of action fails to persuade. The evidence and argument are not there. And the validating phenomenological experience of human personal life is not there. Swidler herself seems to back off of the strong theoretical claims she maintains consistently through her book, conceding near the end that "sometimes culture may affect action, as Weber argued, because individuals hold systematic, unified, consistent worldviews and apply them directly to action" (*Talk of Love*, 179). That late admission, however, does little to soften the force of her central argument. In fact, while Swidler uses the way people talk about love and marriage as evidence for her theoretical case, it is very easy to read the same evidence as actually undercutting her case and instead validating a personalist account. In this view, we simply say that people in fact *do* act in ways motivated to realize determined ends, interests, and goods—in the case of Swidler's interviewees, that being the desire to have a successful marriage, despite the difficulties involved in working that out across the teleologically oriented journey of a lifetime. That is the most parsimonious and obvious interpretation of her data.

121. Aristotle: "The same degree of precision is not to be expected in all discussions" of different kinds of sciences, so "it is a mark of the trained mind *never to expect more precision in the treatment of any subject than the nature of the subject permits*" (*The Nicomachean Ethics*, trans. J. A. K. Thompson [New York: Penguin Books, 2004], 4, italics added).

122. See Herbert Gintis, Samuel Bowles, Robert Boyd, and Ernst Fehr, eds., *Moral Sentiments and Material Interests* (Cambridge, MA: MIT Press, 2005); Joseph Henrich, Robert Boyd, Samuel Bowles, Colin Camerer, Ernst Gehr, and Herbert Gintis, eds., *Foundations of Human Sociality: Economic Experiments and Ethnographic Evidence in Fifteen Small-Scale Societies* (New York: Oxford University Press, 2004); Detlef Fetchenhauer, Andreas Flache, Abraham Buunk, and Siegwart Lindenberg, eds., *Solidarity and Prosocial Behavior* (New York: Springer, 2006); Pierre Moessinger, *The Paradox of Social Order* (New York: Aldine de Gruyter, 2000). For an attempt to squeeze matters of identity into a *Homo economicus* model, see George Akerlof and Rachel Kranton, "Economics and Identity," *Quarterly Journal of Economics* 65 (2000): 715–53.

123. This is true even *to define an object of study*, as Alasdair MacIntyre observes: "An action is identifiable as the action that it is only in terms of the agent's intention. An intention can only be specified in terms of a first-person statement. The expression used in formulating such a statement (even if the agent does not himself formulate it explicitly) will presuppose certain beliefs on the agent's part. . . . So the notion of belief turns out to be ineliminable, and the contemporary project of a science of behavior is seen to invert the proper relationship between beliefs and action. Action must be understood in terms of their character as expressions of belief; beliefs are not simply patterns of behavior plus dispositions to produce such patterns" (MacIntyre, "Rationality and the Explanation of Action," chapter 21 in MacIntyre, *Against the Self-Images of the Age* (London: Duckworth, 1971), 253–55. Hilliard Aronovitch also shows the inescapable "connection between the 'why' and the 'what' of things"—that is, the need in explanation to first identify the nature of the object, event, or condition needing explaining, which

requires some knowledge of the beliefs of the agents involved: "Specific forms of behavior are only identifiable as what they are in light of the given beliefs on the part of those who engage in them. . . . In order to know what people are doing, in order to arrive at an appropriate description of their actions [and then to explain it], we must already know what beliefs they hold" (Aronovitch, "Social Explanation and Rational Motivation," *American Philosophical Quarterly* 15 [1978]: 197).

124. Markus Schlosser, "Agency, Ownership, and the Standard Theory," in Aguilar, Buckareff, and Frankish, *New Waves in Philosophy of Action*, 13–31.

125. See Claudia Strauss and Naomi Quinn, *A Cognitive Theory of Cultural Meaning* (Cambridge: Cambridge University Press, 1997).

126. For an analysis of motivation beliefs framed as "cultural models" that have "directive force," see Roy D'Andrade and Claudia Strauss, eds., *Human Motives and Cultural Models* (Cambridge: Cambridge University Press, 1992).

127. Also see Bertram Malle, "Intentional Action in Folk Psychology," in *A Companion to the Philosophy of Action*, ed. Timothy O'Connor and Constantine Sandis (Malden, MA: Wiley-Blackwell, 2010), 357–65.

128. Thomson, *The Springs of Human Action*, 3–8.

129. Wallis and Bruce, "Accounting for Action," 97–110.

130. See Vaisey, "Motivation and Justification."

131. I agree with Roy Wallis and Steve Bruce, who "do not dispute the value of multivariate analysis and other sophisticated statistical techniques, and accept that they can help to eliminate certain causal stories, and support others. Our view is that we have no way to understand what such correlations mean, or *how* they operate causally, *except* through an action story. When such an action story is secured, the *explanation* lies there, not in the structural correlation. . . . For explanation in sociology, movement to the action level remains an indispensable element" (Wallis and Bruce, "Accounting for Action," 106, 107).

Chapter 3: Against Social Situationism

1. I am indebted to Colin Campbell's critique of situationism, *The Myth of Social Action* (Cambridge: Cambridge University Press, 1996); and to Douglas Porpora, "On the Post-Wittgensteinian Critique of the Concept of Action in Sociology," *Journal for the Theory of Social Behavior* 13 (1983): 129–46; Steve Bruce and Roy Wallis, "Rescuing Motives," *British Journal of Sociology* 34 (1983): 61–71; and Wallis and Bruce, "Accounting for Action," 97–110.

2. Social psychologist Susan Fiske (*Social Beings: Core Motives Approach to Social Psychology* [Hoboken, NJ: Wiley, 2010], 7) calls situationism (the view that social contexts are more important than personality) "the major intellectual contribution of social psychology."

3. Lee Ross and Richard Nisbett's popular 2011 textbook, *The Person and the Situation: Perspectives of Social Psychology* (London: Pinter and Martin) provides a clear example of social situationism from the viewpoint of social psychology.

4. For example, John Doris, *Lack of Character: Personality and Moral Behavior* (Cambridge: Cambridge University Press, 2005).

5. Campbell, *The Myth of Social Action*, 23–37.

6. Gary Fine describes the expanded influences of some of the schools depicted in figure 4, observing that "by the early 1990s many mainstream sociologists were accepting meaning construction, negotiation, impression management, and labeling as components of their sociology. . . . The concepts of interactionism have become the concepts of much sociology" ("The

Sad Demise, Mysterious Disappearance, and Glorious Triumph of Symbolic Interactionism," *Annual Review of Sociology* 19 (1993): 61–87, quote on 67, 81).

7. I am not saying that every sociologist who identifies with the theoretical approaches named in figure 4 above is a social situationist. Some are and some are not. Others may fit the situationist description only somewhat but not entirely.

8. Sheldon Stryker, "Traditional Symbolic Interactionism, Role Theory, and Structural Symbolic Interactionism," in *Handbook of Sociological Theory*, ed. Jonathan Turner (New York: Kluwer, 2001), 213, italics added.

9. Collins, *Interaction Ritual Chains*, 372, 5, 335, italics added. Personal uniqueness thus derives from different social experiences, according to Collins, not the distinct personhood of persons: "[Individual uniqueness] is not the result of enduring individual essences. . . . Individuals are unique to just the extent that their pathways through interaction chains, their mix of situations across time, differ from other persons' pathways" (4).

10. Peter Berger and Thomas Luckmann, *The Social Construction of Reality* (New York: Anchor, 1967), 49, 51, italics added. I do not mean to imply here that Peter Berger was a full-blown supporter of situationism, as he in fact distanced himself from many of the movements inspired by his book.

11. Joel Charon, *Symbolic Interactionism* (Englewood Cliffs, NJ: Prentice Hall, 1989), 65, italics original and added.

12. Erving Goffman, *The Presentation of Self in Everyday Life* (New York: Doubleday, 1959), 252–53, italics in original and added.

13. Alan Blum and Peter McHugh, "The Social Ascription of Motives," *American Sociological Review* 36 (1971): 108, italics added.

14. Whether or not Mead was himself a full-blown situationist or merely a background influence who has been misused in contemporary situationism is debatable.

15. Charles Horton Cooley, *Human Nature and the Social Order* (1902; New Brunswick, NJ: Transaction, 1983), 126, italics in original.

16. George Herbert Mead, *George Herbert Mead on Social Psychology* (1934; Chicago: University of Chicago Press, 1977), 204, italics added. Such older theories have been echoed in new ways by numerous thinkers, as far afield as Michel Foucault, who has asserted, "Individuals are the vehicles of power, not its point of application. The individual is not to be conceived as a sort of elementary nucleus, a primitive atom, a multiple and inert material on which power comes to fasten. . . . The individual . . . is not the vis-à-vis of power; it is, I believe, one of its prime effects. The individual is the *effect* of power." Foucault, *Power/Knowledge* (New York: Pantheon, 1980), 98, italics added.

17. Collins, *Interaction Ritual Chains*, 4. Notice the emphasis on "the individual," not persons.

18. Barry Barnes, *Understanding Agency: Social Theory and Responsible Action* (London: Sage, 2000), 50, 31, 69.

19. Karin Knorr-Cetina, "The Micro-Social Order: Toward a Reconceptualization," in *Action and Structure*, ed. Nigel Fielding (London: Sage, 1988), 21–53, quote p. 25. The "methodological situationism" Knorr-Cetina champions is explicitly "reductionistic," she says (22).

20. Barnes, *Understanding Agency*, 74.

21. Sheldon Stryker, *Symbolic Interactionism: A Social Structural Version* (Menlo Park, CA: Benjamin/Cummings, 1980), 56.

22. Knorr-Cetina, "The Micro-Social Order," 24. Note the telling use of "it" rather than the personal "he or she" to describe "the sociologically relevant person."

23. Note the problematic ways that situationists interchangeably use the different concepts of persons, individuals, the self, people, and humans. These are not the same and their lack of precision contributes to their larger problems. Consider too the kind of personal and social ethics this view could possibly generate and sustain—not a promising possibility.

24. Mead actually argued this in at least one place ("After a self has arisen, it in a certain sense provides for itself its social experiences, and so we can conceive of an absolutely solitary self," Mead, *George Herbert Mead on Social Psychology*, 204), but that possibility has largely been lost in situationist theorizing.

25. For an attempt to transform the physical environment into a "symbolic other" to fit the broadly situationist framework, see Andrew Weigert, "Transverse Interaction: A Pragmatic Perspective on Environment as Other," *Symbolic Interactionism* 14 (1991): 353–63.

26. Stryker, *Symbolic Interactionism*, 59, italics in original. The roles that form people's identities are also entirely defined by "the expectations of others" (62).

27. Sheldon Stryker, "Symbolic Interaction as an Approach to Family Research," *Marriage and Family Living* 21 (1959): 116.

28. Peter Berger, *Invitation to Sociology* (Garden City, NJ: Doubleday, 1963), 106.

29. Mills, "Situated Actions and Vocabularies of Motives," 906.

30. William James, *Principles of Psychology* (New York: Holt, 1890), 291. The qualification of "social" selves softens the point, yet the relation between social and real selves remains unclear.

31. Mead, *George Herbert Mead on Social Psychology*, 218.

32. George Herbert Mead, *Mind, Self, and Society* (Chicago: University of Chicago Press, 1934), 233.

33. Mills, "Situated Actions and Vocabularies of Motives," 913, 910.

34. Alfred Schutz, *The Phenomenology of the Social World* (Evanston, IL: Northwestern University Press, 1967), 9, 32, italics added.

35. Alfred Schutz, *Collected Papers III: Studies in Phenomenological Philosophy* (The Hague: Martinus Nijhoff, 1966), 82.

36. Herbert Blumer, "Society as Symbolic Interaction," in *Symbolic Interaction*, ed. Jerome Manis and Bernard Meltze (Boston: Allyn and Bacon, 1972), 145–51, at 153. Blumer's conclusion does not follow the premises but makes an unwarranted leap. My argument does not depend on Blumer being a full-blown situationist himself, merely that he has been read in a way that has exerted an influence in the formation of situationism.

37. Collins, *Interaction Ritual Chains*, 3, 4.

38. Charon, *Symbolic Interactionism*, 66.

39. Knorr-Cetina, "The Micro-Social Order," 26.

40. Among the many important things missing from this cognitive "knowing-that" emphasis is the crucial importance of practical "knowing *how*" when it comes to the *material* and *bodily* worlds of action—see, for example, Jason Stanley, *Know How* (New York: Oxford University Press, 2011); John Bengson and Marc Moffett, *Knowing How: Essays on Knowledge, Mind, and Action* (New York: Oxford University Press, 2012).

41. Goffman, *The Presentation of Self in Everyday Life*, 239, italics added.

42. Charon, *Symbolic Interactionism*, 125. Also see Aaron Cicourel, *Cognitive Sociology: Language and Meaning in Social Interaction* (New York: Free Press, 1974), 125, italics added.

43. Peter Burke and Jan Stets, *Identity Theory* (New York: Oxford University Press, 2009), 9, italics added.

44. Mead, *Mind, Self, and Society*, 173, italics added.

45. Cooley, *Human Nature and the Social Order*, 81, italics added.

46. Ibid., 119, italics original and added. (Society really exists in the mind?)

47. Ibid., 124, 132–33, italics added.

48. "The imaginations which people have of one another are the *solid facts* of society, and . . . to observe and interpret these must be a chief aim of sociology. . . . The object of study is primarily an imaginative idea or group of ideas in the mind . . . we have to imagine imaginations. The intimate grasp of any social fact will be found to require that we divine what men think of one another" (ibid., 121–22); and "Persons and society must, then, be studied primarily in the imagination. . . . I do not see how anyone can hold that we know persons directly except as imaginative ideas in the mind" (120).

49. Herbert Blumer *Symbolic Interactionism: Perspective and Method* (Englewood Cliffs, NJ: Prentice Hall, 1969), 10, italics added.

50. Brissett and Edgley, *Life as Theater*, 22, italics added and original.

51. Ibid., 204.

52. Barnes, *Understanding Agency*, xi, 72, 98.

53. Mills, "Situated Actions and Vocabularies of Motives," 905, 909, italics and capitalizations in the original.

54. Ibid., 906.

55. Cooley, *Human Nature and the Social Order*, 33–34.

56. Charon, *Symbolic Interactionism*, 124–25, 83, italics in original.

57. Collins, *Interaction Ritual Chains*, 44.

58. C. Addison Hickman and Manford Kuhn, *Individuals, Groups, and Economic Behavior* (New York: Dryden, 1956), 45, quoted in Charon, *Symbolic Interactionism*, 102.

59. Knorr-Cetina, "The Micro-Social Order," 27.

60. Collins, *Interaction Ritual Chains*, 45. The link between particular situations and emotional energy are key for Collins, evident in his expressed wish to "provide . . . a theory of individual motivation from one situation to the next. Emotional energy is what individuals seek; situations are attractive or unattractive to them to the extent that the interaction ritual is successful in providing emotional energy" (44).

61. See John Hughes and Wesley Sharrock, *The Philosophy of Social Research* (Harlow, Essex: Pearson, 1997), 105–15.

62. Goffman, *The Presentation of Self in Everyday Life*, 253. In the midst of all of this, Goffman struggles to express how it is that people or selves can experience any of their own self-direction or agency against the imposing force of the social: "We always find the individual employing methods to keep some distance, some elbow room, between himself and [social expectations]." It is thus, he says, "against something that the self can emerge" (253). But, we might ask, what is the nature of such a self that can resist the social? Here Goffman founders on the rocks of the *Homo duplex* tradition. "Without something to belong to, we have no stable self, and yet total commitment and attachment to any social unit implies a kind of selflessness. Our sense of being a person can come from being drawn into a wider social unit; our sense of self-hood can [also] arise through the little ways in which we resist the pull. Our status is backed by the solid buildings of the world, while our sense of personal identity often resides in the cracks" (Goffman, *Asylums* [Garden City, NY: Anchor Books], 320).

63. Mills, "Situated Actions and Vocabularies of Motives,". 905.

64. Harold Garfinkel, "A Conception of and Experiments with 'Trust' as a Condition of Stable Concerted Action," in *Motivation and Social Interaction*, ed. O. J. Harvey (New York: Ronald Press, 1963), 160, italics added. The total discounting here of what human brains are and

do is astounding. More generally, see Jeff Coulter, *The Social Construction of Mind* (London: Macmillan, 1979).

65. Peter Burke, "The Self: Measurement Implications from a Symbolic Interactionist Perspective," *Social Psychological Quarterly* 43 (1980): 18–29; Peter Burke and Judy Tully, "The Measurement of Role Identity," *Social Forces* 55 (1977): 881–97; Peter Burke, "The Link between Identity and Role Performance," *Social Psychological Quarterly* 44 (1981): 83–92. Also see Nelson Foote, "Identification as a Basis for a Theory of Motivation," *American Sociological Review* 16 (1951): 14–21.

66. Barnes, *Understanding Agency*, 2, 12, 14, 15, 38, 41, 43. However, even if the Wittgensteinian observation is correct that there is no such thing as a private language, that does nothing to validate the idea that people do not enjoy personal lives entailing private dimensions of existence, since personal being and existence involves much more than language use.

67. Robert Wuthnow, *Meaning and Moral Order* (Berkeley: University of California Press, 1987), 334, 336, 340, 63, 338, 65.

68. Steve Derné, "Cultural Conceptions of Human Motivation and Their Significance for Culture Theory," in *The Sociology of Culture*, ed. Diana Crane (Cambridge: Blackwell, 1994), 268, 280.

69. This builds in part on John Dewey, who wrote, for example, that "it is false that a man requires a motive to make him do something." Dewey, "Nature of Motives," in *Human Nature and Conduct* (New York: Holt, 1922), 119.

70. Mills, "Situated Actions and Vocabularies of Motives," 909, 910, 908. How exactly he knows this about the true motives for war is unclear.

71. Collins, *Interaction Ritual Chains*, 6.

72. Blum and McHugh, "The Social Ascription of Motives," 88–89, 103.

73. Winch, *The Idea of a Social Science and Its Relation to Philosophy*, 69, 75–79.

74. Knorr-Cetina, "The Micro-Social Order," 25, 26.

75. Charon, *Symbolic Interactionism*, 132.

76. Cooley, *Human Nature and the Social Order*, 152.

77. Another early statement of this general approach—drawing on Mills, Cooley, Mead, Dewey, and Burke—is Foote, "Identification as the Basis for a Theory of Motivation," 14–21. Foote writes, "Establishment of one's own identity to oneself is as important as to establish it for the other [to define in the situation who others are]. One's own identity in a situation is not absolutely given but is more or less problematic. . . . Faith in one's own self is the key which unlocks the physiological resources of the human organism, releasing the energy (or capacity, as Dewey would say) to perform the indicated act. Doubt of identity, or confusion, where it does not cause complete disorientation, certainly drains action of its meaning, and thus limits mobilization of the organic correlates of emotion, drive and energy which constitute the introspectively sensed 'push' of motivated action" (18–19). Foote thus proposed "identification only as the basis for a situational theory of motivation" (21).

78. Goffman, *The Presentation of Self in Everyday Life*, 13, 242, 304

79. Goffman, *Asylums*, 21, 22, 23, 33, 43, 45, 48, 67, 72.

80. Ibid., 10. Achieving consensus is not conceived in highly mutual and cooperative ways, however, since Goffman views people's actions as oriented toward the self-interested *control* of others: "It will be in his interest to control the conduct of others, especially their responsive treatment of him"; "Informed in these ways, the others will know how to best act in order to call forth a desired response from him"; the person thus "will convey an impression to others which

it is in his interest to convey"; and others know that each person "presents himself in a light that is favorable to him." Ibid., 1, 3, 4, 7.

81. Goffman, *The Presentation of Self in Everyday Life*, 251. Goffman does not seem to realize that this judgment presupposes what he denies to be possible, that is, true knowledge about the subjective states of persons.

82. Goffman, *The Presentation of Self in Everyday Life*, 70.

83. Burke and Stets, *Identity Theory*, 210–18.

84. Ibid., 16, 111, 128, italics in original.

85. Ibid., 8.

86. Blum and McHugh, "The Social Ascription of Motives," 108.

87. Stryker, *Symbolic Interactionism*, 55, 64, 73–79.

88. Knorr-Cetina, "The Micro-Social Order," 25.

89. Terri Orbuch, "People's Accounts Count: The Sociology of Accounts," *Annual Review of Sociology* 23 (1997): 455–79; Colin Campbell, "Reexamining Mills on Motive: A Character Vocabulary Approach," *Sociological Analysis* 51 (1991): 89–97.

90. Mills, "Situated Actions and Vocabularies of Motives," 904, 907, italics in original. Other early statements of this position include Nelson Foote, "Identification as the Basis for a Theory of Motivation," 14–21; A. R. Lindesmith and A. Strauss, *Social Psychology* (New York: Dryden, 1956).

91. Harold Garfinkel, *Studies in Ethnomethodology* (Englewood Cliffs, NJ: Prentice Hall, 1967), 113–14, italics in original and added.

92. Barnes, *Understanding Agency*, 39, 70, italics added.

93. Brissett and Edgley, *Life as Theater*, 203, italics original.

94. Ibid.

95. Berger and Luckmann, *The Social Construction of Reality*, 92, 160, in the context of 156–63, italics in original.

96. Charon, *Symbolic Interactionism*, 130, 131, italics added.

97. Knorr-Cetina, "The Micro-Social Order," 27.

98. Hilliard Aronovitch rightly notes that "discounting the agents' way of describing what they are doing [when we have reason to believe the best explanation transcends their accounts] is not the same as disregarding it. . . . We must start with the agent's own account of their beliefs and behavior and move beyond it only if it does not hold up" ("Social Explanation and Rational Motivation," *American Philosophical Quarterly* 15 [1978]: 200, 204).

99. "The social psychological experiments on which . . . situationists rely looked at all the wrong kinds of situations to test behavioral manifestations of traits. Behavioral consistency across objectively different situation-types was found when situations were defined in terms of the meanings they had for subjects. . . . Empirical psychology does not threaten, but instead, sustains the conception of virtues as global traits. . . . There is good empirical reason to think that personality is coherent and enduring enough to support temporally virtues that are regularly manifested in behavior that occurs across objectively different situation types." Snow, *Virtue as Social Intelligence*, 118, 117, 2. For another balanced assessment of the evidence, see Christian Miller, "Situationism," in Miller, *Character and Moral Psychology* (New York: Oxford University Press, 2014), 85–106.

100. Alasdair MacIntyre rightly notes, "The notion that an agent's having a reason to do something may be the cause of his doing is necessary if we are to distinguish reasons which are genuinely effective from mere rationalizations which are not." MacIntyre, "Rationality and the

Explanation of Action," chapter 21 in MacIntyre, *Against the Self-Images of the Age* (London: Duckworth, 1971), 255.

101. Ignoring the fact, of course, that there are good models of purposive conduct, including that proposed in this book, that are teleological without being utilitarian.

102. Mills, "Situated Actions and Vocabularies of Motives," 905, 907, 908. In Mills's scheme, also working into at least somebody's motivations is the interest in the *social control* of others, as seen in his observation that humans are socially controlled by the limitations imposed on them by available vocabularies of motives, in a way that motives talk is "part of the process of social control" and "anticipations of acceptable justifications . . . control conduct" (906, 913, 907). Exactly who possesses this interest in social control is not stated.

103. Bruce and Wallis, "Rescuing Motives," 63. "This argument does little more than formulate in a more debunking manner the conventional understanding of motives" (64).

104. Barnes, *Understanding Agency*, 74–75.

105. Some psychologists are even conducting research on apes' and monkeys' capacity to infer subjectively significant meanings from events that inform teleological action. Marc Hauser and Justin Wood, "Evolving the Capacity to Understand Actions, Intentions, and Goals," *Annual Review of Psychology* 61 (2010): 303–24; also see Mark Bekoff and Jessica Pierce, *Wild Justice: The Moral Lives of Animals* (Chicago: University of Chicago Press, 2010).

106. Robert MacIver, "The Imputation of Motives," *American Journal of Sociology* 46, no. 1 (1940): 1–12. The quotes below are from pp. 1, 2, 3, 3–4, 6, 6–7, 8, 11, italics added.

107. Smith, *What Is A Person?*, 104–14.

108. Yet even here we are not totally dependent upon people's testimonies about their own subjective states, as Wallis and Bruce ("Accounting for Action," 97–110) point out: "Although the actor has privileged access to the meaning and motivations of his actions, he does not have sole access. The observer may have recourse to others sufficiently close to the actor to understand his behavior well. He may be able to compare the actor's account at one time with accounts offered by him at other times . . . in other forms, or to other audiences. He can often *observe* his behavior at other times to compare it with the actor's reports of his beliefs, actions, and normative motivations. He can even imaginatively locate himself in the same circumstances, to see whether similar responses arise from him. But such methods, while they may provide some grounds for accepting or rejecting actors' accounts, are fallible at best. The search for certainty in method is an enterprise permanently doomed to failure. . . . If lovers and spies can deceive us, and we can even deceive ourselves, what hope can the sociologist have of certainty?" But Wallis and Bruce do not despair: "The fact remains that lovers and spies are often discovered and we do at times even perceive in ourselves motives and beliefs we would rather forget. If the sociologist has no magical recipe for insight into human affairs, there is no reason to believe him condemned to do worse than most of us manage [in ordinary life] most of the time" (103). They rightly commend sociologists to neither dismiss nor readily accept people's accounts of their motivations, but to treat them as "hypotheses" to be tested against the best available evidence (103–7).

109. Guy Swanson, "Collective Purpose and Culture," in *Theory of Culture*, ed. Richard Munch and Neil Smelser (Berkeley: University of California Press, 1992), 207.

110. See Wallis and Bruce, "Accounting for Action." But some research programs—here I think of Daniel Batson's research on empathy—provide models for methods for accessing motivations.

111. Except when the parts of reality in question happen to be our mind-dependent thoughts, ideas, feelings, desires, and such, which are in fact both real and directly constituted by our subjective mental, emotional, and volitional capacities.

112. Blumer, *Symbolic Interactionism*, 5. The following block quote comes from p. 10.

113. The only objective difference in an environment viewed by two different people is the one-person difference in who the other people in the environment are, depending on the observer.

114. See Smith, *What Is a Person*, 119–206. Arguably Judith Butler's *Gender Trouble: Feminism and the Subversion of Identity* (New York: Routledge, 2006) reflects the kind of untenable deployment of radical constructivism.

115. Blumer, *Symbolic Interactionism*, 3–4.

116. Arguably, however, the material relations of objects to humans do in fact shape their meanings to people, as with cows as sources of milk and meat, for instance. To sort this matter out requires further differentiation between "meanings" and "definitions," which situationists sometimes confuse.

117. Blumer, *Symbolic Interactionism*, 10.

118. Mead actually called his approach "social behaviorism" (John Baldwin, "George Herbert Mead and Modern Behaviorism," *Pacific Sociological Review* 24 (1981): 411–40). Jonathan Turner notes, "This line of argument incorporated the driving motive force in utilitarianism and behaviorist theories . . . but made them explicitly sociological" (Turner, "Toward a Sociological Theory of Motivations," *American Sociological Review* 53 (1987):17).

Chapter 4: Human Nature and Motivation in Classical Theory

1. One recent example of the larger resistance to the idea of human nature is Jesse Prinz, *Beyond Human Nature* (New York: Penguin, 2012). Prinz's argument is right as far as it goes, especially in pushing back against illegitimately reductionistic claims, but the argument goes too far, in my view, in its minimizing the role of nature in human personhood, life, and action.

2. First published 1841, *Das Wesen des Christenthums* (Leipzig: Otto Wigand).

3. Émile Durkheim, "The Dualism of Human Nature and Its Social Conditions (1914)," in *Essays on Sociology and Philosophy*, ed. Kurt Wolff (New York: Harper and Row, 1960), 325. Durkheim actually states that sociology "draws on psychology and could not do without it" (325).

4. Harry Alpert, *Emile Durkheim and His Sociology* (New York: Russell and Russell, 1961), 137.

5. Durkheim, "The Dualism of Human Nature and Its Social Conditions," 326, 329, 337. "It is this division that distinguishes us from all other beings" (329).

6. Ibid., 328. Jones summarizes Durkheim's view of "the duality of human nature, [that] in each of us there are two *consciences*: one containing states personal to each of us, representing and constituting our individual personality; the other containing states common to all, representing society, and without which society would not exist. When our conduct is determined by the first, we act out of self-interest; but when it is determined by the second, we act morally, in the interest of society" (Robert Jones, *Emile Durkheim* [Beverly Hills, CA: Sage Publications, 1986], 33, italics in original).

7. Durkheim, "The Dualism of Human Nature and Its Social Conditions," 330.

8. Harry Alpert provides a helpful parsing of five different meanings of Durkheim's view of "the individual," noting that in most cases he was referring to the meaning of "the individual" that we are considering here: "the isolated, organico-psychical individual, the individual qua individual, but considered as he would be were he to live in complete isolation" (*Emile Durkheim and His Sociology*, 136, his full discussion pp. 135–46).

9. Steven Lukes, *Emile Durkheim: His Life and Work, a Historical and Critical Study* (Stanford, CA: Stanford University Press, 1985), 23.

10. Durkheim, "The Dualism of Human Nature and Its Social Conditions," 327, 328, 337, 338.

11. Ibid., 338.

12. That is only a self-perception, however, since Durkheim rejected anything like the metaphysical dualism of body/soul and did not entertain alternative options, such as nonreductionist physicalism.

13. Ann Warfield, *Epistemology and Practice: Durkheim's* The Elementary Forms of Religious Life (Cambridge: Cambridge University Press, 2009), 105.

14. Mark Cladis, "What Can We Hope For?: Rousseau and Durkheim on Human Nature," *Journal of the History of the Behavioral Sciences* 32, no. 4 (1996): 456–72.

15. Jerrold Seigel, "Objectivity and the Subject in Durkheim," unpublished paper, n.d., quoted in Cladis, "What Can We Hope For?," 470–71. Jennifer Lehmann writes: "The war between society and the individual is waged internally between the individual's totally individual body and the individual's totally social soul" (*Deconstructing Durkheim: A Post-Post-Structuralist Critique* [New York: Routledge, 1993], 74).

16. Durkheim, "The Dualism of Human Nature and Its Social Conditions," 338.

17. Émile Durkheim, *Montesquieu and Rousseau: Forerunners of Sociology* (1918, 1919; Ann Arbor: University of Michigan Press, 1960), 121.

18. Lukes, *Emile Durkheim: His Life and Work*, 433. Although he acknowledges that no evidence suggests that Durkheim actually knew of Freud's work, Lukes notes the parallels between the content and tone of Durkheim's last lectures and passages of Freud's *Civilization and Its Discontents*, such as: "Culture has to call up every possible reinforcement in order to erect barriers against the aggressive instincts of men and hold their manifestations in check by reaction formations in men's minds," and "The fateful question of the human species seems to me to be whether and to what extent the cultural process developed in it will succeed in mastering the derangements of communal life caused by the human instinct of aggression and self-destruction" (Sigmund Freud, *Civilization and Its Discontents* [New York: J. Cape and H. Smith, 1930], 86, 143–44). On Durkheim and Freud, see Jay Meddin, "Human Nature and the Dialectics of Immanent Sociocultural Change," *Social Forces* 55 (1976): 382–93.

19. Durkheim, "The Dualism of Human Nature and Its Social Conditions," 335.

20. Durkheim, *Suicide* (1897; New York: Free Press, 1997), 213, emphasis added.

21. Ibid., 318.

22. Ibid., 318–19, emphasis added.

23. Émile Durkheim, *The Elementary Forms of the Religious Life* (1912; New York: Oxford University Press, 2008), 18.

24. Émile Durkheim, *The Division of Labor in Society* (1893; New York: Free Press, 1997), xxx.

25. Ibid., 61.

26. Ibid., 172.

27. Lukes, *Emile Durkheim: His Life and Work*, 435–36.

28. Omar Lizardo, "Taking Cognitive Dualism Seriously: Revisiting the Durkheim-Spencer Debate on the Rise of Individualism," *Sociological Perspectives* 52, no. 4 (2009): 535.

29. Steven Lukes, introduction to *Durkheim: The Rules of Sociological Method and Selected Texts on Sociology and Its Method*, ed. Lukes (New York: Free Press, 1982), 21.

30. Émile Durkheim, *The Rules of Sociological Method* (1901; New York: Free Press, 1982), 131.

31. Durkheim, *The Rules of Sociological Method*, 132.

32. Émile Durkheim, *Essays on Morals and Education* (1904; New York: Routledge, 2005), 127.

33. Émile Durkheim, *Professional Ethics and Civic Morals* (1890–1912; New York: General Books, 2010), 60, also see 90, 116.

34. Émile Durkheim, *Sociology and Philosophy* (1906; New York: Routledge, 2010), 55.

35. Durkheim, "The Dualism of Human Nature and Its Social Conditions," 328.

36. Émile Durkheim, *Moral Education* (1897; New York: Dover Publications, 2002), 119.

37. Jones, *Emile Durkheim*, 50, 73.

38. Émile Durkheim, *Moral Education* (New York: Free Press, 1973), 689. Here, however, by "human nature," Durkheim means not the primordial, individual human nature we have been discussing, but rather the "human nature" that thinkers (who do not understand the importance of society) take for granted as part of an innate and fixed human inheritance—as Jones notes: "Opposing the Enlightenment notion that there is a single, constant 'human nature,' Durkheim began by insisting that a society's ideal conception of a person . . . is relative to each historical period" (*Emile Durkheim*, 194).

39. Durkheim, *Essays on Morals and Education*, 127.

40. Jones and Cladis agree: "The distinctive feature of Durkheim's argument . . . was that discipline was good *intrinsically*, that it was *natural* to human beings because the constraints *themselves* were part of nature" (Jones, *Emile Durkheim*, 195, italics in original); "For most of Durkheim's life, he put forth the view that human nature was radically indeterminate and was not dogged by anything like original sin or artificiality that necessarily impeded human happiness. In Durkheim's view . . . there is no natural antagonism between human nature and social life. His position is that 'the characteristic attributes of human nature come from society.' Human beings are naturally social; culture is a natural phenomenon." (Cladis, "What Can We Hope For?," 469).

41. Durkheim, *Essays on Morals and Education*, 127.

42. One of Durkheim's targets of criticism was the German psychologist and philosopher Wilhelm Wundt's universalist view of human nature, one element of which Durkheim characterized as follows: "Since moral ideas include elements that reappear in every period of history, these elements must consist of certain psychological facts that are derived from human nature in general, for human nature alone remains everywhere the same throughout the extreme instability of historical change." (Durkheim, *Ethics and the Sociology of Morals* [1887; Buffalo: Prometheus Books, 1993], 102). Durkheim's view clearly contradicted Wundt's outlook.

43. Durkheim, "The Dualism of Human Nature and Its Social Conditions," 325.

44. Cladis, "What Can We Hope For?," 464.

45. Lehmann, *Deconstructing Durkheim*, 78–116.

46. Durkheim, *The Division of Labor in Society*, 335.

47. Ibid., 335–36.

48. Durkheim, *The Elementary Forms of the Religious Life*, 320. Durkheim thus wrote consistently about individualistic religions: "The existence of individual cults suggests nothing . . . that contradicts or confounds a sociological explanation of religion. . . . While religion seems to dwell entirely in the innermost self of the individual, the living spirit that feeds it is still to be found in society. . . . Radical individualism that would make religion into something purely individual . . . is a misperception of the fundamental conditions of religious life" (320).

49. Durkheim, *The Division of Labor in Society*, 336.

50. Émile Durkheim, *Sociology and Philosophy* (1924, posthumously; New York: Routledge, 2010), 55.

51. Durkheim, *Moral Education*, 124.

52. Émile Durkheim, *Education and Sociology* (1858–1917; Glencoe, IL: Free Press, 1956), 89–90.

53. Other interpreters—including Talcott Parsons, Jeffrey Alexander, and Richard Münch—

have argued for a supposed shift in Durkheim's thinking over his life from a less to a more socially deterministic view of humanity and society, suggesting that the "early" Durkheim was (or wanted to be) a genuine voluntarist. I find those arguments unpersuasive, agreeing instead with those like Lehmann (*Deconstructing Durkheim*), Frank Pearce (*The Radical Durkheim* [Boston: Unwin Hyman, 1989]), Paul Hirst (*Durkheim, Bernard and Epistemology* [Boston: Routledge and Kegan Paul, 1975]), and Irving Zeitlin (*Ideology and the Development of Sociological Theory* [Englewood Cliffs, NJ: Prentice Hall, 1981]), who argue that "Durkheim is consistently and unambiguously scientific and deterministic in his thinking, which revolves around social realism and social determinism. He is not a voluntarist" (Lehmann, *Deconstructing Durkheim*, 234).

54. Durkheim, *Moral Education*, 319.

55. Durkheim, "The Dualism of Human Nature and Its Social Conditions," 338.

56. Durkheim, *Suicide*, 248.

57. Durkheim, *Moral Education*, 247–48.

58. Durkheim, *The Division of Labor in Society*, 209.

59. Durkheim, *Moral Education*, 248, 250.

60. Ibid., 356. Too much egoism can also lead to society disintegrating: when for an individual "his own goal" becomes "preponderant of those of the community" and "his personality tending to surmount the collective personality" and "recognizes no other rules of conduct than what are founded on his private interests," social disintegration is possible (209).

61. Ibid., 374.

62. Ibid., 213.

63. Steven Lukes, introduction to *The Division of Labor in Society*, by Durkheim, xv.

64. References in this paragraph and the next two are found in Durkheim, *Moral Education*, 43, 44–45, 64, 66, 148, 149, 151, 222, 323–24.

65. Durkheim, *The Division of Labor in Society*, 276, italics added for emphasis.

66. Ibid., 195–96.

67. Durkheim, *The Rules of Sociological Method*, 37.

68. Ibid., 133–34.

69. Durkheim, *The Elementary Forms of the Religious Life*, 2, italics added for emphasis.

70. Ibid., 18.

71. Émile Durkheim, "Marxism and Sociology: The Materialist Conception of History," in *The Rules of Sociological Method* (1897; New York: Free Press, 1982), 167–68; see Camic, "The Matter of Habit."

72. Durkheim, *Moral Education*, 374.

73. Ibid., 258.

74. See Lehmann, *Deconstructing Durkheim*, 86–97.

75. For somewhat alternative readings that tie Durkheim less closely to Kant and more to Aristotle, see Philip Gorski, "Recovered Goods: Durkheimian Sociology as Virtue Ethics," in *The Post-Secular in Question*, ed. Philip Gorski, David Kim, John Torpey, and Jonathan Van-Antwerpen (New York: New York University Press, 2012), 77–104; Douglas Challenger, *Durkheim through the Lens of Aristotle* (Lanham, MD: Rowman and Littlefield, 1995); and George McCarthy, *Classical Horizons* (Albany: State University of New York Press, 2002), 111–56.

76. Although I have not focused on it here, Durkheim well understood the dynamic of *emergence*, by which human actions give rise to irreducibly real social facts and structures, a key idea in critical realism, and he was correct to insist on the existence of fundamental, arational,

prestrategic social bonds of solidarity as the preconditions of any rational contracts, agreements, and exchanges made between individuals.

77. Archer, *Realist Social Theory*.

78. Steven Lukes, "Introduction (1982)," in Emile Durkheim, *The Rules of Sociological Method* (1897; New York: Free Press, 1982), 17. James Coleman offers a similar argument from a rational choice perspective (*Foundations of Social Theory* [Cambridge, MA: Harvard University Press, 1990], 1–23). Lukes repeats the point elsewhere: "It is incoherent to claim that particular circumstances and 'motives and ideas' are irrelevant to the explanation of suicide (or indeed any human action). For these cannot be simply abstracted from actions as though they were merely contingently related to them. Indeed, the actions cannot even be identified independently of them. In general, suicide precisely *is* a motivated act arising out of, and perhaps intended to affect, a particular situation. To put it baldly, explaining suicide . . . must involve explaining why people commit it. . . . Durkheim failed to see that both particular (objective) circumstances and men's subjective perceptions, beliefs, and attitudes and motives are all eminently amenable to sociological inquiry and explanation" (Lukes, *Emile Durkheim: His Life and Work*, 221–22). Lukes also points out that part of Durkheim's error stemmed from his confusion of "ends," "objectives," "objects," "interests," "motives," "ideals," "preconditions," and "causes" (p. 416). Zeitlin points out that "the inevitable result of Durkheim's approach is that it entirely ignores the subjective meaning which . . . beliefs and actions have for the actors concerned. . . . Durkheim's sociology . . . is therefore defective in that it effectively ignores the role of the individual" (Zeitlin, *Ideology and the Development of Sociological Theory*, 279).

79. See Smith, *What Is a Person?*

80. But, based on a slightly different view of what "relativism" means, see Gabriel Abend, "Two Main Problems in the Sociology of Morality," *Theory and Society* 37, no. 2 (2008): 87–125.

81. The term, originally borrowed from Hegel, was used both by Feuerbach and Marx.

82. Karl Marx and Friedrich Engels, *Collected Works*, vols. 3, 4, and 5 (1835–43; London: Lawrence and Wishart, 1975), 4: 141; 5: 55.

83. Marx and Engels, *Collected Works*, 5: 31.

84. Karl Marx, *Capital*, vol. 1 (1867; London: Harmondsworth, 1976), 758–59.

85. Norman Geras, *Marx and Human Nature: Refutation of a Legend* (London: Verso, 1983), 72, 83.

86. Marx and Engels, *Collected Works*, 5: 41–42.

87. Marx and Engels, *Collected Works*, 5: 78, 255, 439.

88. Marx and Engels, *Collected Works*, 5: 437, the italicizing of "needs" is in the original and of "consequently their nature" is added here for emphasis.

89. Marx and Engels, *Collected Works*, 3: 336.

90. Marx and Engels, *Collected Works*, 5: 256, italics added.

91. Marx, *Capital*, vol. 3 (1894, published posthumously; Moscow: International Publishers, 1962), 800.

92. Karl Marx and Friedrich Engels, *Economic and Philosophical Manuscripts of 1844* (1844; Buffalo: Prometheus Books, 1988), 75.

93. Ibid., 76.

94. Marx and Engels, *Collected Works*, 5: 275, 36.

95. Karl Marx and Friedrich Engels, *German Ideology* (1845; Moscow: International Publishers, 1964), 31.

96. Marx, *Capital*, vol. 1, 447.

97. Marx, *Capital*, vol. 1, 283.

98. Marx and Engels, *Economic and Philosophical Manuscripts of 1844*, 154.

99. G. A. Cohen, *Karl Marx's Theory of History* (Princeton, NJ: Princeton University Press, 2000), 345.

100. Jon Elster, *Making Sense of Marx* (Cambridge: Cambridge University Press, 1985), 261.

101. Marx, *Capital*, vol. 1, 20.

102. Cohen, *Karl Marx's Theory of History*, 152.

103. Karl Marx, *Grundrisse: Foundations of the Critique of Political Economy* (1857–58; New York: Penguin, 1993), 494.

104. Marx, *Capital*, vol. 1, 177.

105. Marx and Engels, *Collected Works*, 3: 228.

106. Marx and Engels, *Collected Works*, 3: 229, 315; 5: 58, 295–96.

107. Marx and Engels, *Collected Works*, 5: 292.

108. Allen W. Wood correctly notes: "Marx's language at this point is the Aristotelian language of potency and act. A 'human' mode of life is one which involves the 'development,' the 'exercise,' and thereby the 'actualization' of all the 'human essential powers.'" (Wood, *Karl Marx* [New York: Routledge, 2004], 23).

109. Karl Marx and Friedrich Engels, *The Holy Family* (1845; Moscow: International Publishing, 1956), 31.

110. These include Louis Althusser, Tom Bottomore, Robert Tucker, Robert Cumming, Eugene Kamenka, Wal Suchting, Sidney Hook, Vernon Venable, Colin Sumner, Kate Soper, and István Mézsáros. See Geras, *Marx and Human Nature*, 50–54.

111. Geras notes that many leftists and progressives reject the very idea and existence of any human nature, because political and economic conservatives so often appeal to the limits of human nature (sin, selfishness, and such) in their repudiation of socialism. Yet as Geras rightly points out, "to attempt to respond to that kind of argument . . . by denying that there is a human nature is to meet a powerful ideological opponent with a weapon that is useless" (16). The other source of the error is the failure to distinguish Marx's idea of a fixed human nature from the developmental aspects of human nature.

112. Primarily G. A. Cohen, Norman Geras, and Allen Wood. Cohen, for instance, argues: "Many Marxists will be surprised by our reference to human nature. . . . It is a Marxist tradition to deny that there exists an historically invariant human nature. The point is made against conservatives. . . . But it is not necessary to claim, in response, that there are no quite permanent facts of human nature. All that need be denied is that the particular feature the conservative [critique] emphasizes is one of them. It must be agreed that there are enduring facts of human nature. For man is a mammal, with a definite biological constitution, which evolves hardly at all in some central respects throughout millennia of history. . . . There are permanent attributes of human nature" (Cohen, *Karl Marx's Theory of History*, 155).

113. Marx and Engels, *Collected Works*, 5: 58.

114. Marx and Engels, *Collected Works*, 4: 36, italics added for emphasis.

115. Geras, *Marx and Human Nature*, 73.

116. Marx, *Capital*, vol. 3, 800.

117. Marx, *Capital*, vol. 1, 28.

118. Wood, *Karl Marx*, 29.

119. Geras, *Marx and Human Nature*, 107–8, italics in the original.

120. Cohen, *Karl Marx's Theory of History*, 346–47.

121. Ibid., 347.

122. Ibid., 348, italics in original.

123. Ibid., 348–49.

124. Wood, *Karl Marx*, 29.

125. Weber was the least Aristotelian of the three theorists examined here, the most Kantian.

126. Max Weber, *Economy and Society* (1922; Berkeley: University of California Press, 1978), 13.

127. Quoted in H. H. Gerth and C. Wright Mills, *From Max Weber: Essays in Sociology* (New York: Oxford University Press, 1958), 55.

128. Stephen Kalberg, "Max Weber," in *The Blackwell Companion to Major Classical Social Theorists*, ed. George Ritzer (Malden, MA: Blackwell, 2003), 135, italics in original. How actually new this position is, however, is debatable.

129. Max Weber, "Objectivity in Social Science," in *The Methodology of the Social Sciences*, ed. Edward Shils and Henry Finch (1904; New York: Free Press, 1949), 83, italics in original. Kalberg writes that Weber's interpretive sociology seeks "to comprehend social action in terms of the actor's own intentions" (Kalberg, "Max Weber," 144).

130. Weber, "Objectivity in Social Science," 83.

131. Gerth and Mills, *From Max Weber*, 56.

132. Weber, *Economy and Society*, 11.

133. Ibid., 8.

134. Max Weber, "The Logic of the Cultural Sciences," in *The Methodology of the Social Sciences*, ed. Edward Shils and Henry Finch (1905; New York: Free Press, 1949), 165, italics in original. "For Weber, an agent's 'motive' might be any meaningful 'reason' for behaving in a certain way. Of course some actions are the expressions of a normative standpoint or of an emotion. [But] Weber argued interpreters are well advised to begin by supposing that the actions they observe are rationally selected to *achieve specific ends* . . . [thus advocating] a model of purposively rational action as a useful *starting point*" (Fritz Ringer, *Max Weber: An Intellectual Biography* [Chicago: University of Chicago Press, 2004], 94, italics in original).

135. Max Weber, "The Meaning of 'Ethical Neutrality,'" in *The Methodology of the Social Sciences*, ed. Edward Shils and Henry Finch (1917; New York: Free Press, 1949), 42, italics in original. Mental states can therefore shape the material world: Walter Wallace suggests a number of "broad categories of physical behavior" that he thinks are crucial to Weber's notion of human nature: the constructive acts of labor, work, production, function, performance; the destructive acts of violence and force; and the "transportative" acts of motility [the ability to move spontaneously and actively], transportation, and gestures. These physical behaviors he thinks are "indispensible to Weber's image of human nature, because they represent the elements that . . . are subject to direction by . . . psychical behavior. . . . They are, in short, what the individual's motivation motivates" (Wallace, "Rationality, Human Nature, and Society in Weber's Theory," *Theory and Society* 19 [1990]: 219–20).

136. Weber, "The Logic of the Cultural Sciences," 165.

137. Weber, "The Meaning of 'Ethical Neutrality,'" 18.

138. Gerth and Mills, *From Max Weber*, 70. Weber viewed "charisma" as "a metaphysical vehicle of man's freedom in history. . . . He conceived of individual man as a composite or general characteristics derived from social institutions; the individual as an actor of social roles. However, this holds only for men in so far as they do not transcend the routines of everyday institutions. The concept of charisma serves to underline Weber's view that all men everywhere are *not to be comprehended merely as social products.* . . . Weber's conception of human freedom thus partakes of the humanist tradition of liberalism which is concerned with the freedom of the

individual to create free institutions" (Gerth and Mills, *From Max Weber*, 72–73, italics added). However, Gerth and Mills also rightly note, "Weber represents humanist and cultural liberalism rather than economic liberalism," which he tended to view in the form of capitalism as dehumanizing (73).

139. Weber's approach emphasized "the rational relations of ends and means as the most 'understandable' type of conduct." This "distinguishes Weber's work from conservative thought and its documentary 'understanding' by assimilating the singularity of an object into its [Hegelian] spiritualized whole. Yet by emphasizing the understandability of human conduct, as opposed to the mere causal explanation of 'social facts,' as in natural science," Weber opposed positivistic social science (Gerth and Mills, *From Max Weber*, 57).

140. Weber, "Objectivity in Social Science," 72–73, italics in original. Humans do have a tendency, Weber observed, to engage in "courses of action that are repeated by the actor or (simultaneously) occur among numerous actors since the subjective meaning is meant to be the same" (Weber, *Economy and Society*, 29). Even so, it is only possible to identify certain *tendencies* in actions, which Weber calls "rules," but not positivist laws. Sociologists can identify "certain known empirical rules, particularly those related to the ways in which human beings are prone to react under given situations . . . which has been derived from our own experience and our knowledge of the conduct of others" (Weber, "The Logic of the Cultural Sciences," 74). Thus "statistical uniformities," Weber wrote, are sociologically significant "only when they can be regarded as manifestations of the understandable subjective meaning of a course of social action" (Weber, *Economy and Society*, 12).

141. Weber, "Objectivity in Social Science," 82, italics original. See Philip Woods, "Values-Intuitive Rational Action," *British Journal of Sociology* 52 (2001): 687–706.

142. Weber, *Economy and Society*, 9, 4.

143. Max Weber, "The Social Psychology of World Religions," in Gerth and Mills, *From Max Weber*, 281.

144. Weber, "Objectivity in Social Science," 74, italics original.

145. Weber, *Economy and Society*, 15.

146. Weber, "Objectivity in Social Science," 76, italics original.

147. Weber, *Economy and Society*, 4, italics added. "The historical fact that [the cultural significance of any social phenomenon] plays . . . must be causally explained in order to render its cultural significance understandable" (Weber, "Objectivity in Social Science," 77).

148. Weber, "Objectivity in Social Science," 72, italics original and added. "Persons are capable of *interpreting* their social realities, bestowing 'subjective meaning' upon certain aspects of it, and initiating independent action. . . . There *is*, to Weber, a realm of freedom and choice" (Kalberg, "Max Weber," 142). In his mind, sociology is a thoroughly human practice, and this means recognizing the important ways in which values and interests impinge upon even sociological work. In Weber's view, "we are all 'cultural beings,' and hence values remain inextricably intertwined with our thinking and action; a thin line separates 'facts' from 'values,'" both for ordinary people and social scientists (Kalberg, "Max Weber," 145). This affects, Weber said, what sociologists even define to be worth studying: "The quality of an event as a 'social-economic' event is not something which it possesses 'objectively.' It is rather conditioned by the orientation of our cognitive interests, as it arises from the specific cultural significance which we attribute to the particular event in a given case" (Weber, "Objectivity in Social Science," 64).

149. "It is . . . psychical, rather than physical, behavior that is causally dominant in Weber's image of human nature, a dominance, he says, based on the fact that only the former can confer

'meaning" on the world, and 'Without reference to . . . meaning [the world] remains wholly unintelligible'" (Wallace, "Rationality, Human Nature, and Society in Weber's Theory," 204).

150. Weber, *Economy and Society*, 39, 325, 619.

151. Max Weber, *The Protestant Ethic and the Spirit of Capitalism*, ed. Peter Baehr (1920; New York: Penguin, 2002), 81, 113, 261.

152. Weber, *Economy and Society*, 603, 606.

153. Ibid., 601.

154. Wallace, "Rationality, Human Nature, and Society in Weber's Theory," 209.

155. Max Weber, "The Meaning of Discipline," in Gerth and Mills, *From Max Weber*, 254.

156. Weber, *Economy and Society*, 540.

157. Ibid., 491.

158. Max Weber, "Politics as a Vocation," in Gerth and Mills, *From Max Weber*, 117.

159. Weber, *Economy and Society*, 31, 33–34.

160. Peter Baehr, introduction to *The Protestant Ethic and the Spirit of Capitalism*, by Max Weber (1920; New York: Penguin, 2002), xxxviii.

161. Weber, *Economy and Society*, 21–22; see Camic, "The Matter of Habit."

162. Weber, *Economy and Society*, 24, 494, 602.

163. Ibid., 9.

164. Weber, "Objectivity in Social Science," 96–97.

165. Ringer, *Max Weber: An Intellectual Biography*, 178. Weber "was extremely cautious about" the interpreter's ability to know the causal force of motives, since "motives may be feigned, mixed, or unconscious" (100).

166. "It would be very unusual to find concrete cases of action, especially of social action, which were oriented *only* in one or another of these [four] ways. Furthermore, this classification of the modes of orientation of action is in no sense meant to exhaust the possibilities of the field" (Weber, *Economy and Society*, 24–25, 26, italics original). Even "interests," Weber wrote, can be either "spiritual or material" (ibid., 43). Weber clearly rejected a narrowly utilitarian, instrumentalist, strictly rational-choice view of human action—commonly associated with neoclassical economics—in which individuals always calculate and choose means among options that will increase their utility by increasing rewards and decreasing costs. Human motivations and social life are far too varied in Weber's view to be able to be captured by a simple, utilitarian, instrumentalist analysis. Complexity and multidimensionality, not simplicity, are Weber's watchwords.

167. Weber, *Economy and Society*, 6.

168. Ibid., 85–86.

169. "Weber refused to conceive of ideas as being 'mere' reflections or psychic or social interests. All spheres—intellectual, psychic, political, economic, religious—to some extent follow developments of their own. . . . Weber is . . . eager to state possible tensions between ideas and interests, between one sphere and another, or between internal states and external demands. . . . Weber saw social life as a polytheism of values in combat with one another, and choices were possible among these values," even as he understood that "the decision-making, morally responsible individual is, of course, a specifically modern and Occidental type of personality" (Gerth and Mills, *From Max Weber*, 62, 70). "Even when social action seems tightly bonded to a social structure, a heterogeneity of motives must be recognized" (Kalberg, "Max Weber," 144). "There is nothing in human nature that elevates any one ultimate end above the others: 'the various value spheres of the world stand in *irreconcilable* conflict'" (Wallace, "Rationality, Human Nature, and Society in Weber's Theory," 215, quoting Weber's essay, "Science as a Voca-

tion"). "The search for a single 'guiding hand' . . . remained anathema to Weber. . . . Rather than a causal 'resting point,' he found only continuous movement across . . . political, economic, religious, legal, social strata, and familiar groupings" (Kalberg, "Max Weber," 138).

170. Weber, *Economy and Society*, 36–53.

171. Ibid., 10.

172. Max Weber, "Rebuttal of the Critique of the 'Spirit' of Capitalism," in *The Protestant Ethic and the Spirit of Capitalism*, ed. Peter Baehr (1920; New York: Penguin, 2002), 260.

173. Weber, "The Social Psychology of World Religions," in Gerth and Mills, *From Max Weber*, 291.

174. Weber, "Objectivity in Social Science," 96, italics original.

175. Gerth and Mills, *From Max Weber*, 63.

176. Max Weber, *Roscher and Knies* (1903–06; New York: Free Press, 1949), 193.

177. Ibid., 202.

178. Weber, *Economy and Society*, 1186–87, italics original.

179. More generally, with regard to the doctrine of historical materialism, Weber wrote: "The so-called 'materialist conception of history' as a *Weltanschauung* or as a formula for causal explanation of historical reality is to be rejected most emphatically." However, he conceded, "liberated as we are from the antiquated notion that all cultural phenomena can be *deduced* as a product or function of the constellation of 'material' interests," we can still accept that attention to material factors in social life is a principle of "creative fruitfulness," as long as used "with careful application and freedom from dogmatic restrictions" (Weber, "Objectivity in Social Science," 68).

180. Ibid., 64.

181. Wallace, "Rationality, Human Nature, and Society in Weber's Theory," 220, 216.

Chapter 5: On Basic Human Goods, Interests, and Motivations

1. This is something like what Max Weber called ultimate goals (as opposed to instrumental goals) that informed substantive rationality (as opposed to formal rationality).

2. In addition to the works referenced below, see Maury Silver, "'Purposive Behavior' in Psychology and Philosophy: A History," in *Goal Directed Behavior: The Concept of Action in Psychology*, ed. Michael Frese and John Sabini (Hillsdale, NJ: Lawrence Erlbaum, 1985), 3–17; Kennon Sheldon and Alexander Gunz, "Psychological Needs as Basic Motives, Not Just Experiential Requirements," *Journal of Personality* 77, no. 5 (2009): 1467–92; J. S. Brown, *The Motivation of Behavior* (New York: McGraw-Hill, 1961); W. McDougall, *An Introduction to Social Psychology* (Boston: Luce, 1926); E. Thorndike, *Animal Intelligence, Experimental Studies* (New York: Macmillan, 1911); C. Hull, *Principles of Behavior* (New York: Appleton, 1943); D. G. Winter, *Personality* (New York: McGraw-Hill, 1996).

3. W. McDougall, *Outline of Psychology* (New York: Scribner's, 1923).

4. R. S. Woodworth, *Dynamic Psychology* (New York: Columbia University Press, 1918).

5. Woodworth, *Dynamic Psychology*; Kurt Lewin, *A Dynamic Theory of Personality* (New York: McGraw-Hill, 1935); Hull, *Principles of Behavior*.

6. For example, L. Stevens and S. Fiske, "Motivation and Cognition in Social Life: A Social Survival Perspective," *Social Cognition* 13 (1995): 189–214; Roy Baumeister and Mark Leary, "The Need to Belong: Desire for Interpersonal Attachments as a Fundamental Human Motivation," *Psychological Bulletin* 117 (1995): 497–529; Steven Heine, Travis Proulx, and Kathleen Vohs, "The Meaning Maintenance Model: On the Coherence of Social Motivation," *Personality and Social*

Psychology Review 10, no. 2 (2006): 88–110; H. Tajfel, C. Dlament, M. Billig, and R. Bundy, "Social Categorization and Intergroup Behavior," *European Journal of Social Psychology* 1 (1971): 149–78; L. Festinger, *A Theory of Cognitive Dissonance* (Evanston, IL: Row, Peterson, 1957); A. Tessar, M. Millar, and J. Moore, "Some Affective Consequences of Social Comparison and Reflection Processes: The Pain and Pleasure of Being Close," *Journal of Personality and Social Psychology* 54 (1988): 49–61; C. Osgood and R. Tannenbaum, "The Principle of Congruity in the Prediction of Attitude Change," *Psychological Review* 62 (1955): 42–55; T. Pyszczynski, J. Greenberg, and S. Solomon, "Why Do We Need What We Need?: A Terror Management Perspective on the Root of Human Social Motivation," *Psychological Inquiry* 8 (1997): 1–20; A. Kruglanski, *Lay Epistemics and Human Knowledge: Cognitive and Motivational Bases* (New York: Plenum, 1989); Arnold Gehlen, *Man: His Nature and Place in the World* (1950; New York: Columbia University Press, 1988); Anthony Giddens, *The Constitution of Society* (Berkeley: University of California Press, 1984), 23, 50, 75. Also see E. Tory Higgins and Arie Kruglanski, "Motivational Science: The Nature and Function of Wanting," in *Motivational Science: Social and Personality Perspectives*, ed. Higgins and Kruglanski (Philadelphia: Psychology Press, 2000), 3–4.

7. For an excellent, similar work focused on basic values and goods pertaining to global socioeconomic development, which includes some of the theorists noted below but describes others not examined here, see Sabina Alkire, *Valuing Freedoms: Sen's Capability Approach and Poverty Reduction* (Oxford: Oxford University Press, 2002).

8. H. A. Murray, *Explorations in Personality* (New York: Oxford University Press).

9. Also described in M. D. Vernon, *Human Motivation* (Cambridge: Cambridge University Press, 1969), 99–101.

10. Jacob Alsted, *A Model of Human Motivation for Sociology* (New York: Peter Lang, 2005).

11. Ibid., 87.

12. Ibid., 18.

13. Sometimes Fromm is said, based on his earlier work, to have posited only five basic human needs, though his later work seems to add three more for a total of eight. See Erich Fromm, *Man for Himself* (London: Routledge and Kegan Paul, 1949); Fromm, *The Sane Society* (London: Routledge and Kegan Paul, 1955); Fromm, *The Anatomy of Human Destructiveness* (New York: Holt, Rinehart, and Winston, 1973).

14. Jonathan Turner, "Toward a Sociological Theory of Motivations," *American Sociological Review* 53 (1987): 15–27. Turner's method is eclectic, comparative, and synthetic, like my method in this part of this chapter.

15. Ibid., 15–27.

16. Fiske, *Social Beings*, 14–25.

17. Abraham Maslow, *Motivation and Personality* (New York: Harper and Row, 1954); Maslow, "Some Basic Propositions of a Growth and Self-Actualization Psychology," in *Theories of Personality*, ed. G. Lindzey and C. Hall (New York: Wiley, 1965), 189–202.

18. Clayton Alderfer, "An Empirical Test of a New Theory of Human Needs," *Organizational Behavior and Human Performance* 4, no. 2 (1969): 142–75; Alderfer, *Existence, Relatedness, and Growth: Human Needs in Organizational Settings* (New York: Free Press, 1972).

19. The theoretical and empirical literature on self-development theory is immense, but see Edward Deci and Richard Ryan, "The 'What' and 'Why' of Goal Pursuits: Human Needs and Self-Determination of Behavior," *Psychological Inquiry* 11, no. 4 (2000): 227–68.

20. Richard Ryan and Edward Deci, "Overview of Self-Determination Theory: An Organismic Dialectical Perspective," in *Handbook of Self-Determination Theory*, ed. Deci and Ryan (Rochester, NY: University of Rochester Press, 2002), 3–33, quote on 5.

21. Maureen Ramsay, *Human Needs and the Market* (Aldershot: Avebury, 1992). David Mc-Clelland somewhat similarly argues for the existence of four basic motive systems—namely, the motivation for achievement, power, affiliation, and avoidance (of, for example, anxiety, failure, and such); McClelland, *Human Motivation* (Cambridge: Cambridge University Press, 1987).

22. Manfred Max-Neef, *Human Scale Development: Conceptions, Application, and Further Reflections* (London: Apex Press, 1993).

23. Kai Nielsen, "True Needs, Rationality, and Emancipation," In *Human Needs and Politics*, ed. Ross Fitzgerald (Oxford: Pergamon Press, 1977), 142–56.

24. Ervin Staub, "Basic Human Needs, Altruism, and Aggression," in *The Social Psychology of Good and Evil*, ed. Arthur G. Miller (New York: Guilford, 2004), 51–84.

25. J. B. Watson, *Behavior: An Introduction to Comparative Psychology* (New York: Holt, 1914).

26. E. L. Thorndike, *The Psychology of Learning* (New York: Teachers' College Press, 1913). Also see C. L. Hull, *Principles of Behavior* (New York: Appleton-Century, 1943).

27. W. H. Thorpe, *Learning and Instinct in Animals* (London: Methuen, 1956).

28. Paul Lawrence and Nitin Nohria, *Driven: How Human Nature Shapes our Choices* (Hoboken, NJ: Jossey-Bass, 2002).

29. Michael Argyle, *Psychology of Interpersonal Behavior* (New York: Penguin, 1967).

30. Steven Reiss, *Who Am I?: The 16 Basic Desires That Motivate Our Behavior and Define our Personality* (New York: Tarcher/Putnam, 2000), quote on 10.

31. Ibid., 25.

32. Roy Baumeister, *The Cultural Animal: Human Nature, Meaning, and Social Life* (New York: Oxford University Press, 2005).

33. Ibid., 83–84.

34. Martin Ford, *Motivating Humans: Goals, Emotions, and Personal Agency Beliefs* (Newbury Park, CA: Sage, 1992).

35. Ibid., 22, 43.

36. Ibid., 66–72.

37. Martha Nussbaum, *Creating Capabilities: The Human Development Approach* (Cambridge, MA: Belknap Press of Harvard University Press, 2011).

38. Carol Ryff, "Happiness Is Everything or Is It? Explorations on the Meaning of Psychological Well-Being," *Journal of Personality and Social Psychology* 57 (1989): 1069–81; Carole Ryff and Corey Keyes, "The Structure of Psychological Well-Being Revisited," *Journal of Personality and Social Psychology* 69 (1995): 719–27.

39. Mozaffar Qizilbash, "Capabilities, Well-Being, and Human Development: A Survey," *Journal of Development Studies* 33 (1996): 143–62; Qizilbash, "Needs, Incommensurability, and Well-Being," *Review of Political Economy* 25 (1997): 261–76.

40. James Griffin, *Value Judgment* (Oxford: Clarendon Press, 1996).

41. John Finnis, *Natural Law and Natural Rights* (Oxford: Oxford University Press, 1980).

42. Valued, he says, as a matter of "natural law," by which he means "the set of principles of practical reasonableness in ordering human life and human community," which Finnis believes "can be adequately grasped by anyone of the age of reason," although it is empirically indemonstrable. Natural law, in Finnis's account, is not inferred from speculative principles, from facts, from metaphysical propositions, from a teleological concept of nature, or anything. It is not inferred or proven. Natural law is simply un-derived, self-evident, premoral principles of practical reasonableness, by his account (Finnis, *Natural Law and Natural Rights*, 33–34).

43. Finnis, *Natural Law and Natural Rights*, 92. Very similar to Finnis's 1980 list is that of Germain Grisez and John Finnis, "Practical Principles, Moral Truth, and Ultimate Ends," *American Journal of Jurisprudence* 32 (1987): 99–151.

44. The term "religion," which Finnis puts in quotation marks, he says he proposes "summarily and lamely." By "religion," Finnis does *not* mean specific faith traditions based on belief in divinity or afterlife or nirvana, such as Islam, Christianity, or Hinduism. Instead, he means understandings about more general existential questions about the origins of the cosmic order, human freedom, reason, responsibility, and so on, whether or not their answers involve God or some other religious element (Finnis, *Natural Law and Natural Rights*, 89–90, 403–10).

45. Finnis, *Natural Law and Natural Rights*, 65, 69, italics added. He further argues, "They are objective; their validity is not a matter of convention, nor is it relative to anybody's individual purposes" (69).

46. Ibid., 104, italics in original.

47. Ibid., 111–18. "No element of a good life should be maximized. What is good for someone should take its proper place in his life, falling somewhere in the range of neither too much nor too little. It should not displace all else." Richard Kraut, *What Is Good and Why: The Ethics of Well-Being* (Cambridge, MA: Harvard University Press, 2007), 170.

48. Finnis, *Natural Law and Natural Rights*, 118, italics in original.

49. Readers may question whether the basic human interests and motivations are truly six in number. I am less interested in the precise number and more interested in there being a number that enumerates something real and consequential.

50. I mean here only a starting point, as I do not intend to derive real ontology from the empirical, or to fall into a coherence theory of truth, even if the exercise above does support what follows. I encourage readers to also examine Archer, *Being Human: The Problem of Agency*, 161–90.

51. Robinson, *Aristotle's Psychology*, 77–111.

52. These are the (somewhat modified) rules of Grisez and Finnis, "Practical Principles, Moral Truth, and Ultimate Ends," 99–151. In addition, other criteria we might consider include *ineliminability* (being unable to live a good human life without it) and *irrepressibility* (history suggests it cannot be extinguished from the human experience).

53. The distinction between people being "oriented toward" the good and people always acting good is crucial. The former means that people cannot avoid operating in relation to the good and under its influence; people always act in ways compelled to achieve what seems to be good, even when the "goods" sought are mere privations or mis-directions of genuine goods. Even when people fail and choose the bad, the continual reference point, orienting horizon, and "magnetic attraction" of their doings is nevertheless the proper human good.

54. See Philip Wood, "Values-Intuitive Rational Action: The Dynamic Relationship of Instrumental Rationality and Values Insights as a Form of Social Action," *British Journal of Sociology* 52, no. 4 (2001): 687–706.

55. Robinson, *Aristotle's Psychology*, especially 77–111. Also see Richard Taylor, *Virtue Ethics* (Amherst, NY: Prometheus, 2002); Rosalind Hursthouse, *On Virtue Ethics* (New York: Oxford University Press, 1999); Stan van Hooft, *Understanding Virtue Ethics* (Stockenfield, Australia: Acumen, 2006).

56. Jane Mansbridge, ed., *Beyond Self-Interest* (Chicago: University of Chicago Press, 1990); Rebecca Ratner and Dale Miller, "The Norm of Self-Interest and Its Effects on Social Action," *Journal of Personality and Social Psychology* 81, no. 1 (2001): 5–16.

57. Jonathan Baron and Mark Spranca, "Protected Values," *Organizational Behavior and Human Decision Processes* 70, no. 1 (1997): 1–16; Mark Leary, "Motivational and Emotional Aspects of the Self," *Annual Review of Psychology* 58 (2007): 317–44; George Akerlof and Rachel Kranton, "Economics and Identity," *Quarterly Journal of Economics* 115, no. 3 (2000): 715–53.

58. Further, while the basic goods are incommensurate, they are not all on the same par but exist in some kind of hierarchy—for example, bodily survival and security is a precondition for the other goods (although, to be clear, merely because one basic good depends upon the fulfillment of another does not make the latter purely instrumentally valuable for achieving the first).

59. Julia Annas, *Intelligent Virtue* (New York: Oxford University Press, 2011).

60. Siegwart Lindenberg, Detlef Fetchenhauer, Andreas Flache, and Abraham Buunk, "Solidarity and Prosocial Behavior: A Framing Approach," in *Solidarity and Prosocial Behavior: An Integration of Sociological and Psychological Perspectives*, ed. Fetchenhauer, Flache, Buunk, and Lindenberg (New York: Springer, 2006), 3–19; Thomson, *The Springs of Human Action*.

61. Richard Swedberg, "Can There Be a Sociological Concept of Interest?" *Theory and Society* 34 (2005): 359–90.

62. The "cultural models" view of the "directive [motivational, normative] force" of culture is helpful here; see Roy D'Andrade and Claudia Strauss, eds., *Human Motives and Cultural Models* (Cambridge: Cambridge University Press, 1997).

63. Fiske, *Structures of Social Life*; Siegwart Lindenberg and Linda Steg, "Normative, Gain, and Hedonic Goal Frames Guiding Environmental Behavior," *Journal of Social Issues* 63 (2007): 117–37.

64. Beth Morling and Shinobu Kitayama, "Culture and Motivation," in *Handbook of Motivation Science*, ed. James Shah and Wendi Gardner (New York: Guilford Press, 2008), 417–33.

65. Spiro, *Culture and Human Nature*, 38; Baumeister, *The Cultural Animal*.

66. Lindenberg, Fetchenhauer, Flache, and Buunk, "Solidarity and Prosocial Behavior: A Framing Approach," 23–44.

67. Dave Elder-Vass, *The Causal Power of Social Structures: Emergence, Structure, and Agency* (Cambridge: Cambridge University Press, 2010).

68. Porpora, *The Concept of a Social Structure*; Archer, *Realist Social Theory*.

69. Naomi Ellemers, Dick de Gilder, and S. Alexander Haslam, "Motivating Individuals and Groups at Work: A Social Identity Perspective on Leadership and Group Performance," *Academy of Management Review* 29, no. 3 (2004): 459–78.

70. Fiske, *Structures of Social Life*, 99–111.

71. "True nature having been lost, everything becomes natural. In the same way, the true good having been lost, everything becomes their good." Blaise Pascal, *Pensées* (New York: Oxford University Press, 2008), 7.

72. Christian Smith, "Does Naturalism Warrant a Moral Belief in Universal Benevolence and Human Rights?," in *The Believing Primate: Scientific, Philosophical and Theological Perspectives on the Evolution of Religion*, ed. Jeffrey Schloss and Michael Murray (New York: Oxford University Press, 2009), 292–317.

73. This is not to suggest, however, that moral realism and moral relativism are the only options, my case rather hinges on whether or not humanistic morality can be justified if we lack any substantive, natural good for human persons.

74. Certain kinds of theists can frame all of this within transcendent horizons by adding the need or good of particular kinds of relationships with divine beings, continued personal existence after death, and so on, without violating the essential outlook of the account presented here.

Chapter 6: Toward a Theory of Flourishing

1. Plato argued earlier that the human will is directed toward the good in *Protagoras* 345D, but did not take the empirical, experiential approach of Aristotle that I rely on here.

2. Alasdair MacIntyre, *After Virtue* (Notre Dame, IN: University of Notre Dame Press, 1982); Taylor, *Virtue Ethics*; Hursthouse, *On Virtue Ethics*; Hooft, *Understanding Virtue Ethics*; Stephen Gardiner, ed., *Virtue Ethics Old and New* (Ithaca, NY: Cornell University Press, 2005); Robinson, *Aristotle's Psychology*. For an accessible introduction, see Kraut, *What Is Good and Why: The Ethics of Well-Being*.

3. About whether the diversity and unity of human goods creates tragic conflicts of goods that necessitate doing wrong, see Daniel McInerny, *The Difficult Good* (New York: Fordham University Press, 2006).

4. Alison Gopnik, Andrew Melzoff, and Patricia Kuhl, *The Scientist in the Crib: What Early Learning Tells Us about the Mind* (New York: William Morrow, 2000); Daniel Stern, *Diary of a Baby: What Your Child Sees, Feels, and Experiences* (New York: Basic Books, 1992).

5. Following centuries of modern thinkers, such as John Locke, who wrote, "Happiness . . . in its full extent is the utmost Pleasure we are capable of," and "Happiness . . . seems[s] to me wholly to consist in the pleasure and pain of the mind." Locke, *An Essay Concerning Human Understanding*, ed. Peter Nidditch (1690; Oxford: Clarendon Press, 1975), 258; Locke, *Journals* (1972), f. 1, 335–36, cited in Michael Sherwin, "Happiness and Its Discontents," *Logos* 13, no. 4 (2010): 35–59, at 36.

6. See Julia Annas, *The Morality of Happiness* (New York: Oxford University Press, 1993), 364–84; Annas, *Intelligent Virtue*; for a pessimistic approach to the matter, see Daniel Haybron, *The Pursuit of Unhappiness: The Elusive Psychology of Well-Being* (New York: Oxford University Press, 2008). This sentence, to be clear, expresses a view broader than Aristotle's.

7. This approach parts ways with Kant, who believed, "The more a cultivated reason concerns itself with the aim of enjoying life and happiness, the farther does man get from true contentment. . . . Making a man happy is quite different from making him good." Kant, *Groundwork for the Metaphysics of Morals*, trans. H. J. Patton (1785; New York: Harper, 1964), 63, 109.

8. The root metaphors of Greek thought on this are *biological growth* and *craftwork*, an insight I am grateful to Brian Brock for pointing out. For worthwhile histories of the idea of happiness in Western thinking, see Darrin McMahon, *Happiness: A History* (New York: Atlantic Monthly Press, 2006); Sissela Bok, *Exploring Happiness: From Aristotle to Brain Science* (New Haven, CT: Yale University Press, 2010); Sherwin, "Happiness and Its Discontents," 35–59; Ellen Charry, *God and the Art of Happiness* (Grand Rapids, MI: Eerdmans, 2010), section I. On the empirical study of happiness, see Carol Graham, *The Pursuit of Happiness: An Economy of Well-Being* (Washington, DC: Brookings Institution Press, 2011).

9. Applying this approach to economics is Edward Hadas, *Human Goods, Economic Evils: A Moral Approach to the Dismal Science* (Wilmington, DE: ISI Books, 2007).

10. Aristotle, *The Nicomachean Ethics*, 13, 14, 15.

11. For certain kinds of theists, of course, enjoying some relationship with a divine person or power is central to flourishing—Thomas Aquinas, building on Augustine and Aristotle, offering one highly developed example of such a view.

12. Robert Emmons, *The Psychology of Ultimate Concerns: Motivation and Spirituality in Personality* (New York: Guilford Press, 1999).

13. Aristotle, *The Nicomachean Ethics*.

14. Annas, *The Morality of Happiness*, 227, more broadly, 223–325.

15. David Norton, *Personal Destinies* (Princeton, NJ: Princeton University Press, 1976); Kraut, *What Is Good and Why: The Ethics of Well-Being.*

16. See Smith, *What Is a Person.*

17. Robinson, *Aristotle's Psychology,* 105. On the question of the meaning of the loss of capacities and powers in death, see Aristotle, *The Nicomachean Ethics,* 21–26, 67. Some religious views—again, not required by this account but compatible with it—set the question of human flourishing in this life within larger contexts of different accounts of life beyond death; some of them understand ultimate human happiness to consist of union with divine love.

18. N. J. Dent, *The Moral Psychology of the Virtues* (Cambridge: Cambridge University Press, 1984).

19. On the relationship between virtue ethics and sociology, see Kieran Flanagan and Peter Jupp, eds., *Virtue Ethics and Sociology* (London: Palgrave, 2001).

20. Between the extremes of humility and vainglory is the golden mean of high-mindedness. Right ambition strikes the virtuous balance between lack of ambition and overambition. Other virtues that Aristotle names are good temper (between spiritlessness and irascibility), civility (between surliness and obsequiousness), sincerity (between ironical deprecation and boastfulness), wittiness (between boorishness and buffoonery), modesty (between shamelessness and bashfulness), and just resentment (between callousness and spitefulness).

21. The opposite of virtue in the *eudaimonian* tradition is vice, that is, dispositions and practices known by practical experience to be corrupt and corrupting, which have the effect of diminishing life and stunting human growth and wellbeing. The vices for Aristotle were the far extremes flanking the golden means of virtue. In Buddhism, named vices are shamelessness, absence of embarrassment, jealousy, remorse, drowsiness, distraction, torpor, anger, and concealment of wrongdoing. The central vices in Christianity are lechery, gluttony, greed, sloth, wrath, envy, pride. For Islam, key vices are worldliness, ire, envy, slander, obscenity, intoxicants, and certain instruments of pleasure. One need not be religious, however, to understand and embrace a *eudaimonian* theory of virtue and vice.

22. This implication is practical, not logical.

23. Margaret Archer and Douglas Porpora discuss the importance of personal life "vocations" or "callings" in Archer, *Making Our Way through the World* (Cambridge: Cambridge University Press, 2007); and Porpora, *Landscapes of the Soul* (New York: Oxford University Press, 2001).

24. See, for an overview, Valerie Tiberius, "Well-Being: Psychological Research for Philosophers," *Philosophy Compass* 1, no. 5 (2006): 493–505.

25. Aristotle, *Aristotle's Politics and Poetics* (New York: Viking, 1976).

26. On the relation of rules to the good, see Kraut, *What Is Good and Why: The Ethics of Well-Being,* 29–35; Annas, *Intelligent Virtue.*

27. Smith, *Moral Believing Animals.*

28. See Eugene Garver, *Confronting Aristotle's Ethics: Ancient and Modern Morality* (Chicago: University of Chicago Press, 2006).

29. My approach runs parallel to but is different in certain ways from Martha Nussbaum, *Creating Capabilities: The Human Development Approach.*

30. Love need not be exclusive and pure, unmixed with other motives and concerns, but in empirical life can be and often is blended with other types of interests and actions. That does not diminish the fact and influence of love in the mix.

31. On the political dimensions of participation, see Eugene Garver, *Aristotle's Politics: Living Well and Living Together* (Chicago: University of Chicago Press, 2011).

32. Love of the other also can, does, and often should also extend to appropriate love for animals, land, place, institutions, and cultures.

33. I realize that I have numerous sets of concepts in play at one time here. To reiterate for clarity, human being involves six basic *goods*, and the basic *interest* of human persons is to realize those goods; these basic human interests are also what produce our basic human *motivations*. When persons realize the six basic human goods, through the learning and exercise of virtues, they enjoy personal thriving or *flourishing*. However, being able to accomplish that successfully requires enjoying certain environmental and personal *preconditions*, which are the nine items mentioned just above. Those preconditions are not themselves the basic goods of human life or the definers of flourishing, but rather the conditional prerequisites of realizing the basic goods and thus thriving.

34. But see Beverly Fehr, Susan Sprecher, and Lynn Underwood, eds., *The Science of Compassionate Love: Theory, Research, and Applications* (Malden, MA: Wiley-Blackwell, 2009); Stephen Post, Byron Johnson, Michael McCullough, and Jeffrey Schloss, eds., *Research on Altruism and Love* (Philadelphia: Templeton Foundation Press, 2003); Stephen Post, *Unlimited Love* (Philadelphia: Templeton Foundation Press, 2003).

35. Barbara Fredrickson, *Love 2.0: How Our Supreme Emotion Affects Everything We Feel, Think, Do, and Become* (New York: Hudson Street Press, 2013). I only disagree with the subtitle's reduction of love to an emotion.

36. I am modifying an "orthodox" Aristotelian account, which would insist on the *indivisibility* of flourishing (which is only really finally accomplished after one is dead and one's children do not shame you. Aristotle, *The Nicomachean Ethics*, 21–26, 67), with an insistence on the potential *divisibility* of flourishing, which is part of what makes mine a *neo*-Aristotelian theory. Also see Martin Seligman, *Flourish* (New York: Atria Books, 2012).

37. Aleksandr Solzhenitsyn, *One Day in the Life of Ivan Denisovich* (New York: Signet, 2008).

38. Annas, *Intelligent Virtue*. Some religions teaching a redemptive eschatology claim that perfection or the fullness of happiness is only realized after death or with the final salvation of the world. Samsaric religions, for example—Hinduism, Buddhism, and Jainism—teach that through right understanding and living across reincarnated lifetimes, one can be released from the power of Karma and the sorrows of Maya to realize through Moksha the final happiness of absorption into Brahman and Nirvana. Thomas Aquinas, building on Augustine and Aristotle, taught that temporal happiness is always imperfect, although it can prepare humans for the perfect happiness of the "beatific vision" of God. See Bok, *Exploring Happiness*, 71, and Charry, *God and the Art of Happiness*, 86–110.

39. Kraut, *What Is Good and Why: The Ethics of Well-Being*, 140–41.

40. The experience of crimes against humanity before and during the Second World War leading to the drafting and ratification of the United National Declaration of Universal Human Rights in 1948 is one example of historical learning from failure. How long that learning sticks with humanity, however, is an open question.

Chapter 7: Understanding Failure, Destruction, and Evil

1. Until recently, "evil" was the word commonly used to describe such destructive natural disasters (Susan Neiman, "What's the Problem of Evil?," in *Rethinking Evil*, ed. María Pía Lara (Berkeley: University of California Press, 2001), 27–45).

2. Martha Nussbaum, *The Fragility of Goodness* (Cambridge: Cambridge University Press, 2001).

3. It also presents major problems for anyone who believes in *any* kind of rational order and meaning, much less justice, in the world, though I do not have the ability to address those problems here (but see Susan Neiman, *Evil in Modern Thought* (Princeton, NJ: Princeton University Press, 2002). Different religious traditions will frame the problem of compromise and failure in flourishing within a larger "eschatological horizon" involving samsaric rebirth or resurrection, judgment, and just reward.

4. This type parallels what S. I. Benn calls "self-centered" forms of wickedness ("Wickedness," *Ethics* 95 [1985]: 795–810).

5. M. Scott Peck, *The Road Less Traveled* (New York: Touchstone, 1978).

6. John Kekes, *Facing Evil* (Princeton, NJ: Princeton University Press, 1990); M. Scott Peck, *People of the Lie* (New York: Touchstone, 1983), 74.

7. Here I follow Claudia Card's "atrocity paradigm" definition of evil, which I think is the best, most subtle account going, even if I do not accept all of the implications she develops from it (Card, *The Atrocity Paradigm: A Theory of Evil* [New York: Oxford University Press, 2002]). For the various ways that westerners have thought about evil, see Amélie Oksenberg Rorty, *The Many Faces of Evil: Historical Perspectives* (New York: Routledge, 2001); also see Jeffrey Alexander, "A Cultural Sociology of Evil," in *The Meanings of Social Life: A Cultural Sociology* (New York: Oxford University Press, 2003), 109–19.

8. The *intolerability* of the harms done in evil tends to ruin important parts of people's lives, if not their entire lives; are destructive in ways from which most people are not able to recover (even if some do); and call into question the living of life for its own sake, not merely as a means to another end (Card, *The Atrocity Paradigm*, 3–4, 16). Intolerable harms deprive "others of the basics that are necessary to make a life possible and tolerant and decent (or to make death decent)" (16). The *culpability* of the wrongdoing means that the evil person ought to have acted differently by virtue of having had overridingly good reasons to act differently, in light of the combination of the severity and reasonably foreseeable nature of the harm caused (Card, *The Atrocity Paradigm*, 3–22).

9. Ibid., 16.

10. Following Card (14), we can judge "severity" by various (not all quantifiable) criteria, including intensity of suffering, effects on ability to function in life, impact on quality of relationships with others, extent of the scope of harm, potential reversibility of damage, the possibility of compensations or reparations, the temporal duration of effects, and the number of victims damaged.

11. For a helpful discussion of whether psychopaths are genuinely evil persons or mere moral imbeciles who blithely commit evil deeds, see Benn, "Wickedness," 798–800.

12. This type overlaps with what Benn (ibid.) calls "conscientious" and "heteronomous" wickedness, and what Roy Baumeister (*Evil: Inside Human Violence and Cruelty* [New York: Henry Holt, 1999]) calls "evil as a means to an end" and the "idealistic evil" of "true believers."

13. Persons can also, in theory, according to my definition of evil, commit evildoing *against themselves*, by, for example, knowingly abusing alcohol and drugs for years, despite many good and understood reasons not to, leading to their own foreseeable early bodily deterioration and premature death—though evils committed against oneself are not my primary concern here.

14. Instrumentally evil people and simple avoidant-destructive people (the third type of failure described above) are parallel and perhaps partly overlapping kinds, but not identical. The former knowingly commit evil in order to achieve larger external goals, while the latter do so inadvertently to avoid the pain and loss their own proper personal growth requires. The first deliberately risk and tolerate the suffering they know they may or will cause, while the second

normally work hard to deny that they are causing anyone suffering or destruction. And the first is often expressed at institutional and societal levels, while the second is typically manifest in interpersonal relationships.

15. "The evil action is one in which the agent is entirely impervious—blind and deaf—to the presence of significant reasons against his acting. . . . For him, there is nothing to be outweighed; he has (psychologically) silenced such considerations. . . . The evil act turns out to be one performed by an agent who is suffering from a profound cognitive defect—an inability to grasp the presence of reasons of the first importance. . . . What he fails to grasp is that the pain which the victim is suffering is an overwhelmingly strong reason for him to desist. He fails to see its reason-giving force." Eve Garrard, "Evil as an Explanatory Concept," *The Monist* 85, no. 2 2002): 320–36; also see Garrard, "The Nature of Evil," *Philosophical Explorations* 1 (1998): 43–60.

16. Baumeister, *Evil: Inside Human Violence and Cruelty*, 18–19.

17. Similar to what Benn ("Wickedness,") calls "wickedness of malignity," and what Baumeister (*Evil: Inside Human Violence and Cruelty*) identifies as evil for "the joy of hurting."

18. I qualify suffering with the adjective "destructive," since some forms of imposed suffering can be constructive, perhaps even redemptive. Consider, for example, the genuine suffering an athletic coach puts his or her team through during early training to prepare it to perform its best; or the suffering that a husband or midwife might encourage a wife in the labor pains of a very difficult childbirth to endure, in order that she may eventually deliver a daughter or son. Not all suffering is evil, personalism suggests, a crucial point with important implication about which many modern thinkers, however, seem to be confused. Among the many provocative works on the topic, see Talal Asad, "Thinking about Agency and Pain," chapter 2 in *Formations of the Secular: Christianity, Islam, and Modernity* (Stanford, CA: Stanford University Press, 2003), 67–99.

19. Fred Alford, *What Evil Means to Us* (Ithaca, NY: Cornell University Press), 1997.

20. Erich Fromm, *The Heart of Man: Its Genius for Good and Evil* (New York: Harper, 1964), 23; Simon Baron-Cohen, *The Science of Evil: On Empathy and the Origins of Cruelty* (New York: Basic Books, 2011).

21. Vetlesen, *Perception, Empathy, and Judgment*; Baron-Cohen, *The Science of Evil.*

22. Paul Babiak and Robert Hare, *Snakes in Suits: When Psychopaths Go to Work* (New York: HarperBusiness, 2007); Martha Stout, *The Sociopath Next Door* (New York: Three Rivers Press, 2006); Robert Hare, *Without Conscience: The Disturbing World of Psychopaths among Us* (New York: Guilford Press, 1999).

23. Russell Jacoby, *Bloodlust: On the Roots of Violence from Cain and Abel to the Present* (New York: Free Press, 2011); Michael Ignatieff, "The Narcissism of Minor Difference," in *The Warrior's Honor: Ethnic War and the Modern Conscience* (New York: Holt, 1998), 34–71.

24. Peck, *People of the Lie*, 9–149.

25. See Walker Percy, *Lost in the Cosmos* (New York: Picador, 2000).

26. For an alternative take on different kinds of human bads, see Ronald Milo, *Immorality* (Princeton, NJ: Princeton University Press, 1984). For an analysis of degrees of evil from a psychoanalytic perspective, see Michael Stone, *The Anatomy of Evil* (Amherst, NY: Prometheus Books, 2009).

27. This might also be said to include an *abusus boni* ("abuse or misdirection of the good") account, except that the abuse of the good finally consists of the privation of the proper application of instruction, thought, and action toward the good—so I will speak simply of *privation boni* as meant to include this aspect.

28. "No nature at all is evil, and this is a name for nothing but the want of the good.... Let no one, therefore, look for an efficient cause of the evil will; for it is not efficient, but deficient." Augustine of Hippo, *The City of God* (412–26 AD; New York: Barnes and Noble, 2006), 439, 464–65. Augustine on this point had deeper Neoplatonist roots in Plotinus's *Enneads*.

29. Mary Midgley, *Wickedness* (New York: Routledge, 1984).

30. Martin Buber, *Good and Evil* (New York: Charles Scribner's, 1953), 130. "'Good' is the movement in the direction of home, 'evil' is the aimless whirl of human potentialities without which nothing can be achieved and by which, if they take no direction but remain trapped in themselves, everything goes awry" (Buber, *Between Man and Man* [New York: Macmillan, 1947], 78). Aristotle observes that "evil destroys even itself" (*The Nicomachean Ethics*, 101).

31. Fromm, *The Heart of Man*, 148.

32. Critical realists could press beyond my approach here. Margaret Archer has suggested (personal correspondence) by developing the idea of "relational evils" as emergent, irreducible, and causally powerful—though always activity-dependent and concept-dependent—relationally real facts, a further development that seems well worth expanding.

33. Roy Bhaskar—in what he calls "second wave, dialectical critical realism" (*Dialectic: The Pulse of Freedom* [New York: Routledge, 2008])—argues for the idea that "absence and non-being *exist*," which provides an intriguing point of engagement with my argument, even if the two approaches do not seem to fully harmonize.

34. Fromm, *The Heart of Man*, 149.

35. Also see Ervin Staub, "Basic Human Needs, Altruism, and Aggression," in *The Social Psychology of Good and Evil*, ed. Arthur G. Miller (New York: Guilford Press, 2004), 51–84.

36. See, for example, Douglas Porpora, *How Holocausts Happen: The United States in Central America* (Philadelphia: Temple University Press, 1992).

37. Jonathan Haidt, *The Righteous Mind: Why Good People Are Divided by Politics and Religion* (New York: Pantheon, 2012).

38. Peter L. Berger and Thomas Luckmann, *The Social Construction of Reality* (Garden City, NY: Anchor, 1966), 51–52.

39. McMahon *Happiness: A History*.

40. Haybron, *The Pursuit of Unhappiness*.

41. Aristotle, *The Nicomachean Ethics*, 8.

42. Robinson, *Aristotle's Psychology*, 101. Contrasted to Plato, who "set himself to show that the life of virtue will appeal to every man who thinks clearly about it and that the life of vice will be unwelcome to every man who thinks clearly about it." D. H. Hutchinson, *The Virtues of Aristotle* (London: Routledge and Kegan Paul, 1986), 71.

43. Aristotle, *The Nicomachean Ethics*, 41.

44. Aristotle: "There are two things in which all wellbeing consists: one of them is the choice of the right end and aim of action, and the other the discovery of the actions which are the means toward it; for the means and the end may agree or disagree. Sometimes the right end is set before men, but in practice they may fail to attain it; in other cases they are successful in all the means, but they propose to themselves a bad end; and sometimes they fail at both" (*Aristotle's Politics and Poetics*, 194).

45. Relatedly, see Jessica Moss, *Aristotle on the Apparent Good: Perception, Phantasia, Thought, and Desire* (New York: Oxford University Press, 2012).

46. Smith, *What Is a Person*, 42–59.

47. Anthony Storr, *Human Destructiveness* (London: Routledge, 1991).

48. Jean McGloin and Cathy Widom, "Resilience among Abused and Neglected Children

Grown Up," *Development and Psychopathology* 13 (2001): 1021–38; Mary Harvey, "Toward an Ecological Understanding of Resilience in Trauma Survivors," *Journal of Aggression, Maltreatment, and Trauma* 14 (2008): 9–32.

49. Thomas Wills and Jody Resko, "Social Support and Behavior toward Others," in *The Social Psychology of Good and Evil*, ed. Arthur G. Miller, 416–43.

50. Involving what Aristotle (*The Nicomachean Ethics*) called *proaireses* (choice, purpose), *energeia* (activity, exercise, actualization), *praxis* (action, conduct), and *eupraxia* (good action).

51. Jonathan Turner, *Human Emotions: A Sociological Theory* (New York: Routledge, 2007); Paul Ekman, "An Argument for Basic Emotions," *Cognition and Emotion*, 6 (1992): 169–200.

52. Robert Wuthnow, *Be Very Afraid: The Cultural Response to Terror, Pandemics, Environmental Devastation, Nuclear Annihilation, and Other Threats* (New York: Oxford University Press, 2010).

53. Ernest Becker, *The Denial of Death* (New York: Free Press, 1973); Becker, *Escape from Evil* (New York: Free Press, 1975).

54. Fromm, *The Heart of Man*, 148: "Evil is man's loss of himself in the tragic attempt to escape the burden of his humanity."

55. Jeffrey Kottler, *The Lust for Blood: Why We Are Fascinated by Death, Murder, Horror, and Violence* (Amherst, NY: Prometheus Books, 2011).

56. Joseph Conrad's 1903 novel, *Heart of Darkness*, got this insight right, as did Francis Ford Coppola's 1979 film, *Apocalypse Now*.

57. Not surprisingly, therefore, "Do not fear" and "Be not afraid" are among the most consistent messages spoken by those considered to be our wisest teachers, heavenly messengers, and most compassionate deities.

58. Donald Cozzens, *Sacred Silence: Denial and the Crisis in the Church* (Collegeville, MN: Liturgical Press, 2002); Joy Raphael, *Rape Is Rape: How Denial, Distortion, and Victim Blaming Are Fueling a Hidden Acquaintance Rape Crisis* (Chicago: Chicago Review Press, 2013); Eviatar Zerubavel, *The Elephant in the Room: Silence and Denial in Everyday Life* (New York: Oxford University Press, 2007).

59. Robert Sokolowski, *Phenomenology of the Human Person* (Cambridge: Cambridge University Press, 2008). This is not to deny that some of human life is lived in dreams, fiction, and the imagination — in fact, these can be useful means for putting people in touch with reality — but rather simply to assert the "reality principle" as a key moral standard.

60. Perhaps for this reason a major personification of evil itself in the Western imagination ("Satan") has been called in some religious scriptures "a liar and the father of lies" (John 8:44).

61. René Girard, *The Scapegoat*, trans. Yvonne Freccero (Baltimore: Johns Hopkins University Press, 1986).

62. Francisco Herreros and Henar Criado, "The State and the Development of Social Trust," *International Political Science Review* 29 (2008): 53–71; Roderick Kramer, "Trust and Distrust in Organizations," *Annual Review of Psychology* 50 (1999): 569–59; Sandra Smith, "Race and Trust," *Annual Review of Sociology* 36 (2010): 453–75.

63. See, for example, Helmut Gollwitzer, Kathe Kuhn, and Reinhold Schneider, *Dying We Live: The Final Messages and Records of the Resistance* (Eugene, OR: Wipf and Stock, 2005).

64. "The most important condition for the development of the love of life in the child is for him to be with people who love life. . . . The specific conditions necessary for the development of [the love for life and others are] . . . warm, affectionate contact with others during infancy; freedom, and the absence of threats; teaching . . . of the principles conducive to inner harmony

and strength; guidance in 'the art of living'; [and the] stimulating influence of and response to others." Fromm, *The Heart of Man*, 51.

65. Adam Morton, *On Evil* (New York: Routledge, 2004); Roy Baumeister and Kathleen Vohs, "Four Roots of Evil," in *The Social Psychology of Good and Evil*, ed. Arthur G. Miller, 98–99.

66. Storr, *Human Destructiveness*; Ervin Staub, *The Roots of Evil: The Origins of Genocide and Other Group Violence* (Cambridge: Cambridge University Press, 1989).

67. Jonathan Kellerman, *Savage Spawn: Reflections on Violent Children* (New York: Ballantine, 1999).

68. Nancy Eisenberg, Carlos Valiente, and Claire Champion, "Empathy-Related Responding: Moral, Social, and Socialization Correlates," in *The Social Psychology of Good and Evil*, ed. Arthur G. Miller, 386–415; Staub, "Basic Human Needs, Altruism, and Aggression," 68.

69. Adrian Raine, "From Genes to Brains to Antisocial Behavior," *Current Directions in Psychological Science* 17, no. 5 (2008): 323–28; Essi Viding and Uta Frith, "Genes for Susceptibility to Violence Lurk in the Brain," *Proceedings of the National Academy of Sciences* 103, no. 16 (2006): 6085–86; Andreas Meyer-Lindenberg, Joshua Buckholtz, Bhaskar Kolachana, Ahmad Hariri, Lukas Pezawas, Giuseppe Blasi, Ashley Wabnitz, Robyn Honea, Beth Verchinski, Joseph Callicott, Michael Egan, Venkata Mattay, and Daniel Weinberger, "Neural Mechanisms of Genetic Risk for Impulsivity and Violence in Humans," *Proceedings of the National Academy of Sciences* 103, no. 16 (2006): 6269–74; Avshalom Caspi, Joseph McClay, Terrie Moffitt, Jonathan Mill, Judy Martin, Ian Craig, Alan Taylor, and Richie Poulton, "Role of Genotype in the Cycle of Violence in Maltreated Children," *Science* 297, no. 5582 (2002): 851–54; Luca Passamonti, Francesco Fera, Angela Magariello, Antonio Cerasa, Maria Gioia, Maria Muglia, Giuseppe Nicoletti, Olivier Gallo, Leandro Provinciali, and Aldo Quattrone, "Monoamine Oxidase-A Genetic Variations Influence Brain Activity Associated with Inhibitory Control: New Insight into the Neural Correlates of Impulsivity," *Biological Psychiatry* 59, no. 4 (2006): 334–40; J. W. Buckholtz, J. H. Callicott, B. Kolachana, A. R. Hariri, T. E. Goldberg, M. Genderson, M. F. Egan, V. S. Mattay, D. R. Weinberger, and A. Meyer-Lindenberg, "Genetic Variation in MAOA Modulates Ventromedial Prefrontal Circuitry Mediating Individual Differences in Human Personality," *Molecular Psychiatry* 13, no. 3 (2008): 313–24; Leanne Williams, Justine Gatt, Stacey Kuan, Carol Dobson-Stone, Donna Palmer, Robert Paul, Le Song, Paul Costa, Peter Schofield, and Evian Gordon, "Polymorphism of the MAOA Gene is Associated with Emotional Brain Markers and Personality Traits on an Antisocial Index," *Neuropsychopharmacology* 34 (2009): 1797–809; Terrie Moffitt and Avshalom Caspi, "Evidence from Behavioral Genetics for Environmental Contributions to Antisocial Conduct," *The Explanation of Crime: Context, Mechanisms, and Development*, ed. Per-Olof Wikström and Robert Sampson (Cambridge: Cambridge University Press, 2006), 96–123; Martin Sellbom and Edelyn Verona, "Neuropsychological Correlates of Psychopathic Traits in a Non-Incarcerated Sample," *Journal of Research in Personality* 41 (2007): 267–94; N. Sadeh, S. Javdani, J. Jackson, E. Reynolds, M. Potenza, J. Gelernter, C. Lejuez, and E. Verona, "Serotonin Transporter Gene Associations with Psychopathic Traits in Youth Vary as a Function of Socioeconomic Resources," *Journal of Abnormal Psychology* 119, no. (3) (2010): 604–09; J. Rilling, A. Glenn, M. Jairam, G. Pagnoni, D. Goldsmith, H. Elfenbein, and S. Lilienfeld, "Neural Correlates of Social Cooperation and Non-Cooperation as a Function of Psychopathy," *Biological Psychiatry* 61, no. 11 (2007): 1260–71.

70. Laurence Tancredi, *Hardwired Behavior: What Neuroscience Reveals about Morality* (Cambridge: Cambridge University Press, 2005); Barbara Oakley, *Evil Genes* (Amherst, NY: Prometheus Books, 2008).

71. See, for example, Michael Shermer, *The Science of Good and Evil* (New York: Henry Holt, 2004); Timothy Anders, *The Evolution of Evil* (Chicago: Open Court, 1994).

72. By discipline I do not mean punishment but guided activity that develops or improves a skill, often in accordance with established rules or practices, as in the discipline in training required to become adept at a sport or an accomplished musician.

73. This list relies nearly verbatim on Philip Zimbardo, "A Situationist Perspective on the Psychology of Evil: Understanding How Good People Are Transformed into Perpetrators," in *The Social Psychology of Good and Evil*, ed. Arthur G. Miller, 29, though I omit quotations marks—Zimbardo is the kind of radical situationist I critiqued in chapter 4, although his analysis, when contextualized in a more realist framework, is helpful. Also see Baumeister's process of how evil works (*Evil: Inside Human Violence and Cruelty*, 251–371).

74. Charles Tilly, *Durable Inequality* (Berkeley: University of California Press, 1998). Also see Douglas Massey, *Categorically Unequal: The American Stratification System* (New York: Russell Sage Foundation, 2007).

75. Jim Sidanius and Felicia Pratto, *Social Dominance* (Cambridge: Cambridge University Press, 1999).

76. See Miller, *The Social Psychology of Good and Evil*; Fiske, *Structures of Social Life*, 115–35.

77. Karl Marx, "The Eighteenth Brumaire of Louis Bonaparte," in *The Marx-Engels Reader*, 2nd ed., ed. Robert Tucker (1852; New York: W. W. Norton, 1978), 595.

78. Kellerman, *Savage Spawn*, 57–65.

79. Heidegger, *Being and Time*.

80. Michel Wieviorka, *Evil* (Cambridge: Polity Press, 2012).

81. Stanley Milgram, *Obedience to Authority: An Experimental View* (New York: Harper and Row, 1974).

82. Craig Haney, Curtis Banks, and Philip Zimbardo, "Interpersonal Dynamics in a Simulated Prison," *International Journal of Criminology and Penology* 1 (1973): 90; Philip Zimbardo, *The Lucifer Effect* (New York: Random House, 2008).

83. Zygmunt Bauman, *Modernity and the Holocaust* (Cambridge: Polity Press, 1989), 154, 166, 177; by comparison, see Fred Katz, *Ordinary People and Extraordinary Evil* (Albany: State University of New York Press, 1993).

84. Arne Johan Vetlesen (*Evil and Human Agency: Understanding Collective Evildoing* [Cambridge: Cambridge University Press, 2005], 1–51) is excellent on this point.

85. On Milgram, for instance, "although amounts of obedience can vary as a function of situational manipulations and differ among individuals within the same setting, neither the proposed situational dimensions . . . nor the personality variables studied . . . have accounted for the variations in a consistent, orderly, and predictable manner" (T. Blass, "Understanding Behavior in the Milgram Obedience Experiment: The Role of Personalities, Situations, and Their Interactions," *Journal of Personality and Social Psychology* 70 [1991]: 408); also see J. Sabini and M. Silver, "Lack of Character?: Situationism Critiqued," *Ethics*, 115 (2005): 535–62; Snow, *Virtue as Social Intelligence*.

86. Haney, Banks, and Zimbardo, "Interpersonal Dynamics in a Simulated Prison," 90, italics added.

87. Alford, *What Evil Means to Us*, 29, italics added.

88. Ibid., italics added.

89. Ibid., 71–72.

90. Pearson, *Aristotle on Desires*.

91. Amélie Oksenberg Rorty, "How to Harden Your Heart: Six Easy Ways to Become Corrupt," *Yale Review* 86, no. 2 (1998).

92. Global thermonuclear war is so far one exception, although humans have used nuclear weapons more than once and came close to intercontinental nuclear war during the Cuban Missile Crisis of 1962 and other times.

93. Jack Katz, *Seductions of Crime* (New York: Basic Books, 1988); Eric Wilson, *Everyone Loves a Good Train Wreck: Why We Can't Look Away* (New York: Sarah Crichton Books, 2012).

94. Carol Tavris and Elliot Aronson, *Mistakes Were Made (But Not by Me)*. (Orlando, FL: Harcourt, 2007).

95. Pascal: "Those who lead disordered lives say to those who lead ordered ones that it is they who stray from nature, and believe themselves to follow it; like those on board ship think people on shore are moving away. . . . We need a fixed point to judge it. The harbor judges those on board ship. But where will we find a harbor in morals?" (*Pensées*, 576). "When everything is moving at the same pace, nothing appears to be moving, as on board ship. When everyone is going in the direction of depravity, no one seems to be doing so: the one person who stops shows up the haste of the others, like a fixed point" (*Pensées*, 577). Thomas Aquinas said that evil practices and immoral authorities can make the directives of even natural law opaque to people. *Summa Theologica*, I–II, 2.3.

96. Fromm, *The Heart of Man*, 108–14.

97. Aristotle, *The Nicomachean Ethics*, 63, 146, 278.

98. Neiman, *Evil in Modern Thought*.

99. About evil, "contemporary philosophers find themselves baffled at roughly the same places that perplexed their predecessors; and equally disconcerted by their inability to provide satisfactory solutions to the questions they feel obliged to continue posing" (Rorty, *Many Faces of Evil*, xvi).

Conclusion

1. Archer, *Realist Social Theory*.

2. See Strauss and Quinn, *A Cognitive Theory of Cultural Meaning*, 252–56.

3. Also see Andrew Sayer, *Why Things Matter to People: Social Science, Values, and Ethical Life* (Cambridge: Cambridge University Press, 2011).

4. See Murray S. Davis, "That's Interesting! Towards a Phenomenology of Sociology and a Sociology of Phenomenology," *Philosophy of Social Science* 1 (1971): 309–44.

5. Bhaskar, *The Possibility of Naturalism*; Archer, *Realist Social Theory*.

6. See Xavier de Souza Briggs, Susan Popkin, and John Goering, *Moving to Opportunity* (New York: Oxford University Press, 2010), 23.

7. Charles Taylor, *Sources of the Self* (Cambridge: Cambridge University Press, 1989), 58, 74.

8. Gilbert Harman, "The Inference to the Best Explanation," *Philosophical Review* 74, no. 1 (1965): 88–95; Lipton, *Inference to the Best Explanation*.

9. Hilliard Aronovitch, "Social Explanation and Rational Motivation," *American Philosophical Quarterly* 15 (1978): 197–204.

10. This incorporates the legitimate post-Wittgensteinian criticism of positivist social science without falling headlong into the opposite error posed, for example, by Peter Winch (*The Idea of a Social Science and Its Relation to Philosophy*) and others, of never proceeding in our analyses and explanations beyond the primary agents' own descriptions.

11. Describing the necessary dynamic interplay, Wallis and Bruce write that, "no one will adequately explain social action who does not understand how [persons] interpret their world.

But no one will understand how [persons] interpret their world who is not aware of the social and historical context within which they do it" ("Accounting for Action," 109).

12. Douglas Porpora, "Do Realists Run Regressions?" in *After Postmodernism? Critical Realism*, ed. Garry Potter and Jose Lopez (London: Continuum, 2001), 260–67.

13. Max Weber, *Economy and Society* (Berkeley: University of California Press, 1978), 4–24.

14. For an example of a sociologist who seems to come so close to getting it right, yet in the end fails to do so, see Dietrich Rueschemeyer, *Usable Theory: Analytic Tools for Social and Political Research* (Princeton, NJ: Princeton University Press, 2009), which exemplifies the larger problematic mentalities and conditions in American sociology keeping them from ever getting fixed. Rueschemeyer correctly sees many of the problems and disappointments in normal-science sociology, seems ready to move forward on better terms, takes seriously the complexly subjective dimension of human persons in action, and understands the importance of causation and causal explanation. But in the end he proves stubbornly wedded to the model of deductive-nomothetic theory, covering laws, predictive social science, and rational choice theory. He cannot see the critical realist answers sitting right under his nose. This book thus turns out in the end to be little more than an admission that sociology has not achieved much (by its dominant ideal standards) and a recommendation to move forward provisionally, working instead with Rueschemeyer's idea of "theory frames." In short, it offers the same old stuff in a more chastened mode, all, it seems, with the goal of finally being able to do "ideal-theory" social science down the road (and in that sense reads almost like a New Testament epistle trying to make sense of the fact that Jesus had not yet returned on clouds of glory—only, in this case, the king of glory is positivist social science). In effect, the book actually entrenches the old, failed mentalities it laments by admitting that they have not worked yet still holding onto them as the gold standard. It appears on the surface to be enlightened, creative, realistic, and forward moving, but that only reinforces the illusion that we are getting somewhere new. The phrase "causal mechanisms" is all over the place, for example, even though it is misunderstood, as is the basic idea of causation as well—which only perpetuates the delusion that mainstream sociology today is genuinely postpositivist, when in fact it is not. Rueschemeyer also uses the idea of "emergence" when in fact he does not understand the idea—that he puts it in quotation marks, in fact, communicates that nothing real is really emergent but only "emergent"-like, that is, that it is a term we use but of which have to be wary or skeptical and hold at arm's length (reinforced by the fact that on p. 290 he in confusion directly equates "emergence" with what is "composite," and on p. 34 he recognizes ideas about "emergence" as only "speculations" that are "inconclusive," while only referencing a 2001 *American Journal of Sociology* article). Why, the critical realist wonders, are American sociologists so determined to remain ignorant of and to resist the metatheoretical philosophy of science that actually resolves their problems?

15. For a good starting point, see Donald Brown, *Human Universals* (Philadelphia: Temple University Press, 1981).

16. A few exceptions include Niklas Luhmann, *Love: A Sketch* (Malden, MA: Polity Press, 2010); Wieviorka, *Evil*; Thomas Lewis, Fari Amini, and Richard Lannon, *A General Theory of Love* (New York: Vintage, 2001); and Robert Karen, *Becoming Attached: First Relationships and How They Shape Our Capacity to Love* (New York: Oxford University Press, 1998).

17. Fredrickson, *Love 2.0: How Our Supreme Emotion Affects Everything We Feel, Think, Do, and Become*; Robert Brown, *Analyzing Love* (Cambridge: Cambridge University Press, 2008).

18. Garrard, "Evil as an Explanatory Concept."

Index